Boswell on the Grand Tour
is the fourth of four volumes of The Y
Editions of the Private Papers of James
Boswell to be published as McGraw-Hill
Paperbacks. Other titles in this unique
publishing venture include:

Boswell's London Journal, 1762-1763
(McGraw-Hill Paperbacks 06603, $2.45)

Boswell in Holland, 1763-1764
(McGraw-Hill Paperbacks 50553, $2.75)

Boswell for the Defence, 1769-1774
(McGraw-Hill Paperbacks 70964, $2.65)

**Frederick A. Pottle is Professor of English and
Chairman of the Department at Yale
University. He is also Chairman of the Editorial
Committee for this series.**

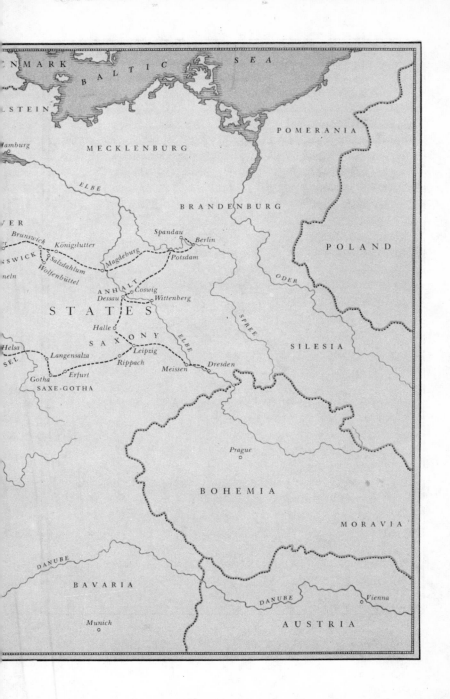

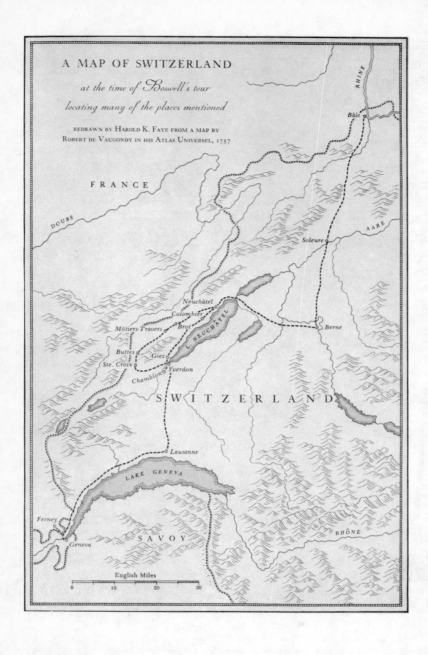

A MAP OF SWITZERLAND

at the time of *Boswell's tour*

locating many of the places mentioned

REDRAWN BY HAROLD K. FAYE FROM A MAP BY
ROBERT DE VAUGONDY IN HIS ATLAS UNIVERSEL, 1757

RHINE

Bâle

FRANCE

DOUBS

AARÉ

Soleure

Neuchâtel
Colombier
Môtiers-Travers   Brot
Buttes   L. NEUCHÂTEL   Berne
Ste. Croix   Giez
            Yverdon
        Chamblon

S W I T Z E R L A N D

Lausanne

LAKE GENEVA

Ferney

Geneva   S A V O Y   RHÔNE

English Miles
0   10   20   30

Boswell

ON THE GRAND TOUR

GERMANY AND SWITZERLAND

1764

EDITED BY FREDERICK A. POTTLE

STERLING PROFESSOR OF ENGLISH

YALE UNIVERSITY

McGraw-Hill Book Company, Inc.

NEW YORK   TORONTO   LONDON

EDITORIAL COMMITTEE

W. S. LEWIS, LITT.D., L.H.D., Fellow of Yale University and Editor of the Yale Edition of Horace Walpole's Correspondence

C. A. MALCOLM, M.A., PH.D., O.B.E., Librarian to the Society of Writers to the Signet, Edinburgh

HENRI PEYRE, DR.ÈS L., Sterling Professor of French, Yale University

L. F. POWELL, M.A., D.LITT., F.R.S.L., F.L.A., Sometime Librarian of the Taylor Institution, Reviser of Hill's Edition of Boswell's "Life of Johnson"

S. C. ROBERTS, M.A., LL.D., Master of Pembroke College, Cambridge

L. W. SHARP, M.A., PH.D., Librarian to the University of Edinburgh

T. B. SIMPSON, Q.C., LL.D., F.R.S.E., Sheriff of Perth and Angus

D. NICHOL SMITH, LITT.D., LL.D., F.B.A., Emeritus Professor of English Literature in the University of Oxford

CHAUNCEY B. TINKER, PH.D., LITT.D., L.H.D., Sterling Professor of English Literature Emeritus, and Keeper of Rare Books in the University Library, Yale University

The Yale Editions of the Private Papers of James Boswell will consist of two independent but parallel series planned and executed for different types of readers. One, the "research" edition, will give a complete text of Boswell's journals, diaries, and memoranda; of his correspondence; and of "The Life of Johnson," from the original manuscript: the whole running to at least thirty volumes. It will preserve the spelling and capitalization of the original documents, and will be provided with extensive scholarly annotation. A large group of editors and a permanent office staff are engaged in this comprehensive undertaking, the first volume of which may appear by 1955. The other, the reading or "trade" edition, will select from the total mass of papers those portions that appear likely to interest the general reading public, and will present them in modern spelling and with annotation of a popular cast. The publishers may also issue limited de luxe printings of the trade volumes, with extra illustrations and special editorial matter, but in no case will the trade volumes or the de luxe printings include matter from Boswell's archives that will not also appear in the research edition.

The present volume is the fourth of the trade edition.

CONTENTS

LIST OF ILLUSTRATIONS

The figures, from left to right, are Maximilian Julius Leopold (1752–
1785), son of the Duke; Johann Friedrich Wilhelm Jerusalem (1709–
1789), tutor of the Hereditary Prince; Friedrich (1711–1763), Margrave of Brandenburg-Bayreuth, son-in-law of the Duke; Sophie Karoline Marie (1737–1817), daughter of the Duke, wife of Friedrich, Margrave of Brandenburg-Bayreuth; Karl Wilhelm Ferdinand (1735–
1806), eldest son of the Duke ("Hereditary Prince"), later Duke of
Brunswick; Friedrich August (1740–1805), son of the Duke; Karl I
(1713–1780), Duke of Brunswick; Philippine Charlotte (1716–1801),
Duchess of Brunswick; Anna Amalia (1739–1807), daughter of the
Duke, widow of Ernst August Konstantin, Duke of Weimar; Auguste
Dorothea (1749–1810), daughter of the Duke, Abbess of Gandersheim;
Elisabeth Christine Ulrike (1746–1840), daughter of the Duke, married
in 1765 to Friedrich Wilhelm II, Prince and later King of Prussia; Wil-
helm Adolf (1745–1770), son of the Duke. The background is a some-

INTRODUCTION

§I

Now that two widely differing volumes of the "reading" edition of Boswell's journal have been published, it is possible for an editor to discern clearly certain features of the situation, and to get enough of a notion of others to enable him to proceed with some confidence in what remains of his task.

The central facts have long been known. The vast majority of literate men and women after they leave school ordinarily read no books more than two years old; and when a piece of eighteenth-century writing does succeed in shaking a large number of such readers out of their accustomed habits, it is unwise to assume that the habits have really been altered. The editor of the book had better regard its extraordinary appeal as due to the casual combination of a large number of factors, not all literary, and continue to plan his volumes for the more predictable portion of the general reading public who do habitually read and relish non-contemporary books. And he knows that by no means everybody in this latter group can be made to take an interest in Boswell. Boswell's personality is not one that permits people to remain neutral: either they dislike him or they feel rather strong affection for him. In short, though other volumes of this series may have as wide circulation as *Boswell's London Journal*, the editor had better assume that Boswell will always be the object of a cult, the delight of the Boswellians.

But though it should not be assumed that all the purchasers of *Boswell's London Journal* were true Boswellians, the true Boswellians are a very numerous body, and their number will increase. There are probably more Boswellians than there are Jamesians or Janeites. And, as in the case of Henry James and Jane Austen, addiction to Boswell is not to any great extent dependent on erudition. Some scholars are Boswellians, some are not; many non-scholarly readers are Boswellians, many are not.

What sets the problem for the editor of the series is not that
many people dislike Boswell, but that the many people who like
him have pronounced and irreconcilable views as to the editorial
policy which ought to be followed. Some Boswellians want only
highly finished narrative, and urge a policy of radical selection.
Some are more interested in psychological revelation, and think
they want to read pretty much the entire collection. And the latter
group has subdivisions. Some want journal or memoranda separated from letters and other documents, so that they can read the
journal straight through for a given period and then read the other
documents; some want the kinds mixed so that they can read according to strict chronology. So far as I can judge from present indications, the majority of the readers of this series do not favour a
policy of radical selection. And I think the editor would make a
mistake if he committed himself to a single formula for the ar-
rangement of the material he has decided to print. It is better to
consider each volume as an independent entity, and to allow the
documents on hand for that period to suggest the editorial plan.

For *Boswell's London Journal*, we had a continuous, book-
length narrative of high literary excellence, plotted by Boswell
himself according to principles of suspense and reversal of situation. In this case it would clearly have been a mistake to intrude
any other documents into the text. For *Boswell in Holland*, on the
other hand, the fully written journal was largely missing, and a
chronological mosaic of memoranda, letters, and other documents
seemed justified. The present volume presents a third variation.
Boswell provides continuous, fully written journal for the entire
period, but the journal has little if any over-all design. In it Dessau
follows Berlin and Leipzig follows Dessau and Dresden follows
Leipzig simply because he happened to be travelling from Berlin to
Switzerland instead of moving in the opposite direction. Several
letters, not copied into the journal, receive prominent mention
there. One of these he himself calls a portion of the account of his
visit to Voltaire; another he regarded as a crucial document that
needed to be read since it could not be described: "It can neither be

abridged nor transposed, for it is really a masterpiece." In editing this volume, therefore, I have presented the entire journal for the period, without cuts, but have ventured to insert in their chronological places several letters and other documents that seemed to me to round out the narrative or to vary it pleasingly. I should be glad of comment from readers on this procedure, because the situation will recur. Do they like expansion of a continuous journal of merely linear organization, or would they prefer the journal straight? Or perhaps straight with a chronological supplement of supporting documents?

§ II

Readers of *Boswell's London Journal* and *Boswell in Holland* have seen Boswell struggling, at times almost desperately, to make himself over into West Digges, or Sir David Dalrymple, or Thomas Gray, or Samuel Johnson. In this volume the struggle is suddenly terminated. "I saw my error in suffering so much from the contemplation of others. I can never be them, therefore let me not vainly attempt it in imagination. . . . I must be Mr. Boswell of Auchinleck, and no other. Let me make him as perfect as possible." Of course he will continue, like a chameleon, to take his colour from his surroundings. To use Geoffrey Scott's nice classification, he was pedantic in Holland, he is princely in Germany and philosophic in Switzerland, and he will be amorous in Italy. But from now on in his roles and disguises he will not be a desperate young man who fears that there are no features behind his essayed mask (Scott again); he will be a citizen of the world, exhibiting the infinite resources of his own versatile and original spirit.

It cannot be said that this refulgent dawning of his ego adds to his attractiveness. On the contrary, readers may find him less *sympathique* in this volume than in any other of the series. Boswell in London ruefully setting down the sequel to that affair with Louisa which he had considered so manly and prudent, Boswell dreary as a dromedary in the fogs of Utrecht, is a more touching and appealing figure than the vaunting and unchastised egoist who dazzles the princess of Saxe-Gotha with his flowered velvet and reads Voltaire a lecture on the soul. In the period covered by this volume Boswell was, for him, almost continuously happy, and Boswell continuously happy is a little overpowering. In his journal, that is. It is noteworthy that the people he met did not consider him either a fool or a puppy. We have confidential reports on that, and they indicate that everywhere he went on this trip he left the impression that he was a remarkably attractive young man. What makes us wince (until we surrender and admit our moral likeness to him) is his shameless setting down on paper of the swelling egotisms we all cherish in our day-dreams but never put in a form that could be used against us.

§ III

Travelling in Germany suited Boswell because it allowed him to satisfy two of his strongest appetites alternately and at brief intervals. He loved splendour, show, the elaborate and stately ceremonial of courts. He loved to deck himself in velvet of five colours and preen himself conspicuously. ("Mr. Boswell! Why, how fine you are!") He was charmed with a country where he could assume the style of Baron without claiming more than German heraldry would have granted to a German gentleman of his standing. It did his feudal soul good to drive by in a state coach and see the people bowing to the earth. But there was also a wide earthy streak in his nature that made it positive pleasure to him to ride through the night in a jolting cart, or to sleep in his clothes ten nights running on the floors of inns or in haylofts. Baron Boswell of Auchinleck resembles Whitehead's simile for an electron: he appears full-blown at the successive milestones (that is, just outside each city gate), but can be located nowhere in between. In between he is replaced by a coarse and resilient young fellow who gets intense pleasure from saving money and who really likes to "campaign," that is, to rough it. And Germany in the eighteenth century provided ample opportunity for roughing it. The roads were atrocious, the public conveyances nothing but great open carts with boards laid across for seats, and, except in cities of some size, there were no inns where one could get a bed, let alone a sleeping-apartment to one's self. Princes and blackguards, gilt rococo and picaresque: but the fact that Boswell gave more vivid expression to the blackguard side of his tour should not cause us to underestimate the princely. The courts of Germany in the latter half of the eighteenth century were really very splendid places. Of those that Boswell described, Anhalt-Dessau was in many ways the most friendly and seems by his account to have been the most homely, but any one who thinks that the Palace at Dessau was homely in any ordinary sense of the word had better take a look at a picture of it. It was as big as a metropolitan railroad station or a seaside hotel, and a great deal grander.

§ IV

A travel journal of Boswell's, though it may make dutiful mention of paintings and buildings, never comes fully alive till it talks about men. In this volume, if we except Lord Marischal, who was Boswell's companion rather than the object of his quest, four men stand out, all monarchs of a sort. Frederick the Great of Prussia was the only man Boswell ever seriously set out to capture without succeeding in his designs. There does not seem to have been any marked inferiority in the letter he composed to rouse Frederick's interest, but kings cannot be caught with that kind of salt, and it did Boswell no harm to find it out. Was he really close to throwing himself at Frederick's feet in the garden at Charlottenburg? If he had, what would have happened? One guesses that the result might have been most unpleasant: the precipitate courtier whacked over the head with the royal cane and hustled out of the garden, perhaps lodged in jail. "This king is feared like a wild beast. I am quite out of conceit with monarchy."

With a monarch, not with monarchy. The glowing reverence

that cooled under the frigid gaze of Frederick of Prussia warmed again to incandescence under the gracious smiles of Karl Friedrich of Baden-Durlach. "From my earliest years I have respected the Great. In the groves of Auchinleck I have indulged pleasing hopes of ambition. . . . My utmost wish has been fulfilled. I have found a grave, a knowing, and a worthy prince. He has seen my merit. . . . He has talked a great deal with me. . . ." One feels that Boswell was never more completely happy than in those moments when he felt sure he would get the Margrave's Order of Fidelity ("Oh, I shall have it. . . . [To his servant] "You shall have a master with a star"), or when, sorting hastily the bundle of letters awaiting him at Geneva, he found one in the Margrave's hand. The end of the affair, since we do not know what really happened, balances in a most unsatisfactory way between comedy and something that is not funny at all. Did Karl Friedrich, after one letter, just get tired of writing? Or were letters suppressed on both sides through bureaucratic meddling? Might Boswell have had his star after all if he and his prince had been left alone? At any rate, it is many pities that he never got it, for he would have made such good use of it. *The Life of Samuel Johnson*, by James Boswell, Esq., Knight of the Order of Fidelity of His Most Serene Highness the Margrave of Baden. . . . James Boswell, painted by Sir Joshua with a star on his coat. . . .

§ V

Boswell chose to record his conversations with Rousseau in French, a language which he spoke and wrote fluently without ever having really mastered it; and he has given us further cause for regret by leaving them in a perplexed and huddled state that falls short by many degrees of the elaborated dramatic dialogue of *The Life of Johnson*. Yet they are historically the most important he ever put on paper. In these conversations we see his mind intimately in contact with that of the greatest literary genius of the century. I believe that no one else has given us so detailed and authentic a portrait of Rousseau the Talker; and in none of the conversations he recorded did Boswell reveal more of himself. They would make even better reading, no doubt, if he had done them over in the style of *The Life of Johnson:* distancing them, muting or suppressing the insistent personal note, posing Rousseau in high light and putting himself in the shadow. But it is a mistake to suppose that we could have had the cool and good-humoured objectivity of *The Life of Johnson* without the intense and at times oppressive subjectivity of the journal. The sketch fixes the matter for ever in the heat of a vivid egotism; the finished picture can afford to be more objective.[1]

The conjunction of the names Boswell, Rousseau, Voltaire is in itself sufficient to awaken enchanting images and expectations. The figures converge with an essential fitness, and, at the same time, an exquisite incongruity. Boswell's powers were fecundated by celebrity, above all by literary fame; and the fame of "Voltaire, Rousseau, immortal names!" was such as to make Johnson's appear merely provincial. The two characters, strongly marked and gaining strength by contrast, were a theme fitted to his hand. At the same time no mind could be less French than Boswell's, and the distance between Auchinleck and Ferney is mentally immeasurable. One foresees that against such a background the biographer's oddity will be accentuated and his feats of self-assurance unequalled.

We see the temperamental hermit in the Armenian dress at Môtiers and the toothless monarch in the dressing-gown at Ferney, but more vividly than either figure, Boswell has shown us his own *impact* upon them; and here he reveals a true if comic quality of genius. To all that is within his grasp at the moment, the visitor

[1] The remainder of this section (that is, to §VI on p. xvii) has been adapted by Frederick A. Pottle from the late Geoffrey Scott's Introduction to the 4th volume of Colonel Isham's privately printed edition of the Boswell papers, 1928. Few changes have been made, but they involve matters of judgment as well as matters of fact. The adaptation bears something the same relation to Scott's original as does the revision of Macaulay's essay on Johnson in the latest edition of the *Encyclopaedia Britannica* to the essay as it first appeared.

is minutely and skilfully attentive; of what lies beyond, he is heroically unaware. He has shut himself within the small circle of his lively perceptions, and reigns there. He hears no whispers. The irony of Ferney makes no prick. Insensibility clothes and shields him like a magic garment. He has the obstinacy of the deaf, the clairvoyance of the blind. Voltaire from the first has "guessed the merit" of his visitor — the merit of a rare specimen, novel even to that unwearied collector of human nature. But under the impact of Boswell, Voltaire's head turns, and he lets himself gently swoon upon an easy chair. (He had, we know, perfected the art of simulated fainting fits.) When he recovers, Boswell is still there. "I resumed our conversation but changed the tone." Boswell has only two days in which to convert the illustrious sceptic to a belief in the immortality of the soul, and he is not to be gainsaid. Voltaire will not only hear him out; the old man will write to him on this topic a letter in which smiling courtesy sharpens the ironic edge.

Thus the enormous intellectual disparity between Boswell and his hosts, while it lends constant comedy to the encounters, is not the last or the most significant of our impressions. In the plane of human reality, he is their equal. "Yes, upon that occasion, he was one individual and I another. For a certain portion of time there was a fair opposition between Voltaire and Boswell." These words will not seem untrue. The universe of Boswell's journal may be comical and confined, but he has the originality to conceive it, the force to maintain it, and (above all) the simplicity to keep himself unaware of any other. Sheer simplicity — his *saturation* with himself — renders him "one individual." Of how many pilgrims to Ferney could this be said? Confronted by the sun of Voltaire, they become at once planets; Boswell remains a small, bright, individual star.

Among his fellow guests at Voltaire's château in December, 1764 was the Chevalier de Boufflers, travelling with his easel as Monsieur Charles. His mind was fitted to entertain and comprehend Voltaire. His letters were the delight of the courts of Luné-

ville and Versailles. There are among them descriptions of Voltaire
written from Ferney at this very date. They are urbane, Latin, and
relevant. But Boswell's irrelevancy is more potent and dramatic.
He assumes for himself by the instinctive right of his egoism —
which is also his genius — a full share of the picture. We acquiesce,
no less instinctively. That he is but twenty-four years of age, utterly
unknown, and to the last degree impressed by the renown of his
two hosts, at Môtiers and Ferney, renders his independence all the
more striking. He goes as an interviewer, but he remains himself
the Object.

§ VI

The principal manuscripts from which this book has been com-
piled are the following:

1. Journal in Holland, Germany, and Switzerland, 18 June
1764 to 1 January 1765: 414 quarto pages, numbered by Boswell
568–587, 508–773, 734–861, but continuous and complete; roughly
9 by 7½ inches, unbound. A good deal of this journal is written in
French.

2. Memoranda and Notes for Journal in Holland, Germany,
and Switzerland, 19 June 1764 to 2 January 1765: 90 unpaged
octavo leaves, nearly all written on both sides; roughly 7¼ by 4½
inches, unbound. Boswell's usual procedure was to fill exactly one
page a day. In the manuscript as we now have it, there are no
entries for 23–25 August and 4–8 September, and there are three
supplementary undated leaves that appear to belong to the middle
of November. Otherwise the manuscript runs straight on with a
dated entry for each day. Many passages are in French.

3. Ten-Lines-a-Day Verses. Dated from 1 October to 22 November 1764: 9 unpaged quarto leaves, written on both sides; roughly
9 by 7¼ inches, unbound.

4. Upwards of 90 letters sent or received by Boswell between
18 June 1764 and 1 January 1765, and 8 letters of later date to or
from the Margrave of Baden-Durlach and Voltaire. All but ten of

these letters are at Yale, and, of that ten, four are represented at Yale by drafts. The letters to Boswell in the Yale collection are originals, as are also the letters from Boswell to John Johnston and Boswell to W. J. Temple. (He retrieved his letters to Johnston from Johnston's executor after Johnston's death; of the letters to Temple, he had asked back all those he wrote from the Continent, meaning to use them for a book of travels.) The other letters by Boswell at Yale are drafts. Nearly half the letters are in French. There is at Yale a Register of Letters sent and received, beginning with 23 September 1764 and running to October, 1766. It is not complete and not entirely accurate, but it is often useful for fixing dates and proving the existence of lost letters.

5. Expense Accounts: "Expenses at Berlin," 8 July to 22 September 1764; "Tour from Berlin, through Several Courts and Cities of Germany to Geneva," 19 September 1764 to 1 January 1765, 2 quarto and 7 folio leaves, unpaged, written on both sides; roughly 9 by 7½ and 12 by 7½ inches, unbound. Entirely in French.

A few other miscellaneous documents will be described at the points where they are printed or referred to.

The journal that appears in this volume was published in 1928 by the late Geoffrey Scott in *Private Papers of James Boswell from Malahide Castle, in the Collection of Lt.-Colonel Ralph Heyward Isham*, an expensive limited edition of which only 570 copies were printed. Boswell's three letters to Rousseau were published in full from the originals in 1924 by Professor Chauncey B. Tinker in *Letters of James Boswell*, 2 vols., Clarendon Press. Two others of Boswell's letters here included have previously been published, one of them by Boswell himself in *The Life of Johnson*. I believe that the remainder of the material is now printed for the first time. Particularly gratifying recent recoveries, not known to Mr. Scott, are the "Sketch of My Life" which Boswell wrote for Rousseau, and two of the eight quarto pages in which he recorded the conversation of Voltaire. I have printed the journal with no cuts, but have felt free to abridge the other documents. Notes saying that certain letters have not been recovered should not be taken as indicating a policy of including all the letters we have for the period, or even all the letters we have that are mentioned in the journal. The purpose of such notes is rather to explain why letters that sound important enough to include in this edition do not in fact appear there.

The spelling, capitalization, and punctuation of the documents have been reduced to accepted modern norms, and abbreviations and contractions have been expanded at will. All quotations in the Introduction and notes, whether from Boswell or other sources, have been standardized in the same fashion. The standard of spelling for all but proper names is *The Concise Oxford Dictionary* (1951). For place-names the English editions of Baedeker's *Germany* (1936) and *Switzerland* (1938) have been followed. Personal names, when the persons are certainly identified, are spelled as in the standard biographical dictionaries, or as they appear in authoritative documents in the local archives. The texts have been broken into paragraphs where such breaks make for easier reading. Names of speakers have been supplied in conversations cast dramatically. A few clear inadvertencies have been put right without notice. Square brackets indicate words added by the editor where the manuscript shows no defect, and where there is no reason to suspect inadvertency on the part of the writer; angular brackets indicate reconstructions by the editor of words lost through defects in the manuscripts, where the reconstruction is not entirely certain.

Documents in foreign languages have generally been given in English translation only. The journal of Boswell's tour in Germany and Switzerland presents a trying problem for the editor of a volume such as this. Boswell wrote the narrative portion for the most part in English, but he occasionally shifted into French in the middle of a sentence. He generally gave the titles of court and government officials in French, as he did frequently the names of buildings and the like. Conversation which was conducted in French (that is, the greater part of the conversation) he recorded in French. I have put most of this French into English, but have left untranslated certain titles and occasional detached words and phrases, my aim being to retain as much as possible of the foreign flavour of the book without really making it difficult for the reader who has no French or who reads it slowly. French that has been retained has been standardized and modernized. I have thought it better, however, to leave Boswell's few attempts at German pretty much alone. His spelling, which is in the main Dutch, could easily have been adjusted, but the resultant forms would still have been highly incorrect. Consequently, I have left the German bits in the text, with translations in the notes, and, except for correcting the spelling of the one word *Herr* (which he invariably spelled *Heer*), have printed it just as Boswell wrote it. Any reader who wishes to see the unmodified text of the journal is reminded that one is available in Colonel Isham's *Private Papers*. The French of Boswell's letters to Rousseau can be consulted in Professor Tinker's *Letters of James Boswell*. And of course our projected research edition of the Boswell papers will give all these documents in the language in which they were written.

The indexes of this series are not mere finding tools, but supplement the annotation. In particular, we usually reserve for the index the function of supplying Christian names of persons mentioned.

The general plan of *Boswell on the Grand Tour: Germany and Switzerland* was worked out in conference by the Editorial Committee after careful study of a long and unselective text which I had prepared. Mr. Liebert provided the artist with materials for the maps, Dr. Metzdorf assumed responsibility for the collection of illustrations, and both they and Professor Hilles read the proofs. Of the larger Advisory Committee Dr. Breuning, Professor Peyre, and Dr. Simpson have read the proofs and have sent corrections and suggestions for changes in the notes.

As has already been mentioned above, the late Geoffrey Scott published a text of Boswell's German and Swiss journals in 1928 as the third and fourth volumes of Colonel Isham's privately printed *Private Papers of James Boswell*. These superb examples of fine book-making, which few people have ever seen because they were expensive and the edition was small, present a scrupulously accurate text with the spelling and capitalization of the manuscripts, accompanied by critical introductions of great charm and penetration. The plan of the volumes precluded footnote annotation, but Mr. Scott provided a translation of the conversations with Rousseau on pages facing Boswell's French. I have used his text as the basis of mine (collating my proofs, however, with the manuscripts), and have made grateful use of his translations and of portions of his introductions.

The long and difficult manuscript containing the memoranda in Germany and Switzerland still remains for the greater part unpublished, but I have at hand a complete transcript with annotation, made twenty years ago as a class exercise by Professor William D. Paden, then a student in the Yale Graduate School. In the same class Professor Joseph Foladare reviewed Scott's text of the German tour and collected annotation for it, and Dean Helen S. Randall performed like service for the Swiss journal. Dr. Charles H. Bennett then reviewed all the exercises, made additions to the annotation, and restudied the text of the memoranda. He also translated the rest of the French dialogue in the journal (Scott's translation not going beyond the conversations with Rousseau), and drafted annotation for a trade or reading edition. Using these stores and others resulting from my own researches, I completed a text for a trade edition as far back as fifteen years ago. The recovery afterwards from Malahide Castle of Boswell's European correspondence and of other papers of the first importance made it necessary to replan the volume and to revise the annotation. Some of the notes appearing in these pages have been rewritten three or four times, I hope to their advantage.

I have been very lucky in having constant access to experts. Mrs. Annemarie Holborn, who prepared the first typed draft of the book and did a good deal of research for the notes under my direction, is German by birth and holds a Berlin doctorate in classics. Professor Curt von Faber du Faur and Professor Konstantin Reichardt, both members of the Department of Germanic Languages at Yale, have answered many questions for me, have furnished me with many of my best notes, and have both read the proofs. Dr. G. R. de Beer, the extent of whose knowledge of matters Swiss is well known, and Dr. Fritz Güttinger of Zürich, who has recently translated Boswell's *Life of Johnson* and *Boswell's London Journal* into German, have also read the proofs and have sent corrections. Dr. W. David Patton, formerly of the Department of French at Yale, has patiently compared the translations with the French originals, and has given me invaluable assistance with some of the notes, especially those dealing with Rousseau and Voltaire. Professor Robert Warnock, who spent February to August of last year in Germany and Holland searching the archives for materials with which to annotate the forthcoming research edition of Boswell's journal, sent me preliminary reports from which I was able to extract some useful notes for this edition, besides fixing the spelling of many family names and supplying many Christian names which we had formerly lacked. Through Professor Warnock's presence in Germany we were able to acquire from the archives at Karlsruhe texts of the correspondence between Boswell and Karl Friedrich of Baden-Durlach and to locate two of our best illustrations: the Ducal Family of Brunswick reproduced opposite page 14, and the sketch of Karl Friedrich opposite page 180. For securing us photographs of these pictures I wish to thank Dr. Gerda Kircher of Karlsruhe and Dr. H. Vogel, Director of the Picture Gallery of the Hessisches Landesmuseum; for the key to the picture of the Ducal Family (p. vii), Dr. August Fink, Director of the Duke Anton Ulrich Museum in Brunswick. My note concerning Rietberg on page 9 was furnished by Dr. Bernhard Winter, Director of Studies in the Municipal Foundation High School, Rietberg.

My old friend and collaborator, Dr. Charles H. Bennett, whose services in preparing the text have already been mentioned, has added to the long list of my obligations by reading the proofs. And how shall I express my general and enduring obligation to Professor Chauncey B. Tinker, the only begetter of all Boswellian studies at Yale?

To the following learned colleagues at Yale and elsewhere I acknowledge help with particular problems which I cannot take room to specify: Roland H. Bainton, Robert S. Bosher, Lewis P. Curtis, Edward R. Hardy, Harry M. Hubbell, Wallace Notestein, Henry B. Richardson, Norman L. Torrey, Marshall Waingrow, Ralph L. Ward, C. Bradford Welles, and L. Pearce Williams. And finally I tender my warm thanks to all the members of the office staff of the Yale Editions of the Private Papers of James Boswell during the last year: Mrs. Jane H. Carroll, Mrs. Dorothy B. Moravcik, Mrs. Marion S. Pottle, Joseph W. Reed, '54, Mrs. Ellen R. Weld, and Thomas M. Woodson, '53. Mrs. Patricia B. Wells is mainly responsible for the index.

F.A.P.

Yale University, New Haven
1 August 1953

JOURNAL OF A TOUR
THROUGH THE COURTS OF GERMANY

What a singular being do I find myself! Let this my journal show what variety my mind is capable of. But am I not well received everywhere? Am I not particularly taken notice of by men of the most distinguished genius? And why? I have neither profound knowledge, strong judgment, nor constant gaiety. But I have a noble soul which still shines forth, a certain degree of knowledge, a multiplicity of ideas of all kinds, an original humour and turn of expression, and, I really believe, a remarkable knowledge of human nature.... With this I have a pliant ease of manners which must please. I can tune myself so to the tone of any bearable man I am with that he is as much at freedom as with another self, and, till I am gone, cannot imagine me a stranger. [29 DECEMBER 1764]

Journal of a Tour
through the Courts of Germany
by James Boswell, 1764

SKETCH OF BOSWELL'S LIFE TO JUNE, 1764. James Boswell was the eldest son of Alexander Boswell, a Scottish laird and judge who took the style Lord Auchinleck (then generally pronounced Affléck) from his estate in Ayrshire. The family was ancient and well connected; and it was felt by the neighbours that the Boswells of Auchinleck showed at least as much pride as their descent and possessions entitled them to. Lord Auchinleck's father had been a lawyer before him and had prospered in his profession; and it was for the law that Lord Auchinleck destined his eldest son. Young Boswell rebelled and remained stubborn in revolt. He did not know exactly what profession he wished to embrace, but his chief delight lay in scribbling and publishing; he was fascinated by the theatre and enthralled by actresses. In 1760, when he was in his twentieth year, he ran away to London and made his submission to the Roman Catholic Church. Lord Eglinton, an Ayrshire peer living in London, diverted him from this sincere but precipitate commitment by turning him into a rake and convincing him that what he really wanted was a commission in the Foot Guards. Lord Auchinleck refused to purchase a commission in the Guards and continued to press for the law. After struggling for two years with his unhappy but obstinate heir, he allowed him to go up to London with a modest allowance to see if he could obtain a commission through influence. Shortly before starting on this expedition, Boswell had begun the portentous journal which was to be the central achievement of his life. The London journal of 1762–1763, long believed to have been lost, was discovered by Professor C. Colleer Abbott at Fettercairn House in 1930, and was first published in 1950.[1]

Ever since the course of instruction he had received from Eglinton in 1760, Boswell had been very much a man of pleasure. Though he was sincerely pious and had an unusual capacity for devotion, he accepted with pride the *bonnes fortunes* which his youth and personal attractiveness threw in his way, and resorted frequently to the grosser indulgence which the streets of London offered him. But towards the end of his stay in London, he met the great moralist, Samuel Johnson, was greatly impressed, and resolved to reform. The quest for a commission having proved futile, as his father had predicted and as he himself wished though he did not know it, he gave in to his father and consented to be a lawyer. It was agreed that he should go to Utrecht for a winter to study Civil Law, and that he should then be allowed to visit Paris and some of the German courts. He did not at the time think it prudent to ask for more, but it was his intention from the first to secure his father's consent to a much more extended tour.

To Utrecht he went in August, 1763, and there he remained until the middle of the following June.[2] He did reform: studied law with reasonable assiduity, improved his Latin and Greek, and worked really hard to acquire a fluent command of French. Having excellent introductions and being himself descended from a noble Dutch family, he met all the most prominent people at Utrecht and The Hague. He suffered a brief but violent passion for a beautiful and rich young widow, Madame Geelvinck, and towards the end of his stay in Holland began to entertain more than friendly feelings for Belle de Zuylen, a Dutch girl of noble family, who will

[1] *Boswell's London Journal, 1762–1763*, McGraw-Hill Book Company, Inc. (New York) and William Heinemann, Ltd. (London).
[2] See *Boswell in Holland, 1763–1764*, McGraw-Hill Book Company, Inc. (New York) and William Heinemann, Ltd. (London).

appear frequently in the present volume under the *nom de plume* Zélide.

Not only was Boswell studious in Holland, not only did he try to acquire greater reserve of character, but he also remained strictly chaste. It would be gratifying to report that he was happy, but the facts are otherwise. He had always been subject to fits of depression. So long as industry and virtue remained.novel, they stimulated him and filled him with solid satisfaction, but when his strict regimen became a routine, he suffered the worst attack of low spirits he had ever been called on to endure. As usually happened on such occasions, melancholy brought with it a horrified conviction of the truth of the doctrine of necessity; and as usual he found he could escape from the coils of necessity only by relaxing the strictness of his religious and moral convictions. He was assisted in his emancipation by Rousseau, whose ideas as stated in "The Creed of a Savoyard Vicar" he came upon at this juncture, and by a Dutch physician named Hahn who assured him that unaccustomed continence was bad for the health. By the end of the Utrecht period he had adopted very grand and extensive notions of God's benevolence, and needed only opportunity to revert to his old grossness. The end of the Utrecht journal shows him restored and in eager high spirits, preparing to start on a tour of the German courts.

THE GERMAN STATES AND THE GERMAN EMPIRE. Germany in the eighteenth century was a nation but hardly a state. The area comprising roughly the countries of Germany, Czechoslovakia, and Austria, as they stood between 1920 and 1935, constituted what was known as the Holy Roman Empire, and this entity was presided over by an august personage who bore the style of Emperor. In theory, each emperor, as the Imperial throne fell vacant, was elected by nine of the great German princes, the Electors. Actually, the Empire was the loosest sort of federation of principalities and free cities, and the Electors as early as the fifteenth century had got into the habit of choosing the successive heads of the House of Habsburg, that is, the reigning archdukes of Austria. In 1764 (the male line of the Habsburgs having died out) the title was held by Francis I, husband of the Habsburg Archduchess and actual ruler of Austria, Maria Theresa. Outside his own dominion the Emperor exercised few powers except the granting of titles. The Empire had no army, except as the constituent states raised one for a given war, and no police force. It was in fact a collection of virtually independent powers subscribing to a symbol that tended to foster national consciousness, but not to produce political unity. And there were very many of these independent states. The territories and the titles of the Electors had for some time been descending undivided according to the principle of male primogeniture, but the other principalities were treated as though they were the personal properties of the successive reigning princes, and had come to be divided and sub-divided among different lines of the same family. Boswell, for example, visited two Brunswicks, two Anhalts, and two Badens; there were at the time five duchies of Saxony besides the Electorate. Some of these principalities, by modern standards, were ridiculously small. Yet even the small ones maintained splendid courts, with a staff of officials and a show of public buildings, painting, and music out of all proportion to their size. The court language and even the court culture of Germany was French, the native German speech and culture being considered too homely for such exalted display.[3]

THE SEVEN YEARS' WAR AND FREDERICK THE GREAT. The present-day reader who comes with no historical preparation to the reading of Boswell's German journal will find that, so far as customs and manners are concerned, Boswell himself provides all that is really needed. He, too, was strange to the scene, and, being strange, noticed and reported on most of the details of difference in dress, food, means of travelling, amusements, etiquette, and the like that we wish to be told about. There is perhaps no other document extant that transmits so vividly as this journal the feel of Ger-

[3] For the English reader the best general introduction to the politics and culture of eighteenth-century Germany is still Carlyle's *History of Friedrich II of Prussia*. Though extremely long and violently opinionated, it presents the personalities of the time with incomparable brilliance.

man *Kleinstaaterei* at the middle of the eighteenth century. But the
reader will perhaps not find amiss a word about the Seven Years'
War and Frederick of Prussia, for though Boswell makes a good
deal of reference to both, he never fills in the military-political
background in any coherent fashion.

Seen in its simplest relations, the political history of western
Europe during the first half of the century had consisted of attempts by the Habsburgs on the one hand and the Bourbons
(headed by the Kings of France) on the other to extend by war and
diplomacy the territorial sway of their respective dynasties both
inside and outside the Empire. England's policy had been to throw
her weight now this way, now that, in accordance with the principle of the balance of power. Prussia, under two remarkable rulers,
had followed a consistent programme of building up the most for-
midable army in Germany.

The chief issue of the half-century, so far as the continent of
Europe was concerned, was the emergence of Prussia as a first-rate
power. The Hohenzollerns had long been Margraves and Electors
of Brandenburg, but the title "King of Prussia" was recent and was
considered rather pretentious. Frederick II, the young king who
succeeded in the year of Boswell's birth (1740), took advantage of
the dispute over Maria Theresa's succession to snatch from Austria
the extensive territory of Silesia. The Seven Years' War, which
began in 1756 and ended in 1763, was a tremendous coalition of
formerly hostile powers — Austria, France, Russia, Saxony, Sweden, and the Empire — to crush Frederick and dismember his
state. England, his only ally, furnished him with a subsidy, but
since the war had turned for her into a world-wide naval and colo-
nial struggle with France, could give him only limited military
support. A smallish Anglo-Hanoverian army serving in western
Germany under the command of Frederick's general, Ferdinand
of Brunswick, won great glory for itself at the Battle of Minden (1
August 1759).

In spite of expert preparation, of brilliant generalship and
amazing victories in the face of greatly superior numbers, Fred-

erick by 1761 was brought to the verge of defeat. Old George II of England had died in 1760, and the government of his successor wished a speedy ending of the war, which had brought the British Crown tremendous additions of territory in America and India. The British contingent in Germany was reduced and the subsidy was withdrawn. Frederick lost most of Silesia, and on one occasion Russian and Austrian troops entered Berlin. But early in 1762 he was saved by the death of the Empress of Russia, which removed Russia from the coalition against him. He emerged from the war with his territory intact, the Prussian state recognized as a power of the first rank, and the numeral which was his own distinguishing style replaced in popular reference by the emphatic designation "the Great." When Boswell saw him in the summer of 1764, less than a year and a half after the signing of the Peace, he was fifty-two years old. Because he thought that England had let him down in his hour of greatest need, he had no great love for Englishmen.[4]

BOSWELL'S TRAVELLING-COMPANIONS. The other figures that momentarily cross the kaleidoscope of Boswell's narrative are too numerous to be comprehended in a single survey. Boswell fortunately is the most precise, the least allusive of diarists, and explains each episode as it occurs. It may however be useful to say something of the travelling-companions with whom he sets out. Had Boswell ever given his tour a more literary form, it is likely that the Earl Marischal would have been accorded a conspicuous place. It is true that in Berlin they parted company and, though the Earl returns later in the narrative, it is but for a brief interval. Nevertheless his thread in the story is longer than any other. The picturesque past of the old warrior, his position at the Court of Prussia, his romantic physical demeanour and personal eccentricities — all these (coupled with his friendship for Boswell) fit him for a principal part. But in the journal as it stands he is rather a

[4] The two paragraphs that follow are by the late Geoffrey Scott, slightly revised by Frederick A. Pottle. They were first published in 1928 as part of the Introduction to the 3d volume of Colonel Isham's privately printed *Private Papers of James Boswell*.

George Keith, tenth Earl Marischal of Scotland, from a painting
in the Historical Museum of Neuchâtel.

fellow spectator than part of the spectacle; and Boswell who en-
larges at length on many trivial encounters finds few occasions for
delineating him.

Lord Marischal's is one of the odd cosmopolitan careers of the
eighteenth century. He was born well within the seventeenth, and
had held a commission under Marlborough. His Jacobite sym-
pathies were fearless from the first. He had wished to proclaim the
Pretender at the head of his troops in 1714; he entertained him in
his house and fought at Sheriffmuir in 1715; four years later he
commanded a Spanish expedition which suffered disaster in the
west of Scotland; escaping disguised to Spain, he continued to further by intrigue the cause which had been lost in arms. Disillu-
sioned, and bitterly critical of Prince Charles (on this head we gain
some interesting light in the journal here printed, p. 237), he took
no part in the '45, and thereafter threw in his lot with Frederick
the Great, going as his Ambassador to the courts of Paris and
Madrid. In 1754 he was appointed Governor of Neuchâtel, where
he became the friend and protector of Rousseau. In return for diplomatic services to the British Government he was pardoned and
granted a sum of money which enabled him to buy back his forfeited Scottish estates; but he remained faithful to Frederick, and
at the date of our narrative he was on his way to Potsdam in answer
to the King's entreaty. There he was to remain, and there he died
in 1778. He had adopted a Turkish girl named Emetulla, whom
his brother, Marshal Keith, brought back from the siege of Ocha-
kov. Of this lady (Madame de Froment) all that is known is her
infinite capacity for unbroken silence. This then is the strange
trio in the coach which lumbers out of Utrecht towards Germany:
the heroic rebel, the speechless Turk, and Boswell of Auchinleck.

MONDAY 18 JUNE 1764. . . . At seven we set out in a coach and four. My blood circulated just as briskly as in my days of youth.[5] I was drowsy, and now and then nodded. My Lord Marischal was pretty silent. So was Madame de Froment. I laid my account with little conversation.[6] We came at night to Nymwegen. I met Captain Mungo Graham of Gordon's regiment, who accompanied me round the ramparts. We saw a very ancient castle, in which it is said that Julius Caesar lived. We also mounted a tower from whence we had a most extensive and noble prospect.[7] At night I was in a charming frame, quite blissful.

TUESDAY 19 JUNE. François has given me an excellent character.[8] We dined at Kleve. I went and paid my respects to Monsieur and Madame Spaen at Bellevue, from whence there is indeed a fine prospect.[9] It was pleasant to see the German baron's castle: a hall adorned with guns; an English clock that plays ten tunes and cost £1000. At night we came to Wesel, where we had a jolly, talking

[5] Boswell was at this time in his twenty-fourth year.

[6] "I expected little conversation." (A Scotticism later accepted as English.)

[7] The "very ancient castle" was the Valkhof, a palace built by Charlemagne on Roman foundations in 777; it was demolished by French Revolutionary troops in 1795. Guide-books continued to connect it with Julius Caesar until long after Boswell's time. The "tower" was the Belvedere, a seventeenth-century structure built on the foundations of one of the old towers.

[8] Boswell had written a letter of recommendation for his servant François, whom he was leaving behind in Holland, insisting at the same time that François should give him a "character" as master. François had presented it, sealed, just as Boswell was leaving. It is printed in *Boswell in Holland,* following 18 June 1764.

[9] Boswell has now entered Germany, the Duchy of Kleve being a principality of the King of Prussia. — Alexander Sweder, Baron von Spaen, descended from a noble family of the Duchy of Minden, was a favourite of Frederick the Great during Frederick's youth, and had been involved with two other young officers, Lieutenants Katte and Keith, in Frederick's plot to flee from Germany in 1730. The plot being discovered, Keith saved himself by flight, but Katte was arrested and, by express command of Frederick's father, was beheaded. Spaen, who is said to have swallowed the one incriminating paper in his possession, got off with a brief imprisonment and exile. Entering the service of the States General, he rose to the rank of major general. Boswell

landlord. I find Madame de Froment very lively, although she has an indolence, or, as the French say, a *nonchalance*, that is terrible. She does not dress. Scarcely even will she speak. I talked with her in rather too gallant a strain.

WEDNESDAY 20 JUNE. We pursued our journey peaceably but were still silent in the coach. At night we had a sad inn.[1]

THURSDAY 21 JUNE. We were now in a Roman Catholic town. It was *fête-Dieu*,[2] so that there was to be a procession. I went into the church, adored my God and resolved to be a worthy man. All seemed noble and well. At night we came to an inn in the territory of Cologne where Maréchal Broglie has slept.[3] A dreary inn it was. I was laid upon a table covered with straw, with a blanket and a sheet; and above me I had a sheet and a feather bed. Thus was I just in the situation of a bold officer. Thus did I endure the very hard-ships of a German campaign which I used to tremble at the thoughts of when at Auchinleck.

FRIDAY 22 JUNE. My Lord told me so many curious stories that I began to think faith very uncertain. Yet I resolved to main-tain a decent system of mild Christianity. He told me that he had never been oppressed with religious prejudices. At night we came to ——, a Popish town. I walked without the gates in delightful humour. I was struck at the sight of an image of the Pope, with a crucifix in one hand and an olive-branch in the other.[4] I was filled

---

had become intimate with him at The Hague in the previous winter. His wife, with whom Boswell kept up a correspondence, was a Dutch lady, niece of the Count of Nassau, the chief magistrate of Utrecht.

[1] At Haltern, as the memoranda show.   [2] Corpus Christi.

[3] Shown by the memoranda to have been at Vellinghausen. The Maréchal Duc de Broglie attacked Ferdinand of Brunswick's army at that point on 15–16 July 1761, and no doubt spent the night of the 15th in the village; but he was driven out with heavy losses the next day, mainly by the English troops under the Marquis of Granby. Boswell is mistaken, however, in plac-ing Vellinghausen in the territory of Cologne; it was in the County of Mark, which belonged to the King of Prussia.

[4] The "image" identifies the town as Rietberg, in the County of the same name. It is not a statue of the Pope, as Boswell thought, but of St. John

with pleasing reverence. I kneeled, and with warm devotion adored my God and was grateful to the Saviour of the World. A poor man came to me; I gave him alms. I was very happy. I slept upon a great table in the common hall of the inn.

SATURDAY 23 JUNE. My Lord was eloquent in the praises of Spain, where he passed twenty years. He talked of the beautiful country, the charming climate, the excellent people, who were never known to betray their trust. My desire to go to Spain was increased.[5] His Lordship also talked of the Scots Highlanders with respect and affection, as the most brave and most generous people upon earth, and abused the harsh absurdity of our Government for taking their clothes from them and extirpating their language, by which means they will be at last reduced to a level with the other inhabitants of Scotland, and so we shall lose the best militia upon earth.[6] The proper method was surely not to destroy the Highlanders, but to render them attached to the Government, which would be no difficult matter, as the chiefs are no longer disaffected.

We came at night to Herford. I found myself a new man. My ideas were altered. I had no gloomy fears. I talked with Madame de Froment, who had been educated Mahometan and who still believed that the Great Prophet was sent from God. This opened my mind. I resolved to be prudent, nor to own my many waverings. I was quite happy. I determined to get free of the clouds which hung upon me. I determined to be manly and content.

SUNDAY 24 JUNE. We dined at Minden. But I had not time to view the field of battle. I went into a Roman Catholic church and heard mass, and was devout, and had not one Scots Sunday idea. My religion now is chiefly devotion. Pomp of worship aids me in

---

Nepomuk, the patron saint of Bohemia, and was erected in 1723 by Count Maximilian Ulrich von Kaunitz, who had married the heiress of Rietberg.

[5] At least twice in 1763 Johnson had urged Boswell to go to Spain, remarking that much of it had not yet been "perambulated."

[6] After the suppression of the Jacobite Rebellion of 1745, the British Government had made it a penal offence for a Highlander to carry weapons, to use the tartan, or to wear any part of the distinctive Highland garb.

this. I see a probability for the truth of Christianity. I shall be an amiable man. My "life shall be in the right."[7]

We came at night to an inn in the territory of Hanover.[8] Thus was I laid. In the middle of a great German *salle,* upon straw spread on the floor, was a sheet laid; here "great Boswell lay."[9] I had another sheet and a coverlet. On one side of me were eight or ten horses; on the other, four or five cows. A little way from me sat on high a cock and many hens; and before I went to sleep the cock made my ears ring with his shrill voice, so that I admired the wisdom of the Sybarites, who slew all those noisy birds. What frightened me not a little was an immense mastiff chained pretty near the head of my bed. He growled most horribly, and rattled his chain. I called for a piece of bread and made a friendship with him. Before me were two great folding doors wide open, so that I could see the beauties of the evening sky. In this way, however, did I sleep with much contentment, and much health.

MONDAY 25 JUNE. My Lord joked on the tea-spoons, which seemed of gold: "Ay, ay, the money of Old England in the Hanoverian dominions."[1] He assumed the character of Dictionary Johnson in order to joke in this manner. He talked of somebody having stolen gold spoons. "Very natural," said I. "Hear the Scotsman,"

[7] For modes of faith let graceless zealots fight:
He can't be wrong whose life is in the right.
                    Pope, *Essay on Man,* iii. 305–306
[8] Somewhere in the vicinity of Hameln.
[9] In the worst inn's worst room, with mat half-hung,
The floors of plaster, and the walls of dung,
On once a flock-bed, but repair'd with straw,
With tape-tied curtains never meant to draw . . .
Great Villiers lies.
                    Pope, *Moral Essays,* iii. 299–305
[1] The Duchy of Hanover was completely independent of the British Crown, but its sovereign, the Elector of Hanover, happened also to be King of England. It was a constant gibe of the anti-Court party in England that the English were being beggared by taxes to protect and foster the King's foreign domains. Lord Marischal, it will be remembered, had risked his life to prevent the succession of the House of Hanover.

said he. We came to Hanover, where we dined. My Lord went and waited on the Countess of Yarmouth.[2] My old Mrs. Webster ideas of King George's Palace at Herrenhausen, &c., were all realized.[3] We had a very amusing day of it. I made my Lord laugh by saying that all the girls we met were like the princesses of our present royal family.

TUESDAY 26 JUNE. We arrived at Brunswick before dinner. My Lord dressed, dined, and went to Court. I strolled about; found it a large and handsome town, with a number of old buildings. At night Madame de Froment and I supped tête-à-tête. She talked of the hypochondria, which she had severely felt. She understood it perfectly. She told me of a gentleman whom his friends wanted much to settle in business, but he said he would not stir two steps to get two thousand pounds. She said that the imagination and all the faculties of the mind were confounded, and could judge of nothing, so that all things appeared one undistinguished black mass. Exercise and dissipation, with moderate enjoyment, she said, were the only remedies. I was amused with all this, but kept myself snug.

WEDNESDAY 27 JUNE. The fiend laid hold of me. I was heavy and gloomy and awkward and lazy. At breakfast we had Mr. Mackenzie of Seaforth, a lively, pretty young man, with the most perfect elegance of manners, having been abroad a great many years.[4] I was bashful before him. Such is the effect of a narrow education. At eleven I waited on Monsieur de Feronce, Privy Coun-

[2] Amalie Sophie Wallmoden, a young married woman of the Hanoverian Court, had taken the fancy of George II, and had become his mistress with the knowledge and professed approval of Queen Caroline. After the Queen's death he brought her to England, caused her to be created Countess of Yarmouth, and maintained her as his favourite for twenty years. On his death in 1760 she returned to Hanover.

[3] This probably means that Boswell's aunt, Mrs. Webster, had described to him a visit to Herrenhausen, near Hanover, the favourite residence of the first two Georges. Her husband, Dr. Alexander Webster, was a devoted Hanoverian, and had been chaplain to Frederick Prince of Wales.

[4] He was twenty years old, and would have been Earl of Seaforth if his grandfather had not taken an active part in the Rebellion of 1715.

cillor, &c., of the Duke of Brunswick. I had a letter for him from young Count Bentinck at The Hague.[5] I found him a man of polite science, lively and easy. He sent to all the Grands Maréchals and Grands Maîtres, and all the great folks, who appointed me to be at Court by two. Feronce went with me. He presented me to Monsieur de Stammer, a Knight of the Teutonic Order, for whom I had also a letter from Count Bentinck. I was next presented to all the Grands, &c., and to the Dames d'honneur. Next the Duke came out, to whom I was presented, and next to the Duchess. At three we sat down to dinner. I was quite struck to find myself at table in the Palace of Brunswick, with that illustrious family. I sat opposite to Prince Ferdinand, whose presence inspires animated respect. He absolutely electrified me. Every time that I looked at him, I felt a noble shock.[6]

We had a splendid dinner and plenty of burgundy and other wines. After dinner we went into another room and had coffee, after which Monsieur de Stammer went with me to the Court of the Hereditary Prince. I kissed the hand of the Princess, and I was politely received by the Prince.[7] I next went with the gay Feronce

[5] A grandson of the first Earl of Portland and Captain in the British Navy. His wife was a cousin of Belle de Zuylen, and he was serving as intermediary in the correspondence between Belle and Boswell.

[6] Karl, Duke of Brunswick from 1735 to 1780, is particularly remembered for his lavish expenditure in the cause of learning and the arts. His Duchess, Philippine Charlotte, was a sister of Frederick the Great. (See opposite p. 14 the reproduction of a picture of the Duke's family painted not far from the time of Boswell's visit. The separate figures are identified in the key on p. vii.) Prince Ferdinand, a younger brother of the Duke and a great general, had led the British troops in the Seven Years' War. If Boswell had served a German campaign, he would have fought under him.

[7] "Hereditary Prince" means "heir to the Reigning Prince." (The rulers of the German principalities bore the varying styles of Archduke, Grand Duke, Duke, Margrave, Landgrave, &c., but the term "prince" could be applied to any of them.) Karl Wilhelm Ferdinand, a famous general, succeeded his father as Duke of Brunswick in 1780. In 1792, because of his reputation for liberality and benevolence, he was offered the supreme command of the French Revolutionary army, but refused, and accepted instead the command

and paid some visits to ladies whom he presented me to, and at seven I returned to the Reigning Court, where I played at whist. We had here of English, Lord Hope and his tutor Mr. Rouet, and his brother of the Guards; Mr. Richards, an amiable Dorsetshire man, and Mr. William Hall of Scotland. We supped with the Court. All was noble and fine. Yet did my abominable speculation analyse all into insipidity at last.

THURSDAY 28 JUNE. I waited on Lord Hope and the other English; found them at breakfast, talking like virtuosos. Left them soon. Waited next on the Abbé Jerusalem, for whom I had a letter from Count Bentinck. I found him a learned, agreeable man with a pleasing simplicity of manners.[8] He told me he had a conversation of two hours with the King of Prussia, whom he found as great a man as fame had reported him to be. He talked on a variety of subjects with a remarkable force and fluency. The Abbé said that he lost all fear for the King, so that at last he wished to bring him on the subject of religion, on which he doubted not to give His Majesty some arguments that would not be without weight. The Abbé said he defended no sect, but the genuine Christian religion itself. He said he had been twice just a-dying and took up Plato's *Phaedo*, which was the support of the ancients in the gloomy hour. "I was struck," said he, "to find it so weak. I applied to the religion of Jesus, and had full contentment of mind. Thus," said he, "I have had a trial of my religion." I was pleased with this anecdote of the worthy and amiable Abbé. But I was not at ease myself. My faith

---

of the opposed Prussian forces. He was mortally wounded in the battle of Auerstedt, 1806. His "Princess" was Augusta, sister of George III; she had married him five months before Boswell's arrival in Brunswick. "Monsieur de Feronce" (later Finance Minister) had gone to England as Minister Plenipotentiary to arrange the marriage.

[8] Johann Friedrich Wilhelm Jerusalem, celebrated Protestant divine, was tutor to the Hereditary Prince and director of the Collegium Carolinum. He preached a new kind of "clear Christianity" which Boswell at this stage of his religious progress would naturally have found interesting. He appears in the picture of the Duke's family opposite: the figure in black, standing behind the young prince's horse.

The Ducal Family of Brunswick, from a painting (1762) by Johann Heinrich Tischbein, in Schloss Wilhelmshöhe, formerly the summer residence of the Electors of Hesse. (For identifications of the persons, see p. vii.)

was confused. Objections rose thick against revelation. Yet I hoped at last to attain stability. I said to the Abbé that in travelling we meet with painful circumstances. We make a good acquaintance and we must be obliged to quit. "I find," said I, "that I could be very happy with your conversation; and tomorrow I must leave you and perhaps shall never have the happiness of seeing you again."

I dined with the Hereditary Prince. The Princess was excessively affable. She talked to me with the greatest ease of the Catch Club, Lord Eglinton, Lord March, and other English topics.[9] After dinner she spoke English to my Lord Marischal, Mackenzie, Richards, and me. She was just a free English lass. "I can get no bread and butter here of a morning," said she. "The butter is bad and they have only brown bread." A Cumberland squire's daughter could not have been more easy.

I then paid a visit to Feronce, saw his library, which was not great, but very well chosen and elegant. I was gloomy and talked to Feronce of that distemper. He said it was merely corporeal; for he had heard of a girl of twelve who hanged herself, and she could not have much thought. I then went to the Reigning Court. The Palace is ancient, and the rooms filled me with respect. The great court looks noble, although the front is only wood cut in imitation of stone, except a small part of it newly built.

I ought to be tied to the halberds and lashed unmercifully for neglecting to relate that this day at two I was presented to Prince Ferdinand. He received me in his bedchamber. It was splendid. The canopy was sumptuous. He had a number of pretty pictures and an elegant collection of books. He talked a good time to me. It was luxury. I stood with a mind full of the ideas of the last glorious war. I was talking to a distinguished hero. He had a force and yet an affability of address. He seemed a man of strong judgment and clear ideas. He told me that the Scots Highlanders were happy

[9] Lord Eglinton and Lord March, along with Lord Sandwich, Hugo Meynell, and others, founded the Catch Club in 1761 to encourage the composition of catches, canons, and glees. The club has continued down to the present time.

when they met with heath, but complained that it was short, and nothing like their heath. All my speculation could not annihilate the satisfaction of this interview.

At night Rouet and I talked a good deal. He was a sensible, forward fellow. After supper the Duke of Brunswick honoured me with a pretty long conversation, and I am sure that his Highness was pleased. Here now do I find myself in the very sphere of magnificence. I live with princes, and a court is my home. I took leave of the Duke, and a cordial adieu of all the courtiers. I found myself already liked by them with affection. They asked me to return to Brunswick in August, when I would see the Fair. I said I probably should have that pleasure. I went home in vast spirits. I could scarcely sleep.

FRIDAY 29 JUNE.[1] After a restless night, I rose fallen not a little. At six we set out. We had a so-so day of it.

SATURDAY 30 JUNE. I was exceedingly melancholy, but I had fortitude enough to conceal it. My thoughts were horrid, yet my manners were cheerful. I lost all foreign ideas. I thought myself just in Scotland. How strange is the mind of man! How are our ideas lodged? How are they formed? How little do they depend upon realities!

In the afternoon my Lord was very chatty. He told me that the Marquis d'Argens was a good-natured, amiable man, and much liked by the King of Prussia.[2] He is now old. He has married an actress, whom he keeps in great subjection. He has made her learn Greek, and I don't know how many things, merely to make her of use to him in his studies. He is a miserable being, for he is hypochondriac and terrified for death. He had worn a flannel under-

[1] " . . . Be gay; mem. firm, Laird of Auchinleck, habits of *retenue,* prudence, &c. Manage Father with affection" (Memorandum, 29 June).

[2] The Marquis d'Argens, a dissolute and adventurous French nobleman, was the author of a number of frothy books which attracted the attention of Frederick, who admired French literature and held the German language in contempt. Frederick invited him to Potsdam and made him Chamberlain and Director of Fine Arts in the Berlin Academy. He had remained Frederick's faithful friend for more than twenty years in spite of Frederick's habit of playing rough jokes on him.

waistcoat four years and durst not take it off for fear of catching cold. The King drove out one fear by another, and told him that if he persisted to wear that waistcoat, his perspiration would be entirely stopped, and he must inevitably die. The Marquis agreed to quit his waistcoat. But it had so fixed itself upon him that pieces of his skin came away with it. My Lord, as usual, laughed at religious gloom. I told him he had the felicity of a sound mind, which everybody has not. Good heaven! how fortunate is one man above another! We slept at Magdeburg.

SUNDAY 1 JULY. I was in moderate spirits and pretty well.

MONDAY 2 JULY. We talked of the Spaniards. My Don Quixote humour got up. I said I should be infinitely happy to be a colonel in the Spanish service. My Lord amused us with a fine fanciful story of my making a conquest of Portugal and marrying an infanta, and afterwards called me constantly the great Colonello. At night we arrived at Potsdam, which is a very pretty town. The King has built houses like those of the people of quality in London, and has let them to tailors and shoemakers and other tradesmen.

TUESDAY 3 JULY. My Lord Marischal carried me to the Palace, where he has an apartment assigned him by the King. He seemed just like one who comes to a good friend's house in the country, when the friend is of somewhat higher rank than the guest. Just as I come to Eglinton. It was fine to see the old Scots nobleman lodged in the Palace of Prussia, just as if he had been in the Abbey of Holyroodhouse. At ten he carried me to the Parade, which was full of Prussian officers, all bold-looking, all gay, all well dressed. He presented me to the Prince of Prussia,[3] calling me "of a very good house, and very much a gentleman." He also presented me to Count d'Anhalt, the lover of Zélide; he has never seen her, but has heard so much of her charms that he has sent formal proposals to her. I then waited on Mr. Catt, Reader to the King, to whom I had a letter from Monsieur de Zuylen. He was sick and could not go out with me, but he was civil. I found him dry and even insipid.[4]

[3] Frederick's nephew and successor, Frederick William. His reign was not of great distinction.

[4] Friedrich, Count of Anhalt, son by a morganatic marriage of Hereditary

Madame de Froment and I dined tête-à-tête, after which we went and were shown the Palace, which is magnificent. The King's concert-room is very elegant. We looked through a glass door and saw his bedchamber and a neat little library. All his books were bound in red Turkey[5] and handsomely gilt. They made me think of my dear Temple. They would have pleased him much. In the antechamber were a good many books, but our conductor would not allow us to lift any of them, for he said the King knew the exact place of every one of them. I saw *Œuvres de Voltaire*, and a fine quarto edition of the *Œuvres du Philosophe de Sans Souci.*[6] Great and pleasing were my thoughts.

At night Madame de Froment told me how hypochondriac she had been. "All my thoughts were gloomy. The beauties of Nature mocked me. I was in despair. Yet without any change in the external world I suddenly became perfectly happy. My imagination was gay. In the evening I found myself alone in my room; I wished for company, to tell them of my felicity. I opened my window. I was delighted with everything I saw: the moon, the stars, the fields, the lake, all bore their most cheerful aspect. I said to myself, 'Good heavens! is it possible? Where does all this joy come from?' The fact is, Sir, that our happiness depends on the way in which our blood circulates."

This description struck me very much. Some weeks ago at Utrecht when I felt an amazing flow of sudden felicity, I thought

---

Prince Wilhelm Gustav (d. 1737) of Anhalt-Dessau, was at this time aide-de-camp to Frederick and later became his Adjutant General. He had heard of Zélide only through Catt, who had once been tutor to her brothers. Henri Alexandre de Catt was a Swiss, who, while studying at Utrecht, had met Frederick travelling incognito on a canal boat, and had made so favourable an impression that the King had invited him to Potsdam to be his Reader. His function actually was not so much to read to the King as to afford him opportunities for animated conversation on the many subjects that interested him. Catt's *Memoirs* are an important source for the life of Frederick.

[5] What would now be called Levant, or Levant morocco.

[6] That is, of Frederick himself, who was a voluminous writer in prose and verse, his complete collected works running to thirty volumes. Why he was called so is explained in the note following this.

it quite singular; but I find that I have just had the very same distemper with my Turkish lady. This is curious, to find the same
spleen over the whole globe. I was in the humour of gallantry tonight. I was pleased with the romantic idea of making love to a
Turk. However, I talked morality at last and thought myself a
Johnson. She seemed too indolent in body and too vivacious in
mind to be a very rigid lady. Besides her ideas were quite different
from mine. Her religion was of a kind very different from mine.
Bless me! what are mortals?

WEDNESDAY 4 JULY. At nine the Inspecteur of the gallery at
Sans Souci waited on me, and I carried him in a coach to the retreat
of the great Frederick. The King has here apartments for himself
and four friends. The building is light and elegant. But the gallery
is truly superb. It is very long, very lofty, and very richly finished.[7]
The collection of pictures is not as yet very numerous, but they are
all fine pieces; and I was told by Lord Marischal that there is not a
better collection in one place, even in Italy. I was unlucky enough
to be gloomy, and could not relish this rich scene as Boswell himself relishes beauty. I speculated on the ennui of terrestrial existence. I waited on Lord Marischal, who, as one of the King's particular friends, is lodged here. I then saw the foundation of an
immense palace which the King is building near this.[8] I returned
to Potsdam, dined quiet, journalized and walked and chatted till
bedtime.

THURSDAY 5 JULY.[9] I hired post-horses for my Lord's coach,
and set out free and happy to conduct Madame de Froment to
Berlin. We had a pleasant jaunt, and arrived about two at Rufin's

[7] Sans Souci ("Free from Care") was a one-story building of modest dimen-
sions which Frederick built (1745–1747), partly from his own plans, to
serve as an occasional retreat. It became his favourite residence. The picture-
gallery was a separate building.

[8] The "New Palace" was not completed until 1769.

[9] "Yesterday . . . too familiar with [Mme de Froment]. Have a care. At
night merely from talking, grew well. This day, be alive, be manly; fear
not censure. If pleasure be a deception, so is pain. Enter Berlin content.
Pursue Plan. Forget dreary ideas and sensual Turkish ones. Be Johnson. But
take fresh German, &c." (Memorandum, 5 July. By "Plan" he means the

in the Post Straas.[1] Here we found Monsieur de Froment, a lively
Frenchman, pretty much mellowed, and Lieutenant Lauchlan
Macpherson, late of Fraser's Highlanders. He is son to Breakachie.[2]
He is a fine, honest, spirited fellow. We dined, and then I dressed
and Macpherson accompanied me to Mr. Mitchell's, the British
Envoy, and to my bankers, but we found none of them at home. I
was struck with the beauty of Berlin. The houses are handsome and
the streets wide, long, and straight. The Palace is grand. The pal-
aces of some of the royal family are very genteel. The Opera-House
is an elegant building, with this inscription: "Fridericus Rex Apol-
lini et Musis." At night we sauntered in a sweet walk under a grove
of chestnut trees by the side of a beautiful canal,[3] where I saw a
variety of strangers. The foul fiend fled.

FRIDAY 6 JULY. I went to my bankers, and found Mr. Schickler, a fine, jolly, generous fellow, and young Splitgerber, a good
bluff dog; he has been three years in London.[4] He went with me to
look for lodgings, but I found none to my mind. He then carried me
in his coach to the *campagne* of Herr Schickler; that is to say, a
house and garden. We dined in a handsome summer-house, which
projects upon the river and commands a view of Berlin and its
beautiful vicinity.[5] We were fifteen or sixteen at table. I was enlivened by seeing the hearty Germans. After being three hours together at table, we played at ninepins. I then took a tour in Schick-

scheme of conduct he called his Inviolable Plan. See *Boswell in Holland*,
Appendix I.)

[1] That is, *Strasse*. See p. xx for a statement of the editorial policy followed
in this volume with regard to the spelling of Boswell's German.
[2] That is, to the Laird of Breakachie in Inverness-shire, Duncan Macpherson.
[3] Probably in the famous promenade, Unter den Linden. See p. 86. The ave-
nues of trees contained chestnuts as well as lindens, and in 1764 a canal ran
parallel with them.
[4] The title of the banking-firm was Splitgerber and Daum; it was the most
important Berlin banking-house of the eighteenth century. "Young Splitgerber" was the son, and "Mr. Schickler" the son-in-law, of the founder, who
had recently died.
[5] From the entry for 29 August we learn that this *campagne* was near Treptow, some four miles up the river Spree from the centre of Berlin.

ler's boat. At nine we had a cold collation and good wine. Splitgerber carried me home in his elegant coach and sung many English songs in *The Jovial Crew, Artaxerxes,* &c.⁶ I was firm and gay
and sound as ever. Am I indeed the dull dog of Utrecht?

SATURDAY 7 JULY. If ever man underwent an alteration, it is
the man who writeth this journal. I drank punch at the lodgings of
Captain Wake, a Scots privateer.⁷ At night I was Young Boswell of
Auchinleck upon his travels, and had with me Macpherson, a
brave Highlander. He was quite the man for me. He had good
health, good sense, and good humour. He awaked well. He never
speculated. He was gay. I was the same, and gloom fled from my
mind.

SUNDAY 8 JULY. I waited on Mr. Mitchell and found him a
knowing, amiable, easy man.⁸ He was very polite. He talked of
Mademoiselle de Zuylen: "She has a great deal of wit." "Yes," said
I, "too much for the Dutch." And who was in the room but Mr.
Verelst, the Dutch Envoy! Mr. Mitchell turned it off with a smiling reply: "Sir, you are paying a fine compliment to the Minister
of Holland." Blockhead that I was! Let never man blunder out reflections against any country when he does not very well know his
company.

I dined too heartily this day, and Macpherson and I must needs
have our sleep after dinner. I dozed like a very bum-bailiff, but
when I awoke, relaxed were my nerves, and like unto a lump of
clay on a barrel of Edinburgh twopenny was my mighty head. It
was indeed fitter for knocking other people down than for holding

⁶ Thomas Arne's opera in the Italian style, the libretto translated from
Metastasio's *Artaserse*, was first produced at Covent Garden in 1762. *The
Jovial Crew*, a great favourite of Boswell's, was in its original form a comedy
by Richard Brome (d. 1652); it had been turned into a very successful comic
opera in 1731.
⁷ Boswell tells later why he was in Berlin. See p. 86.
⁸ Andrew Mitchell (knighted in 1765), an Aberdeenshire Scotsman, Minister
Plenipotentiary and close personal friend of Frederick the Great, whom he
accompanied on several of his campaigns. Carlyle regarded his letters as one
of the most valuable sources for the biography of Frederick.

itself up. However, out went the Highlander and I, took a dish of coffee and a game at billiards, and then away we went and took a hearty walk in the Park,[9] which is a noble thing just by this beautiful city. It has a variety of walks both for coaches and horsemen, as well as for those who love the milder movement of their own limbs. We grew as fresh and as strong and as content as men of the last century. Macpherson is a true philosopher though he knows not what philosophy means.

MONDAY 9 JULY.[1] Who will say that I am not a man of business, I who write my journal with the regularity of the German professor who wrote his folio every year? I waited this day on Professor Castillon, whom I had known at Utrecht.[2] He received me well, and I saw him with other eyes than when I groaned in gloom. I drank tea at the house of the Président de Police, Monsieur Kircheisen, a hearty cordial Saxon. I found his lady well bred and his son lively. My worthy Monsieur Schickler recommended me to the President, who agreed to let me have an apartment in his house at the rate of fifteen crowns a month.

TUESDAY 10 JULY. At night I entered to my apartment. I had a handsome parlour, gaily painted and looking to St. Peter's Church, a noble building.[3] I had a genteel, large alcove with a pretty silk bed. I was quite happy, quite Digges, quite as if I had never felt the heavy hand of the demon of gloom. I find that my happiness depends upon small elegancies. I am a kind of Baron Maule. I will take care to have all the elegancies of life.[4]

[9] The Tiergarten.

[1] On this day Boswell wrote the most important of his letters to Belle de Zuylen, according to Geoffrey Scott "the finest document of masculine complacency which has ever escaped the flames." See *Boswell in Holland*, No. 4 of the Correspondence with Belle de Zuylen.

[2] A well-known mathematician. Frederick had called him from Utrecht in 1763 and made him a member of his Academy.

[3] This places his landlord's house in either Scharren Strasse or Gertraudten Strasse, in the oldest section of Berlin.

[4] West Digges was an actor whom Boswell had long regarded as a model of worldly elegance; John Maule of Inverkeillor, one of the Barons of the Court of Exchequer in Scotland. "A man whom in my early years I had

WEDNESDAY 11 JULY. Monsieur de Froment took lodgings
very near me. I agreed with him to dine at his lodgings when not
otherwise engaged. He had dinner from a tavern and we paid half
an écu a head.[5] This regulation is exceedingly convenient for me.
I am always sure of dining agreeably.

THURSDAY 12 JULY. I was advised by Mr. Mitchell to accompany Macpherson to Potsdam, in order to see some of the entertainments given to the Court of Brunswick. I was indolent, but resolved. In the morning I waited on Madame la Présidente, and was
presented to Mademoiselle.[6] She was seventeen, comely, fresh,
good-humoured, and gay, and had an ease of behaviour that
pleased me greatly. I was quite in pleasing frame. I must observe
of myself that from my early years I have never seen an agreeable
lady but my warm imagination has fancied as how I might marry
her and has suggested a crowd of ideas. This is very true, but very,
very absurd.

At twelve Macpherson and I got into the *journalière,* a sad machine but cheap, for you pay but twelve gross for four German
miles. We had with us a Polish colonel, a sulky dog, but Macpherson's *braid* sword kept him quiet. We had a dusty journey to Pots-

---

viewed in a grand style," wrote Boswell on hearing of his death (*Journal,*
3 July 1781).

[5] The English equivalent of "écu" is "crown." "At Berlin, and in most of the
King of Prussia's dominions, the moneys are expressed by crowns or rixdollars, grosses, and fennins [in German, Reichsthaler, Groschen, Pfenninge].
They have two sorts of rixdollars, the old and the new; the old rixdollar is
worth about three shillings and sixpence sterling, and is valued at twenty-
four grosses; the new rixdollar, which is the dollar most generally current
in Germany, and is worth about four shillings and sixpence, is valued at
thirty grosses . . . " (Thomas Nugent, *The Grand Tour,* 2d ed., 1756, ii. 61).
Boswell's écu is apparently the "old" rixdollar; on p. 31 he gives it the value
of three shillings, but on p. 120 equates six écus ("dollars") with a pound
sterling, which is not far from Nugent's figure. American readers will get
approximate values by rating an écu at seventy-five cents and a gross at
three cents.

[6] "Madame la Présidente" is Frau Kircheisen. "Mademoiselle," her daughter,
bore the name of Caroline.

dam.[7] We waited on Captain Scott of the Prince of Prussia's regiment. We found him a worthy, plain, hearty Caledonian. He is an Aberdeenshire man, son to Scott of Auchty-Donald, a branch of the family of Galashiels. He has been fifteen years in the service, and has distinguished himself as a very brave officer. He gave us a good supper, English beer and good wine, and Macpherson and I were laid upon the floor, on two hard beds and clean straw, like two immense Highlanders. Hearty were we, and as content as human existence could allow.

FRIDAY 13 JULY. I rose fresh as a roe on the braes of Lochaber. I find that if I had got a commission in a Highland corps, I should have been as stout a Donald as the best of them. I waited on my good Lord Marischal, whom I found as contented and as cheerful as ever. I then went to the Parade. I saw the King. It was a glorious sight. He was dressed in a suit of plain blue, with a star and a plain hat with a white feather. He had in his hand a cane. The sun shone bright. He stood before his palace, with an air of iron confidence that could not be opposed. As a loadstone moves needles, or a storm bows the lofty oaks, did Frederick the Great make the Prussian officers submissive bend as he walked majestic in the midst of them. I was in noble spirits, and had a full relish of this grand scene which I shall never forget. I felt a crowd of ideas. I beheld the king who has astonished Europe by his warlike deeds. I beheld (pleasant conceit!) the great defender of the Protestant cause, who was prayed for in all the Scots kirks.[8] I beheld the "Philosophe de Sans Souci." I have really a little mind, with all my pride. For I thought one might well endure all the fatigues of war, in order to have an opportunity of appearing grand as this monarch.

My Lord Marischal told me I could see no shows here and ad-

[7] The *journalière* was probably the regular post-wagon, an uncovered cart moving at the rate of about three English miles an hour. (See p. 50.) The four German miles were equivalent to eighteen English. Nugent (*The Grand Tour*) refers frequently to the sandy roads of northern Germany.

[8] In his recent war with Austria and France, Frederick had posed as a Protestant Defender of the Faith, in spite of the fact that Sweden and the Empire (which included several Protestant states) were allied with Maria Theresa.

vised me to post back to Berlin and get introduced at Court. Scott
was this day upon guard. Macpherson and I dined with him, then
played at billiards and walked, then supped with him. Never were
fellows more jolly. Scott gave us stories of Prussian wars, and Macpherson of American ones. I saw that Prussian officers live just as
well as others; and for the common soldiers, they placed themselves
on a seat before the guardroom and sung most merrily. My ideas
of the value of men are altered since I came to this country. I see
such numbers of fine fellows bred to be slaughtered that human
beings seem like herrings in a plentiful season. One thinks nothing
of a few barrels of herring, nor can I think much of a few regiments
of men. What am I then, a single man? Strange thought! Let it go.
I slept sound one night more as a Highlander.

SATURDAY 14 JULY. I left Macpherson at Potsdam, where he
waits the instructions of Lord Marischal, who took a liking to him
in Scotland and made him come to Berlin to see the world a little
at his Lordship's expense. This is very genteel in my Lord, who is a
kind of Lowland chieftain of the Macphersons. I rumbled in the
journalière to Berlin, having for company, amongst others, Mademoiselle Dionisius, daughter to the cook of Prince Ferdinand of
Prussia. I talked words of German to this lass. I dined at Froment's,
and after dinner went to Mr. Mitchell's. We talked of Sir Joseph
Yorke,[9] whom he called Sir Joé. I told him that he seemed so anxious lest people should not know that he was Ambassador that he
held his head very high and spoke very little. And as in the infancy
of painting, people generally wrote, "This is a cow," "This is a
horse," so from Sir Joé's mouth cometh a label with these words,
"I am an Ambassador." What a difference between this buckram
knight and the amiable Mr. Mitchell! The family of my good Herr
Président were happy to see me.

SUNDAY 15 JULY.[1] I dined at Mr. Mitchell's. He has an elegant
house and a good table. He is polite and easy. His servants are good
people, civil and attached to their master. After dinner, I played at

9 The British Ambassador at The Hague.
1 " . . . This day, church. Be grave and think, and at nine for health — "
(Memorandum, 15 July).

billiards with Mr. Burnett, secretary to Mr. Mitchell, a very good, solid, clever young fellow. At six the Envoy carried me to Monbijou, the *campagne* of the Princess of Prussia.[2] Here I was presented to the Queen, with whom the King has never lived.[3] She has been handsome, and is very amiable, although she stammers most sadly. I was presented to I don't know how many princes and princesses. I was awkward, but not afraid.[4]

MONDAY 16 JULY. I dined with Monsieur Verelst, the Dutch Minister, and dined heartily. His Excellency was phlegmatic, but not unjolly. We formed a trio at table with the assistance of a German count who had great vivacity and *usage du monde*. I had old Abbey, Lord Somerville ideas.[5] I drank tea at home (for so I call my landlord's), then went with Herr Président in his chaise and took a drive in the Park, came home, supped with the family, and after supper went with the ladies and the young Kircheisen and walked *sous les marronniers*.[6] Is not this living? It is. I am quite a new man.

TUESDAY 17 JULY. Our family carried me at five to Herr Behmer's, a Conseiller de guerre,[7] where was a fine ball. I must ex-

[2] Louisa Amalia, widow of Frederick's brother, Augustus William, and sister to his queen, Elizabeth Christina; mother of his heir, Frederick William II.
[3] That is, with whom he had never consummated his marriage. He had of course resided with her for considerable periods of time while his father lived but now saw her very infrequently. See p. 83.
[4] The memorandum continues, "Home, undressed [that is, changed from court dress] and street. Black girl — had no condom [and so refrained]. Walked, came home."
[5] Lord Somerville, a man somewhat older than Lord Auchinleck, had been kind to Boswell as a boy and had encouraged him in his scribbling and publishing. He had rooms in Holyroodhouse. Boswell recorded his affectionate gratitude in a note in *The Life of Johnson*.
[6] Friedrich Leopold Kircheisen, at this time only fifteen, became a distinguished jurist, held the post of Prussian Minister of Justice, and was ennobled in 1798. *Sous les marronniers* ("under the chestnuts"), as explained above, is probably the street better known as Unter den Linden.
[7] Member of the War-Council (Kriegsrat). Behmer, a well-known lawyer and judge, had drawn up a formal defence of Frederick's title to Silesia.

plain this matter a little. Mademoiselle Schartow, an amiable young lady, lost her parents in her infancy. My worthy President Kircheisen took her to his house, where she has lived as if she had been their own child. Herr Stielow, who has a little office that enables him to live genteelly, made love to her and was accepted. Herr Behmer is her uncle, and gave this ball to the *promis* and *promise* and their friends. Here I saw the vivacity of German ladies and counts and captains and Herren. We had at ten o'clock a collation in the garden; three or four tables with cold meat and pastry and sweetmeats and fruits and wine of different sorts. Behmer was a big, gallant Allemand; his wife, hearty even to excess. She was a most singular figure. She had no cap, and her hair dangled about her head. While she ran from table to table, with bottles in her hand and health most florid in her face, she seemed quite a female Bacchanalian. I was just celebrating the *orgies*. Her daughter was little and lively and kind. "Do have a taste of this, Sir, I beg you," was her byword. I eat much and drank much and found animal life of very great consequence. I danced a great deal, and was an easy man, without affectation and timid consequence. We went home late.

WEDNESDAY 18 JULY. Young Kircheisen showed me his prints and pebbles, and Mademoiselle her drawings and books and china. I love young people who have tastes of this kind. They never tire. I dined with Herr Président. The young couple were there. At five the company came and we had tea and coffee; and at seven a Lutheran parson performed the ceremony of marriage according to the German service-book. It was very decent. We then had cards, and at ten a most elegant supper. It was quite German, quite hearty, and quite easy; for although this nation loves form, custom has rendered it easy to them. We had sugar figures of all sorts. A gentleman broke these figures in a lady's hand, and in the ruins was found a device, one of which is curiously baked in each figure. They are generally amorous or witty. I sat by my dear Mademoiselle Caroline, whom I find more and more agreeable. She said she imagined the British nation to be rude like Russians or Turks. How excellent was this. What would I have given that Mr. Samuel Johnson had heard a German talk thus! Herr Président embraced me with cordiality and cried, "My dear Englishman, no man ever had a better heart. Your being sent to my house was an act of Providence." Prodigious! Is this the gloomy wretch who not long ago laid it down as an impossibility that he could ever have a happy hour? After this can I dare to oppose sickly theory to bold practice? I hope not. I hope to be free of sickly theory.

After supper we conducted the young couple to the house of Herr Stielow. I mounted on the back of the calash, quite English. At Herr Stielow's we had a collation and good wine. We laughed much and many a joke went round. The ladies were free and vivacious. We put the bridegroom and bride to bed in night-gowns.[8] They got up again, and wished us good night. How pleasant a scene was this! And how innocent! Some years ago it would have quite filled my imagination with fine sentiments. But now I am too old; I have seen too much. My taste is too much corrupted. However, here was one day of sure satisfaction.

THURSDAY 19 JULY. At eleven I waited on young couple. Our jokes were still gayer. We had a fine breakfast. The weather was charming, which gave me delicious spirits. I was too *high* at Froment's. He said, "My friend here is beside himself." Madame said, "You are naturally too serious. You have great need of gay company." This is exceedingly true.

I found among my Lord Marischal's books *An Inquiry into the Human Mind on the Principles of Common Sense*, by Professor Reid of Aberdeen. I found it a treasure. He discovered strong reasoning and lively humour. He insisted much on the original principles of the mind, which we cannot doubt of, and which cannot be proved because they are really axioms. He drove to pieces the sceptical cobweb. I found myself much refreshed and very happy.[9] At

[8] The modern term would be "dressing-gowns."
[9] The book was new, having appeared in this year. It established Reid as the head of the "Scots School of Common Sense" and had won him in May election to the professorship of moral philosophy at Glasgow. The "sceptical

night I walked with the young Kircheisen *sous les marronniers.* He
was too forward. I checked him.

FRIDAY 20 JULY. I passed the morning with Mr. Mitchell,
who talked of Parliamentary affairs while he sat in the House.[1] He
revived in my mind true English ambition. I dined at Herr Schickler's. At six in the evening I went in our family coach to Herr Splitgerber's garden, where the young couple gave a fine ball and most
excellent supper. I danced a great deal and was in true, gay, vigorous spirits. I must mention a particular circumstance or two in a
German marriage. There is a poem of hymeneal guise composed,
and every guest receives one. The bride stands in the center of a
ring of gentlemen, and they dance around her. She is blindfolded,
and holds in her hand an emblematical crown of virginity, which
she puts on the head of what gentleman she pleases, and he is considered as marked out to be the first married of the company. He
again takes the bride's place, and in the same manner crowns a
lady. I was rather too singular. Why not? I am in reality an original character. Let me moderate and cultivate my orginality. God
would not have formed such a diversity of men if he had intended
that they should all come up to a certain standard. That is indeed
impossible while black, brown, and fair, serious, lively, and mild,
continue distinct qualities. Let me then be Boswell and render him
as fine a fellow as possible.[2] At one we went home. I made Made-

cobweb" to which Boswell refers is the empirical system of David Hume,
who had argued that we can know nothing but our own ideas and therefore
can have no certain knowledge of external realities. Reid maintained that
this is not what experience (Hume's final authority) really teaches. We have
an intuitive belief in a material external world and in the existence of the
soul which is anterior to all philosophical constructions and should be im-
pregnable against any doubts raised by the rational process. Boswell, who
was always tortured during his fits of depression by sceptical and neces-
sitarian arguments, found Reid's system very comforting.
[1] Mitchell had been M.P. for Aberdeenshire and later for the Elgin burghs.
[2] This entry is crucial, for it marks the occasion on which Boswell turned
from his usual pattern of anxious admonition to be West Digges, or Sir David
Dalrymple, or Samuel Johnson, and contemplated with complacency the
idea of being himself. The memorandum for 21 July is even more revealing

moiselle play me a sweet air on the harpsichord to compose me for gentle slumbers. Happy man that I am!

SATURDAY 21 JULY. Scarcely had I got up when Mademoiselle sent me a rural present of luscious cherries. At dinner Froment talked of Scotland and the grievous dulness of our women, who stand around yawning all the time. Nor did he neglect to mention the sad familiarity amongst our men. "A fellow there will call you by your first name: 'O Jack!' — and perhaps give you a kick in the backside." He said I must lay my account to be very miserable in Scotland for fourteen or fifteen years. This sounded very hard. But I hope it shall not be so.

At three I had a coach, and carried three Germans to Charlottenburg, one of which was Herr Hübner, a clerk in Chancery, a genteel, even-tempered, fine fellow, much at ease. We went to Herr Wegely's, a rich merchant who had a *campagne* here.[3] We went and saw the garden at Charlottenburg, which is spacious and elegant, and afterwards to a *comédie française*, played for the entertainment of the Court of Brunswick. No strangers were invited to the feasts, so I was only a simple spectator. I had a full view of the King. I was very well amused.[4] I spoke some time with my Lord

than the entry in the journal, for it records some of the other ideas running through Boswell's mind: "Be self. Be original. Be happy. You *was* so, certainly. Add to this learning and taste and devotion and *retenue*. Marry not, but think to have fine Saxon girls, &c., and to be with Temple. Continue journal. Keep firm abroad another year — or marry Zélide. Go home with design to *try* [the law], and if bad, Spain or France, &c., &c., &c."

[3] Wegely was founder of the first porcelain factory in Berlin. The factory, however, had lost heavily, and had been converted into a manufactory of woollens.

[4] "Boswell went from Berlin to Charlottenburg while the entertainments were there on account of the betrothing of the Princess Elizabeth of Brunswick to the Prince of Prussia. All the ladies and gentlemen pressed eagerly to get places at the windows of the Palace in order to see the royal families at supper. Boswell found this a little ridiculous, so came up to his acquaintances and said . . . , 'Come, come, pray do let us go see the second table. I assure you it is more worth while. They eat more than the others' " (*Boswelliana*, ed. Charles Rogers, 1874, p. 237).

Marischal, who at seventy-five is as much pleased with shows and gaiety and ribbons and stars as any young courtier in Christendom. With all this he is the old Scotch earl and has strong sense and much knowledge. It is hard that I can see him so little. We returned to Wegely's and supped, and went home gay.

SUNDAY 22 JULY. I entered a moment St. Peter's Church, was devout and not gloomy. I hope to get free of my dreary associations of sadness to public worship in any form. I fear however that the Presbyterian *Kirk* cannot be overcome. I went to Charlottenburg and dined with our family at Monsieur Wegely's. His garden is splendid. We dined in a grotto richly adorned with shells and seaweed and all manner of fine things. After dinner I played at a game which I know not the name of. We were seated upon elbow-chairs fixed on a round plane of boards which was whirled about very fast. Every one had a pole in his hand, with which our business was to catch some iron rings which were loosely fixed in a beam above the plane on two sides. I was blockhead enough to bet against a lady, an écu (three shillings) each ring. I lost eighteen écus. I have really the spirit of gaming. Happy is it for me that I am tied up.[5]

We next went to the royal garden and amongst other spectators heard or saw a concert. I also saw the King a long time in the garden. General Wylich, cousin to Mr. Spaen, whom I was recommended to, stood by me. I was quite enthusiastic and talked of the King with prodigious warmth. The gallant Wylich held me by the arm and said, "Calm yourself, Sir." An excellent anecdote. As I stood among the crowd, the Duke of Brunswick walked past. He made me a most gracious bow, and made me come out to him; took me by the hand, and talked to me some time. I told him I intended to have the honour of paying my respects at Brunswick at

[5] This variety of the merry-go-round was called *Ringelstechen* or *Ringelspiel*. A picture of a similar device, Paris, 1775, appears in *Der Grosse Brockhaus* under the heading *Karussell*. It has a canopy and seats for four players, and appears to have been turned by two men standing in the middle. — To pay his gambling debts, Boswell had borrowed from Thomas Sheridan, promising not to lose more than three guineas at a sitting. See p. 52 *n.* 2.

the *Foire*. He said I should be very welcome. How worthy and how amiable a prince is this! He made me very happy. The Hereditary Prince also named me. I returned to Wegely's and eat a bit of supper. There was here a Mademoiselle Scheenemark, very handsome and very clever, but too theatrical. She pleased me not a little. I went home calm.[6]

MONDAY 23 JULY. Lord Marischal dined with us at Froment's. He and I talked of Jacobitism, as how there was something pathetic and generous in it, as it was espousing the cause of a distressed and ancient royal house. My Lord however owned that they deserved to lose the throne of Britain. I own so too. I am sorry for them. I wish to forget them; and I love from my soul "Great George our King." In the afternoon I was a little hipped, but by walking hard was cleared. How easy is now an attack of this kind!

[Boswell to William Johnson Temple][7]

Berlin, 23 July 1764

MY DEAR TEMPLE, — Is it possible for you to believe that, notwithstanding the intimacy of our friendship, I never can begin a letter to you without feeling a degree of anxiety? Strange as this may seem, it is really true. Indeed, my friend, your dignity of virtue and delicacy of taste throw a certain amiable awe upon my mind. It is a pleasing restraint. I would not wish to be free from it.

[6] " ... You sat by Mademoiselle Scheenmark. You was too open. You must learn *usage du monde de badiner sans que le cœur s'y mêle* [the polite mode of gallant small talk without allowing your feelings to be involved] ... " (Memorandum, 23 July). The lady's name should probably be spelled Schönemark or Schönmark. The memoranda show that it was she to whom Boswell lost the eighteen crowns, a debt which he had not paid by 3 September, though he probably discharged it on that day.

[7] William Johnson Temple, an Englishman from Berwick-on-Tweed, had been one of Boswell's two most intimate friends since they had met as boys of fifteen in a Greek class in the University of Edinburgh. Temple went on to Cambridge to study law, and kept chambers in the Inner Temple, where he was at the time this letter was written. He was now thinking of taking holy orders.

I have at present so many things to say that I am at a loss which to say first. My head is crowded with a variety of brilliant ideas. All appear equally charming. All appear equally worthy of being presented to my friend. . . .

I have been at Berlin some weeks. It is the finest city I have ever seen. It is situated on a beautiful plain, and like London has its river. The streets are spacious and the houses well built. I have been presented to the Queen and all the princes and princesses, but have not yet had an opportunity of being presented to the King. This ceremony can only be performed at Berlin, whither His Majesty comes very seldom, for he cannot bear the vain forms of a court. However, I am determined to see him before I leave this. I despair not to make him speak. I will let him see that he has before him a man of no common clay. You see me now, Temple, restored to myself, quite *The Great Man*. Don't laugh. . . .

I am now, Temple, really happy. I have a genteel wardrobe. I have a very clever Swiss for my servant. At seven in the morning I go to the manège and ride the great horse. At ten a French fencing-master comes to me. I read an agreeable French author. I write French letters. I have health of body and cheerfulness of mind. . . .

Trace me only from the time when first our congenial souls united, when they separated themselves from the *profanum vulgus*[8] at college and united in elegant friendship. Since that time what variety has there been in my mind! Trace me only since I left London. What a gloomy winter did I pass at Utrecht! Did I not speculate till I was firmly persuaded that all terrestrial occupations and amusements could not compose felicity? Did I not imagine myself doomed to unceasing melancholy? . . . And yet, my friend, I am now as sound and as happy as a mortal can be. How comes this? Merely because I have had more exercise and variety of conversation. . . . One great lesson to be learned is that man is a practical being. It is hard, but experience proves it to be true that speculation renders us miserable. Life will not bear to be calmly

[8] "The uncultured herd" (Horace, *Odes,* III. i. 1.).

considered. It appears insipid and ridiculous as a country dance. Yet nothing is more certain than that the dreariest of all speculatists may be made to think as agreeably as others, provided he will rouse himself to action like them. Let you and I then, my dearest Temple, keep our blood a-circulating and the faculties of our minds in due employment . . .

Pray, what do you intend to do? Are you still for the surplice? For my own part, I am not so fixed as I could wish. My mercury is again put in motion. It is with much reluctance that I think of returning to Edinburgh and enrolling myself in the profession of an advocate, where I shall be excelled by sober drudges who have not half my parts. And yet, Temple, this must be done, for my worthy father has it quite at heart. I have agreed to please him in this, and I am determined to pursue my purpose. I will however gain as much time as I can to be abroad, so that I may be as much a man as possible. I hope to pass the winter at Rome. Pray, Temple, encourage me. Tell me that I shall pass many agreeable days at my ancient seat of Auchinleck; that I need not be a slave to the law, but may get into Parliament or be made a Baron of Exchequer and have really *otium cum dignitate.*[9]

To be plain with you, my friend, neither you nor I seem intended for making a great figure in active life. We want firmness of mind and steadiness of application. Upon my soul, I think so. No real object has arrested our view. We excel in no branch of science or of art, while our fellow collegians are jogging along the plain road and always getting on.[1] What can this mean, Temple? What say you to it? It is certainly true; and yet it does not make me think meanly of us. No, we have brilliance of imagination, polite learning, elegance of taste and manners, and elevation of soul. Perhaps we are beings superior to this life. However, since

[9] "Dignified leisure" (Cicero, *Pro Sestio*, xlv. 98).
[1] He means in particular Henry Dundas, their junior by two years, who was already in practice at the Scottish bar. Dundas's "jogging" had been called to his attention by Lord Auchinleck, who had sent him one of Dundas's legal papers to read — a sufficiently broad hint that he himself had better not waste time. See *Boswell in Holland,* following 14 April 1764.

we are placed in the world, let us make the best of it. . . . Let us be directed by practice. Johnson has taught me this, and I am every day more convinced of its force. While my blood stagnated in the fogs of Utrecht and my sullen mind beheld the whole creation with horror — while my imagination ranged over the face of the earth, considered all that could be seen and all that could be done and concluded that all was dismal — had I been told that by being drawn some hundreds of miles in a certain machine, seeing another assemblage of houses and some more of those miserable two-legged animals called human, hearing them talk, capering with them to the sound of an instrument of music, and pouring now and then into my stomach a certain liquid, getting upon the back of an animal and moving in certain directions, pushing at a fellow with a piece of steel and performing several more actions — had I been told that by doing thus, I should feel myself a happy man, should view the Creation in an agreeable light and should feel time fly pleasantly along, I should most certainly have treated him who told me so as a great philosopher treats a very ignorant fellow. And yet the reality of this effect is proved to me by the strongest experience. I now believe, Temple, that it is possible to keep a man in a great measure constantly happy. . . . To be sure, if we were all Pitts and Johnsons and Grays, we should be much nobler beings. But if, by studying to be great when we are intended for being agreeable, we become sour and discontented, in that case, I think the vivacious and happy French and Italians may with some justice laugh at us. . . .

And now, Temple, for another conjugal scheme. You already know the character of Mademoiselle de Zuylen. Some days before I left Utrecht, I saw her as often as I could and talked to her with more affection than formerly, for indeed I was sorry to part from her for ever. I had always appeared to her in the character of a lively but firm philosopher, had warmly reproved her levity of conduct and declared to her that I would not be her husband to be King of the Seven Provinces. Notwithstanding all this, such is woman that the charming Zélide actually imagined me in love with her, which was to me a certain indication that she was in love with me. Don't wish to knock me down as the vainest of all mortals, for you yourself shall judge if I could think otherwise. I passed my last evening in Holland in a party of pleasure with her and some more ladies. She seemed unquiet and tender. She talked of her own character, and that she had never been really in love, for she had never remained long constant to any one inclination. I seriously upbraided her on this account. She said that she had not yet met with the man that could properly attach her to him; and she said that perhaps *one* might meet with (here she described me in such a manner that it was impossible for me to mistake her meaning), for whom *one* might have a serious and lasting passion, but might not have an opportunity of proving it. I was embarrassed, and with an affected ease replied, "You are quite right. It must be admitted that love is a very risky affair." When I took leave of her the tear was in her lovely eye. She had agreed to correspond with me while upon my travels. But she now gave me a letter, with a degree of hesitation and confusion. And what was this letter, think you, but eight quarto pages in which she defended her own character, paid me some elegant compliments on mine, told me she had imagined me her lover, that this had rendered her *distraite*, formed pleasing schemes of being a wife and a mother — in short, discovered all her heart, concluding with, "I have said everything; or at least I have said much." I was flattered not a little with this confession, but was honest enough to leave her a note in which I assured her with the gravity of a Cato that I was not her lover but should ever be her faithful friend. Upon my arrival at Brunswick I was amazed to find a letter from Zélide (as she calls herself) lying for me in the house of Monsieur de Feronce, Privy Councillor of the Duke. In this letter she would fain have persuaded me that she was not in love, but had only a fanciful and light inclination. She was piqued at my indifferent epistle, and was anxious to show me that she was evens with me. But the amiable creature betrayed her real situation. Judge from the following expressions: "My friendship is yours for ever. . . . I will be a little more tender one day than another, but every day you will be dear to me. . . . My heart will always be the same towards you. I hope, all your life, you will be glad of it." Temple, seest thou not the meaning of all these sallies? I have written to her from Berlin and continued my old serious dictatorial style.[2] But I find strange fancies coming into my head that I might not do amiss to bring home with me the daughter of one of the first nobles of Utrecht: that I might by that means have an immediate independent fortune of £1000 a year; that I might live in supreme happiness with a handsome and most accomplished lady. But, on the other hand, Zélide is of a bad constitution. Her spirits are unequal. She is either wretched or excessively blessed. She has no prudence, and although she has the best heart in the world, her ungoverned fancy may make her do many wrong things and make a husband very uneasy. Then, Sir, she is a metaphysician and a mathematician too. Is not all this too much? After the first year should I not be very miserable with such a woman? And then, Temple, you know my whimsical disposition. Should I not curse myself for having married a Dutchwoman? Take care of me, my worthy friend. I can have her if I please. But ought I not to delay marrying till I am fairly fixed to a certain plan of life? And must I not have an English wife, as you and I have always planned? Yes, yes, so must it be. So it shall be. There's enough.

I must give you a most curious observation how much our sentiments depend upon circumstances. In the gloom of Utrecht I had fixed so rigid a system that Venus seemed a frightful divinity; and when you asked me if the Dutch women "were alive all over," I thought you a sad libertine.[3] Was I then the very Boswell whose history you know? Since I left England I have been chaste as an anchorite. Now, my mean scruples are gone, but rational morality directs me to do no harm to others or to myself. I have

[2] These letters are all printed in *Boswell in Holland.*

[3] "Have you been chaste since you left us, or do Dutch women feel it all o'er as ours do, and is human nature in that respect everywhere the same? Strange questions these, Boswell, but not unnatural ones" (Temple to Boswell, 7 February 1764, in *Boswell in Holland,* following 15 February 1764).

not yet had an opportunity of indulging my amorous genius. But I have hopes. What think you, Temple, of this immense epistle?[4] . . . Believe me ever your most affectionate friend,

JAMES BOSWELL.

. . . Advise me how to manage matters with my father. . . . Adieu.

TUESDAY 24 JULY. This morning at ten I had with me a French fencing-master, a soldier in the Prussian service. He was a tall, black Gaul, and rattled away with his national volubility. I am now quite in the humour of exercises, as will appear from this my journal.

I dined at Mr. Mitchell's. At table I was stupid. After dinner he and I were left alone, and fell into most agreeable conversation on the small effect of systems of morality, and on the great importance of early impressing upon the mind just sentiments which never leave us. He talked of Thomson, whose friend he formerly was in London.[5] He said that Thomson had more genius than knowledge; that notwithstanding of his fine imitation of Ovid on the Pythagorean system,[6] he was an egregious gormandizer of beefsteaks. He observed that the drama was not his province. He was too descriptive. When a sentiment pleased him, he used to extend it with rich luxuriance. His friends used to prune very freely, and poor Thomson used to suffer. Mr. Mitchell said now and then, "This is fine, but it is misplaced. *Non est hic locus.*" Thomson used to sweat so much the first nights of his plays that when he came and met his friends at a tavern in the Piazza, his wig was as if it had been dipped in an oil-pot. Mr. Mitchell just recalled my London ideas, and made me very happy. At night I supped with the family and then walked with the ladies.

[4] Three sheets (twelve folio pages) completely filled, with a postscript written on the outside. Temple had to pay 4s. 6d. postage.
[5] James Thomson, the poet of *The Seasons,* had been dead only sixteen years. In 1764 the two greatest names in recent English poetry were those of Thomson and Pope.
[6] *Spring,* ll. 358–370; *Metamorphoses,* xv. 116–126. By "Pythagorean system" Boswell means no more than "vegetarianism."

WEDNESDAY 25 JULY.[7] At seven in the morning I went with young Kircheisen to the manège of Comte Schaffgotsch, the King's Master of Horse, where he has two principal grooms that give lessons. I put myself under the direction of Mr. Galliard, a French German. He was active and lively, and talked with the authority of a master. I was a little timorous at first. But the exercise warmed my blood and I got into the true spirit of a cavalier. I do well to apply thus to the exercises of the academy. I shall at least receive some benefit.

I drank tea at home. I said to Mademoiselle that I would not take her with me to Brunswick as I feared to tire of her in two or three days. This was true, but too free. I must really learn a little of that restraint which foreigners call politeness, and which after a certain time becomes quite easy.

I am much pleased with my servant Jacob. He is a Bernois, a genteel, active fellow. I liked this specimen of him upon our journey to Potsdam from Utrecht. He was always alert and ready to put everything right. One day the postilions were at a loss for a machine to carry water in to cool the wheels. Jacob sprung away to the side of a brook, tore from its place a young tree that had fixed its roots in the humid soil, and bringing with it a lump of watery earth, he plashed against the wheels, as a London maid does against the stairs with her moistened mop. There was invention and execution, too, of the very epic kind. He is quite sober, has good Christian principles and even generous sentiments. He would fight for his master, and gold could not tempt him to marry a woman he did not like. He had a most extraordinary adventure before he left Holland. A young officer of the regiment where his master served was uncommonly civil to him, and even used him like a friend. He used to invite him of an evening to the tavern, and give him a bottle of wine, and show a strange fondness. He at last asked Jacob if he would come and live with him. Jacob began to suspect that the young dog was a man of Italian taste. The offi-

7 " . . . This day resume. *Chase libertine fancies.* Happiness upon whole as Milton's 'wedded love' . . . " (Memorandum, 25 July).

cer however told him, "I am not what you think me," and opening his breast discovered himself to be a woman. She was of a good
family and fortune, but had run away from her friends. Jacob
however would not marry her upon any account.

THURSDAY 26 JULY. I put my ladies of the family in a passion by affirming that I would not marry any woman whose fortune was less than £10,000. They were seriously shocked, and
gave me all the good common arguments against low interested
matches. Very well. But my purpose is fixed: my wife shall have
a handsome fortune and that will always be something sure. However, I need not say so. Let me above all strive to attain easy
reserve.

In the evening, I went with Hübner and young Kircheisen to
the Garden of Corsica, a kind of little Vauxhall, and indeed a very
little one.[8] We supped and drank cherry wine, which I found delicious. At night when I got home I resolved ever to cultivate
sublime devotion, to be a Baron of Exchequer and a Laird of
Auchinleck.

FRIDAY 27 JULY. I dined with Mr. Mitchell, who always
gives me agreeable views. He said that, in living, every man must
be his own director, for our tastes are extremely different. He said
if lawyers had a fixed salary, they surely could not drudge as they
do. But the little refreshing presents keep them alive. He coun-
selled me much to pursue the law in Scotland, as I might by that
means attain a useful and honourable station. Yet he owned that
some people could not follow that profession. I said nothing, but

[8] "A burgher of Berlin by the name of Corsica has bought the garden of
Oemcken the bankrupt [in the Tiergarten], and serves supper there for all
comers with great neatness of table-furnishing and china. All the people of
superior rank go, and the rich burghers as well. This garden, with its more
than fifty small tables, all laid, where every one sups with company to his
liking, makes a very pleasant impression on a visitor. The foreign diplomatic
corps goes there frequently" (From the diary of Count E. A. H. Lehndorff,
22 July 1764, ed. by K. E. Schmidt-Lötzen as *Dreissig Jahre am Hofe Frie-
drichs des Grossen*, 1st Supplement, 1910, p. 407, translated). Vauxhall was a
famous pleasure garden across the Thames from London.

had a secret satisfaction to find that my aversion to the law was
not absolutely absurd.[9]

At six we got into his Excellency's coach. I told him that the
Abbé Jerusalem had wished to dispute with the King of Prussia
on religion. "Indeed," said Mr. Mitchell, "they had better save
themselves the trouble; for the King has heard all the Abbé's
arguments, and the Abbé has heard all the King's, and after they
have said a great deal, each will retain his own opinion." "Then,
Sir," said I, "you think Truth is at the bottom of the well." "Yes,"
said he, "and I suppose will remain there some time." We went to
Monbijou and paid our respects at Court. Dull enough.

SATURDAY 28 JULY. At five in the morning, I set out on a
party with Herr Hübner and a councillor. We had a clever chaise
and drove by Spandau to the *campagne* of Mr. Stoltz, who should
have been sent *chargé d'affaires* to England.[1] He was a good genteel young fellow, and spoke English not amiss. We eat currants;
we reposed ourselves in the sun; we dined cheerfully. We walked
about his place, which is sweet and romantic. I was more and
more convinced that hypochondria is ill health, and resolved to
live like Baron Maule.[2] We drove back to Berlin by nine.

SUNDAY 29 JULY. Honest Hübner went with me to look at
some of the Lutheran churches here. I was pleased with their decent ornaments. I drank tea at home, and talked Latin with a fat
Lutheran parson. Then I made a tour in the chaise with Madame
and Mademoiselle, who looked sweet and cheerful and had her

[9] Mitchell had himself been admitted to the bar in both England and Scotland.

[1] Abraham Louis Michel, the Prussian Minister, had just been recalled at
the request of the British Government. Frederick had appointed as Secretary
of Legation (he declined to send another Minister) Monsieur Baudouin,
librarian of his sister, the late Margravine of Bayreuth. "Mr. Stoltz" (or
Stoltzen, as he is named in a letter Boswell afterwards received from
Hübner) is not mentioned in Frederick's political correspondence; perhaps
he was Andrew Mitchell's candidate.

[2] " ... Resolved ... to keep principles to self, being always a friend of Johnson
and moderate Christian ... " (Memorandum, 29 July).

green silk parasol and looked like an Indian princess. We walked
in the Park with Mesdemoiselles Behmer, &c. I then came home as
agreeably as I went out, and very happy I was.

MONDAY 30 JULY. I did my exercises nobly. I was in superb
spirits. Mademoiselle Stensen[3] and other young ladies drank tea
at our house. I was very gay. They begged me to repeat to them
something in English. I repeated Erskine's beautiful stanza, "I
fly, yet I love you, my fair."[4] They thought it Russian. I also repeated Mr. Johnson's verses, "On Thames's banks," &c.,[5] and they
thought them no less rude. How curious is this! Here are human
beings who don't understand English; and to whom Mr. Samuel
Johnson does not exist, and Erskine seems a savage. Mademoiselle
Stensen taught me a sweet song, "Je reconnais les atteintes, qui
m'ont autrefois charmé," &c.[6] It touched me sensibly and made
me own, "That brings back to my mind a married woman with
whom I used to be deeply in love."[7] I must be on my guard.

[3] The name should probably be spelled Steensen.
[4] The last stanza of "A Pastoral Ballad in the Manner of Shenstone," by Boswell's friend, Andrew Erskine:

> Farewell to the flocks I have fed!
>   Farewell to the flow'rs I have rear'd!
> Farewell to the sweet-breathing mead,
>   Where so often with you I've appear'd!
> I fly, yet I love you, my fair;
>   Perhaps you'll repent when I'm gone;
> My bosom shall nourish despair,
>   And I'll sigh that all pleasure is flown.
>   Alexander Donaldson's *Collection*
>   *of Original Poems*, i. 94

[5] On Thames's banks, in silent thought, we stood,
> Where Greenwich smiles upon the silver flood;
> Struck with the seat that gave Eliza birth,
> We kneel, and kiss the consecrated earth.
>   *London*, ll. 21–24

[6] "I experience again the spells by which I was once bound." I have not found
the author.
[7] Probably Mrs. Heron, daughter of Lord Kames, one of Lord Auchinleck's
colleagues on the bench. Boswell was feeling a strong compulsion to talk

TUESDAY 31 JULY. This morning I was out of order. But by making my blood circulate, I became quite well. I went with Hübner to the Garden of Richards[8] in the Park, and supped.

[Boswell to Henri de Catt. Original in French. First draft][9]

[Berlin, *c.* 31 July 1764]

I TAKE THE LIBERTY, SIR, of writing to you. I hope that you are completely recovered and are able to enjoy again the good fortune for which I envy you so much. Yes, Sir, I am not ashamed to confess my envy of a man who spends his hours in the company of the King of Prussia.

I have already told you of my enthusiastic wish to be presented to your monarch. I am not quite so easy to please as the English knight who made the trip from London to Potsdam solely to see the King, and when he had seen him on the Parade, went quietly home again. I am like the ancient philosopher who said, "Speak, so that I can see you."[1] I have already had the honour of seeing His Maj-

---

about this affair, and finally did discuss it with Rousseau, though without naming names. See pp. 123, 212 *n.* 3, 234, 254.

[8] The "Richardsche Kaffeegarten," another open-air restaurant beside the Tiergarten. It faced what is now Königgrätzer Strasse.

[9] This letter, now first published, is worthy of comparison with the famous cajoling epistle which Boswell was to write to Rousseau in December of this year (below, p. 218). He has had no success in securing a presentation to Frederick through Lord Marischal or Andrew Mitchell, and has come to fear that unless he makes a frontal attack, he will not be presented at all. In writing to Catt he is really writing to Frederick; that is, he hopes that Catt (who, as Reader, sees the King on informal terms) will put the letter into the King's hands, or at least will read portions of it to him. The letter which he actually sent has not been recovered, but Boswell preserved a first draft showing a good deal of subsequent toning down by deletion and substitution, and a second draft which carried the letter still further in the direction of sobriety. I have printed only the first draft, ignoring much of the revision, my aim being to present the document in the first flush of its artful naïveté.

[1] Socrates, according to Erasmus, who was probably Boswell's source. A rich man had sent his son so that Socrates might look him over and judge of his talents. "Well, then, my lad," said Socrates, "speak, so that I can see you"

esty two or three times. Imagination may do much, but I am sure that he has an aspect of superior guise. Upon my soul, I was struck. He electrified me. Every time I looked at him, I felt a shock of the heroic. You, Sir, whose blood does not circulate so rapidly as mine, may laugh at a stranger. No doubt I seem to you like a child who gazes open-mouthed at a picture of Alexander or Julius Caesar. Well and good. I am willing to keep something of the spirit of childhood. Ah, dear Sir, it is a pleasant age: one feels then in full force that admiration which to my way of thinking is one of the most agreeable of passions.[2]

I am not satisfied with having seen the King. If it is possible, I should like to hear him speak. Mr. Mitchell gives me very little hope of succeeding. On the road here, I said to my worthy conductor, Lord Marischal, that it was a great pity that the King did not have the lesser vanities as well as the greater: that he did not like to show himself in person to strangers as well as to make his brilliant conquests. My Lord replied that if the King had been in love with little things, he would not have accomplished great ones. Nevertheless, it is a real loss to the rest of us and especially to me, who in a sense flatter myself for feeling such admiration for him. The sage said, "Οὐκ εἰμὶ σοφὸς ἀλλὰ φιλόσοφος."[3] It is certain that I am not a great man, but I have an enthusiastic love of great men, and I derive a kind of glory from it. I am told that at least I can sometimes conceive an idea of greatness of soul. How many fine things should I not do if I were not hindered by the fear of appearing absurd! How often should I not follow the lively inclinations that come into my mind! Do you know that one evening at Charlottenburg I was very near the King in the garden, and that I felt a powerful impulse to throw myself at his feet and risk telling him how much I had wished to see His Majesty? But I thought a

---

[Loquere igitur, inquit, adolescens, ut te videam]. Erasmus continues, "meaning thereby that a man's character is reflected less fully in his face than in his speech" (*Apophthegmata*, iii. 70).

[2] The manuscript has the alternative *sensations*.

[3] "I am not a wise man but I love wisdom" (A remark attributed to Pythagoras, preserved in Latin by Cicero, *Tusculan Disputations*, V. iii. 8).

little, and my heated imagination cooled. Yet I am sure that I showed something of unusual agitation, for General Wylich said to me with a serious but cordial air, "Calm yourself, Sir." I shall not forget that little anecdote. I am truly the old Scottish baron: I might have said the old feudal baron. I am haughty towards the tenants on my estate. But for a superior like the King of Prussia I have prodigious[4] veneration. Do not reason with me. What I am describing to you is a fixed sentiment. I find that sentiments firmly impressed have much more power than arguments proved up to the hilt; and it is to sentiments that I always return.

What makes me wish still more to see your monarch and what makes me still more regretful that the pleasure is so difficult to obtain, is that I know the Philosopher of Sans Souci so well. Am I not reading him every morning? Has he not fired my soul? Have I not criticized him without ceremony? Are you aware that he has perhaps no greater admirer and no freer companion than myself? Are you aware that he has done me real good, that he has often roused a noble ambition in a heart, alas! too pensive and listless, and that I feel for him much sincere gratitude? I shall not cite passages. It is not necessary to advance proofs. But may I tell you also that I would give a great deal if my royal Philosopher had not written the epistle to my countryman, Marshal Keith? Is it possible that he entertained such thoughts at one moment of his life? Where was that *sentiment* which is so dear to me? How could he uphold the gloomy doctrine of annihilation and at the same time show the fire of an immortal spirit?[5] How striking a paradox! Dare I say that it is a piece of philosophic coquetry, exactly like that of a woman of

[4] "Prodigious" is in English, and stands a little above the line. Boswell could not recall at once the French adjective he wished and put the English word down to record the sense. He later substituted *étonnante* and then *la plus profonde.*

[5] James Keith, Lord Marischal's younger brother and like him a Jacobite exile, had been one of Frederick's most trusted generals and had held the rank of field marshal in the Prussian Army. He was mortally wounded at the battle of Hochkirch (1758). The epistle to which Boswell refers (No. XVIII) is entitled "To Marshal Keith, on Empty Fears of Death and the Terrors of Another Life."

extraordinary beauty who looks at you and, as she shows you her charms, says, "No, I am not good-looking at all"? Ah, no, great King! You shall never be destroyed. Not only shall your name live for ever, but your soul shall be immortal too; and I shall certainly speak to you in the other world, though I may not in this.

Will you have the goodness, Sir, to let me know if you think there is any chance that I may be presented to the King somehow or other before his departure for Silesia? It is perhaps a piece of un- reasonable curiosity on my part, and perhaps I might repent of it, for I should probably be so timid that His Majesty would consider me an egregious blockhead. Nevertheless you will afford me a very lively pleasure by giving me your advice in this matter. It will seem exceedingly hard to me to have been in Prussia and not to be able to tell my grandsons that I paid my respects to Frederick the Great. Next week[6] I plan to make a tour to Brunswick and to pass some weeks at a court which I love and respect, where I have received extraordinary attentions, and where I hope not to be forgotten.

I hope, Sir, that you will be able to understand my bad French.[7]

WEDNESDAY 1 AUGUST.[8] I dined at Mr. Mitchell's, where was Mr. Formey, Perpetual Secretary to the Academy of Sciences at Berlin.[9] He was facetious, but vain. He talked of his books, and he

[6] The manuscript has the alternative "next Monday." He actually left on Saturday.

[7] Catt wrote a polite but non-committal reply on 4 August, saying that no presentations could be made at Potsdam, especially since Frederick was always at Sans Souci, but that there still remained the possibility of a presentation at Berlin, either before Boswell went to Brunswick or after he came back. He himself, he said, could not do more than mention Boswell to the King and tell the King how much Boswell wished to hear him speak.

[8] "... Still keep in mind being Baron and Laird of Auchinleck, and shun wild ideas, for you're Mr. Samuel Johnson's friend" (Memorandum, 1 August).

[9] Formey, born at Berlin of French parents, had been pastor of the French Church at Berlin and professor of philosophy in the French college. He was a good executive, and was esteemed in his own day as a popularizer of philosophical ideas, but his name now is perhaps principally kept alive by Rousseau's sarcastic references to him in the footnotes to *Émile.* — In his

talked of his lectures. He said, "When you hear the drum roll at
nine o'clock in the evening, you can say, 'Formey is abed.' " He
told us that Mr. Gualteri, a French minister here, was so hypochondriac that he caused tie his legs together at night, lest he
should get up and do himself some mischief. How strange a distemper is this! When he was gone, Mr. Mitchell and I talked on the
difference of sentiment among mankind, and of the infinite number of books which deluge the field of literature.

I then got into my coach and paid a number of visits to the
ladies of my acquaintance. In particular, I waited on Madame de
Brandt, to whom I was presented at Charlottenburg, having by
mistake accosted her daughter who lives with her, thinking that it
was her daughter who is lady of honour to the Queen. Madame de
Brandt was lady to one of the great officers of the Prussian Court.
She has been very handsome and is still a fine figure. She has a very
courtly address and is clever. She asked me to supper.[1] I accordingly returned and found there another lady and gentleman, whose
names I did not hear and had no inclination to ask. Madame de
Brandt told us of a shrewd Saxon who loved his dinner, that when
asked after his friends and neighbours, replied shortly, "They are
all dead," so kept all the company busy with lamentation till he
had eat as much as he chose; after which he gravely began and told
that all the good people were come alive again. I was here quite at
my ease, but too vivacious. I really believe that I must, for some
years yet, now and then give scope to my vivaciousness.

THURSDAY 2 AUGUST. This was a dreary wet day, and my
nerves were soaked in the moist ether, so that I was a little dreary
myself. I dined at Mr. Mitchell's, who after dinner talked with me

---

memorandum for 2 August Boswell records a remark of Voltaire's, evidently
repeated to him by Formey: "I am going blind, like Tiresias, but not because
I pried into the secrets of heaven."

[1] Louise von Brandt was the widow of Christian von Brandt; he was a cousin
of Frederick's beloved "Mama," Madame de Camas. As a young woman she
corresponded with Voltaire, and appears to have been a friend of Madame
de Wreech, who is reputed to have been Frederick's mistress. Boswell mistook
her daughter Friederike, who was not a "lady of honour," for her daughter
Sophie, who was.

on metaphysics, fate, free will, the origin of evil, and all those beautiful themes. In support of free will I maintained that Omniscience could not foresee the actions of men; and that it was nobler to create a being with such powers that God knew not how it would act than to create a mere machine, of whose motions he should be certain. "Then," said Mr. Mitchell, "it is more ingenious to make a child than to make a watch." This pleasantry has a colour, but the question is if a man can make a child: if a man can give a child the spark of celestial fire. In short his Excellency and I ended our conversation with affirming that dark speculations were to be shunned, and man kept busy and cheerful.

FRIDAY 3 AUGUST. A Swiss gentleman who dined with us at Froment's told me that Lord Baltimore was living at Constantinople as a Turk, with his seraglio around him. He said that this nobleman was quite the man of English whim. He lived luxuriously and inflamed his blood, then he grew melancholy and timorous and was constantly taking medicines. In short, he is there leading a strange, wild life, useless to his country, uneasy to himself, except when raised to a delirium, and must soon destroy his constitution. The Swiss very sensibly observed that the greatest kindness my Lord's friends could do him would be to put him aboard a ship, feed him moderately on wholesome food, and make him work hard. By this means he might be restored to health and soundness of mind; after which they might put his estate into his hands, which he then might truly enjoy. Lord Baltimore was a beacon to me. I trembled to think of my wild schemes.[2]

[2] So far as I know, Boswell nowhere explains what his own "wild schemes" had been, but the fantasy of thirty concubines which he later confessed to Rousseau can probably be taken as representative. — Frederick Calvert (born 1731), sixth and last of the Lords Baltimore, proprietors of the colony of Maryland, printed a *Tour in the East in the Years 1763 and 1764* which has received no praise from those who have read it. At the beginning of 1763 he was at Rome making life miserable for the great German archaeologist Winckelmann, whom he had engaged to show him the antiquities of the place. Winckelmann's caustic reports in letters to his friends furnish the best account we have of this most unpleasant man: "My Lord is an original and deserves to be written up. He thinks he has too much brain and that it would

At night Madame Muller, a young widow, supped with us.[3] I was too ludicrous, but it was in order to kiss the widow; and heartily did I smack her little lips.

SATURDAY 4 AUGUST. This day I had fixed to set out for Brunswick. I dined Herr Président's, and after dinner Madame made

---

have been better if God had substituted brawn for a third part of it. He has wearied of everything in the world; we went through the Villa Borghese in ten minutes. Because of ennui he is going to make a tour to Constantinople, where he will stay some years, how many he does not know himself. His retinue consists of a young and pretty English girl, but he is looking for a male travelling-companion; he will have difficulty in finding one here" (To Usteri, 1 January 1763). "Nothing pleased him but St. Peter's and the Apollo Belvedere. . . . He finally got so unbearable that I told him what I thought of him and shall have no more to do with him. He has £30,000 sterling of annual rent, which he does not know how to enjoy" (To Franke, 15 January 1763). "I left my Lord to his own devices two weeks ago because I could stand him no longer. He is one of those sensual, unhappy Englishmen who are weary of everything in the world. He . . . was married to a daughter of the Duchess of Bridgewater, by whom he has no children, though he has plenty by other women . . . " (To Usteri, 29 January 1763). In 1768 Baltimore stood trial at the Kingston Assizes on a charge of rape on the body of a girl named Sarah Woodcock, a milliner. He was acquitted, to the great disappointment of the public, and went abroad again. Count Maximilian von Lamberg professes to continue his story from that point: "In 1769 my Lord was travelling with eight women, a physician, and two negroes, whom he called his *corregidores,* who were entrusted with the discipline of his little seraglio. With the aid of his physician he conducted odd experiments on his houris: he fed the plump ones only acid foods and the thin ones milk and broth. He arrived at Vienna with the train I have described; when the chief of police requested him to declare which of the eight ladies was his wife, he replied that he was an Englishman; and that when he was called upon to give an account of his sexual arrangements, if he could not settle the matter with his fists, it was his practice to set out instantly on his travels again" (*Le Mémorial d'un mondain,* 1774, pp. 110–111, translated). Lamberg's book, which is in large part a *chronique scandaleuse,* swarms with obvious errors; and it may be that his account of Baltimore's harem in 1769 is actually a version of the same gossip that Boswell heard in 1764. Baltimore died at Naples in 1771, leaving the Province of Maryland to a schoolboy named Henry Harford, his illegitimate son. The Revolution shortly afterwards made the bequest nugatory.

[3] This name should probably be spelled Müller.

fine *gâteaux* (diet cakes) for me to eat upon my journey. Never was a fellow so kindly used as I am here. This little instance of attention shows a true cordiality.[4] I was quite a Spaniard, a gallant gentleman. I had hesitated much how to travel. I found that hiring a machine or horses would cost me very dear, and I did not choose to join company with any merchants or merchants' clerks. I therefore took places in the *Postwagen*. Herr Hübner saw me mount and fairly set off. The *Postwagen* is a remain of barbarity of manners. It is just a large cart, mounted upon very high wheels, which jolt prodigiously. It has no covering, and has three or four deal boards laid across it to serve for seats. In this manner do the Germans travel night and day. It was wet, and I began to fret. However, I fell upon an expedient. I fixed my attention on the Court of Brunswick, which I was going to visit, where I should be very happy, and therefore all the intermediate time was to be considered as nothing.

As I passed through a wood before I entered Potsdam, a branch struck my eye and hurt me a good deal. It made me muse on the risk I had run of losing the half of one of my senses. I had time in the dark silence of night to ruminate on the great question concerning Providence. Should I now have said that Providence preserved my eye? But, I pray you, why did Providence permit the branch to strike me? Oh, that was a natural event. Very well, and the degree of force was natural too; so that very naturally I have not lost my right eye. For shame, divines, how dare you bring in Providence on every trifling occasion? *Nec deus intersit nisi dignus vindice nodus.*[5] 'Tis true, our heavenly Father sees every sparrow

---

[4] The memoranda for this day contain the direction "Buy parasol"; the expense account shows an entry of four crowns, not for a parasol but for a "pair of large pigeons." The parasol would pretty certainly have been a going-away present for Madame or Mademoiselle Kircheisen; the pigeons, which were actually bought, may have been a gift to young Friedrich Leopold. Mademoiselle already had a parasol, as Boswell well knew; he later bought her an expensive etui.

[5] "Nor must God intervene except in great matters" (Horace, *Ars Poetica,* l. 191).

that falls to the ground. Yes, the universal eye perceives every-thing in the universe. But surely, the grand and extensive system employs the attention of God, and the minutiae are not to be con-sidered as part of his care; at least, we are not to presume that he interests himself in every little accident. At Potsdam we stopped two hours. I laid myself down upon a timber stair and slept very sound.

SUNDAY 5 AUGUST. I was well jaded. I had a Jew and many other blackguards with me. I passed by the name of Herr Sheridán, Français, Coufman nag Berlin.[6] I was too tired to speculate.

MONDAY 6 AUGUST. My ideas alter. Very well, let them alter back again. We stopped some hours at Magdeburg. I felt an un-usual glow of feeling at this renowned city, so famous for its dread-ful sack by the Austrian general Tilly, of which the King of Prussia speaks in one of his cantos on the art of war.[7] It is a large city, very well fortified, and has many good houses. Prince Ferdinand of Brunswick is governor of it.[8] It was a sweet, warm day. I went and saw the great church, which is noble. I saw there several relics. I was all devotion, and fit to enter into the society of blessed spirits. All my former sufferings did me no harm. I heard *horae* solemnly sung. I was quite happy. Why do I, like Wharton, indulge the "lust of praise"?[9] Why seek to please all? Why fear the censure of

[6] "Mr. Sheridan, Frenchman, merchant at Berlin." He has assumed this style because travelling in the post-wagon was *infra dig.* for a gentleman, let alone an ancient feudal baron.

[7] The sack of Magdeburg, an incident of the Thirty Years' War, occurred in May, 1631, when the combined armies of the Empire and of the Catholic League burned most of the city and massacred the greater part of its in-habitants. Frederick (*L'Art de la guerre*, Chant IV) makes Tilly an example of the cruel general.

[8] As deputy of the King of Prussia, to whom the Duchy of Magdeburg belonged.

[9] The reference is to Pope's lines on Philip, Duke of Wharton:

> Wharton, the scorn and wonder of our days,
> Whose ruling passion was the lust of praise.
> *Moral Essays*, i. 180–181

those whom I despise? Let me boldly pursue my own plan. I now adored my God with holy confidence and implored his influence to preserve my mind from the clouds of gloom, above all from sad notions of his infinite majesty.

I began an *Epistle on Parliament* to Dempster. I was rich in ideas.[1] I wrote a letter to Mr. Sheridan, in which I said that all my extravagancies had been occasioned by my nervous disorder, which he himself was also subject to. I wrote well and with vivacity, yet discovered a despondency of making any considerable figure.[2] To make a fair trial how much I depend on my body, I went to bed in noble glow, and by only sleeping a few hours with my clothes on in a soft bed, I was relaxed so as to get up sick and dismal.

TUESDAY 7 AUGUST. I jogged on. I stopped at Königslutter, having taken an extra post for the last stage, in order to enter Brunswick as a gentleman. In the churchyard of Königslutter I met an old gentleman in a dark shabby dress. I asked him if he was a clergyman. "Non," said he, "cantor sum."[3] I went and saw the great church here. It stands high, and is an excellent old building. At night I arrived at Brunswick, and put up where my Lord Marischal and I were, at the Gulden Arm. I was quite the Laird of Auchinleck, serious and calm.

WEDNESDAY 8 AUGUST. I paid visits to Feronce, Stammer, and to Monsieur de Bassewitz, Lord Chamberlain to the Duke. I had immediately an invitation to dine at Court. I went before two, and found an agreeable reception from everybody, and was again

---

[1] George Dempster, a Scots laird eight years older than Boswell, had since 1761 been one of his principal literary cronies. He represented the Forfar and Fife burghs in Parliament, and was an accomplished politician. The *Epistle on Parliament*, of which considerable fragments are preserved among the Boswell papers at Yale, does not appear to have enough general interest to warrant publication in this edition.

[2] This letter has not been recovered. Thomas Sheridan, actor, theatrical manager, and teacher of elocution, father of the more famous Richard Brinsley Sheridan, had at one time been adopted by Boswell as his principal mentor. See p. 31 *n.*

[3] "I am a precentor" (other possibilities, "schoolmaster" or merely "singer").

presented to the reigning family. Baron de Pless, aide-de-camp to
Prince Ferdinand, is a brave, worthy, amiable young man. He
said, "Duke Ferdinand is a worthy man. He is always busy. He
reads and writes a great deal. He is an extremely devout prince.
Every morning regularly he says his prayers and reads the Scriptures. He is always polite, and is very even-tempered. During the
war he did all he could to alleviate the inevitable suffering, whereas
the King of Prussia had no human feeling. I have seen him pass by
a group of poor wounded men and turn his eyes the other way."

After dinner I waited on the Hereditary Prince and Princess,
then went to a German comedy, then supped at Court. It was a
glorious change after all my posting fatigues.

THURSDAY 9 AUGUST.[4] I walked with Feronce in the Fair,
where I was agreeably light-headed. I dined *chez* the Hereditary
Prince, and talked lively but too young, from my sad timorous education. At night I was very gay at a pretty *opérette*. I sat in the
Duke's *loge* and was fine with the ladies of the Court. Was not this
quite as I could wish? My mind was clear and firm and fertile. It
contained in itself both male and female powers: brilliant fancies
were begotten, and brilliant fancies were brought forth. I saw my
error in suffering so much from the contemplation of others. I can
never be them, therefore let me not vainly attempt it in imagination; therefore let me not envy the gallant and the happy, nor be
shocked by the nauseous and the wretched. I must be Mr. Boswell
of Auchinleck, and no other. Let me make him as perfect as possible. I think, were I such a one, I should be happy indeed; were I
such another, I should be wretched indeed — without considering
that were I really these people, I could not have the same ideas of
their situation as I now have, for no man has of himself the notion
that other people have of him, especially those who know him lit-

---

[4] " . . . Remembered Mother, her tender care, and resolved to be good-
humoured and by superior strength of mind to make her gay. This is real.
Write her so, and God will assist you. . . . Have a care or health and purse
ruin. You're well and can be with no girls except sure ones" (Memorandum,
9 August).

tle. I considered also the absurdity of my reasoning in low spirits. What gloomy nonsense have I often imagined! I recollected my moments of despair when I did not value myself at sixpence, because, forsooth, I was but an individual, and an individual is nothing in the multitude of beings. Whereas *I* am all to myself. I have but one existence. If it is a mad one, I cannot help it. I must do my best.

Amidst all this brilliance, I sent forth my imagination to the Inner Temple, to the chambers of Mr. Samuel Johnson. I glowed with reverence and affection, and a romantic idea filled my mind. To have a certain support at all times, I determined to write to this great man, and beg that he might give me a "solemn assurance of perpetual friendship," so that I might march under his protection while he lived, and after his death, imagine that his shade beckoned me to the skies. Grand, yet enthusiastic, idea![5]

FRIDAY 10 AUGUST. The little gloom which I now feel of a morning seems a mere trifle. Instead of those thick heavy clouds which pressed me down at Utrecht, I find only thin dusky vapours, and they are soon dispersed. After dining at Court, De Pless and I walked in the piazzas of the Palace, and in the garden. He asked me what could occasion melancholy, and with easy composure I gave him a lecture on that distemper. Then he talked of religion, and carried me to see a Catholic church.

I then went to the opera, which at Brunswick is very noble. The house is large, and the decorations much finer than in London. The performers were very good. The piece was *Enea in Lazona* — Aeneas in Latium. He who played Turnus was no eunuch, and had a bold manly voice, with which he did wonders. One air in which occurred *rivale*, and another in which occurred *la traditore*, struck me prodigiously.[6] I had no notion of being so

[5] See p. 64 *n.*

[6] The best known opera with the title *Enea nel Lazio* was that by Niccolò Jommelli, Kapellmeister to the Duke of Württemberg; it was first produced at Stuttgart in 1755. The libretto was by Mattia Verazi. But since in the libretto as preserved the words *rivale* and *traditore* occur only in recitative passages, it is not certain that Jommelli's was the "noble opera" that Boswell heard.

much affected by music. My hypochondriac deadness is almost forgot. How happy am I now! I dined at Court, and after this noble opera I returned to Court and supped elegant and grand.

[Boswell to Caroline Kircheisen. Original in French]

Brunswick, 10 August 1764

To SHOW YOU, MY DEAR FRIEND, how completely I am a man of my word, I take the risk of exposing my ignorance of the French language. I have found ways of hiding it somehow or other in the volubility of conversation, but when you read at your leisure what I have written, you will see that your Scots Spaniard has such contempt for the frivolous nation that he has scorned to learn its language.

Have you ever seen a man so vain as I am? I am sure you never have. I cannot divest myself of vanity for a single instant. I assure you that I began quite sincerely to make excuses for my bad French, and yet I could not get to the end of a sentence without taking a high tone and priding myself on my very ignorance. Well! you are good enough to pardon me all my faults: I am only too sure of it. If I correct them, it is from motives more generous than that of fear. You know it, my dear; and you behave towards me in a manner very different from that in which I imagine that I should behave towards my wife, if I had one. . . .

How are you coming on with the harpsichord? Labour to improve your playing, I implore you. You will perform miracles one day. In the mean time, you have the satisfaction of contributing sensibly to the pleasure of a very worthy man, who (between ourselves) receives a pretty large share of your admiration. Charming creature! do not blush. You were offended when I told you that you admired me. Perhaps you will not take it amiss if I write the same thing. At any rate, I should like to try it and see.

I beg you to give my regards to Monsieur and Madame Kircheisen. At present I shall say no more. I must be far, far away before I tender them my feelings of gratitude. My compliments to the young horseman. He has no other occupation so far as I know.

No, he is not a woodcutter.[7] May I venture to entrust you with compliments for Mesdemoiselles &c., &c., &c.? Fill in the names as you please. Such confidence do I have in your judgment and sense of propriety that I give you full power to distribute my endearments as you think best.

I beg you to write by the first post. Be assured that I am your sincere friend and also (as the formula runs) your very humble servant,

Boswell.

SATURDAY 11 AUGUST. I breakfasted with Sir Joshua Vanneck's son and his Swiss governor. They answered precisely to my ideas.[8] I then waited on Monsieur l'Abbé Jerusalem, who received me with cordial joy. I found him in his library. It pleased me, and I resolved to have a very large and good one at Auchinleck. He gave me an exact idea of the King of Prussia's mind. "He has, Sir, a great deal of imagination. He lays hold of the first idea which presents itself agreeably; and I am sure if the Christian religion were presented to him in the right colours, he would be struck all of a sudden by its beauty." "And perhaps," said I, "he would be the greatest of enthusiasts, and would write a magnificent poem in praise of his faith." We started fate and free will. The good Abbé was afraid to doubt of a quality which he had been always accustomed to attribute to the Divinity, to wit, an universal prescience even of the actions of men, and would maintain the scholastic notion that certain foreknowledge did not restrain the liberty of acting. I boldly opposed the prescience, and clearly defended my liberty.

I believe I have not yet mentioned in this my journal the melancholy story of Monsieur Gualteri who travelled with young Mackenzie of Seaforth. It happened just before I was first at Brunswick.

[7] The "young horseman" is Caroline's brother, Friedrich Leopold, who seems to have been attending the same manège as Boswell. The joke about being a woodcutter is unexplained. Boswell on at least one occasion had found Friedrich "forward" and had "checked" him. See pp. 29, 39.

[8] Sir Joshua Vanneck was a great London merchant.

He was a mighty pretty man, but dreadfully melancholy. He supped at the Hereditary Prince's, where he seemed very happy and played charmingly on the flute. That very night he was seized with a dismal fit, got out of bed, and threw himself from a window three storeys high. He was not killed, but bruised in the most shocking manner, so that he was at this time half putrefied and in horrid anguish, wishing for immediate death yet finding that the cruel enemy approached him with slow steps. The Abbé said, "He said he was sorry that the blow had missed him; but now I believe that he has juster thoughts, and that religion brings him consolation. His brother has the disposition of an angel but likewise the gloomiest ideas, and extreme impatience. He came here to see the poor fellow, but dared not remain, for fear that he would do the same as his brother."

The Abbé then owned to me that he himself had suffered most severely from the hypochondria. "It is astonishing," said he, "what power the imagination can exert, even when you are in full possession of your reason and are convinced that your imagination is diseased." He said that he had great satisfaction from having borne it with patience, and that God had helped him. He said he was often terrified lest in some moment of despair his imagination should drive him to kill himself.[9] It is impossible to conceive the satisfaction which I had at hearing that this excellent person had fought with the demon as I have done, and that he had conquered him; for he told me, "That is all a thing of the past." I told him freely what I had endured at Utrecht, and how I thought myself a hero. When I rose to leave him, he took me cordially by the hand and said, "My dear Sir, be assured that my esteem for you is firmly fixed. It is not because of your birth, but because of your character, your heart, and your manner of thinking. You can go wherever you wish, into the farthest corners of the earth: I shall never forget

[9] The Abbé's only son, Karl Wilhelm Jerusalem, committed suicide in 1772. He was in some sense the original of Goethe's Werther. See D. Van B. Hegeman, "Boswell and the Abt Jerusalem," *Journal of English and Germanic Philology,* 44 (Oct. 1945). 367–369.

you." This sincere compliment from a learned and amiable Lutheran abbé who had the honour to educate the Hereditary Prince of Brunswick gave me uncommon satisfaction. I shall remember it all my life. He agreed to correspond with me.

After dining at Court I went to the French *comédie.* At night indolence made me think, why give myself so much labour to write this journal, in which I really do not insert much that can be called useful? Beg your pardon. Does it not contain a faithful register of my variations of mind? Does it not contain many ingenious observations and pleasing strokes which can afterwards be enlarged? Well, but I may die. True, but I may live; and what a rich treasure for my after days will be this my journal.

SUNDAY 12 AUGUST. I breakfasted with my worthy Baron de Pless, and then he conducted me to the Duke's Chapel, where I heard a psalm performed with magnificent music, eunuchs and other singers from the opera, an organ, a French horn, flutes, fiddles, trumpets. It was quite heaven. I adored my God, and I hoped for immortal joy. It was really grand to see the serene family of Brunswick at their devotions. After chapel was the levee of the Hereditary Princess, this day being her birthday. The Court was in grand gala. Unluckily, I did not think of this before I left Berlin, so had only with me two suits of silk clothes. However, I passed very well. Upon occasion were presented to the Princess, English verses by "G. L. Hertel, Lector and Teacher of the English Language at the Julius Charles University in Helmstedt." But such verses not Sternhold could exceed. He said he had imagined it was very difficult to write poetry, but when he tried it now for the first time, he found it very easy. I asked him if he just found a kind of sudden inspiration. He said yes. I wrote verses to him in his own style, of which the following was a stanza:

> Ye Muses nine! on English wings
>   A poet German sails!
> Now may in Greenland hams arise,
>   And in Westphalia whales!

As I found him a good creature, I did not present them to him. I have them together with his.[1]

We had a prodigious company to dine at Court, and a most magnificent dinner. I sat by Madame de Boick, Gouvernante to the young princesses, an amiable, pleasant old lady.[2] Grand music played in an apartment adjoining, and round the table was a vast crowd of spectators. I confess that I was supremely elevated. I had the utmost pleasure of contrast by considering at this hour is assembled Auchinleck kirk and many a whine and many a sad look is found therein. But how shall I support it some time hence? I know not, and let it not disturb me at present. However, let me firmly resolve to drive off the *veteres avias*.[3] Let me not encourage

[1] Boswell's copy of Herr Hertel's verses has not come down to us, but Professor Warnock has found the complete text in the Bibliotheca Augusta at Wolfenbüttel. Two of the twenty-eight stanzas will suffice:

> Her native shores Augusta left
>   To bless a foreign clime;
> Old Brunswick was the happy place
>   She chose to pass her time. . . .

> The princes and princesses all,
>   The present and the absent,
> Bless them in their high dignity,
>   To them be always present.

Boswell's parody contains three stanzas in addition to the one he copied into his journal. His last stanza reads,

> Great bard, accept this tax of praise,
>   Let it a trophy be;
> Thou sing'st of Brunswick's *hups* Princess,
>   I sing, great bard, of thee.

To this he appends the following note: "For the information of the English reader, it is necessary to say that in the German tongue *hups* [that is, *hübsch*] signifies 'beautiful' or 'pretty.' "

[2] This name remains a mystery. If it is German, the spelling should probably be Boeck; if Dutch, Buick. (In the memoranda Boswell actually uses the latter spelling.) But no such name occurs in the Brunswick court lists.

[3] "Foolish old prejudices" (Persius, v. 92).

the least gloomy idea of religion, but let me be firm and cheerful.

After dinner we walked in the garden, then had a concert at Court, and then grand court in the Duke's bedchamber, where every Sunday he receives the compliments of his subjects. I played at whist. I was not invited to supper, and was weak enough to go home vexed a little. Such is a mind rendered too delicate by fine living. I however recollected that when there was such a crowd the Maréchal might easily forget me.

MONDAY 13 AUGUST. There came into my room this morning the sweetest girl I ever saw, a *blanchisseuse*,[4] eighteen, fresh, gay. I spoke German to her with unusual ease, and told her that I would not for the world debauch her to give myself a few days' pleasure, but if she would go with me to England and then to Scotland, I would be very kind to her. She was really innocent. Her beauty thrilled my frame. I thought that I might be an old patriarch upon occasions and could not see any harm in taking her with me. She refused to go, but promised to come back from time to time.

I called on Feronce, as I do indeed almost every morning, and if I find him not, amuse myself with his books. I said, "I am perplexed by a swarm of ideas which mingle confusedly in my head." "But," said he, "as time goes on, each idea will settle in its own cell." This is well. I met at Court the Marquis Cavalcabo, an Italian nobleman of ancient family, not rich, but very knowing and extremely clever. He told me, "I was sadly troubled with a weakness of the stomach and a relaxation of the nerves. But I have cured myself by taking ice. The water, Sir, when it is mixed with the food, makes it soft, and the chill of the ice gives elasticity to the fibres of the stomach; and you digest as though you had millstones in your belly." His system pleased me much and his vivacious expression made me relish it more. I determined to try it, and he promised to teach me how to make ice.[5]

[4] Laundress.

[5] It does not seem as though Cavalcabo could have taught him any practical way of making artificial ice that did not involve the use of natural ice and salt. It was known that one could produce a freezing-mixture by taking ad-

After dinner I was at the noble entertainment of rope-dancing, at which was the Duke and all the Court. I have omitted in this my journal to mention that one day last week we had a ball at Court, where I danced most agreeably. I asked to dance a minuet with the Hereditary Princess. She graciously consented, but we had just made our reverence when the fiddles struck up a country dance which the Hereditary Prince was to begin. So we were stopped. Oh, I was a mortified gentleman. This evening was again a ball. No sooner did the amiable Princess perceive me than she came up to me with a smile celestial and said, "Mr. Boswell, let us finish our minuet." Accordingly I danced with Her Royal Highness, who danced extremely well. We made a very fine English minuet — or British, if you please, for it was a Scots gentleman and an English lady that performed it. What a group of fine ideas had I! I was dancing with a princess; with the grand-daughter of King George whose birthday I have so often helped to celebrate at Old Edinburgh; with the daughter of the Prince of Wales, who patronized Thomson and other votaries of science and the muse; with the sister of George the Third, my sovereign. I mark this variety to show how my imagination can enrich an object, so that I have double pleasure when I am well. It was noble to be in such a frame. I said to the Princess, "Madam, I return your Royal Highness a thousand thanks for the honour you have done me. This will serve me to talk of to my tenants as long as I live." I was next taken out to dance by the Princess Elizabeth, who is to be Queen of Prussia, and by the

---

vantage of the property possessed by certain salts, such as ammonium chloride, of lowering the temperature of water in which they are dissolved, but it seems quite certain that the method had not been adapted to domestic use. Ice was harvested and stored in the eighteenth century and appears to have been widely used to chill liquids and make frozen desserts, though it was probably considered a good deal of a luxury. But if one had natural ice, why bother to make artificial ice? I can suggest two explanations, neither, I am afraid, very plausible: (1) the natural ice (or snow) which was stored in the eighteenth century was commonly too dirty for direct consumption; (2) by "ice" Boswell really means "ices" — frozen confections of flavoured water.

Princess Dorothea. My spirits bounded; yet was I solemn, and stretched my view to the world of futurity. It was fine to be in the Palace of Brunswick, and see the illustrious family brilliant and gay, and the Prince diverting himself after his scenes of heroism.

I don't know if I have as yet mentioned in this my journal the Comte Shuvalov, Chamberlain to the Empress of Russia.[6] He was a little, lively man, had a knowledge of the names of books, if not more, and much easiness of manner. He and I were very well. On Sunday night we stood in a window with the Hereditary Prince, who said, "It is very difficult to combine business and pleasure"; and, when he had talked of warriors hazarding so much for glory, he said, "It is folly." He said too, "I once did a generous thing for a man who was my enemy. He is dead, but I give you my word that the recollection always gives me genuine pleasure." This night again I did not sup at Court.

TUESDAY 14 AUGUST. This morning at six I went to the Collège de Caroline, to young Fawkener, son to Sir Everard.[7] He and I and a Mr. de Bloem, a German, took horses and went to Wolfenbüttel.[8] As we rode along, I was as pleasant and gay as when in my boyish years, and all the horrors that I have since endured had left no mark on my mind. Well then, may I not be in heaven at last? It was a charming day. Fawkener is a genteel, pretty, amiable young fellow. The country between Brunswick and Wolfenbüttel is very fine. At Wolfenbüttel, which is not a bad town, we saw the Palace, the ancient residence of the Dukes. We saw the noble Library. The room is a spacious rotunda, and contains 10,800 books and 5000 manuscripts. This library was made by the Duke Antonius Ulricus, great-grandfather to the present Duke. There is a cata-

[6] Andrei Shuvalov was cousin to the Czarina Elizabeth's lover, Ivan Shuvalov. He later visited Voltaire, who spoke well of him.
[7] The Collegium Carolinum was a preparatory school, conceived and headed by the Abbé Jerusalem. "Young Fawkener" was not over fourteen. His father, Sir Everard, had been Voltaire's host during the greater part of Voltaire's stay in England, and may also have been known to the Abbé Jerusalem, who also was there from 1737 to 1740.
[8] Seven and a half miles from Brunswick.

logue of it in four thick quarto volumes, written by his own
hand. He has also marked with their titles the backs of the manuscripts and of many of the books. He was a man of learning, in
the taste of the times, and has written a treatise on the game
of chess, and some other pieces.[9] We saw here Luther's ink-
horn, which he threw at the devil's head when he appeared to
him. He hit him with such force that the ink-horn, which is of lead,
has a deep dimple in it, and is very much crushed. A very just
emblem of the outrageous temper of this reformer. We next went
to Salzdahlum, where we saw the garden, in which is a Parnassus,
adorned with the nine Muses, poor enough.[1] But the Palace is
noble, and has a gallery of pictures, which contains many valuable
pieces, and a gallery of china, the finest thing of the kind that I
ever saw. The china is magnificent, and disposed with excellent
taste. I rode briskly back to town, was all glowing and gay, and
dined at Court with pleasure. In the evening I was at the Grand
Opera, where the Russian Comte Shuvalov invited me to his *loge*
and said, "Come, Sir, and sit by my wife. I assure you that I have a
great regard for you." I shook his hand and was pleased.

WEDNESDAY 15 AUGUST. I passed the morning with my
worthy Abbé Jerusalem. He said the Duke was a worthy man, but
passionate, and sometimes he gives way to terrible rages. I said,
"The Prince seems pensive and even melancholy." "Sir," said he,
"he has always loved war; from his youth he has been charmed by
it. He has a restless spirit. He needs much occupation and great
aims. At present he is not well. The greatest court is not equal to
a camp. So he is not the great man that he was. After having had
so much to do, he is now quite idle. Besides, he is obliged to please

[9] The famous Lessing was librarian of this library from 1770 to his death in
1781. Anton Ulrich, Duke of Brunswick-Wolfenbüttel (d. 1714), wrote in
verse as well as in prose. He was an able statesman, and married his grand-
daughter to the Emperor Charles VI, father of Maria Theresa.

[1] Salzdahlum was the favourite summer residence of the Dukes of Brunswick
in the eighteenth century. The background of the picture which appears
opposite p. 14 is a somewhat idealized representation of the "garden" Boswell
is referring to.

the Duke. Every morning regularly he must be at the parade; thus
his morning disappears insensibly. Next he must dress, go to
Court, receive people, go to the theatre: in short, he must spend his
time in a manner which he finds beneath him."

This description pleased my discontented mind. I saw that all
ranks must take their portion of evil. I saw the Prince was with his
father just as I must be with mine. He is obliged to attend the parade, just as I must be obliged to attend the day-labourers. The
Abbé also told me that the Prince had good principles of religion,
and would never give up Christianity, although often carried away
by his passions. His Highness came lately to the Abbé and complained that, by dissipation and keeping company with infidels, he
found his principles wavering, and therefore begged that the Abbé
would draw up for him a neat summary of the proofs of Christianity, which might always keep his mind settled. The Abbé most
kindly promised me a copy of this summary. He told me that the
Duchess of Brunswick had much of the genius of her royal brother.
Formerly, when she read an infidel book, her imagination was
struck *tout d'un coup*, and she was thrown into uncertainty. The
Abbé was sent for, solved the objections and calmed her mind. Now
she is more constant and is a true Christian, especially in practice.
At night was French comedy.

THURSDAY 16 AUGUST. I passed the morning at home, in
writing. I have attempted to write to Mr. Johnson every day since I
formed the resolution of demanding a charter of his friendship, but
have not yet been able to please myself.[2] Want of motion flattened

---

[2] The memorandum for this day concludes, "Be firm and stable by [imitat-
ing] Johnson. Amen." The earlier memoranda contain several reminders to
write to Johnson, as well as jottings of ideas which he intended to include:
" ... Thought to write Johnson and swear everlasting attachment while
alive and shade when dead. ... Give some of your wild dreary fancies and
conclude you'll be directed steady by him ... Say to Johnson, as in Preface
to *Dictionary*, that all, all were empty names to you." The last hint probably refers to the last sentence of Johnson's Preface: "Success and mis-
carriage are empty sounds ... " The letter appears not to have been written
until 30 September, and was not then sent. See pp. 117, 118.

me. I was not much amused at the *opérette*. At Court at supper I cleared up. I came home gay. I had store of delicious ideas. I considered that mankind are sent into the world to gather ideas like flowers. Those who take their ideas from books have them at second hand, as flowers from a stall in Covent Garden. Whereas those who take them from real life have them fresh from the garden, pull them themselves. Care is to be taken in gathering these flowers. Vices are weeds, pretty enough when fresh, but when faded have a most terrible stench. Virtues are often beautiful when fresh, and when faded have always a pleasing odour. Let us lay up our flowers in some order. Let us pull flowers of size and figure, nor fill our repository with trifling ones which have neither colour nor scent. However, let us not despise a flower because it is small. The violet, though scarcely perceived among the grass, has many sweets.

FRIDAY 17 AUGUST. Quanten, a Swede, an officer in the service of Brunswick, was kind enough to entertain me with some music this morning. He plays delightfully on the German flute, and composes very well in a singular taste, with quick transitions from high to low notes, very hard to play. He paints too. He is a lively, genteel, brisk young man. He brought to my mind many ideas of healthy, accomplished foreign officers. He told me there were many of my name in Sweden. Some generations ago, four sons of our family went over to the service of Gustavus Adolphus.[3]

I was at the German comedy in the evening. I was hurt with wavering ideas. I found myself obliged to write my letters twice over. I determined to check fanciful, warm inclinations to write, and to have a moderate chosen correspondence.

SATURDAY 18 AUGUST.[4] Hypochondria was at me. I however walked hard round the ramparts, from whence I had a fine prospect. I then saw the parade, which merits to be seen. Then the Mar-

[3] Actually only three sons, as Boswell learned later. August Ferdinand and Christoph Leopold Boswell, descendants of one of these, were living in East Prussia (probably in Tilsit) in 1791, in which year the family was ennobled. On 10 June 1791 Boswell sent them a diploma of their pedigree "formally and authentically made out with the family arms emblazed upon it."
[4] " . . . Temperance is virtue" (Memorandum, 18 August).

quis Cavalcabo and I went and saw the Duke's cabinet, which is a very valuable one. It is very rich in medals, precious stones, antiques of different kinds, and natural curiosities. There is here an onyx formed into a cup, of which Montfaucon has given a description. I then waited on the worthy Stammer, who had fallen from his horse and broken an arm. I dined *chez* the Hereditary Princess; then saw a very clever pantomime. Harlequin changed himself into a centaur and into a sentinel, both which changes went very well. The centaur was formed with two harlequins. I thought to mark these for my friend Love.[5]

I must here record my romantic consideration. Before I set out from Berlin, I took up thirty ducats from my banker, by way of journey-money for my Brunswick jaunt, and enough it was for three weeks. But a rogue of a tailor and a rascal of a shoemaker came and picked my pocket of seven or eight of these same pieces, so that I was left bare enough. I did not however perceive it till I had been a week at Brunswick. When I called on my trusty Jacob and told him my case and asked him, "Have you any money?" "Yes, Sir," said he, "I have five louis." "Well, Jacob, keep those five louis. They will pay expenses in returning to Berlin. And as for me, I shall now put up three ducats for two days in different papers. I have enough for six days. When my ducats are spent, we shall go away." This plan I followed most exactly. I was so good an economist that I had money sufficient to keep me three days longer than the six days, and these three days I stayed.[6]

This night I had an adventure. I had no chair to bring me home from Court, and my servant had brought no lantern. Indeed he had not come for me at all, so that I was obliged to trudge home by

[5] James Dance, brother of the architect George Dance and of the painter Sir Nathaniel Dance-Holland, assumed the name Love when he went on the stage. Boswell had been intimate with him in Edinburgh, where he had been manager of the theatre. At this time he was engaged at Drury Lane in London. Besides acting comic roles, he was the author of plays and pantomimes.
[6] According to the tables in Thomas Nugent's *The Grand Tour*, 2d ed., 1756, ii. 60–66, thirty ducats was approximately £15 sterling, five louis a little more than £4-10-0, three ducats about £1-10-0.

myself in the dark. It is a regulation at Brunswick that if any person is found on the streets after ten o'clock at night without a light, the patrol shall carry him to the Guard. I dreaded this, and as I was posting along, up came a couple of musketeers on horseback. I tried to escape, but in vain. They rode me up to the wall. I told them, "Ich bin ein Herr das von der Hoft comt. Your servant." The cavalry answered, "Er moes met oons geen."[7] However, after pausing a little, they asked me where I lodged. Upon which they separated, and one of them followed me to my inn, taking special care that I should not run away from him. I imagined that he was only to tell the people of the house that I was his prisoner, and then carry me to the Guard; so I offered him money to go away. No — he would not be bribed. I therefore resigned myself to my fate. Happy was I to find that he allowed me to enter my quarters in peace, saying, "Das is een Herr, das ich hab op straas gevonden."[8]

SUNDAY 19 AUGUST. I was again at the Duke's Chapel, but so hipped that I could hardly relish in any degree the noble music. By reason, however, I maintained my devotion and my immortal hope. De Pless and I then walked in garden. He said he was very melancholy, and all of a sudden so, without any reason for it. I explained to him that miserable distemper, and bid him ride and be gay. He told me he lived with a *danseuse*, an Italian girl. He said, "I shall never marry. I should be jealous as a fiend. I will not trust my honour with any woman living." He had also a religious disposition, was devout, and did not think keeping a girl any sin. He carried me to the Romish Chapel, where we saw his charmer.

This day I saw at Court Lady Mary Coke,[9] who came hither from Hanover, chiefly to see the Hereditary Prince, who went away several days ago to meet the King of Prussia in Silesia. This night after supper some of the ladies of honour complained to me of their

[7] "I am a gentleman coming from the Court." . . . "You must go with us."
[8] "This is a gentleman whom I found on the street."
[9] Lady Mary Coke, the widow of Edward, Viscount Coke, was the daughter of a Scots duke (Argyll) and a friend of Boswell's patron, the Scots Earl of Eglinton. She was much given to visiting foreign courts, and kept a diary, which unfortunately makes no reference to this meeting with Boswell.

not having time enough to themselves, &c., &c. What! is discontent
heard to murmur amongst the fair ladies of a gay court? Well,
Life! I call thee sad.

MONDAY 20 AUGUST. Baron Bassewitz told me that he kept a
regular book of all the strangers that came to the Brunswick Court.
This idea pleased me. He marks their titles, their employments,
when they came, how long they stayed. There came this day a
Count of the Empire and some more strangers. I could see a certain
joy in the faces of the courtiers when strangers are announced. No
wonder. It furnishes them with new ideas. And indeed I could
observe their Highnesses also pleased.

I wrote all this afternoon. I supped *chez* the Hereditary Princess, where was a very great company. I was vexed with Lady Mary
Coke, in whom I found all the absurd distance of manners by which
the English ladies petrify people. She rendered me just as I used to
be at Lady Northumberland's. I stood like a pillar of "dull, cold
marble" and looked at her without daring to approach.[1] At last I
stepped up to her and said, "How comes it, Madam, that I can
speak to all these foreign ladies with ease, and can scarcely say a
word to your Ladyship?" "Sir," said she, "we have not the same
ease with them." Some more syllables feebly muttered in the air,
and then our lips were again glued — not hers to mine and mine to
hers, but as if each had been afraid that the other would bite and
had got them bound over to the peace. O sad manners! Avaunt!

[Received *c.* 20 August, Caroline Kircheisen to Boswell.
Original in French]

Berlin, 18 August 1764

SIR: . . . The mistakes you say you have made in your letter
do you honour, for they prove that you need not reproach yourself
for having wasted much of your time in study. . . .

[1] "Dull, cold marble": Shakespeare's *Henry VIII*, III. ii. 433. While in London in 1762–1763 Boswell had been a great deal at Northumberland House in
order to pay court to Lady Northumberland, who, he hoped, would exert her
influence to procure him a commission in the Guards.

I was delighted to hear that the Court of Brunswick does justice
to your merit. Between ourselves, does this not nourish that slight
tendency towards vanity that you have? Admit frankly that I have
guessed right in thinking that it is nectar to you. I fancy you will
come back a perfect Spaniard, and woe to whoever does not treat
you humbly and respectfully. I shall already have prepared myself in advance. . . .

The fair ones to whom I was commissioned to distribute your
endearments appeared to be sensible of the honour. I performed
my task very discreetly, for I was afraid they would be unduly
flattered by the distinction and might make themselves troublesome to you.

I commend myself to the honour of your remembrance, and
am, Sir, your affectionate friend, and (neither as mere formula nor
quite seriously) your servant,

CAROLINE KIRCHEISEN.

TUESDAY 21 AUGUST. Cavalcabo paid me a visit. He told me
that he had been "so wretched that if I had not had the care of my
sister-in-law and her children, I should have been capable of blow-
ing out my brains with a pistol." I told him, "Indeed, Sir, I was
extremely gloomy. But I thought, what is the difference? It is all
the same whether I suffer or not. I am only a single individual."
"Well, Sir," said he, "you had certainly fallen into a fine melancholy. It all comes from the body, and can be cured by diet. Happy
is the man who knows his own body." I found him the true *bon
catholique*, for he talked with ease of having women, and yet told
me of a distemper that he had brought on himself by fasting.

This was my last day at Brunswick. I talked at Court, "I shall
come back in twenty-five years to see who are dead and who are
still living." I dined in a kind of luxurious sorrow. I must not forget
to mark that I fell in love with the beauteous Princess Elizabeth.
I talked of carrying her off from the Prince of Prussia, and so oc-
casioning a second Trojan War. Madame de Boick was my con-
fidante. I was also smitten by Lady Mary Coke.[2] Madame de Boick

[2] There are some grounds for thinking that Boswell knew Lady Mary a great

would ask me, "Well, Sir, is it the English or the German lady who takes your fancy most this evening?" At the opera this evening, I was quite ravished. It made me recollect a story of Dr. Colquitt's,[3] how at some fine music in London dukes and lords cried they'd dash out their brains against the wainscot. I owned to Feronce, "I could almost have wished that some one would cut my throat." Feronce agreed to correspond with me. So did Pless. I shall have a pretty correspondence in all at Brunswick.

I said to Cavalcabo, "People talk a great deal about the lightness and vivacity of the French, but indeed they have better judgment than the English. They always have *some* rules. The English have none at all." "Sir," said he, "the French appear to have more giddiness, but actually they do not have so much. A Frenchman jumps and sings in front of his mistress, but he is nevertheless master of himself. The Englishman, however, is all caprice; and with all the composure in the world he goes about setting the house on fire."

I was pensive at Court. I had taken leave of the Hereditary Princess. I mused on the life of a courtier here. Putting myself, by strong imagination, in every one's place, my gloomy temper found all their situations uneasy, even the Duke's. Yet I recalled the best ideas and felt pleasing regret. I took leave of the Duchess shortly. I have seen in her room a portrait of the King of Prussia, the only one for which His Majesty ever sat. It is very like, but it stoops too much.[4]

deal better than one would infer from the casual way in which he mentions her here — that she was in fact the "lady of quality," masked always in his journal by the pseudonym "Lady Mirabel," to whom he laid inconclusive siege in London during the winter of 1762–1763. The absence of any reference here to that episode counts neither for nor against the identification, for he has named Lady Mary, and the code of gallantry enjoined the greatest circumspection when the lady had a reputation to lose.

[3] The Reverend Edward Colquitt was a raffish young priest of the Church of England whom Boswell had known in Edinburgh, 1760–1762. See p. 243, 244 *n.* 1. The "Doctor" is jocular.

[4] It was painted by Antoine Pesne. Frederick never sat for his portrait after

When I took leave of the Duke, I said, "Sire, you have had people at your Court more brilliant than I, but never a better man, nor a man more sensible of the politeness which your Highness has shown to him." The Duke of Brunswick replied, "Sir, I am very glad that you have been pleased with your visit here." I expected still more civilities than I received, because forsooth the Duke spoke to me at Charlottenburg. I magnify all events in my own favour, and with the wind of vanity blow them up to size immense. I took a tender leave of the ladies and gentleman of the Court and said, "Is it not sad that we shall never see one another again?"

WEDNESDAY 22 AUGUST. I was hippish. I went upon the Parade and saw the Duke once more. I wondered how he could plague himself every morning with making men march about. I was convinced that all situations are judged of by comparison, so that he who has been Laird of Auchinleck ten years feels himself as great as he who has been Duke of Brunswick ten years. I then took leave of Ap Herusalem, as they call him here. I don't know how it is, but I am always gloomy on leaving a room where I have lodged. I could get no extra post, which vexed me a little. I however hoped the Court would suppose me gone in some company. I mounted the post-wagon without the gate, and away we went.

THURSDAY 23 AUGUST. Rumbled along.

FRIDAY 24 AUGUST. Why relate that I had blackguards with me, that I was sorely shaken, that the night air began to grow cold, that I slept at every stage? I had, however, a very bad custom of running always to the stable, making a bed of straw or of lint, throwing myself down, and making Jacob call me when the horn sounded. This was very dangerous. I might have easily been robbed. The horses might have broke loose and trampled me to death in the dark.

SATURDAY 25 AUGUST. This morning I arrived at Potsdam and breakfasted with honest Scott, who told me that Lord Marischal and all his family were at Berlin. I took an extra post and came

he became King (1740), but he no doubt sat for the others which Pesne painted of him as Crown Prince.

briskly to town. I immediately waited on his Lordship and found him well. I then went home and was kindly welcomed by the ladies.

I received a packet of letters, one of which was from Monsieur de Zuylen. I have never mentioned that at Brunswick I received a second letter from Zélide, disclaiming love, but vowing strong friendship, and charging me to write much to her. I did write her a long letter a few days after my arrival at Berlin. I wrote to her with the serious freedom of a friend, convinced her that she could never have me for a lover, and assumed the tone of a preceptor. Her conduct shows me that she was just titillated by love, for I have had no answer. But let me not blame her. Let me wait a little.[5]

At eight I waited on Lord Marischal, told him how I was subject to melancholy, and said his Lordship relieved me at Utrecht, as the man was relieved who fell into a coal pit and imagined himself fifty fathoms from the bottom, when in reality he was not two feet. My Lord said I must have occupation, and must avoid gloomy or absurd company. It is fine to see his peace of mind.

SUNDAY 26 AUGUST. My Lord and all of us dined at Mr. Burnett's, where we were exceeding well. My Lord chatted finely, and said, "I am old enough to remember stories told me by those who lived in the reign of Charles the Second."

MONDAY 27 AUGUST. I dined and supped at home. But I was too free and too merry. I was introduced to Mr. Aschersleben, half-brother to Madame la Présidente. He was captain of cavalry, but was so much wounded that he quitted the service. He is a changeable, splenetic, unhappy man. He was feverish with gaiety this night. He hurt me. But he taught me a German song. Hübner and I had been this morning to see the prints of Schmidt. He works very well. But engraves only heads. 'Tis pity.[6]

TUESDAY 28 AUGUST. On Sunday last I complained to the Pro-

[5] See p. 22 *n.* 1.
[6] The prints shown must have been a selection. Schmidt engraved portraits of all types; he also did imaginative subjects and book illustrations, among them illustrations to the works of Frederick the Great.

fessor Castillon that my memory was bad.[7] He bid me recollect every evening what I had learnt during the day. "It is painful at first, but it will become easy, and will be very useful."

I dined this day tête-à-tête with Mr. Burnett, after which he carried me in his chaise to the Park, where we had a fine drive. He told me that during the last war Marshal Keith was one day riding out, when there came up to him an Englishman, who called himself John Tibi, Esq. His story is curious; but I find it too long for my journal, so shall mark it in another place.[8] Burnett said that Marshal Keith was a noble fellow. He had not much vivacity, but he had what was a great deal better, much knowledge and strong sense. He spoke very slow. His manners were courtly and amiable. I found Burnett a solid, clear-headed fellow, much better than myself. We passed the afternoon well.[9]

[Boswell to Andrew Mitchell][10]

Berlin, 28 August 1764

You MAY BELIEVE, SIR, that I was a good deal surprised to hear upon my return to Berlin that *onze gezant*[1] was gone. There was

[7] He must mean his memory for things he had made a matter of formal study, like law or "antiquities."

[8] If he did "mark" it, the paper has not yet been recovered.

[9] " . . . Yesterday . . . at night you *resolved* to please worthy father as at Auchinleck: month October wood fire, coffee; and to be *retenu*. So compose mind, and stay here fortnight" (Memorandum, 29 August).

[10] The original of this letter is among Mitchell's papers in the British Museum. If Boswell kept a copy, it has not yet been recovered. Our text is from *Letters of James Boswell*, 2 vols., 1924, with the kind permission of the editor, Professor C. B. Tinker, and of the Clarendon Press, Oxford. It is one of Boswell's most elaborate and skilful exercises in the art of persuasion. The reader will note how the tone of these cajoling letters is adapted to the correspondent. In the letter to Catt it was naïve and enthusiastic, here it is deferential but manly.

[1] "Our envoy" (Dutch). Boswell is trying to establish a tone that will be intimate without being forward: "as we Scots who have studied in Holland say."

indeed a surmise at Brunswick that you intended to return to England this season. I was asked if it was true, and very innocently affirmed that there was nothing in it. I find however that when a man leaves a minister at a foreign court but a fortnight, he is not sure of finding him upon his return.

Your departure is a good deal unlucky for me, not only as it deprives me of conversation which gave me uncommon pleasure and insensibly accustomed me to rational thinking and honourable sentiment, but because I now particularly stand in need of your prudent and kind counsel with respect to my travels. I have had another letter from my father, in which he continues of opinion that travelling is of very little use, and may do a great deal of harm.[2] I shall not repeat what I have formerly said of my father's particular character. I say "particular," for rarely will you find a man of so excellent a frame of body and so noble a mind as to have passed through life with uniform propriety of conduct.

For my own part, I own that I am not such a favourite of Nature. Think not that I intend to plead machinery[3] and escape from the censure due to the faults which I have committed. I only would have you consider that judgment is a natural gift, as well as imagination, and force of mind in a great measure independent of our endeavours. Think of me as I am, and pronounce accordingly. I esteem and love my father, and I am determined to do what is in my power to make him easy and happy. But you will allow that I may endeavour to make him happy and at the same time not be too hard upon myself.

I must use you so much with the freedom of a friend as to tell you that, with the vivacity which you allowed me, I have a melancholy disposition. To escape from the gloom of dark speculation, I have made excursions into the fields of amusement, perhaps of folly. I have found that amusement and folly are beneath me, and

[2] Not recovered; probably two letters are missing. Boswell found one waiting for him when he arrived at Brunswick on 26 June, and wrote next morning in his memoranda, "Father's letter to restrain; resolved to manage." On 29 June he wrote, "Manage Father with affection," and on 29 July, "See Mitchell and fix Italy."   [3] Fatalism: see p. 48.

that without some laudable pursuit my life must be insipid and wearisome. I therefore took the resolution of leaving London and settled myself for the winter at Utrecht, where I recovered my inclination for study and rational thinking. I then laid my account with travelling a couple of years, but found my father's views to be entirely different.

You saw the letter which I wrote him from this, and I flatter myself that you approved of it. I cannot expect his answer for some weeks. In the mean time he tells me that he would not oppose my passing another winter at Utrecht, so that he does not grudge the time which I ask. As for the money, I should think for one year a little extraordinary expense is not thrown away when it is also to be considered that what I spend now I shall not have some years hence. My father seems much against my going to Italy, but gives me leave to go from this and pass some months in Paris.

I own that the words of the Apostle Paul, "I must see Rome," are strongly *borne in* upon my mind. It would give me infinite pleasure. It would give me taste for a lifetime, and I should go home to Auchinleck with serene contentment. I am the more confident in my request that I am no libertine and have a moral certainty of suffering no harm in Italy. I can also assure you that I shall be as moderate as possible in my expenses. I do not intend to travel as a *milord anglais*, but merely as a scholar and a man of elegant curiosity; and I am told that in that character I may live in Italy very reasonably. I obviate your objection of my being obliged to live like others by assuring you that I have none of that second-rate ambition which actuates most young men of fortune upon their travels. After passing four months on classic ground, I would come through France and go home, as I said to my father, *uti conviva satur.*[4]

Now, Sir, tell me fairly if I am unreasonable. Upon my honour, I cannot think that I am. I give you my word that my father's inclinations shall be as inviolable laws to his son. But don't you think I may first remonstrate before I consider an act as passed? Don't you

[4] "Sated like a guest who has dined" (Horace, *Satires*, I. i. 119).

think that rather than go home, contrary to what I much desire and cannot help thinking very proper, don't you think it worth while to humour me so far as to allow me my year and a reasonable sum, after which I return clear and contented, without any pretence for my gloomy disposition to murmur at? I would beg, Sir, that you may write to my father your opinion as to this matter, and put it in the light which you may think it deserves. In the mean time, I can see little advantage to be had at Berlin. I shall however remain here a fortnight, after which I intend passing by Mannheim and one or two more of the German courts to Geneva. I am there at the point from whence I may either steer to Italy or to France. I shall see Voltaire. I shall also see Switzerland and Rousseau. These two men are to me greater objects than most statues or pictures.

I take this opportunity to assure the loved and respected friend of my father that I am sincerely happy at having obtained his acquaintance. I would hope that I shall not be found unworthy of his regard; and I wish very honestly for an opportunity of showing my real esteem for such a character as I could draw to anybody else but to himself.

I am, Sir, your obliged humble servant,

JAMES BOSWELL.

I would be much obliged to you for an answer as soon as you are at leisure to write.

WEDNESDAY 29 AUGUST.[5] At manège I found that all things seem insipid when a man is sluggish and his blood stagnates. But set him on horseback and make his blood circulate, and all things seem gay. This is an original principle. I examine no farther.

At eight a captain of artillery carried Castillon and his family and several more and myself by water to Treptow, a public house almost opposite to Monsieur Schickler's *campagne*. We dined and danced and were hearty. But the company did not please me. Be-

---

[5] "Etui for Mademoiselle Kircheisen, eighteen crowns" (Expense Account, 29 August). See p. 50 *n.* 4.

fore dinner Castillon and I walked out, and brought free will on the carpet. He said he could conceive the most perfect prescience without restraining liberty. This is absurd. He said that God must leave his creatures free because they neither can add to or diminish the happiness of the supreme Creator. I asked if it was possible to give free will, as every effect must have its cause. "Sir," said he, "I distinguish. Most effects have, to be sure, their causes. But there are others which contain their causes within themselves. The will of God is a *dernier ressort*. It is not influenced by extraneous force. It now and then is no doubt moved by circumstances. But it can pronounce merely from its own determination. God having been pleased to communicate a portion of his own nature to man, man has the same will in a certain degree. This we feel to be fact. The common instance of two eggs proves that we may determine without a motive."[6] I liked to hear this reasoning. It is just and clear. Castillon complained of Utrecht. I said, "Sir, is it not curious to suppose a philosopher so situated that his chief duty is to hide his finest qualities? But you were in that condition at Utrecht."[7]

THURSDAY 30 AUGUST. This morning I was hurt to find how little I had done after being employed several hours. I must learn more quickness, acquire more spring in action. I did not dine, but at three went with our ladies to the garden of Gotskowsky, a great banker. Here we had coffee, then walked, then saw the china manufactory,[8] then supped in a very handsome room in his garden, which is very large and well laid out. He is a gallant German, stupid, comely, cordial. She was a *danseuse*, and he married her

[6] I suppose this means that instead of being paralysed when faced with the necessity of choosing between two apparently identical objects, a man does in fact choose one, though it is impossible to assign any convincing motive for his choosing that one in preference to the other.

[7] Because at Utrecht (where the atmosphere was Calvinistic) his notions concerning free will would have given offence.

[8] Gotskowsky, after the failure of Wegely's venture, had established the porcelain manufactory at the instance of Frederick, to compete with the wares of Saxony. The factory prospered, but he was ruined by other ventures and died poor.

for love. She is a stout, good-looking *Frow*, but struck me as if she had been the greatest beauty. I raved, "Heavens! what a charming woman," &c., &c., and told the husband, "You are the most fortunate man in the world." He was pleased, and made us dance a minuet together. She sung well, and I was in raptures. So fiery is my imagination that if an object furnishes only a spark, I am very soon all in flame. As we went home I said, "If I had been born simply to adore that woman, it would have been enough." Oh, can I not tame this turbulence of mind!

FRIDAY 31 AUGUST. I dined at Burnett's, who said that the young English were really mad. He gave me an instance of young Madan of the Guards, who was with him at an academy in London. He came in one day, and said, "By the Lord, a glass was never broke with guineas," and immediately took out some guineas and broke a fine mirror.

SATURDAY 1 SEPTEMBER.[9] I dined at Rufin's, where Nehaus, an Italian, wanted to shine as a great philosopher, and accordingly doubted of his existence and of everything else. I thought him a blockhead, and recollected with wonder my scepticism at Utrecht. In the afternoon I talked much with Mademoiselle Kircheisen, whom I like much. She has good sense and enough of vivacity, and she is comely. She is the only girl I ever saw constantly agreeable. She has but one fault. She loves too much to *badiner*,[1] and thence is now and then a little impolite. She is a mimic, and that is dangerous.

SUNDAY 2 SEPTEMBER.[2] Spleen pressed me down. Young

[9] "Yesterday you dined Burnett... Home all evening; too gay. Sat up till one, but was bad. Resolved never so. You're in fine train, and one night may break constitution. So go on with regular non-naturals, and rather stay in whole days and bring up journal. Calm mind. Think old lairds of Auchinleck better than little tickling pleasure.... This day, journal; house all day for once to recover." (Memorandum, 1 September; "non-naturals" in the old medical terminology meant food and drink, sleep, exercise, excretion, &c.)
[1] Jest; rally.
[2] " ... *Think;* be good. Every year you're growing better. For shame, pay Mademoiselle Scheenmark Monday" (Memorandum, 2 September).

Kircheisen carried me to the Dooms Kirk,[3] where are the tombs of several of the princes of Brandenburg, next to the Garnisoon Kirk, and then to a Catholic chapel. I got a letter from my brother John, telling me that he had quitted the Army, and was going to England to learn to be a farmer. I was vexed and angry. But, recollecting his hypochondriac disposition, I resolved to make the best of it and be as kind to him as possible.[4] At four I went with the family to Gotskowsky's garden. Burnett was there, and an English lady, wife to a German merchant in London. She was detestable. We had coffee, and a fine supper, and a dance. I was again too fiery.

[Boswell to Lord Marischal][5]

[Berlin, 2 September 1764]

MY LORD: — Mr. Burnett and I intend to have the honour of eating an olio with your Lordship at Potsdam on Wednesday next. You will then have an opportunity of judging in some measure of my talents as a Spaniard; and I hope you will be kind enough to tell me freely if you can recommend me to the Court of Madrid, and if I may flatter myself with the splendid ideas of conquering Portugal and marrying an infanta.

Allow me, my Lord, to take this opportunity of talking a little to you, which I can do with much more ease in a letter than when in your Lordship's presence. Will you forgive me for complaining of your Lordship's coldness of manner, by which any ardour that I may have is constantly repressed? You made me not a little uneasy upon our journey, for my extreme sensibility made me afraid that

[3] That is, the Dom-Kirche, and, below, the Garnison-Kirche.
[4] John, who was at this time about twenty-one, suffered from periodical insanity and was at all times eccentric.
[5] This letter is not quite of the same sort as those to Catt and Mitchell, and later to Rousseau. No doubt Boswell's main purpose in writing it was to get Lord Marischal to introduce him to the King, but the appeal for more cordial relations is heartfelt and might have been made in much these terms if Boswell had had no ulterior design.

you disliked me; and this, you may believe, was very mortifying. By seeing your Lordship with others whom you certainly liked, and observing that they were affected in the same way that I was, my apprehensions were removed. I perceived that in your Lordship's presence the Frenchman Froment and the mountaineer Macpherson, instead of showing a briskness of gesture and striving who should speak most, became still and silent like Presbyterian divines at the table of a Member of Parliament.[6]

In respected characters this quality is highly proper. I admire it; but I complain that I have been restrained by it from expressing the warm regard which I entertain for your Lordship. Whatever faults I may have, I am surely honest; and I believe your Lordship is already convinced that I have got sentiments which are rarely to be found in a Scotsman on the south of Tay and I fear are but too much decayed on the north. I say, my Lord, a man who has such sentiments is a superior being, for to have disinterested attachments is to have greatness of soul.[7] I am however no Jacobite. I am sorry that the conduct of our ancient Royal Family was such that the Nation was obliged to choose another. But I now find the British Government properly settled. I find a Sovereign to whom I can attach myself with enthusiasm, and a Court that will be pleased to hear me own myself a Tory.

My Lord, you may believe me when I tell you that I have always honoured the character of my Lord Marischal, and that upon

[6] The letter, which is a draft and much revised, shows the following deletion at this point: "My father keeps those around him in awe much in the same manner. If he does not choose it, I defy the most vigorous talker to speak in his company."

[7] This sentence originally ran, " . . . superior being. Is it not greatness of soul to have a disinterested attachment to a king, to a chieftain, to a kinsman?" Boswell then wrote, and deleted, the following passage: "It is not English whim, my Lord. It is founded on excellent principles. I wonder that none of our religious Whigs have attended to the history of the children of Israel, God's chosen people. They might there have seen strict loyalty and the clanship which they are such enemies to. I own indeed that the Jewish tribes of Israel acknowledged no chieftain, nor did they know anything of heritable jurisdictions. With all this, my Lord . . . "

acquaintance I have found my expectations exceeded. But I would also have your Lordship to know that I have peculiar satisfaction in your company; for I have a set of agreeable old-fashioned ideas which make me regard with reverence the representative of the illustrious family of Keith, and heartily rejoice to find a Scots earl so much respected in a foreign country, so much loved by Frederick the Great.

My dear Lord! why do I see you so seldom? Is it not hard that one who values your conversation so much should have it so little? I shall never forget your Lordship's kindness in carrying me with you to Germany. It has made me appear in the most advantageous light. But your Lordship must not now lose sight of me. As I have begun my travels under your protection, I hope you will assist me to finish them.

Be assured, my Lord, that I am not undeserving of your good offices. My desire is to be a worthy laird of Auchinleck and as useful a member of society as I can. I have told you that I am unhappy enough to be subject to melancholy. I would not make it an excuse for idleness, but it must have some indulgence. As my father is anxious to have me at home as soon as possible, I would wish to make the most of my time. I beg to know if it will be possible for me to hear the King talk. Cannot your Lordship procure me that satisfaction? Were it not for the hope of that, I should set out immediately for Geneva, see Voltaire, and be ready to pass into Italy or France. I must entreat your Lordship to give me a recommendation to Rousseau. With that advantage I despair not to pass some precious hours with that amiable wild philosopher. I am, &c.

MONDAY 3 SEPTEMBER.[8] Hübner went with me to see the Royal Library of Berlin. It is large. The manuscripts are numerous. It has received many presents. Amongst others who have added to the library of Frederick the Great is Walter Harte, one of the canons of Windsor, who has here deposited his *Life of Gustavus*

[8] "Encouragement to Jacob, two crowns eighteen groschen" (Expense Account, 3 September). The "encouragement" was the same as Jacob's weekly wage; that is, this week Boswell gave him double pay.

Adolphus, bound superbly. An inscription is written on the initial blank leaf: "Accipe, Princeps illustrissime," &c.⁹ I dined with Monsieur le Professeur de Castillon. I talked to him of hypochondria. He said, "Sir, I have suffered greatly from that malady. After the death of my first wife, there was a year during which I dined alone; and I swear to you that all that time, I never touched my knife and fork without wishing to kill myself." This was another proof to me that I am not a singular victim to the dire disease.¹

At night I was the guest of Stoltz at an ordinary for supper. I did not like it much. After supper, Hübner and Blanchot and some more of us went to a Berlin bawdy-house, which I was curious to see. We found a poor little house, an old bawd, and one whore. I was satisfied with what I saw.

TUESDAY 4 SEPTEMBER. Hübner went with me to the Park, where I saw a Prussian regiment exercised. The soldiers seemed in terror. For the least fault they were beat like dogs. I am, however, doubtful if such fellows don't make the best soldiers. Machines are surer instruments than men. Were I to knock down a scoundrel, I would rather take a stick than take a child by the heels to give him a blow with. I also saw a deserter pass the *baguette* twelve times. He was much cut. It made me sick to see it.²

⁹ Harte was travelling tutor to the Earl of Chesterfield's natural son, whom Boswell was to meet at Dresden. Lord Eliot, another of Harte's pupils, said that the *Life of Gustavus* was a very good book — after it had been translated into German.

¹ As of course he was not, though his hypochondriac constitution (which was partly, at least, a family inheritance) made him particularly susceptible to the prevailing *mal du siècle*. In the earlier half of the eighteenth century the inhabitants of Great Britain had talked and written so much about "melancholy" and "the spleen" that depression of spirits came to be called "the English Malady." By the 1760's self-conscious hypochondria seems to have been about as common in Germany as in England. This vast uneasiness was basically a reflection of the strain imposed upon religious faith by the new scientific outlook — the "mechanical philosophy." See Professor Margery Bailey's able essay, "Boswell and His Audience" in the Introduction to her edition of Boswell's *Hypochondriack*, 1928.

² "Pass the *baguette*" means "run the gauntlet." Though Boswell does not

I had Stoltz for my guest to dine at Rufin's. In the afternoon, I walked four hours with Blanchot, who is in the service of the Swedish Ambassador. He entertained me much, being a fellow of knowledge and clear expression. He said the French music was a contrast to the French temper. The French are gay. Their music is grave. A Frenchman never looks so serious as when he sings a song. He said the King of Prussia had been sadly debauched in his youth, for he used to go to the common bawdy-houses as well as to divert himself with the ladies of the Court. "He is now," said Blanchot, "quite impotent."

At night Blanchot and Hübner drank a glass of wine with me at my lodgings, and Blanchot showed me on the map my route to Geneva, so as to take several German cities and courts in my way.

WEDNESDAY 5 SEPTEMBER. Some days ago I wrote to my Lord Marischal that Mr. Burnett and I intended this day to have the honour of eating an olio with his Lordship. At six we set out in a clever chaise. The day was good. My spirits were fine. We talked of spleen. Burnett said that Mr. Mitchell was sadly distressed with it; that sometimes he would sit without speaking a word, and say, "Well, I could not have thought that this could get so much the better of me." All this was really owing to his being costive, to prevent which he took every proper method. He had his own box, which was constantly tied behind the coach, and with Mr. Locke's regularity did he attempt the necessary operation.[3]

We found all well at Potsdam. My Lord gave us an olio which I found excellent. After dinner we went and saw the garden and house at Sans Souci. I looked with pleasure at the King's study, which is elegant, and has its books finely bound, as at Potsdam. In his bedchamber I found some verses on a table. We then went to the gallery, where I saw the noble room and rich pictures with true relish. We then looked at the foundation of the house which

___

say so in the journal, he gave the flogged soldier four groschen (Expense Account).

[3] See John Locke's *Some Thoughts concerning Education*, Sections 23–28. The pertinent passage is quoted in *Boswell in Holland*, 11 October 1763.

the King is going to build for my Lord, which makes his Lordship very happy.

At night Macpherson and I dressed ourselves in the Highland dress, of which Macpherson had two suits, and a fine frolic did we make of it. We wrote a card, "To the Right Honourable George, Earl Marischal of Scotland. Two Highland gentlemen, Messrs. McDonald and McIntosh, beg leave to have the honour of paying their respects to the Earl of Marischal. They ask pardon for troubling him at so untimely an hour." The direction and the word "untimely" were excellent.[4] Away we went, and Scott and Burnett behind us, passed the sentinels, and went to my Lord's apartment in the Palace. I asked the servant in German for my Lord, and delivered the card. His Lordship made us welcome. We stood just within his door, bowing much. He cried, "Come in, gentlemen, come in." He advanced and immediately knew us, and asked how cows sold. He took our joke in good part. We marched home again. Going and coming we were followed on the street, for we spoke a barbarous language. I did, at least, for I made it. We supped on sowens hearty, and were *canty chields.*[5] Burnett had a bed, and in the same room the Highlanders lay on straw. Thus did I talk. Thus was I merry.

THURSDAY 6 SEPTEMBER. I rose stout and well. After breakfast I disputed against the Union.[6] Burnett was my antagonist. After much warm disputation, I said, "Sir, the love of our country

[4] The direction, presumably, because of its Jacobite flavour (Lord Marischal had been pardoned, but his honours had not been restored). "Untimely," perhaps, because it is equivocal, and might be taken to mean either "so late at night" or "now that he has forsaken the cause."

[5] "Brisk lads." Sowens is a preparation of oatmeal.

[6] The crowns of the kingdoms of England and Scotland had been united in 1603, when James VI of Scotland succeeded to the throne of England, but the two countries maintained separate parliaments for a century more. By the Legislative Union, 1707, the Scots Parliament in Edinburgh was abolished, and Scotland began sending representatives to a Parliament of Great Britain, sitting at Westminster. Boswell believed that this tended to extinguish Scots nationality, and to turn an ancient and proud kingdom into a province — a view shared by many other Scotsmen of his day and since.

is a sentiment. If you have it not, I cannot give it you by reason-ing." I waited on Lord Marischal. I had written to him from Ber-lin, complaining of his coldness of manner which prevented me from enjoying with ease his excellent conversation, telling him what esteem I had for him, and how I had "old-fashioned ideas" which made me have a particular veneration for the "representa-tive of the illustrious family of Keith." I also begged his advice as to my travels. I found that my letter had pleased him. He was more affable than usual.

I owned to him that I was afraid I could not do great things as a Scots lawyer, and could wish to be in some other employment. "As for the Army," said he, "it is too late." "Then, my Lord, might I not be employed abroad?" "Sir, you must begin as secretary, and if you are not with a man to your mind, you are very unhappy. Then, if you should be sent Envoy, if you are at a place where there is little to do, you are idle and unhappy. If you have much to do, you are harassed with anxiety." "Well then, my Lord, I would get into Parliament." "No, Sir, you would be obliged to stick to a party, right or wrong, through thick and through thin, or you must be singular, and be thought absurd." "My Lord, if you go on, you'll chase me out of existence altogether. What say you to my following the law in Scotland moderately? jogging on between the Parliament House and Auchinleck, and so doing pretty well?" "Indeed, Sir, I'm for your jogging on. Your father will see that you do your best. He has a great liking for you, and you'll do very well together." "Then, my Lord, will you write to him, that in the mean time he may allow me to travel a year?" "I will."[7] His Lordship then gave me my route by Switzerland, Italy, and France. I was very happy, quite in the humour of revering the old earl. I thought on the Abbey of Holyroodhouse. I thought on worthy Johnston. I talked with my Lord against the Union, and how we had lost our spirit. I said, "You find Scotsmen in the Highlands. But very few south of Tay. I ought to be valued, my Lord, as a rare Scot."

[7] Lord Marischal kept his promise and sent a letter which must have been very influential. See p. 88.

He took down from his bookcase the history of Robert the Bruce in old verse, and made me a present of it, writing upon it, "Scotus Scoto,"[8] and saying, "Now you must read this once every year." I had almost cried before the good old man. We dined with his Lordship. After dinner Burnett and I set out. He was excellent company. His stories flew thick. He insisted that I should sup with him. I did so, and merry we were. Yet my gloomy eye saw the situation of an envoy in an unpleasing light. I am an unhappy dog.

FRIDAY 7 SEPTEMBER. The civility of Mr. Burnett is very great. I dined with him today, in company with Captain Wake. I don't know if I have as yet mentioned Captain Wake in this my journal. He is a good Prestonpans man, but has been all his life at sea, and during the last war had the King of Prussia's commission to go out with a privateer. He took some Swedish ships. He cannot get the prize-money, having carried them into the port of ———, where they are retained.[9] He has been two years at Berlin, pleading before a court of justice, in order to recover them.

SATURDAY 8 SEPTEMBER.[1] Was splenetic; dined Herr Président's; was rude. Madame made me say in Germans the equivalent of *léchez-moi le cul*.[2] I knew the meaning of it, and yet repeated it several times to an old maiden in the company. At last I said, "I know very well what it means." Bad, bad. At six after playing cards to help away time, I walked Unter Linden with Mademoiselle Stensen and others. I thought them poor beings. I supped at home. I was still unruly. Something of Houston Stewart. Let me take care.[3]

[8] "From one Scot to another." The poem was John Barbour's *Brus* (1375).

[9] See p. 21. Captain Wake, in his ship *Emden*, took a Swedish vessel off the North Spanish coast in January, 1759, and seven more in the Mediterranean that summer. The port Boswell could not recall was Cagliari in Sardinia.

[1] "Irish soldier, sixteen groschen" (Expense Account, 8 September).

[2] See p. 210. "Germans" for "German language" is by analogy with Dutch forms.

[3] Boswell's early journals, and more particularly his memoranda, are strewn with the names of men whose conduct he considered in one way or other admirable, and whom he admonished himself to resemble: Sir David

SUNDAY 9 SEPTEMBER. It must be the bad weather that over-turns me. I am just as much hipped as ever. All things displease me. I am even timorous. I dined this day at Rufin's with Prussian offi-cers, and thought them madmen to endure fatigues and risk their lives. Mean thought! One of them, a Saxon, walked with me after dinner and said, "Our king has neither religion nor humanity." I said, "I am glad to hear you speak so freely." He said of the Prince of Prussia, "He's a weak character." I called on Hübner, and pitied him and found him insipid. I went with him and some ladies to the Park and saw fireworks of magnificent and brilliant structure. Thought of Canongate — Johnston — Mrs. Bird's tarts.[4]

MONDAY 10 SEPTEMBER. I took leave of the riding-school. I was glad to do so, for I had the spleen. I drove it off by writing all day. At night I supped with the family. Mademoiselle made me a present of a book to keep an *album amicorum*, a great custom in Holland and Germany and the northern countries. You present your book to a friend, who writes something in it of his own, or a quotation from some author, and writes his name below; or, if he can draw, designs you something. Thus you have a remembrance

---

Dalrymple, Lord Chesterfield, West Digges, Johnson, Thomas Gray, Lord Eglinton, and many more. Similarly he had always before him several ex-emplars of conduct which he considered unworthy of the future Laird of Auchinleck: James Montgomerie of Lainshaw, Lord Kellie and the other members of that family (some of whom, nevertheless, he was fond of), and particularly Houston Stewart (later Stewart-Nicholson), a frivolous com-panion of his youth whom he seems to have outgrown very early.

[4] "My honest Johnston, I am going to recall a chain of curious ideas. I am going back to the time when I was first acquainted with you, when you had a straw-coloured lining to your coat and I thought you quite the genteel gentleman. When you used to walk to Leith with Mr. Dun and me on a Saturday, come in by the Abbey Close and eat Mrs. Bird's tarts . . . " (Boswell to Johnston, 19 July 1763). From this it seems probable that Mrs. Bird was a pastry-cook with a shop in the Canongate, the whole length of which Mr. Dun and his charges would have walked on the way back to Lord Auchin-leck's house in Parliament Close. From the present reference in the journal it appears that Boswell also associated the Canongate with displays of fire-works.

of your friends. It is not a bad contrivance, but a little ridiculous. Mademoiselle said she would write in mine: "Grand Roi, cesse de vaincre, ou je cesse d'écrire."[5] She however would not do it, as it was not *convenable.* I raged at her, being so much pleased with the conceit, and exclaiming, "It is noble, you have outdone yourself. You do not understand the force of your own idea, whether you intend it as a compliment or as an exquisite sarcasm." I raged in the cause of pride, and said my greatest satisfaction was to have power over others, to have which I would suffer many evils; and I thanked heaven for having given me noble sentiments and the rule over lands. They talked of contentment. I said it was a poor thing. Indeed, I was too fiery.

[Received *c.* 10 September, Lord Marischal to Boswell]

Sunday [9 September 1764]

SIR: — I have writ as you desire to try if your father will indulgence you in your project of travelling a year more. I have also told him that as travelling is dearer than only short excursions, I think you will want two hundred pounds sterling extraordinary, which I dare say will do. In Italy one can have a chaise for two at about a gold ducat a day, horse, chaise, eating, and all included. I remember I paid a ducat (per head) from Venice to Augsburg. I heartily wish you a good journey, having the honour to be, with particular regard, Sir, your most humble and obedient servant,

MARISCHAL.

I send two letters for friends at Neuchâtel, and a packet of seeds. The letter to Mademoiselle Bord à Rochefort, only to be put into the post at Neuchâtel.

I have told Lord Auchinleck that you will wait at Geneva his orders. If Splitgerber should make any difficulty to advance you two or three months allowance, I shall send it you with pleasure. Bon soir.

[5] "Cease, great King, to conquer, or I cease to write" (Boileau, *Épîtres,* viii. 1, addressing Louis XIV).

[Boswell to John Johnston of Grange][6]

Berlin, 10 September 1764

My dear Sir, — Why have you not written to me since I left Utrecht? Davy[7] would have given you my address. But I excuse you; for although I wrote you the last letter, you are waiting for a letter from Berlin.

How do our minds alter with the times! How easily do we submit ourselves with contentment to circumstances! While I was in London, you would have been very uneasy if you had been a week without hearing from me; and when you now and then neglected a post, you was sure to receive from me a very warm letter, in which anger, anxiety, and affection were mingled so as to show the heart of a most sincere friend who suffered so much from the apprehensions of a tender and gloomy mind as really to upbraid him whose innocent neglect caused his uneasiness. Now our situation is very different. We are at such a distance from each other that frequent correspondence cannot be carried on but at a great expense. We have therefore set our minds at ease, and as we have no fixed time of expectation, we are never disappointed. Yet, my friend, believe me, three months is a long time. I think we might correspond once in two months. What say you?

To give you my history since I emerged from Holland would be to transcribe or abridge my journal, neither of which would I wish to do. For I hope to have the satisfaction of reading it with you at length. . . .

[6] John Johnston, Boswell's most intimate friend after W. J. Temple, was laird of a small property in Dumfriesshire and practised law as a "writer" (attorney) in Edinburgh. Boswell appears to have formed close ties of friendship with him by his own fifteenth year, and leaned heavily on him for a kind of sympathy that Temple could not furnish. He suffered like Boswell from melancholia, and shared Boswell's enthusiasm for Scottish scenery and antiquities.

[7] Boswell's younger brother, at this time about sixteen. He was apprenticed to a banking-house in Edinburgh.

As to the course which I am next to steer, I cannot as yet exactly inform you. I would wish to pass four months in Italy, but my father is averse to my going to that intoxicating region. He wishes to have me pass the winter at Geneva, and go to Paris in the spring. I however still beg to be allowed to see Rome. My Lord Marischal and Mr. Mitchell have both written in my favour, so that I am not without hopes that my request may be granted. In the mean time, I am to leave this in ten days, make a tour by Dessau, Dresden, Gotha, Mannheim, and some more courts to Geneva, where I shall receive my father's final determination, and from whence I have a plain passage into France, or a mountainous one into Italy. If my father is absolutely against my going to Italy, I shall see how I like Geneva. If it is agreeable, I shall stay there till the spring. If otherwise, I shall go to some university town in France. I shall however have an opportunity of seeing Voltaire and Rousseau. I hope to be very well amused in the German courts which I intend to visit. You shall hear from me when I get to Geneva. In the mean time, do you write me a long letter proving that you are alive, that you have not forgot me, your absent friend, and that you have no antipathy at the Abbey of Holyroodhouse, or at the noble mountain of Arthur's Seat. Let your letter be sent to the care of Messrs. Splitgerber et Daum, à Berlin.

I pray you, Johnston, give me consolation against the hour of antiquity.[8] Both you and I must lay our account to suffer such hours. Let us assist each other. I study hypochondria as a science. I am always picking up more knowledge with regard to it. My dear friend, I feel sincerely the want of you to talk with. God grant that we may yet be much together. Encourage me in my plan of following the law in Scotland. May I not do pretty well between the Session House and Auchinleck, with now and then a jaunt into England? You know my sad changeable humour. Help me to get the better of it.

You are now at Grange. Walk out on a sunny day and indulge

[8] Boswell's and Johnston's private term for "melancholy," or, as we would say, "depression."

pleasing meditation. One thing is most sure: that after the blackest gloom we may be quite happy. Strange is our existence. Let us hope for a better world and do as well as we can in this. Pray be kind to Davy. . . .

Believe me, my dear Johnston, your affectionate friend,

JAMES BOSWELL.

TUESDAY 11 SEPTEMBER. To punish my extravagant rodo-montading, and to bring up my affairs and compose my spirit, I had sitten up all night. Grievous was it to the flesh till seven in the morning, when my blood took a fine flow.[9] I was quite drunk with brisk spirits, and about eight, in came a woman with a basket of chocolate to sell. I toyed with her and found she was with child. Oho! a safe piece. Into my closet. "Habs er ein Man?" "Ja, in den Gards bei Potsdam."[1] To bed directly. In a minute — over. I rose cool and astonished, half angry, half laughing. I sent her off. Bless me, have I now committed adultery? Stay, a soldier's wife is no wife. Should I now torment myself with speculations on sin, and on losing in one morning the merit of a year's chastity? No: this is womanish. Nay, your elegant mystics would not do so. Madame Guyon was of opinion that sin should be forgotten as soon as possible, as being an idea too gross for the mind of a saint, and disturbing the exercise of sweet devotion. Her notion is ingenious. I am sorry that this accident has happened, I know not how. Let it go. I'll think no more of it. Divine Being! Pardon the errors of a weak mortal. Give me more steadiness. Let me grow more perfect. What a curious thing is it to find a strict philosopher speculating on a recent fault! Well, I shall not be proud. I shall be a mild and humble Christian.[2]

I was made happy at twelve by a visit of Messrs. Scott and Macpherson. We all dined at Burnett's. Scott had taken it into his head to think of Mademoiselle Kircheisen for his wedded wife, though

[9] The passage illustrates a constitutional oddity of Boswell's: going without sleep, instead of depressing him, often put him in high spirits.

[1] "Have you a husband?" "Yes, in the Guards at Potsdam."

[2] See the entry for 18 November.

he had never seen her. I carried him and Macpherson to the President's to drink coffee. The Highlander pleased much. But Scott not at all. Poor fellow! His manners are not taking. I must put his courting project far from him. We supped at Burnett's. Captain Wake was there. He sung,

> Wat ye wha I met yestreen,
> Coming down the hill, my Joe,

and some more Scots *sangs*. They were a little too free. But I was master of myself.[3]

WEDNESDAY 12 SEPTEMBER. Mademoiselle joked too much with me this morning, and somewhat in the Scots biting way. I was angry with her, and said, "You say that I am not so polite as I should be, yet I never say anything that might seem rude without making clear that I say it in jest or from heedlessness. But you really do say biting things through spitefulness, and that is to be lacking in true politeness."

Burnett and all of us Scots lads dined with honest Wake. Good biscuits adorned his jolly board. His dinner was substantial and his punch strong. I wish he had not mixed three Germans with us, and had not given us a bawdy song. At night Wake and Scott and Macpherson eat crawfish and drank Rhenish at my lodgings. We were hearty.

THURSDAY 13 SEPTEMBER. The captains went away. I passed the morning with Burnett, who is now *chargé d'affaires* here. I dined *chez* Castillon. At four he carried me to the Royal Academy of Berlin. The building is large. Below are the King's stables, and above assemble his literati, which made a wag put this inscription on the Academy: "Musis et mulis."[4] I saw a poor collection of natural curiosities, except indeed the collection of dried plants of the Levant made by Tournefort. The Academy assembled before

---

[3] "Silk for a suit, twenty-one crowns twelve groschen; tailoring, lining, &c., twenty-four crowns twelve groschen; a riding-coat, twenty-eight crowns; omitted, fireworks, one crown four groschen." (Expense Account, 11 September. He had seen the fireworks on 9 September.)

[4] "[Dedicated] to the Muses and to mules."

five. Formey read a letter from a physician at Truro in Cornwall concerning some astronomical phenomenon. He wrote sad Latin, and, when he wanted a word, mixed still worse Greek. I was ashamed of him. Monsieur Francheville next read a dissertation on the art of making ambergris, with which I was not greatly edified.[5] After he had done, not a word was said. The Academicians grinned and separated. A poor affair this.

I then went to Madame de Brandt's, where I imagined I was invited. But I had mistaken Tuesday for Thursday, and she punished me by a recital of the fine *partie* that she had, as it was her daughter's birthday. How she had a fine supper and a fine ball and all the company were dressed *à la turque;* and how a dress was ready for me. She asked me to stay this evening with her. Much she talked of gallantry and of the Duke of Portland, who was here some years ago.[6] Young Comte Schaffgotsch supped with us, and after supper we played at "seek the pin." One is sent out of the room till the pin is hid, and when he enters he must seek it. In proportion as he approaches it, one beats harder and harder upon the table, till at last he finds it.

[5] Francheville, a second-rate man of letters who owed his place in the Academy solely to Frederick's passion for French literature, dismissed various theories of the origin of ambergris (including the correct one), and maintained that it was formed from a mixture of honey and wax which had floated from the sea-side nests of the wild bee. In the interest of history, it is a pity that Boswell did not hear a paper by one of the really great scientists of the Academy (Euler, Marggraf, Gleditsch), but it is doubtful whether he would have been much "edified" by scientific papers in any case. Lessing, on whom it would be most interesting to have Boswell's remarks, had been made a non-resident member in 1760 — much to Frederick's disgust — but was not at this time in Berlin.

[6] The Duke, who was only two and a half years older than Boswell, is known to historians as a sober, formal, high-minded, and rather dull statesman who twice held the office of Prime Minister. Family letters recently explored by Professor A. S. Turberville show, however, that during his youthful Continental tour he managed to spend over £3000 a year and otherwise to cut a pretty wide swath (*A History of Welbeck Abbey,* 1938–1939, ii. 36–41). He was very handsome.

Mademoiselle[7] said, "One gets terribly bored at Berlin." I believe it. She said too, "Mr. Mitchell used to be very gloomy sometimes, and had to be left to himself; and at last he grew cheerful. Lord Tyrconnel also, who was Ambassador from France here, was sometimes very sad. He had a charming wife, who made him gay."[8] I passed this evening perfectly well.

FRIDAY 14 SEPTEMBER. In the morning Castillon and I went and saw the collection of natural curiosities of Mr. Gerhard.[9] In metals, not amiss. I dined at Burnett's, where was Schmidt, the engraver. Burnett was hearty. At four Castillon and I went and saw old Marggraf, the chemical professor, a very industrious and able man in his profession.[1] But a strange old fellow. It thundered and lightened. He cried, "I love to see my God in flames," and he laughed always when he spoke. Such is man. He must have defects. He may have health and manners. But then he is ignorant. He may have knowledge. But then he is sick or awkward. Marggraf showed us glasses of his making, and a composition by which he can imitate all kinds of precious stones. He gave me a piece like sapphire. His minerals were very complete. I promised to send him some from Scotland.

Castillon went home with me. He said we ought to revere God; but all affections exercised towards the Supreme Being were only in the fancy of fanatics. He owned that the Gospels were all that

[7] Mademoiselle de Brandt, the daughter for whom the birthday party was given.

[8] Tyrconnel was a Jacobite title. Richard Talbot, Earl and titular Duke of Tyrconnel, an Irishman, had commanded the forces of James II in Ireland, and of course had been attainted. His nephew, who would have inherited his honours but for the attainder, assumed the style of Earl of Tyrconnel and fled to France. It was the son of this nephew, a brigadier general in the French Army, who had been French Ambassador to Prussia.

[9] A well known mineralogist who held various important posts in the Prussian government.

[1] Andreas Sigismund Marggraf, one of the last great chemists of the phlogiston school, conducted important researches on phosphorus, on aluminium and other metals, and was the first to extract sugar from beets. He was at this time director of the physics class in the Academy.

he owned as truly Christian scriptures. The Epistles he thought only good pieces which might be of use sometimes. He said the Christian religion had not added much to morality. What would he be at? He left me at eight. I amused myself with a street girl as in London. Idleness — no great harm.[2]

SATURDAY 15 SEPTEMBER. Some time ago I was taken in by Castillon for a dreary dinner at Treptow, of which Captain Durand of the artillery paid the expense. Castillon and I could not do less than give such another treat, so I could not shun being once more taken in. We went to Stralau and had a sad house. I tired terribly. At dinner I was sulky, and I railed against the French. Durand came and seated himself by me, saying, "It is better that I, rather than my sister,[3] should hear these little impertinences which are flying about." "Sir," said I, "I hope that you have not been offended by what I have said." "Yes, Sir. You have spoken against the French. I, Sir, am a Frenchman; and no one can speak in such a way against an entire nation unless he is a scoundrel." This last word gave me a blow on the heart. It was a clear affront which could not be put up. I bowed and said, "I am sorry, Sir. I had no intention of being impertinent." It happened luckily in the middle of dinner, so that I had time to think. I found fear working with me. I recalled old David, Laird of Auchinleck, my great-grand-father, and thought he called to me to support the honour of my family.[4] I had also my honour as a Scotsman, my character as a man, at stake. I must do myself the justice to say that I was fully determined for the worst. Yet I wished that the affair could be made up, as I was really in the wrong. I felt myself in the situation which I have often fancied, and which is a very uneasy one. Yet upon my honour, so strong is my metaphysical passion that I was pleased

[2] " ... Then girl, breast. Necessity. Care. Just idleness ... " (Memorandum, 15 September).

[3] Boswell has neglected to identify the Captain's sister.

[4] David, the sixth Laird, was nephew to the fifth, who had passed over his own daughters to keep Auchinleck in the male line. Hence it behoved David's descendants to justify the choice.

with this opportunity of intimately observing the working of the human mind.

When dinner was over, I took the Captain to a walk behind the house and said, "I am very sorry, Sir, for what happened today. I was much in the wrong. I should wish, if it is possible, to avoid a quarrel. But you made use of an expression which a gentleman cannot endure, and I must have satisfaction." "Whatever you wish, Sir," said he; "I am ready for anything." "Sir," said I, "I wish that you would own that you were in the wrong to speak to me as you did. I shall own first that I was impolite to speak as I did against the French." By this time one of his brother officers and another gentleman came up to us. To excuse me, they said, "The gentleman was only joking." I replied, "Excuse me. No, I shall not deny my feelings. I was in earnest, Sir. I own that I have an antipathy, or, if you wish, a prejudice against your nation. I own also that I ought not to mention it in a company I am not certain of. Sir, will you own that you were in the wrong?" He said, "Sir, everything you wish. I am very sorry that I used such an expression; for you did not mean that, because I am French, I am not a gentleman."

Castillon also came, and he owned his fault before three or four gentlemen, and Castillon said, "Then everything is arranged. Mr. Boswell, you could ask no more." However, I was still uneasy. The affront had been given before all the company. It was necessary that all the company should see it repaired. Some went by land, the rest of us in the boat. I sat in great uneasiness. We supped all at Durand's very well. After supper I filled up a bumper of hock, and called to him, "Sir — Captain Durand — I repeat here what we said in private. I am very sorry that I spoke today in an impolite manner. I hope that you will say as much." He replied, "I am very sorry, Sir, that I was so hot-headed and that I spoke to you in an impolite manner." I cannot remember our very words. I said, "Sir, I should only like to make you see that a man can speak as I have done and be imprudent or impolite, but not a scoundrel." "O Monsieur," said he with concern. We drank to each other, and all was

fully and genteelly settled. When I got home I reflected with a
Lucretian suavity on the *mare magnum* that I had escaped.[5] In
time coming, I shall be more on my guard, and be truly polite.

SUNDAY 16 SEPTEMBER. At Burnett's I found old Gualteri, a
fine lively little man, who snapped his fingers at every little sally
that he gave us.[6] He said Voltaire had all his life assumed characters. When he was at Berlin he played the arrant miser. Now he
acts the most generous man alive. When Gualteri was gone, Wake
came in and I said, "Gentlemen, I ask you as my countrymen, have
I done right or not?" I told them the story of my quarrel, and they
agreed that I had got into a very ugly scrape, but had brought
myself out of it very properly.

I dined with Burnett tête-à-tête. He said if a man owned
honestly that he was a coward, he would still esteem him. "But,"
said he, "a coward will fight upon occasions." He has found me
several words for my Scots Dictionary.[7]

At night I walked with Wake. I supped at home and after supper told Madame my story. She was pleased to find that I had got
off so well and bid me by all means avoid being impolite. I asked
her if I had been really so sometimes. She said, "It must be admitted that sometimes you have been extremely rude." I explained
to her how it proceeded from a flow of vivacious humour. But that
will not do. Lord Kellie has the same. Let me then be master of
myself. Let me be mild and agreeable.

[5] "It is pleasant, when the *mighty deep* is roused by winds, to stand on shore
and watch another man struggling painfully with the waves; not because
one really gets pleasure from seeing other people in trouble, but because it
is pleasant to see dangers and know that you yourself are free from them"
(Lucretius, *De rerum natura,* ii. 1–4).

[6] "Old Gualteri" was a French Protestant pastor who had forsaken the cloth
and had been ennobled by Frederick the Great.

[7] This work, the most ambitious of Boswell's unrealized literary projects,
was conceived in January, 1764 at Utrecht, and occupied a good deal of his
thought during the remainder of his stay in Holland. For a description of
the method he intended to follow, see *Boswell in Holland,* following 24
February 1764.

MONDAY 17 SEPTEMBER. I breakfasted with Burnett on Scots oatmeal pottage and English porter. This is one of the best methods that can be taken to render the Union truly firm. I went to take leave of Gotskowsky. He very kindly kept me to dinner. I saw there an old officer of eighty-nine, who was page to Charles the Ninth of Sweden, and had made the campaigns of Charles the Twelfth and of the King of Prussia. There was a tale to brag of. He told me that the soldiers were much happier under Charles than under Frederick. He said he had served the latter as captain ten years, and he had now no greater pension than ten crowns a month. Very hard indeed. I took a cordial farewell of Gotskowsky, who is indeed what the French call *un galant homme*. He has shown me very great civility and in an easy, hearty way, which is not easy to feign. He asked me to write to him. I shall certainly do so.

At three I waited on Monsieur Durand and sat half an hour with him. We talked away with genteel ease, as if nothing had happened. I observed a large cut on his forehead which he had got in a duel. I was happy to have avoided any such mark. When I took leave of him, I once more resumed our quarrel. He said to me, "Sir, to tell the truth, both of us were at fault. I have made all the reparation I could, and I hope you are satisfied." I replied, "Sir, I shall always esteem you. You have acted in a manner which does you a great deal of honour." "Sir," said he, "I have acted as one ought to act with gentlemen, of whom I believe you to be one." Upon my word, this is a fine fellow. I parted from him on the best terms.

At night I had a long chat with Madame and Mademoiselle, and owned that I had the misfortune to be *changeant* in a most unaccountable degree. "You will not be able to believe it, Mademoiselle, but sometimes it has given me great pain to see you in the morning, and to hear you play." The amiable ladies were sorry for me, and said that they had observed something about me *d'extraordinaire*, and that I would appear sorry one day for what I had said on another. Madame Kircheisen said, "You must take care, or you will become hypochondriac. You must drink a great deal of water and take a great deal of exercise. My husband used to be very melancholy. He thought every one had a grudge against him. He wanted to stay in this room. I had his bed brought here, and I lay on the settee. Then he would say, 'I should be better off on the settee,' and we would change. Well, I pretended to go to sleep. He would remain then without closing his eyes, get up, wander about the room; he was always restless. He tried to write. He couldn't. He was gloomy and complained bitterly. I would rise. I would talk to him. I would quote him consolatory passages from the Bible. He would be somewhat soothed. He would begin again. So I said to him, 'Why, you will kill me and yourself too, staying awake like this, and what will become of our family?' I would talk like that just to rouse him a little. Then he would be sorry. He made an effort. He conquered his humour. He began to sleep."

This history gave me infinite pleasure. I wish I may have such a wife. Madame la Présidente is between forty and fifty. She is still a handsome woman. She is of a genteel family. She has excellent common sense and much ease of behaviour. Yet the *bourgeoise* appears at times. She is a most estimable mother and mistress of a family. She is penetrating, and she can conceal her sentiments, so that I know her not so perfectly as I have known many a character. Of the strangers whom I make acquaintance with, I shall not draw regular characters. The little anecdotes which I mark serve to point them out well enough. Madame Kircheisen has an excellent, neat, descriptive talent. She has often talked to me of the *bel* Abbé Bastiani of Breslau, who lodged in her house, and many pretty little anecdotes she has of him. She is quite the Scots lady in one particular. She makes all fine cakes and conserves. Every morning I get some good thing or another from her.

TUESDAY 18 SEPTEMBER. For the last time I dined at Burnett's. I then paid my visits *pour prendre congé*, having fixed tomorrow for my day of departure. We went and saw old Gualteri, who said, "Vous faites une visite à la Nicodème" to Burnett and me.[8] I then sat some time at Madame de Brandt's, who was mighty civil and said, "You are the second whose departure I regret in-

8 "You come at night" (John, 3. 2).

finitely. Chevalier Silva, the Spaniard, was the first. Oh, but he was a fine man!"[9] I said, "Madame, if I had stayed here longer, I am sure you would have liked me better." In short I gave her to understand that I should have been happy as her very humble servant. She was still a fine woman, and has the most perfect elegance of manners. Her gallantries have been notorious, "from the King to the herdsman," if one can trust gossip.[1] She made me a present of a handsome little crayon and case. I was really sorry to leave for ever a lady who might have greatly formed me. I supped at home for the last night, and upon my word, I felt no small regret and tender melancholy.

WEDNESDAY 19 SEPTEMBER. I received a kind letter from worthy Dr. Boswell,[2] and one from Mr. Francis Gentleman proposing to dedicate to me a second volume of *A Trip to the Moon*. I answered him immediately, and politely refused his offer. These letters recalled fully my former days. I felt myself greatly improved.[3] My worthy Lord Marischal offered to advance me what money I should need for three or four months if Mr. Schickler made any difficulty; which however was not necessary, for my hearty banker freely gave me what I asked. I run about all morn-

[9] If Madame de Brandt was not indulging in irony, she was paying Boswell a considerable compliment. Mariana de Silva (just Boswell's age) won distinction both as author and painter.

[1] In French in the original: "Du Roi jusqu'au berger, à ce qu'on dit."

[2] Boswell's uncle, a physician of Edinburgh. He and Boswell resembled each other in temperament. The letter has not been recovered.

[3] In 1760 Gentleman, a none-too-reputable Irish actor who had also been an officer in the Army, had dedicated to Boswell a version of Southerne's *Oroonoko*; and in the same year the two perhaps collaborated in a pamphlet entitled *A View of the Edinburgh Theatre*. Gentleman had probably received a genteel present of guineas from Boswell for the dedication of *Oroonoko*, and certainly would have expected one if Boswell had accepted the dedication he was now offering. The first volume of *A Trip to the Moon*, *containing an Account of the Island of Noibla, its Inhabitants, Religious and Political Customs, &c. by Sir Humphrey Lunatic, Bart.*, was reviewed in the *Monthly Review* for May, 1764. The proposed second volume seems never to have been published.

ing. I recalled all my scenes of pleasure at Berlin, where I was cured of the black hypochondria. Yet I was glad to go. So much do I love change. I dread that this love may increase. But my warm regard for the old Auchinleck shall ever fix me.

I took cordial leave of my good President before dinner. I did not dine, but run about taking leave. I eat a bit of apple pie at Castillon's. I was not sorry to leave *him*. He is a peevish being, and if he has knowledge, it does himself little good and others far less. It was humbling to see in this man of how little value the possession of knowledge may be. No more of this. At three I came home. I gave every one of the servants drink-money, and they bid me adieu with regard.[4]

Before I quit this house, let me mark some ideas which I shall like to recall. The President's regular employment. The easy uniformity of the family. Three machines.[5] Five good horses. The courtyard with the walnut tree. The stork. The little temple of ease. Curtzin, the neat little maid. I now walked through the dining-room with that kind of agreeable agitation which I always feel at quitting a place where I have been well. My stay here appeared like a dream. Bless me! In two months' time have I formed so kind a connection with this family? Well, my agreeable talents must be great. I sent away my servant and baggage by the *journalière* to Potsdam. I took leave of the ladies very tenderly, and set out upon post-horses. Young Leopold accompanied me half way. I was quite the Laird of Auchinleck, and he was a Bruce Campbell.[6] I rode briskly along to Potsdam, went to Froment's, found there my Lord Marischal and Scott and Macpherson; talked well, supped Froment's. Slept at Scott's.

THURSDAY 20 SEPTEMBER. All the morning was employed in writing. I dined Froment's, and after dinner we all walked.

[4] He paid thirty crowns to the President for two months' lodging, and distributed fifteen crowns in tips (Expense Account).

[5] Carriages.

[6] The young laird of Mayfield, a second cousin of Boswell's descended from the family of Auchinleck in the female line. Boswell means that he respected and liked young Kircheisen but felt superior to him.

Madame la Turque said to me, "You have a turn for melancholy.
It makes you extremely variable." I said, "Then what country
ought I to adopt?" She replied, "Europe." "And who should be my
wife?" Froment exclaimed, "A post-wagon." Very ludicrous and
well applied. I supped at Scott's, and told stories like a Charles
Cochrane.[7]

FRIDAY 21 SEPTEMBER. The whim struck me to put on a blue
bonnet and appear quite a Scots gentleman.[8] I went in this dress to
the parade of the Prince of Prussia. The Prince observed me and
asked Scott, "What is that little cap which that gentleman is wear-
ing?" Scott said, "It is the kind of cap which Scottish gentlemen
wear." The poor Prince did not like it much, nor could he think
that he was a lord's son who wore it. No matter. I was pleased, and
boldly did I march upon the Parade before the Palace, where I
again saw the King. But he did not look towards me. However, I
was pleased to have shown the first blue bonnet on the Prussian
Parade. I dined heartily at honest Scott's, and supped too. I was
healthy and cheerful, and just Father.

SATURDAY 22 SEPTEMBER. This morning I called on General
Wylich, who told me he had been *très hypochondre*. Said he, "You
must eat little, especially at night; for if you have supped, you
have frightful dreams, and when you awake next morning, you
are — I don't know how." I see the good General knows it. He said
the King has a little of the malady too, but he is so busy that he
never has time to encourage it. The General said of hypochondria,
"I do not find it a bad kind of temperament."

[7] Boswell's grand-uncle, an advocate, brother to Basil ("Commissioner")
Cochrane and to the eighth Earl of Dundonald. He had died when Boswell
was in his twelfth year.
[8] The rest of the entry shows that this donning of outlandish headgear was
not all whim: it was in part at least a scheme for catching the King's eye. —
If what Boswell says is to be taken at its face value, it means that the tradi-
tional soft flat cap of Scotland had not by 1764 become the distinguishing
mark of a ploughman or a petty laird, as the term "bonnet laird" shows it
later did become. And in fact the Oxford English Dictionary lists no oc-
currence of the term "bonnet laird" before Scott's *Antiquary* (1816).

Frederick the Great, from an engraving by Frederik Christian
Carstens in the Metropolitan Museum of Art.

The Hereditary Prince of Brunswick was now at Potsdam. I waited upon him in the Palace, and talked some time. On the Parade I stood by Wylich, who had promised that if it was possible he would present me to the King. But an opportunity did not present itself.[9] This King is feared like a wild beast. I am quite out of conceit with monarchy. I dined at Froment's. Then Madame and I took a drive in my Lord's coach. We once more talked of hypochondria, and when I mentioned many gloomy ideas, she said always, "You must be ill to think in that fashion." She is really right. We paid a visit to Catt and his lady, two poor beings. At night we all met at Froment's. We played at faro, I for the first time. I grew monstrously keen. We supped. Again the bank went on. I am happily tied up from gaming.[1]

SUNDAY 23 SEPTEMBER. Once more I saw the King of Prussia. My father had proposed to me to pass the winter at Geneva. But I was anxious to go to Italy. Mr. Mitchell wrote in my favour, as did my worthy Lord Marischal. In the mean time I resolved to go to Geneva, but to make a long tour of it by visiting several of the German courts. My Lord Marischal approved of this. I passed part of the morning with his Lordship, who gave me his good advices with an accuracy and a vivacity that amazed me. He is absolutely free of affectation, which I cannot understand, for I am sadly plagued with it. He joked with me and said, "Well, Colonel! May you not only conquer Portugal, but Africa, and so triumph over the Moors." I took leave of him with a most respectful and affectionate embrace, saying, "My Lord, you may always reckon upon me as upon a most faithful servant." My heart was big when I took my last adieu of the venerable Scots nobleman. I yet hope to see him again. I almost cried. At this moment the tears are in my eyes.[2] I

[9] Boswell's failure, after all his wiles, to secure a presentation to Frederick was his great European defeat; perhaps the major social defeat of his life.
[1] See p. 31 *n.*
[2] He never did see him again, for Lord Marischal remained at Potsdam until his death in 1778. He kept up an affectionate correspondence with Boswell, however; consented in 1767 to stand godfather for his illegitimate child, and lent him money for the purchase of Dalblair.

dined at Froment's and took leave of my poor Turk with regret. Well, she and I have passed curious hours together. Honest Scott said, "If I come within sixty miles of you, I shall see you." Macpherson and Froment walked with me till I was out at the gate, and then took leave. All these circumstances mark my being regarded. I mounted the post-wagon. I found it cold and really hard enough. Courage.[3]

[Lord Marischal to Boswell. Original in French][4]

[Potsdam, *c.* 23 September 1764]

LORD MARISCHAL sends Mr. Boswell his wishes for a good trip, and hopes he will have health, pleasure, and profit from the fine things he will see in Italy.

He begs him if he sees Monsieur Rousseau to pay him many compliments on Lord Marischal's part, and to inform Lord Marischal of the state of Monsieur Rousseau's health, concerning which he is more than ordinarily disturbed, since he has had no reply to the letter he wrote him on his arrival at Sans Souci.

MONDAY 24 SEPTEMBER. About noon I arrived at Coswig, the residence of the Prince of Zerbst, who is a strange, wrong-headed being.[5] He has got his troops, forsooth, to the number of 150 foot

[3] "At Bostorf, straw for sleeping on, four groschen" (Expense Account, 23 September).

[4] This letter was probably delivered at Froment's to Boswell, after he and Lord Marischal had taken leave of each other. It will be remembered that Boswell had finally written the old man a letter asking point-blank for a presentation to the King and a recommendation to Rousseau. (See p. 81.) Lord Marischal, when they met, seems to have said nothing as to either request, but he did *not* present Boswell to the King, and this brief "card" was as far as he was willing to go in recommending Boswell to Rousseau. He held a privileged position with both Frederick and Rousseau, and did not propose to take advantage of it. — After Boswell left Berlin, he received few letters till he reached Neuchâtel on 6 December, when he found a packet of fourteen waiting for him. Two of the better ones from the accumulation will be presented at that point.

[5] He was the last of his line. His greatest claim to remembrance is that he was the brother of Catherine the Great of Russia.

and 30 horse, and, during the last war, he took a fancy that the King of Prussia was coming to attack him. So he put in readiness his little battery of cannon, and led out his 180 to make head against the armies of Frederick. He was not here at present, but at Vienna, as he has a regiment in the Austrian service. So I had no opportunity of paying my court to him. The appearance of his little dirty town, his castle, and his sentinels with sentry-boxes painted in lozenges of different colours, like the stockings of Harlequin, diverted me a good deal. I walked about, and, to have a little German talk, I asked every sentry, "Vie veel troepen hebt der Furst?"[6] One soldier, whose head resembled that of his prince, had marked me with serious political attention, and, dreading that a foreign spy had got into his Highness's dominions, and that a conspiracy was forming against the state, followed me close, and at last when I came to the grenadier before the Castle-gate, he laid hold of me, charged the sentry with me, and bringing a party, conducted me to the main Guard. I was heartily entertained with this adventure, and marched with all the formal composure of a state prisoner. When I arrived at the Guard, there was a hue and cry around me as if I had entered a kennel of dogs. I could not explain myself well enough in German, and stood for some time like the stag at bay. At last a blackguard dog of a soldier said, "Dominus forsitan loquitur Latine."[7] I told this fellow that I was a stranger, a gentleman of Scotland, and that I had asked the number of his prince's troops to amuse my curiosity, and that I supposed I had done no harm. He repeated this in German, and most of the troops seemed content. But my foolish fellow of an accuser would see more into the matter, and so away they carried me before the Burgmeester, while I laughed and cried "Beast." My interpreter repeated my defence to the Burgmeester, and this judicious magistrate smiled at the fellow and dismissed me immediately.

> Solvuntur risu tabulae, tu missus abibis.
> My Lords the judges laugh, and you're dismissed.[8]

[6] "How many troops does the Prince have?"
[7] "Perhaps my Lord speaks Latin."
[8] Horace, *Satires*, II. i. 86.

This is really an adventure to tell. My interpreter told me, "Studui Lipsiae."[9] I suppose he has been a very sad dog.

At three I arrived at Dessau, and immediately dressed. I sent immediately my compliments as Monsieur de Boswell, Scotsman, to the Maréchal of the Court, begging to have the honour of waiting upon him and being presented to the Court. He asked to see me at Court at five. Immediately I had from the Prince an elegant coach and footman well laced, and at five I drove to Court. This now is quite the thing. My good fortune put me in a flutter, and I became timorous, like a peasant upon whose back is clapped a suit of rich clothes. The Maréchal spoke no French, which was a little awkward. I presented a letter to the Prince Jean George from Count d'Anhalt at Potsdam. I was presented to three princesses and to the Prince Albert. I never saw a family that pleased me more. It was one of the grand court days. We had a concert. The Reigning Prince was not at home, which I regret much, as he has been in England, loves it, speaks the language, and is fond to see the British.[1] Neitschütz, his Master of Horse, who was also in England, was now at Dessau, and very kind he was to me, as was also a Monsieur de Berenhorst.[2] I supped at Court where all was very well. The two princes spoke only German, so that I had difficult conversation of it. However, I did so well that I was liked, and I was honoured with the distinction of being offered one of the Prince's horses to go a-hunting with, which I most thankfully accepted. I got into true spirits.

TUESDAY 25 SEPTEMBER. Like a bold hunter I rose at five.

[9] "I have studied at Leipzig."

[1] Johann Georg and Albrecht (aged respectively sixteen and fourteen) were younger brothers of the Reigning Prince; the sisters were Henriette Katharina Agnes (aged twenty), Maria Leopoldine (aged eighteen), and Kasimire (aged fifteen). Friedrich, Count of Anhalt, was their first cousin. The Reigning Prince (later Duke) Leopold Friedrich Franz, two months older than Boswell and still unmarried, was one of the more enlightened rulers of the day. He had only recently returned from his English tour.

[2] Natural son of Leopold I ("der Alte Dessauer"), grandfather to the Reigning Prince. He was later ennobled by the Emperor.

Monsieur de Berenhorst presented me to Prince Diederic,[3] uncle to the Reigning Prince. I found him a tall, comely old man of sixty-two. He was formerly Velt Marischal in the Prussian service. He has loved hunting all his life. He now keeps two packs of good hounds. He is just one of the old Germans, rough and cordial. He took me by the hand, and showed me his stables, and then we went out. The old gentleman went in his open chaise to the rendezvous. The pack consisted of fifty couple. The hunters were pretty numerous, and had a genteel uniform of red and blue. There were a great many noble *cornes de chasse*, the sound of which roused my blood. The forests of Dessau are magnificent, all of fine oaks, some of which are immensely large. I was mounted on a trusty old white, very quiet, very sure-footed, and by no means slow. For this day, however, I kept by the young Prince Albert, who cut the wood by neat, pretty roads which are made in different places. A large stag was singled out, and away we went after him. It was the first time that I saw this sport, and a most noble one it is. Macfarlane would say, "Then it might be a marquis, for Most Noble is his title."[4] The chase lasted more than two hours. At last the stag took the Elbe and was half worried, half drowned, half slain by the hunter's *coup de grâce*. The horns then sounded, and we all assembled. The princesses came out of their coach. I must mark a little anecdote not quite according to strict decorum. The Prince's mistress was in a chaise, just behind the coach. She did not, however, come out.[5]

After we had paid our respects to Prince Diederic on his chase, a collation of cold meat, bread and butter, and wine was served round. In the mean time the deer was skinned and the best pieces

[3] That is, Dietrich. He had acted as regent during his nephew's minority.

[4] Boswell's elderly friend Walter Macfarlane of Macfarlane, an antiquary, might be expected to be punctilious in such matters. The proper style of a marquis is "Most Honourable."

[5] She was perhaps Johanna Eleonora von Neitschütz, who had borne him a son (Franz Johann Georg, later Count of Waldersee) a little over a year before. But to identify any particular mistress of a German prince is a matter of great perplexity. Augustus the Strong, Elector of Saxony and King of Poland (d. 1733), acknowledged 354 illegitimate children.

of venison laid by. The rest of him was cut to pieces, while the old Prince sat very composedly with his muster-roll, and named all the dogs to see if they were all there. I was vexed that they could not answer to their names, especially as there were several English dogs among them. They were then well whipped in, till their hunger increased almost to fury. The skin and horns were placed above the minced pieces, and then all at once the pack were let loose, and the moment that they attacked the image of the deer, the skin and horns were removed, and they were allowed to devour with full freedom. Prince Diederic then presented me with the stag's foot, saying, "My dear Sir, this is a mark of distinction." This pleased me. It shall be laid up in the museum at Auchinleck, with an inscription on a plate of gold or silver, telling that Laird James the Fourth had it in a present from a German prince with whom he had the honour of hunting, when upon his travels.[6] We all had oak garlands in our hats, and returned gaily to Dessau. I recollected my old Edinburgh vapours — Lord Galloway — "By chase our long-liv'd fathers earn'd their food," &c.[7] I resolved to take daily vigorous exercise.

We dined at Court in boots, as the ladies were not with us. At three I waited on the Countess d'Anhalt, mother to the Count at Potsdam.[8] She had three daughters, strong, bouncing women. One of them is very clever. In the evening we all met again at Court. I must not forget to mention one personage, Captain O'Grady, an Irish officer in the Saxon service, a good, honest, light-headed fellow. He keeps a girl at Dessau, and is very much there. At supper this night he talked a vast deal of bawdy concerning a Mademoi-

[6] Boswell's great-grandson and heir to Auchinleck, the late Lord Talbot de Malahide, reported that he knew nothing of this souvenir. But Boswell certainly got home with it, and he may have carried through his design of identifying it for posterity, for his unpublished correspondence with Sir David Dalrymple in the papers at Yale shows that Dalrymple composed a very elegant Latin inscription for the purpose.

[7] Author unidentified. And the reference to Lord Galloway is obscure.

[8] See p. 17 *n.* 4. She is said variously to have been the daughter of a brewer (*Brauer*) or of a peasant (*Bauer*).

selle Stenix, who sat near me. I looked grave, and seemed to give
no attention to his discourse, by way of reproving him. At last he
said that "she would go like a pair of lobster's claws." This ludicrous idea struck me so much that I burst out into a fit of laughter,
and Master O'Grady was heartily pleased.

WEDNESDAY 26 SEPTEMBER. I had some conversation with
Mr. L'Estocq, who formerly was a tutor to the princes. He said
their father had a curious whim that he would not allow them to
learn any Latin.[9] After dinner I waited on Princesse Wilhelmine,
aunt to the Prince. She was a large jolly princess, very high and
mighty, but her pride was of the best kind. It did not show itself in
silent disdain but in splendid magnificence. Her Highness has her
Master of Horse, her *Grande Maîtresse*, her *Dame d'honneur*, and
in short the true state of a court in a certain degree. I was asked to
return at six. I did so, and found there a little party, eight in all.
We played at cards till eight, when we supped, and exceedingly
well. She was very hearty, and conversation went well on. There
was just as much restraint as pleased me. Well, I am at present a
happy fellow. Where are all my gloomy speculations at Utrecht,
when I imagined that I knew all the circumstances that could arrive in human life, and that the result was only insipidity? Castillon gave me no bad answer to this. "You know," said he, "all the
circumstances of human life, as you know the ingredients of which
a dish may be made; but in neither of the cases can you know what
will be the effect of a selection and mixture, till you try."

THURSDAY 27 SEPTEMBER. While I was on bad terms with
my worthy father, I was treated with great kindness by Lord
Kames.[1] His Lordship's house was a home to me. We corresponded

---

[9] It was L'Estocq who related to Boswell perhaps the most famous of the
anecdotes preserved in *Boswelliana:* "When Voltaire was at Berlin, he used to
be rude to the King of Prussia. The King came into his room one day when
he had before him on a table a great parcel of His Majesty's verses, which he
no doubt put in order very freely. The King called to him, 'What are you
doing, Voltaire?' He replied, 'Sire, j'arrange votre linge sale [I am sorting
your soiled linen]' " (p. 227 of Rogers's edition, 1874).

[1] See pp. 1, 234. Henry Home, Lord Kames, an elder colleague of Boswell's

while I was in London. But since I have been abroad, I have not written to him. This day I wrote him a long letter, of which I shall mark the principal passages:

After a silence of thirteen months, you may believe, my Lord, that Boswell finds some difficulty in beginning a letter to your Lordship. I feel that my conduct has not been altogether right. I should have written to you before now. Indeed I should. I can make no other apology than reminding you of the strange nature of man, of whose unaccountable conduct I have had so many instances that I am fully confirmed in the belief of human liberty, and that the doctrine of motives is only imaginary.

I reserve a detail of my travels for the entertainment of those evenings which I hope to pass with your Lordship in Scotland, when I hope to be better company for you than you have formerly found me. I hope to be company for you in a better style. I am making a tour through the German courts. I am behaving as my best friends could wish. Wherever I come I find myself loved. My dear Lord! is it possible for me not to be flattered when I find that in a day or two I can make strangers of all kinds regard me? Sure I am this could not be done without external merit. As to my internal worth I am always certain. To talk philosophically, a man's acquitting himself well or ill depends extremely on the situation in which he is placed. Take me at present as I am. During this portion of my existence in which I am visiting the courts of Germany, I am acting with perfect propriety. I am fulfilling every duty that my station requires, and when the sun goes down, I review my day with satisfaction. Place me as a student in the Temple, as an officer in a garrison, as a laird upon his estate, or as an advocate in the Court of Session, and I fear my review would not be so pleasing. However, I hope the best. I am every day becoming more temperate in mind. I am every day more convinced that imagination forms false views of life, and that in all human affairs there is not

---

father on the bench, was a prolific writer on law, agriculture, philosophy, and theory of criticism. He was able and not without kindness of heart, but his manner was sarcastic and overbearing.

so much mystery as a young man is apt to think. Is not this true, my Lord? Speak, thou sage, for well thou knowest mortal man.

Is it not amazing to find Voltaire writing still with so much vivacity? I am pretty well informed that he wrote the critical letter on *The Elements* in the *Gazette littéraire de l'Europe*. Was there ever such an old rogue? He gives the French no more idea of your book than if he had written a love-song or a drinking-catch. I must, however, own that his letter bears hard against your chapter on Ridicule. For, notwithstanding the value which I have for your book, it seemed ridiculous for a minute or two after reading the letter.[2]

I believe I told your Lordship before I left England that I had obtained the friendship of Mr. Samuel Johnson. I look upon this as the happiest incident in my life. The conversation of that great and good man has formed me to manly virtue, and kindled in my mind a generous ardour which I trust shall never be extinguished. I hope your Lordship shall one day see Mr. Johnson. His conversation on subjects of importance is not more excellent than is his strong humour. Mr. Garrick said to me that he preferred the latter, and Garrick surely knows to judge of humour. Mr. Johnson accompanied me to Harwich, and since I have been abroad has honoured me with his correspondence. My Lord, if I should die tomorrow, I have not lived in vain.

Pray, my Lord, what is your son[3] doing? Will you allow me to say that I think the original plan for him was not a very good one? I think, my Lord, we have honoured trade enough in our island, by allowing the younger sons of gentlemen to follow it without disparaging their families. To make merchants of our eldest sons is going too far. Let us not abolish distinctions from which mankind have received more benefit than harm.

[2] The review of Lord Kames's *Elements of Criticism* (1762) was indeed by Voltaire, who had been nettled by Kames's strictures on his plays. Boswell's ostensible naïveté is of course malicious.

[3] George Home Drummond. (The "Drummond" was added after he became heir to his mother's estate of Blair Drummond.) Boswell had seen a good deal of him in the winter of 1762–1763 in London, where he was then settled as a merchant, or preparing to be one.

Since I have been abroad, several circumstances have concurred to make me think in a manner more serious than when I had the honour of being with your Lordship. Upon the whole, I think myself a good deal improved. While I thus talk to you without reserve, it would be cruel to laugh or to suspect me of affectation. Pray, my Lord, be kind enough to forget my former extravagant love of ridicule.

Such was my letter. I think he must be pleased with it, and I expect he will write me a good answer.

After dinner my worthy Neitschütz carried me through the Palace, which has many noble rooms. I saw a very pretty beginning of a collection of pictures, which the Prince has made, and a very handsome library of French, German, and English books. His Highness's English library is very well chosen. It gave me pleasure to find there Johnson's *Dictionary*, and my respected friend *The Rambler* in good attire.

We then mounted a couple of the Prince's horses, after having seen his stables in town, and went and saw his Polish and Hungarian cattle, for which he has excellent pasture. They are generally of a bluish colour and resemble the Scots Highland beasts. They are indeed larger; but, like our Highlanders, they are lean and firm, and when brought to rich feeding make excellent beef. We saw also the young horses, of which the Prince has a vast many. I was very well amused with these rural sights, and quite in the humour of being a clever farmer at Auchinleck. A Scots baron cannot do better than travel in Germany. When he goes to Italy and France, he lives with artificial men cooped up in towns and formed in such a manner that Nature is quite destroyed. Yet is an art so agreeable substituted in its place that these people feel themselves happy, although the true manly character is melted into elegant ease. If the Scots baron were to pass all his life abroad, he would not perceive his imbecility more than they do. But as he must return to his own country, he should not render himself unfit for it. Let him then go and visit the German courts, where he can acquire French and polite manners, and at the same time be with people who live

much in the same style that he must do at home. He may thus
learn to support his character with dignity, and upon his paternal
estate may have the felicity of a prince.[4] Let him make a tour into
the delicious countries of the south, to enrich his mind with a variety of brilliant ideas, and to give his manners a still finer polish.
But let him not stay there too long. Let him not remain in the Italian sun till his Caledonian iron is melted.

At night we had *grande cour.* A lady asked me for the Marquis
of Annandale, whom she had seen at The Hague. I told her with
concern his melancholy fate.[5]

FRIDAY 28 SEPTEMBER. Again we went a-hunting. We went
to another part of the forest from that where we were last day. We
were obliged to wait a long time till the stag was found. I went into
a farm-house, where I learnt a piece of German housewifery. The
country people here have in their gardens a great many plums of
the bluish-red kind which we call burnets at Auchinleck. They
skin them and take out their stones and then throw them into a
great cauldron with a certain quantity of water. They put them
over a brisk fire of wood, and keep stirring them till they are sufficiently boiled. They mix no sugar with them, as their juice makes
them sweet enough, and being well boiled they can be kept a great
while. They throw this rustic jelly into a large tub. They call it
Floum Moose.[6] When butter is dear, they spread it very thick on
their brown bread, and a very good relish it makes. I took a hearty
bit of it, for which, bread and all, I paid a groschen.

At last the stag was put up, and a glorious chase we had, much

[4] This remained with Boswell a conviction and a program. An amusing passage in his journal sixteen years later shows him scolding his wife for oppos-
ing him when he tried to inculcate the same attitude in his heir Sandy, then
five years old. "She said . . . that our [the Boswells'] pride and high estima-
tion of ourselves as if German princes (my phrase) was ridiculous in the
eyes of other people, who looked upon us not only as no better than any other
gentleman's family, but as a stiff and inhospitable family" (6 January 1780).
[5] He was insane, and had been so since 1744. David Hume, when a young
man, served a year as his companion.
[6] *Pflaumenmus,* plum sauce.

better than the first. I acquired venatic courage, took made roads no more, but rushed boldly along with the Herr Overstalmeester, as they called my friend Neitschütz. The stag did not get to the river. But when run down, he couched three several times, and three several times took another race, and stood at last at bay. Of all this we had a full view. At last he sunk, the dogs laid hold of him, and the *coup de grâce* laid him dead on the field. Poor animal! the agitation of sport prevented us from pitying him so much as we ought. All the ceremonies which I mentioned last day were again performed, and then we returned in triumph. A great parcel of us dined *chez* Prince Diederic, who made a respectable figure at his own table with his white locks. He was a plain, warm-hearted old man. A servant of Princess Wilhelmine's came to invite us to dinner next day. "Bid him *in com*," said the Prince; and when the fellow entered, "Ah, myn lieber Jan!" said his Highness, and asked him kindly questions. Jan kissed the Prince's garment, as is the custom in Germany, and was ordered a glass of wine.

In the evening at Court, a Brandenburg gentleman made a bank of faro. The Prince Jean George, the Princesse Marie, and I played. I lost six écus. I am always unlucky at play, and always keen. The Brandenburger, who was a canon of Halberstadt, bid me be upon my guard against play. "For," said he, "there are many people in Germany, even princes, who live by gaming; and they can play a thousand tricks." "Ah," said I, "how is that?"[7] — and a little after, "There was a Jew at The Hague who showed me some very fine tricks." Said he, "So, my good Sir, you already know what you have just asked me." "No, Sir," said I; "I didn't know it was possible to play such tricks at faro." I did not well know how to take this speech of his. It looked as if he suspected me to be an adventurer. However, I took no notice of it, for I did indeed deserve it with my thoughtlessness. The canon was thoughtless from conceit, although a real clever young fellow. I told him, "I said to this Jew, 'Sir, your tricks are excellent. You can deceive everybody. I don't dare learn them.' " The canon, eager to get to the other side of the

---

[7] " 'How is that?' " is an editorial conjecture to complete the sense. Boswell inserted a caret after "I," but did not supply the missing words.

room, yet willing to say a polite thing, replied, "Sir, you are right." Which was as much as saying, "You are right to fear that you would learn to cheat." By the by, the faro and all this story happened last night.[8]

SATURDAY 29 SEPTEMBER. We assembled in the palace of the late Prince Maurice, which now belongs to the Princesse Wilhelmine. She gave there this day a splendid entertainment to Prince Charles of Saxony, Duke of Courland, of which last dignity the Russian tyrant has deprived him.[9] I was presented to him, and found him a charming prince, perfectly gay and affable. I admired much a Saxon general who was with him, a Piémontais, a genteel man about forty, with the most perfect ease of manners that I ever saw, quite master of himself. He had that *esprit* which is excellent in conversation, talked of *l'homme machine*, and *un corps bien organisé.*[10] He had a most agreeable laugh at command. I, who am a good player myself, could perceive it was made; but it was so nicely managed that one in a hundred could not see the finesse. I was presented to Prince Eugene, another uncle of the Reigning Prince. His name made me think of Sir Roger de Coverley.[1] He was a Saxon general, and a most curious figure, quite a countenance of the last age, venerable and yet queer. Had he been hung up on the side of the room, you would have sworn it was a portrait by a master long since dead.

We had a magnificent dinner. The *noblesse* of Dessau was assembled. We were in all forty-seven. Music played in the next

[8] In the memorandum for 29 September is preserved the following reminder: "Say today, 'Sir, you have suspected one of the best men in the world. But I cannot blame you.' " For the sequel to this episode see p. 131.

[9] Prince Karl (1733–1796), son of the late Elector of Saxony (who was also King of Poland), was formally declared Duke of Courland in 1758, but in 1763 had been forcibly deprived of lands and title by Catherine the Great.

[10] Probably referring to works by two French philosophers who had been patronized by Frederick: *L'Homme machine* (1747) by La Mettrie and *Essai sur la formation des corps organisés* (1751 and 1754) by Maupertuis.

[1] Because in January, 1712 Addison brought Sir Roger to London for a glimpse of another Eugene, François Eugène de Savoy, the great general of the Austrian forces whose deeds were so closely associated with Marlborough's. See *The Spectator,* No. 269.

room, and by what strange chance I cannot tell, they played among other tunes the Scots country dance, "The Campbells is coming, Oho! Oho!" This caused in my mind a most curious mixture of German and Caledonian ideas. I was very healthy and very happy. I had just the same sensations as when a boy at Culross and Valley-field.[2] I find it is no impossible matter to be just what one has formerly been. It is no more than having the mind filled with the same ideas. After dinner we had coffee, and chatted an hour or so. Coffee and tea I never drink since I heard the Marquis Cavalcabo display their sad effects.[3] In the evening we had a splendid ball. The Duke of Courland danced the best of any man I ever saw. I danced with all the three princesses. We had a cold collation, with wine carried about. In short it was a complete thing.

In the great hall where we dined and danced was a most singular piece of antiquity. Leopold, Prince of Anhalt-Dessau, grandfather to the present Prince, was a great warrior.[4] He commanded ten thousand Prussians in the Allied Army under the Duke of Marlborough in the War of the Succession. The sieges and battles which he was at are marked upon the windows. Not on the glass, I hope. No, on the good hard boards. When he came home from the war, he assembled his brave grenadiers, and has a complete company of them painted from the life, with their names under each picture. They are drawn with long blue cloaks, which was formerly the Prussian uniform, and with their arms and accoutrements. I was much pleased with this idea. It has a most singular effect.

SUNDAY 30 SEPTEMBER. After the gay fatigues of the ball I got up at six, took post-horses, and rode four German miles to Wittenberg in Saxony. I found it an old town sadly ruined by the late war. I saw the convent where Luther lived, and I went to the old church in which he first preached the Reformation. It has been miserably shattered by the bombardments. But the tomb of Luther

[2] The scenes of his mother's youth.

[3] There is no reference to this in the journal, unless it is implied in Cavalcabo's brief mention of diet, above, p. 69.

[4] For this wonderful old man, "der Alte Dessauer," see Carlyle's *Frederick*, *passim*. He invented the iron ramrod and perfected the Prussian system of military drill.

is still entire, as is that of Melanchthon, just opposite to it. They are nothing more than two large plates of metal fixed on the floor. They have inscriptions in raised letters.

LUTHER'S:

Martini Luteri S. Theologiae D. Corpus H.L.S.E.
Qui An. Christi MDXLVI. XII. Cal. Martii Eyslebii in Patria S.
M.O.C.V. Ann. LXIII. M.II. D.X.

MELANCHTHON'S:

Philippi Melanchthonis S.V. Corpus H.L.S.E.
Qui An. Christi MDLX. XIII. Cal. Maii in Hac Urbe
M.O.C.V. Ann. LXIII. M.II. D.II.[5]

I was in a true solemn humour, and a most curious and agreeable idea presented itself, which was to write to Mr. Samuel Johnson from the tomb of Melanchthon. The woman who showed the church was a good obliging body, and very readily furnished me with pen and ink. That my paper might literally rest upon the monument, or rather the simple epitaph, of this great and good man, I laid myself down and wrote in that posture. The good woman and some more simple beings gathered round and beheld me with wonder. I dare say they supposed me a little mad. Tombs have been always the favourite resort of gloomy, distracted mortals. I said nothing of hot-headed Luther. I only mentioned the mild Melanchthon, and that at his tomb I vowed to Mr. Johnson an eternal attachment. This letter must surely give him satisfaction. I shall not send it till I see if he gives me a favourable answer to my two last letters. It is really an excellent thought. The letter shall be a valuable remain.

I got a Saxon drummer to walk with me about the town,

[5] "In this place lies the body of Martin Luther, Doctor of Sacred Theology, who died at Eisleben, his birth-place, on 18 February 1546, at the age of sixty-three years, two months, and ten days." (It should be "sixty-two years, three months," but Boswell copied correctly.) "In this place lies the body of Philip Melanchthon, a man of holy life, who died in this city on 19 April 1560, at the age of sixty-three years, two months, and two days." (M.O.C.V., an unusual abbreviation, stands for "mortem obiit cum vixisset.")

called him "Myn lieber Trummel," and took him to my inn and made him sit down with me, and he and I eat bread and cheese, and drank brandewine.[6] What a transition! I am mighty whimsical and even low sometimes. I have had enough of this. Let it be no more.

I returned at night to Dessau, as if it had been my home, dressed, supped at Court, and took leave of the princes and princesses. The eldest princess is a comely, black, amiable young lady. The other two are very well. The Prince Jean George is very handsome and very affable. The Prince Albert is a good-looking, blunt, bold little fellow. The table here was plain but good. The removes were made by degrees, without obliging us to rise. Half a bottle of Rhenish was placed between two people. You might call for as much more as you pleased. We were served by footmen, which is much better than pages. A hussar and a Pole drew my notice. I shall not forget the luscious venison with currant jelly. The Castle is guarded by a few old soldiers. This court is much like the residence of an old British baron.

[Boswell to Samuel Johnson][7]

[Wittenberg] Sunday 30 September 1764

MY EVER DEAR AND MUCH RESPECTED SIR: — You know my solemn enthusiasm of mind. You love me for it, and I respect myself for it, because in so far I resemble Mr. Johnson. You will be agreeably surprised when you learn the reason of my writing this letter. I am at Wittenberg in Saxony. I am in the old church where the Reformation was first preached and where some of the Reformers lie interred. I cannot resist the serious pleasure of writing to Mr. Johnson from the tomb of Melanchthon. My paper rests upon the gravestone of that great and good man, who was undoubtedly the

[6] Brandy. "Dinner and brandy for me and drummer, fourteen groschen" (Expense Account, 29 September).

[7] Boswell decided that this letter was "at once too superstitious and too enthusiastic," and did not send it to Johnson until June, 1777. He printed it in *The Life of Johnson,* from which it is here reprinted.

worthiest of all the Reformers. He wished to reform abuses which had been introduced into the Church, but had no private resentment to gratify. So mild was he that when his aged mother consulted him with anxiety on the perplexing disputes of the times, he advised her to keep to the old religion. At this tomb, then, my ever dear and respected friend, I vow to thee an eternal attachment. It shall be my study to do what I can to render your life happy, and if you die before me, I shall endeavour to do honour to your memory and, elevated by the remembrance of you, persist in noble piety. May God, the Father of all beings, ever bless you! And may you continue to love your most affectionate friend and devoted servant,

JAMES BOSWELL.

MONDAY 1 OCTOBER. Monsieur de Guericke, who educated the Reigning Prince, sent me his *album amicorum*, which was very splendid. I wrote thus in it:

Never has a foreigner relished his travels more than I. I travel as a philosopher. I am not so rude as Diogenes, but I am, like him, in search of men: beings worthy to uphold the dignity of human nature. Among such beings I make bold to name Monsieur de Guericke. Remember, Sir, a good Scots gentleman who has the honour to be, with the highest regard, your most humble and most obedient servant,

BOSWELL OF AUCHINLECK.

For Prince Diederic and for the Princess Wilhelmine, I wrote the following card: "Baron Boswell, to take leave, and to return his most humble thanks for all the courtesies with which he has been honoured by His [Her] Most Serene Highness." (I think proper to take the title of Baron in Germany, as I have just the same right to it as the good gentry whom I see around me.) Is not this card in the true style? I am made for travelling. The Prince was at the hunting. The Princess received me, and I appeared in my travelling-dress, quite at my ease. I then went to Guericke's, who thanked me for what I had written, but told me, "I shall show you what the Prince of Courland has written, and although you write well, Sir, I believe you will own that his Highness writes still better." My curiosity was excited, and I prepared myself to admire a specimen of this Prince's fine genius. But what did I find? Nothing but a commonplace French sentiment taken from one of their poets, with a commonplace assurance of sincerity, &c. "Look," said my good Guericke, "is not that fine?" In short I found that it was the fine hand which he admired, and that a writing-master would make the best figure in his *album amicorum*.

He showed me some pretty good pictures which he has got, and some excellent portraits by the painter to the Court, Liszewski. His father was a painter at Berlin. The son does remarkably well both large portraits and miniatures. Guericke is a sensible, dry, cordial man. He said to me, "Stay longer with us. Believe me, you are greatly liked here." Let me give this testimony to Dessau: I have passed here a full week, during which time I have not had half a day of hypochondria in all. Let this then be ever a sure consolation for me; for after all my dire gloom at Utrecht I have had much clear joy.

The Princes of Dessau have been remarkable for a numerous progeny of natural children. Each of them has a pension of six hundred dollars (£100) and they are educated as gentlemen.[8] The amiable De Berenhorst is one. He is uncle to the Reigning Prince. I shall correspond with him and Neitschütz. At every court where I go, I shall establish a correspondence.

I began this day a most curious scheme. I would not wish to make my friend Johnston pay postage for frequent letters while I am abroad, yet to write to him often is agreeable and keeps alive friendship. I shall therefore, at every court and city where I reside any time, write him a letter. These letters I shall direct and seal, so that I shall have as little to do with them as if they were really sent off. I shall number them and put them up in a bundle; and when I

[8] "... Was quite renewed in old laird and family ideas. Prince gives six hundred dollars to each natural child. Some of them genteel. Do you the same ... " (Memorandum, 28 September). At this rate a dollar or crown equals 3s. 4d., which is probably a more precise evaluation than the round figure 3s. which he gave in the entry for 22 July.

return to Britain, he and I shall open them and read them at
leisure; and a luxurious entertainment it will be.[9]

I had this morning the coachman, groom, and footman of the
Court with me. I gave each of 'em drink-money, and they were
humble and thankful.[1] I have been here like a very prince. While I
drove by in my coach, the people bowed to the earth.

My plan was originally to be at Geneva the end of November,
and get to Rome at Christmas, so as to see the splendid Christmas
Eve in St. Peter's Church. But I find that if I follow this plan, I
shall not be able to see the half of the German courts that I intended, and be hurried to get through Switzerland, so that I should
be in constant anxiety, and lose seeing many fine courts and passing many hours with Voltaire and Rousseau, which would be
losing many real advantages of which I may think with pleasure
all my life — merely for the solemn satisfaction of a single evening, which, too, would in all probability not come up to my expectations. I therefore at once gave up this scheme, and my mind
was at ease. I shall go on leisurely and enjoy fully my tour.

At two I mounted the post-wagon for Halle. It was sad weather.
I had for companion a Felt Preher (chaplain) to a Prussian regiment. He and I conversed in Latin and German. He was a clumsy
dog, but understood something of language. This day I resumed
my whim of writing ten lines a day.[2]

[9] This entire series, numbered by Boswell from 1 to 51, has survived. Some
extracts from the fourteen written in Germany and Switzerland are included
in the present volume, beginning with 20 October 1764.

[1] The coachman three crowns, the footman and groom two each, the "fille"
and "garçon" one each. He also records payments of one crown six groschen
for laundry, and thirteen groschen for having his stockings and linen mended
(Expense Account).

[2] An exercise in self-improvement begun by Boswell at Utrecht, and occasionally resumed at least as late as 1780. The present series extends without
a break from 1 October to 22 November 1764. Boswell's object was to write
ten lines of heroic verse as rapidly as possible on the first topic that came into
his head. Though, as Mr. Leonard Bacon has said, they are comically bad as
poetry, they occasionally contain interesting biographical information. A
few are included in the present volume, beginning with 3 October 1764. —
On this day also (though he does not mention it) he wrote to Belle de Zuylen

TUESDAY 2 OCTOBER. This morning at three I arrived at Halle, very jaded. I went to an inn and was put into a cold room. At seven I rose, having dozed a little. I was sadly hipped. All seemed dismal. But reason remained and assured me that in an hour or two I should be well. I took exercise in my chamber and grew more healthy. At ten I called on Monsieur Kircheisen, student here, eldest son to my good landlord at Berlin. He seemed a good, homely fellow. But the male part of this family is nothing like the female. The male seem formed of a much coarser clay. The President indeed makes up for this by his rough warmth.

I saw Halle with some curiosity, because Lord Elliock[3] studied here. It is a very old town. I saw the salt-works, which are very simple. There is here a salt-spring from which they draw water from a prodigious depth. They boil it, till the saline particles are left at the bottom. They then take out the salt and form it into large loaves, which they dry and harden in a room well heated by stoves. It is then fit for being transported. This manufactory yields the King of Prussia a great deal of money. I should have thought boiling and baking the salt very unwholesome, but it is not so. An old fellow told me here that he had wrought at it I think fifty years. I saw also the Orphan-House, which is immensely large; as also the College Library, which is numerous. I saw Halle students here. I was glad I was not one of them. At night I was alone. Pen and ink ever amuse me.

[Boswell to Caroline Kircheisen. Original in French]

Halle in Saxony, 2 October 1764

IT WAS NOT BECAUSE I WAS PROUD that I failed to write to you from Potsdam to return you many thanks for your dear little letter. Believe me, it was rather out of a kind of prudence. I wished to wait until I could at the same time give you some news of myself, and thus (to use a ludicrous Scots saying) kill two dogs with one

complaining that his letter written at Berlin had not been answered. See *Boswell in Holland.*

[3] James Veitch, one of his father's colleagues on the bench.

stone. I have passed a week at Dessau very agreeably. Tell me if I am not a true philosopher? a solid man? a man who is master of himself? I am about to give you proof of it. After having tasted all the delights that an amiable stranger can taste at an amiable court, was I enfeebled? No. Not at all. I seated myself with perfect tranquillity on the post-wagon, and in spite of the rain, the wind, and the darkness of a wretched night, I made my way in excellent humour to Halle, where I am at present.

Do you know that on the road I composed some French verses? You can well imagine what kind of French verses a man would make if the year before he did not have enough of the language to ask for meat or drink. I shall write them down for you nevertheless. When has a man ever shown such boldness?

VERSES WRITTEN ON A POST-WAGON,
ADDRESSED TO MADEMOISELLE KIRCHEISEN

Autrefois j'étais poète,
  Et je faisais tous les jours
Des chansons sur une brunette,
  Qui m'inspirait de l'amour.

La brunette était galante,
  Elle avait un tendre cœur;
Et (comme Cavalcabo se vante)
  Elle m'aimait à la fureur.

Ces jours sont passés comme une ombre;
  Adieu l'amour! adieu ma lyre!
Je ne suis que froid et sombre,
  Je n'ai plus mes beaux désirs.

Ah! ma jolie Caroline,
  Qui me charma tant de soirs!
Par vos yeux doux je devine
  Que vous ne voulez pas me croire.[4]

I am always your, &c.

[4] "Formerly I was a poet, and every day I made songs about a dark lady who

WEDNESDAY 3 OCTOBER. I set out at nine, and had a disagreeable journey through bad roads to Leipzig, where I arrived at night. I found high houses as in Edinburgh, and had some of my old ideas, when I saw families living on others' tops. Wappler's, the inn to which I was directed, had no room for me, so I was at a loss. They procured me, however, quarters in a private house, Gabriel's, barber in Peter Straas. As it was Fair time, the town was full.[5] I was obliged to pay a ducat a day for lodging for myself and servant. The people were very civil and of the better sort. I had a damp alcove to sleep in, but a very handsome chamber. So I caused Jacob spread my bed on the floor of the chamber, and thus I lay with my clothes on, a good coverlet above me, and my head reposed on a pillow laid on one of my trunks. This operation however was performed after the good folks of the house were abed, for I would not shock them by letting them know that I could not bear their dormitory. This is in some degree benevolence.

WEDNESDAY 3 OCTOBER

Of all mankind beneath the northern sky,
Without dispute the happiest am I:
Of an old fam'ly in the Shire of Ayr
My fate has made me the apparent heir.

---

inspired me with love. The dark lady was amorous; her heart was tender; and (as Cavalcabo boasts) she was madly in love with me. Those days are gone like a shadow; farewell love! farewell my lyre! I am now but cold and sombre, I no longer feel those fine longings. Ah, pretty Caroline, who charmed me so many evenings! From your calm gaze I guess that you are unwilling to believe me." In a copy of this poem in the Bodleian Library, Boswell has added a note to explain the reference to Cavalcabo: "An Italian marquis, who employed this expression in speaking of a lady." Boswell was no doubt trying to impress Caroline (who was only seventeen) with this glimpse into his burnt-out heart, but the amorous dark lady was not a fiction. See pp. 212 *n.* 3, 234.

[5] Leipzig, a city in the Electorate of Saxony situated at the intersection of several trade-routes, had attained great commercial importance by the fifteenth century. The fairs were held at New Year's, Easter, and Michaelmas (end of September, early October); they lasted fifteen days.

Health, youth, and gold sufficient I possess;
Where one has more, five hundred sure have less.
Yet if I all my qualities must name,
Dire Hypochondria mixes with my frame.
Ah, my poor mortals, are you formed so
That none amongst you is exempt from woe?

THURSDAY 4 OCTOBER. Lying on the floor did me much good. I sprung up cheerful. Experience shall ever be my great guide. I find that to sleep on a very hard bed prevents my nervous system from being totally unstrung, and so prevents me from being clouded, except when I have eat too much and so caused obstructions. My room was hung with tapestry, adorned with battles well painted. I went and saw the Fair, where there is a concourse of all nations, even of Turks. Such a scene gives me an agreeable agitation of ideas. I was pleased to see the Saxon troops all genteel fellows, very neat and clean, though their livery is white and they are clothed only once in three years. They have every year a frock. I then found my worthy Neitschütz, who was here to sell some of the Prince's horses, and O'Grady, who was here to sell some of his own. It seems he had freighted a ship from Ireland. He talked German with great facility, swore in it, and abused the Germans for not being able to know good cattle when they saw them. "There now," said he, "they are all fond of that ugly animal because he goes with a spring, and that is because he is weak. A right strong nag moves firm and easy." We dined together with some more Germans in a house on the Horse-Market, where we were mighty well.

I then went and called on the Professor Gottsched, one of the most distinguished *literati* in this country. It was he who set a-going the true cultivation of the German language, of which he has given an excellent grammar. He has also written several pieces, both in verse and prose.[6] I found him a big, stately, comely

[6] Boswell's account of German authors seems woefully scant until one considers chronology. In 1764 Goethe was fifteen, Schiller only five. Herder was twenty, but had published nothing of importance. Klopstock (forty years old) was at Copenhagen. The one German writer now considered first-rate

man, with an ease of manners like a man of the world. Although I
had no recommendation, he received me with a perfect politeness.
We talked of Scotland, of its language and the difference between
it and English. I mentioned to him my plan of a Scots dictionary,
and promised to show him a specimen of it. He said the Preface to
Johnson's *Dictionary* was one of the best pieces he had ever read.
Said he, "He knows his subject to the bottom." He advised me to
wait upon Mr. Bel, Professor of Poetry. I did so, and found him a
lively Hungarian, with a degree of French manners. He had a very
good library. I should have mentioned that Gottsched and I were
quite easy together in a few minutes, and I was at once among his
books. Both he and Bel promised to be of what service they could to
me during my stay here.

FRIDAY 5 OCTOBER. At ten I went with Bel and saw the University Library.[7] It is in a great old room which was formerly the
Cloister Sancti Paulini. At the Reformation it was seized. One old
monk of a venerable character would not come out. He said he had
lived there all his life, and they must just allow him to die in peace
in his convent. His request was granted, and he was nourished
there till the day of his death. His effigy is preserved in the Library.
There is here a very numerous collection of books arranged according to their subjects. There is also a number of portraits of learned
men. Every professor is obliged to give his portrait to the Library.
I was in a true classical humour, quite *doctus*. I resolved to add to
the number of books. I resolved to have a noble library at Auchinleck. I saw here a volume of original manuscript letters of famous
learned men in Germany. I saw Luther's Bible, in which the verse
of St. James which says that the three which bear record in heaven
are *one*, is not to be found.[8] Bel sent my name to Gellert, a professor

whom Boswell might have met was Lessing, but he was at Breslau, far off
the line of Boswell's route. Failing him, Gottsched and Gellert (whom he
met next day) were really about as big game as the country afforded.
[7] Besides being Professor of Poetry, Bel was Librarian of the University.
[8] Not St. James, but I John 5. 7, the famous *Comma Johanninum*. It is now
generally regarded as an interpolation, and is omitted in the Revised Version.

here, who appointed me to come to him at three. I dined with
Neitschütz, O'Grady, &c., and merry were we all. I am every day
more strong, and less liable to be put out of order by little circumstances. I have seen the time when a dinner would have overturned
me quite. Now I defy it.

At three I went to Gellert. They call him the Gay of Germany.
He has written fables and little dramatic pieces. I found him to be
a poor, sickly creature. He said he had been twenty years hypochondriac. He said that during a part of his life, every night he
thought to die, and every morning he wrote a fable. He said, "My
poetry is at an end. I no longer have the power of mind." He spoke
bad Latin and worse French, so I did my best with him in German.
I found him a poor mind, with hardly any science. His conversation was like that of an old lady. You saw nothing of the ruins of a
man — ruins have always something which mark the original
building. He has just had a tolerable fancy and a knack of versify-
ing, which has pleased the German ladies and got him a mushroom
reputation. Poor man, he was very lean and very feeble, but
seemed a good creature. I did not form my judgment of him till I
had seen him several times, which I did during my stay at Leipzig.
I shall not mark them in this my journal. He translated to me in
Latin one of his fables, and I promised to learn German so as to
read him well. Yet alas! how unpersevering am I! Where is my
Greek? Where is my translation of Scots law?[9] Well, all will come
about yet.

I passed the evening at Bel's. He was till his sixteenth year in
Hungary, where his father was Lutheran minister. He read me his
Preface to the *Acta eruditorum* for this year, which he was just
sending to the press.[1] The Court of Saxony grants him the privilege

[9] This was another ambitious scheme conceived during the previous spring
at Utrecht. He was to translate into Latin John Erskine's *Principles of the
Law of Scotland*, and his professor of Civil Law, Christian Heinrich Trotz,
was to supply notes. He gave it up after several days' hard labour. See the
Index of *Boswell in Holland*, section III. a. 9 of the article Boswell, James.
[1] "There is a monthly work published here, being a sort of *Journal des
savants*, or memoirs of literature, containing an account of all remarkable

of being director of this work, the property of which belongs to the widow of a bookseller whose family began and carried it on. Bel employs what assistants he pleases, but is despotic prince to insert or cut out as to him seemeth good. It yields him only about £50 a year. I am very fond of Leipzig. The professors here are easy men of the world. I said I regretted that I had not studied here myself, but I would go home and marry and send a son. "Give me your hand on that," said Bel. I gave it him that I would send my son to his care. Let me remember this.[2] I supped with him in an easy way with his family. Is not this being treated with much civility? If I ever laugh at Germans, I am a villain.

SATURDAY 6 OCTOBER. My old friend at Utrecht, the Baron van Qualen, was now studying at Leipzig. I waited upon him this morning, drank chocolate and talked over our winter's parties. We then went and saw some gardens here, which I liked much. One of them is noble and extensive. It has the Dutch taste improved. There are in it four large stone statues of excellent workmanship; indeed the best of the kind that I ever saw. One finds here and there choice pieces which are hardly known. Honest Qualen insisted that I should dine with him. A very good dinner he gave me. We had with us Herr Rogler, M.A., who has made a surprising progress in the English language. He has given a dictionary, German and English, which is properly a translation of the *Dictionary* of Mr. Samuel Johnson, as he says in his title-page. But from the unlucky inclination to be voluminous, which is so remarkable in Germans, he has *enriched* it forsooth with three thousand words taken from *others*, so that he has amassed all the rubbish which Mr. Johnson has with so much judicious care kept out of his book. *O quale caput!*[3] I gave him it pretty plainly. He was however very obliging,

---

pieces in all branches of learning, and entitled *Acta eruditorum Lipsiae*, which shows that music, anatomy, natural philosophy, and the mathematics are very much cultivated in this city" (Thomas Nugent, *The Grand Tour*, 2d ed., 1756, ii. 226).

[2] Boswell's son and heir Alexander did spend some time at Leipzig in the winter of 1795–1796, but was not formally enrolled in the University.

[3] "What judgment!" Boswell misread Rogler's title-page, which describes the

was charmed to hear a specimen of my Scots Dictionary, and mentioned to me a correspondence which may be of great service to me,
to wit that of Monsieur Riisbrigh, a learned Dane and remarkable
for his talents in etymology, and the famous Pontoppidan, Bishop
of Bergen, of whose son Riisbrigh was tutor. He said I might freely
write to both, and might be sure of a good answer from each. I shall
not neglect such opportunities. It has been my wish since I first
thought of my Dictionary to establish correspondences in the
northern parts of Europe. I am very lucky hitherto.

After dinner Qualen and I went with Gottsched and saw the
Magistrates' Library. There is a very noble room, and the great
collection of books is well arranged. I saw here Anderson's
Diplomata Scotiae. My old spirit got up, and I read them some
choice passages of the Barons' letter to the Pope.[4] They were struck
with the noble sentiments of liberty of the old Scots, and they expressed their regret at the shameful Union. I felt true patriot sorrow. O infamous rascals, who sold the honour of your country to a
nation against which our ancestors supported themselves with so
much glory! But I say no more, only Alas, poor Scotland![5]

I then went to a sale of the effects of the Comte de Brühl, which
was truly a curious sight. There were upwards of seven hundred

---

work as a third edition, revised, of Christian Ludwig's *Dictionary* (first published in 1706), "augmented with more than twelve thousand words taken
out of Samuel Johnson's English *Dictionary*, and others."

[4] Dated from Arbroath, 6 April 1320. The Pope (John XXII) supported
Edward II of England in his campaigns to crush Scottish independence, and
had sent bulls commanding Bruce to consent to an unfavourable truce. When
Bruce refused to submit, the Pope excommunicated him and his adherents
for contumacy. The letter of the "Barons" (really of the Parliament of
Scotland) asserted the independence of Scotland in the most spirited manner.
Four years later Boswell chose a ringing sentence from this letter to serve
as motto for his *Account of Corsica*. In English it would run something as
follows: "We do not fight for glory, wealth, or honours, but solely for that
liberty which no virtuous man will survive."

[5] An exclamation attributed to the Young Pretender while he was a fugitive
in the Hebrides. See Boswell's *Journal of a Tour of the Hebrides*, ed. Pottle
and Bennett, 1936, p. 131, where Boswell records it in the form "O God! poor
Scotland!"

snuff-boxes in gold, and many of them very rich with diamonds. There were many fine fire-arms, and a variety of other things of value. The room seemed like the shop of three or four rich Jews. These are pretty remains of a minister of state. His sovereign paid for all this magnificent trumpery.[6]

I then went to Mr. Gottsched, with whom I had left a specimen of my Scots Dictionary. He was much pleased with it, and advised me by all means to go on with it, as it would not only be a most agreeable present to my countrymen, but would give much pleasure to the curious etymologists of every nation; and therefore he advised me to add to each word its signification in Latin. This I shall do, as I did in the specimen. Mr. Gottsched allowed me to search his etymological library and take thence a list of such books as may assist me in compiling my Dictionary. He also promised to correspond with me.

At eight I had Bel with me, and gave him bread and butter and cheese and fruit and wine. I called it *cena Pythagorica;* but I found that our good Professor would have chosen to be of a sect that lived a little better. We were, however, very merry, and renewed our literary covenant to send each other mutual accounts of the state of learning in our different countries. I would gladly know, O my enemies! if any young fellow in Britain would have done more at Leipzig.

SUNDAY 7 OCTOBER.[7] I breakfasted with honest Qualen, who was quite eager to show his regard for me. My worthy father used now and then to upbraid me that I had no friends. I must take the

---

[6] Heinrich Count of Brühl was instrumental in placing the Elector of Saxony on the throne of Poland as Augustus III. As a reward he was appointed Prime Minister, a position which enabled him to assume the powers of dictator. He was personally responsible for the policy which entangled Saxony in the alliance against Frederick, and led to its ruin in the Seven Years' War. His personal extravagance (for which see Carlyle's *Frederick*) was fabulous: he kept twelve tailors continually employed and wore a new suit every day. He died on 28 October 1763.

[7] " ... Swear solemn with drawn sword not to be with woman *sine* condom *nisi* Swiss lass" (Memorandum, 7 October).

liberty to think otherwise upon the evidence of facts. My father's friends have been ever ready to oblige him. I have surely more people who would be ready to oblige me. The difference is that my father formed his friendships very slowly, whereas I have formed mine quickly. Can I help it if I find mankind take an affection for me at once? Besides, my father's friends are only rational connections. He has no friends for whom he feels that enthusiasm of affection which I feel for Temple or for Johnston.

At one I mounted the wagon for Dresden. It was charming weather. For several miles there fell around us white flakes as of fine thread. My foolish companions told me that they fell from the *Sterne* (the stars). I dismounted and picked up a little of the stuff, which I found to be a sort of field-spider's webs which the wind had carried from the bushes into the air, and was now falling down again. I know not if we have such webs in Britain.

Let me here mark an anecdote which occurs. After I became acquainted with the chanoine at Dessau, who had taken me for an *aventurier*, I told him, "Sir, you made me a little angry the other evening." Yes, Sir?" said he. "If that was so, I very cordially ask your pardon." I explained the thing to him. He was sorry, and when we parted, he said to me, "I like you, Sir, and I hold you in esteem." So this rub was well smoothed.

MONDAY 8 OCTOBER. After sleeping all night in a thick mist on the post-wagon, I awaked much out of order. My blood was quite stagnated, and my teeth were loose.[8] I was alarmed. When we came to a *station*, I got down and danced with much vigour, which by degrees brought me to myself. I must really take care on these wagons. I now wrap myself up, head and all, in a great cloak. But even thus the cold gets at me. Besides, when so wrapped up, I am quite an Egyptian mummy and have no use of my arms, so that if the wagon were overturned, I should be quite helpless, and probably be bruised and broken. Let me then take care.

This day I had a pleasant drive between Meissen and Dresden. We went along the side of the Elbe. On each side of the river were

[8] Not to be taken literally: he was numb and his teeth chattered.

beautiful rising grounds covered with vines. Pray may we not have the same in Scotland? Surely our climate differs little from that of Saxony. I saw too, here and there, old castles, Heerschaften's houses, seats of gentlemen. It pleased me. It was Scottish. In Brandenburg I don't remember to have seen any, and I believe they are extremely scarce.

I got in good time to the beautiful city of Dresden, put up at the Hôtel de Pologne, an excellent house, dressed in scarlet and gold, and went immediately to call on Mr. Stanhope,[9] the British Envoy, for whom I had a letter from Mr. Burnett at Berlin. He was not at home. I returned to my inn, and went comfortably to bed. This was a degree of luxury to me, for I had not been undressed for ten days. I am really campaigning in Germany. I like it much.

TUESDAY 9 OCTOBER.[1] This morning I was in delicious spirits. I stood calm in my chamber, while the sun shone sweet upon me, and was *sure* that after gloom I may be *quite well.* This is a corporeal change. No matter. No philosophizing. Mr. Stanhope sent me his compliments, and said he'd carry me to Court at twelve. He came very politely, and took me in his coach. Scarcely had we gone two yards when he called out, "Stop!" and catching hold of me, said, "You can't go to Court." In short the Court of Saxony was in mourning, and I had not a black coat.[2] As I intended staying here only three or four days, Mr. Stanhope said it was not worth my while to make a suit of mourning. But he advised me never to be without a black coat, as so many accidents may happen.

I was set down at my inn, where I dined at the table d'hôte. It was in a large room, as in an old earl's castle. There was a very good dinner. The *légumes* and lesser dishes were put upon the table. The soup and the large dishes stood on a sideboard, and the waiters brought his portion to each of the company. A very clever

[9] Philip Stanhope, Lord Chesterfield's natural son, to whom the famous *Letters* were addressed.

[1] " ... Try for condoms.... At eight ... <ha>ve sweet lass ... " (Memorandum, 9 October).

[2] The Court was in mourning for the Elector Friedrich Christian, who had died nearly a year before.

method this. There was very good company, mostly officers: Swiss, Brabançons, and others who spoke good French. The only objection to this table is that after dinner one of the company generally makes a bank at faro, and this brings on a little gaming.

I strolled about and viewed the city. It is finely built of freestone. It gave me great pain to see the ruins made by the Prussian bombardments. I hated the barbarous hero. He was under no necessity to bombard Dresden. It was from mere spite that he did it.[3] I admired the new Catholic church, which is an elegant building, finely adorned with excellent statues. I admired the noble bridge over the Elbe. There is an excellent police here. Those who are going towards the Catholic church (for I know not the points of the compass) must walk upon one side of the bridge, and those who are going from the church, upon another. By this means there is no confusion amongst the passengers. If a blundering fellow takes the side of the bridge which he should not, the sentry drives him to his place.

I waited this evening on Monsieur Vattel, Privy Councillor of the Court, and author of the *Principes du Droit des gens*. I had a recommendation to him from Froment. I found him a mild, sensible, pretty man. He said he composed his book while Saxony was all in confusion, and he expected to lose all that he had. But he said composition preserved him in tranquillity. He presented me to Madame Vattel, a handsome young Polish lady. He said he was engaged to pass the evening *chez* Monsieur l'Envoyé de Danemark, who was his particular friend; so he begged I might accompany him and Madame Vattel. I did so. The Envoy, Count Schulenburg, was a mighty agreeable man. We had four or five more gentlemen

[3] The siege of Dresden, "one of the rapidest and most furious ... anywhere on record, [filling] Europe with astonishment, expectancy, admiration, horror" (Carlyle), occurred in July, 1760. Frederick was driven off by much superior Austrian force before he could reduce the defences. Boswell's comment reflects a view commonly held at the time, that Frederick could not really have hoped to take the city in the brief space of time he knew his enemies would allow him, and that consequently the bombardment was mere *Schrecklichkeit*.

there. We played at whist and chatted by turns. I was in the very best spirits. Sir James Macdonald could not have made a better figure.[4] I however complained to Vattel that I was ill educated, and had but little knowledge. He said, "Excuse me, Sir, you are well educated." The Envoy did not let this pass; he looked at me as one looks at one whom he admires, without well knowing for what. Vattel and I talked of learning in general, of the late war in Germany, of fate and free will, or more properly the origin of evil. He was for the chain of beings. I stood well against him.

We had this evening something curious. The Envoy begged pardon for not giving us a formal supper. We continued to sit as we pleased. The servants entered, and gave each of us a napkin. They then brought each a plate of soup. Then each a plate of ragout, and knife and fork. In short, we had a suite of six or seven dishes, with bread to each, a plate of genteel dessert, called for wine when we pleased, and drank also good punch. His Excellency just saved a table and table-cloth. For it was indeed an excellent supper. I was much pleased.

WEDNESDAY 10 OCTOBER.[5] I went and saw the grand gallery of pictures, which I was told is the noblest in Europe. The gallery is properly two rooms, one within the other. In the outside room is the Flemish and Dutch School, and in the inside room the Italian School. There are of both schools an infinite number of noble pieces. I was luxuriously entertained for two hours. I saw also a chamber full only of crayons. I dined at Mr. Stanhope's. He is natural son to the Earl of Chesterfield, but has received the education of a nobleman and been always considered by my Lord, his father, in the best light. He is little and young, but much of a gentleman.[6] He abused the King of Prussia. He talked lightly of the

[4] Sir James Macdonald of Sleat, a young man of twenty-two, had already acquired an international reputation for learning and elegance. Boswell had met him at Oxford in April, 1763. He died at Rome less than a year after the date of this entry.

[5] " . . . This day resolve to be independent and love fine women and profit of talents, yet store [mind with ideas]" (Memorandum, 10 October).

[6] Boswell must mean that his conduct was "young," for Stanhope was his elder by eight years.

Saxon Court, and said he tired sadly at Dresden. This was not quite the formed man. But I liked him the better. He showed me that being employed abroad was not so very mysterious a matter. His secretary (Mr. *Carroll*, though by no means a jolly dog) was an Irish officer of Marines. He was an obliging sort of man, but very formal. He was just Mr. Carron at Utrecht in regimentals.[7] After dinner came in Colonel Brown, an Irish officer in the Saxon service, a very sensible worthy gentleman. In the evening I must needs go and look at the Dresden street-walkers, and amuse myself as I used to do in London. Low, low.[8]

THURSDAY 11 OCTOBER. I went and saw the Elector's Library. It is put up in four different rooms, part of a superb building called the Zwinger. It is numerous, and has a good many manuscripts. But what can a man see of a library from being one day in it? I dined at my inn. At three I returned to the Zwinger and saw the noble museum. It made me think of honest James Bruce, with whom I have talked of it so often.[9] I must remark that at Dresden strangers pay monstrously dear for seeing the fine things, which is shameful when they are the property of a prince. My *valet de louage* told me that I must pay a ducat to the library-keeper and a florin to his man,[1] which I was fool enough to do, as I would be genteel, forsooth. It seems, too, I must pay at the museum a louis to the principal keeper, two écus to another, and a guilder to the servant. Instead of this I made two guilders do the business.[2] I know not how I divided it between the upper keeper and the servant. I forget, but no matter. The fellows looked strange and I saved six écus. The museum has indeed many great curiosities, but some of its richest pieces have been sold to repair the ruins of the war. I then walked

[7] Mr. Carron, whose mother was an Englishwoman, was clerk of the English-speaking church at Utrecht. Boswell had engaged him as teacher of French.
[8] " . . . Wrong, low, punish, but in Suisse have sweet girl. . . . Resume reins. Let Father force you to be a man" (Memorandum, 11 October). The expense account enters eight groschen for "petite aventure."
[9] James Bruce was at this time overseer at Auchinleck; he may, as personal servant, have accompanied Lord Auchinleck on his foreign travels.
[1] About twelve shillings in all.
[2] He made something less than five shillings do the work of twenty-five.

to the garden, where I saw some fine antiques in bronze. I went to the French *comédie*, which is very pretty here. I saw the Elector, Prince Xavier,[3] and several more of the Court. I was enlivened with new ideas.[4] Yet again I went with those easy street girls, and between their thighs — , merely for health. I would not embrace them. First, because it was dangerous. Next, because I could not think of being so united to miscreants. Both last night and this they picked my pocket of my handkerchief. I was angry at myself. I was obliged to own to my servant that I had been *avec des filles*. Man is sometimes low.[5]

FRIDAY 12 OCTOBER. Mr. Mackenzie, a relation of the Seaforth family, who has been a very long time abroad, waited upon me this morning. He was a genteel, pretty man, and spoke French like a Parisian. He found me a-dressing to go to Court; for, as I was curious to see it, I begged Mr. Stanhope to present me as a British officer. I accordingly put a cockade in my hat and tied a crape round my arm, and was presented at the Court of Saxony as "an officer in Loudoun's regiment." "Who? Laudon the Austrian?" "No. The English Lord Loudoun."[6] It was a great palace. The Court

[3] The Elector, Friedrich August III, was at this time a boy of fourteen. Prince Xavier, his uncle, was "Administrator" during his minority.

[4] Boswell himself at some time deleted what follows to the end of the entry by carefully covering all the words with the sort of scrolls that one uses in trying out a pen.

[5] " . . . Then had girl, merely *saluberrima lumbis*. Then *comédie*. Then girl. Pocket picked; obliged to own to servant. Swore never to be with girl till you see Rousseau. This day Court. Prepare journal. Never be cast down, but punish and go on. Support Utrecht character. Command self" (Memorandum, 12 October). *Saluberrima lumbis* means "most healthful to the loins." Boswell is adapting an old rhyming Latin tag which lauds the healthful effect of breaking wind while emptying the bladder (Mingere cum bumbis/ Saluberrimum est lumbis).

[6] An officer in uniform was considered to be in mourning if he merely put a piece of black crape around his sleeve. Boswell's expense account shows that this cheap substitute for a black coat cost him nine groschen. — John Campbell, fourth Earl of Loudoun, had formerly been Commander-in-Chief of the British forces in America; Baron Gideon Ernst von Laudon was a famous

went from room to room, I believe to visit different princes. I called
it *une chasse de princes*. Prince Xavier had something the look of
Dempster. The Elector was a sweet prince.[7] His governor, l'Abbé
Victor, was a very pretty man. This court lives at present very
sparingly. Three times a week a few strangers are asked to the
table. I was too short a while there to be asked. The Saxon officers
wear white cockades. It looks pretty. I hope there's no offence.[8] I
was diverted at the conceit of being an officer for a day.

I dined at Mr. Stanhope's. The Elector's Master of Horse was
there. He looked at my coat, and said, "Sir, that is not a uniform."
I replied, "No, Sir, not properly speaking. But in our country, if
you have a red coat, you are an officer; it is enough." Mackenzie
was there. He said the Danish Envoy told him, "You have a countryman here, Mr. Boswell. He has been well instructed." I smiled
in my own mind. Perhaps I was wrong. Perhaps I am really now
well instructed. Secretary Carroll had a particular phraseology.
He talked of Mr. Stanhope's servants. "They will do well, Sir.
Now, that heavy, *material* fellow there, he'll make an excellent
servant." I really love Stanhope. He and I were mighty well together. We agreed to renew our acquaintance in London.

I went to my inn, put on my travelling-dress, paid visits of
congé, and at seven mounted the post-wagon. I was vexed to find
that to return to Gotha I must take Leipzig in my way, and so just
return the way I came. I had for companion a little German clergyman who talked French by way of improving himself. Every
phrase that he made use of, he turned and turned in his mouth as a

---

field marshal of the Austrian Army. It has been maintained that the names
are ultimately the same, Marshal Laudon being descended from a Campbell
of the Loudoun family who settled in Livonia in the sixteenth century, but
the *Scots Peerage* is sceptical.

[7] He refused the crown of Poland in 1791, fought against Napoleon until
Jena, then became Napoleon's ally and assumed the title of King of Saxony.
He was taken prisoner after the Battle of Leipzig, 1813, and the Congress of
Vienna gave half his kingdom to Prussia.

[8] Either for impersonating a British officer or for approving of white cockades
(Jacobite emblems).

man would a piece of sugar-candy, seeming to say, "This I have well." Poor man, he was very angry with me for running to the stables and not eating and drinking, as all passengers are obliged to do. He said he might raise an action against me. I suppose *actio de non edere nec bibere.*[9]

SATURDAY 13 OCTOBER. Upon this jaunt I sleep immensely. When I came to Leipzig at night, I found the post for Gotha engaged. This was a sad scrape. However, I made the best of it, and engaged an extra. I supped on a dozen of larks. They are remarkably fine in this country, and prodigiously numerous. The excise, or rather the custom, upon larks at Leipzig comes to seventeen thousand écus a year, although the duty upon each is a mere trifle; I believe no more than a pfenning.

SUNDAY 14 OCTOBER. I thought it better to keep myself snug here, without being seen. At twelve I set out. I was somewhat melancholy in the Glasgow style. At night I was miserably cold.

MONDAY 15 OCTOBER. I was obliged to go on very slowly, as they sometimes made me wait five hours for horses to my machine.[1] I resolved never again to take an extra. I strolled about in a village in search of the ugliest woman I could find. I restrained myself. Such inclinations are caused by disease.

[Boswell to Baron de Pless. Original in French]

Rippach in Saxony, 15 October 1764
FORGIVE ME, DEAR BARON, for writing to you on a piece of paper that is almost brown in colour. Ever since I had the honour of meeting you, I have often thought of writing to you, and as often I have been interrupted. I have therefore come to see that when one is

[9] "An action for not eating or drinking." There is no such action at law, but if there were one, that would be its designation.
[1] And this in spite of the fact that he had bribed the postmaster for better service. The Expense Account for 14 and 15 October records payment of "Smear Gelt" at each of the stations on the way to Gotha: Leipzig, Rippach, Naumburg, Oberstadt, Buttelstedt, and Erfurt.

travelling, one is not master of one's time, one cannot shut one's self up in one's closet and write peacefully to one's friends. It is for that reason that I am now seizing a moment when I have to wait for horses. The postmaster has supplied me with the paper you see. I hope you will be able to read what I have written on it.

Believe me, Sir, I shall always remember with pleasure mixed with regret the days that I passed at Brunswick; and be assured, dear Baron, that you did much to make my visit there pleasant. From the first moment that I had the honour to speak with you, I found your character amiable; and the better I came to know you, the more I esteemed you. I shall never forget our walks in the garden of the Palace. I shall never forget the conversations we had on subjects sometimes serious, sometimes tender. It is in such conversations, Sir, that I find satisfaction with myself; that I find myself a being superior to coarse libertines.

Now, I have a favour to ask of you. I am in some sort a virtuoso. In all the countries where I travel, I wish to make a collection of the silver coins struck in the year that I was there. I forgot to do this at Brunswick, and I beg you to repair my neglect. Unless I am mistaken, your new coins are a florin, a half-florin, pieces of four, of two, and of one groschen. If there are still more, you will have the goodness to add them. Since I should like to have the pieces quite new, not scratched in the least, I beg you to procure them from the Mint, where you can get them in the condition I wish. I shall be at Kassel until the 28th of this month. I hope you will be able to send them before that time, and if they arrive two or three days too late, they can be sent to Mannheim, where I shall be till the 10th of November.

I ask a thousand pardons for having taken the liberty of giving you so much trouble. I shall take care to send you the value of the coins. One must be strict even in little things. Do not think of making me a present of them. I absolutely do not wish it. After saying so much, I shall be offended if you consider it for a moment. I need no remembrance from Monsieur de Pless, and if I wanted one, it would not be of silver. I am, &c.

[*c.* 15 October. Maxims in the Manner of La Rochefoucauld.
Original in French]²

1. It is not those whom we love the most that we make love to.
It is those who happen to be alone with us when our passion is
strongest.

2. The regret we feel on quitting our best friends is nothing
more than the indolence which makes us dislike leaving one place
for another.

3. We always become uneasy when we stay long in one place.
The bustling joy that fills us when we go to see our best friends is
nothing but the relief we feel at escaping from this uneasiness.

4. It is vain to preach patience as a virtue: a virtue it can never
be. When we see a wretch complaining, we should say, "There is a
man whose strength is badly proportioned to his sufferings"; and
when we see a wretch who does not complain, we should say,
"There is a man whose strength is well proportioned to his sufferings." Our more or less of strength is the gift of Nature.

TUESDAY 16 OCTOBER. I came to Erfurt, which is partly
Catholic. There are some convents here, but none very magnificent.
I heard afterwards that there is here a Scots convent. The block-
heads at my inn told me nothing of it.³ I saw the great clock called
the Grosse Susanne. I saw here some troops of their prince, the
Elector of Mainz. They had a singular piece of exercise. When an
officer passed by, the whole ranks pulled off their hats. It had a
very good effect. It was a charming day. I arrived in good time at
Gotha. I was pleased to see the pretty green hills around and the

² These are written on the same brown paper as the copy of the letter to De
Pless. Boswell had picked up a copy of La Rochefoucauld's *Maxims* at Halle
on 2 October (Expense Account).
³ The "convent" was St. Peter in Erfurt, a Benedictine monastery of very
ancient foundation. Boswell was understandably misled by the German term
Schottenkloster, which does not mean a monastery inhabited by Scots but
rather one founded by British missionaries in the days when *Scotus* meant
indiscriminately a native of Ireland or of what is now called Scotland.

Castle on a lofty eminence. I had a good inn. A light agreeable supper put me in pleasant humour. I read and wrote cheerfully.

WEDNESDAY 17 OCTOBER. Last night I had seen some of the
courtiers, and found them all in mourning.[4] This alarmed me. I
sent this morning to the Baron de Keller and Monsieur de Gotter,
for whom I had recommendations, but they were both out of town.
However, Madame de Gotter opened my letter, so that it was
known that I was a gentleman. I sent to the Baron de Thüngen,
Hof Maréchal, and said there was a circumstance which rendered
it absolutely necessary that I should pay my respects to him before
I durst cause myself to be announced at Court. He received me, and
I found him a sensible, polite man. I told him the circumstance,
which was the want of mourning. But he told me that it was now
almost over, and that I could be presented without it. We talked of
the Duke of Württemberg's excessive gallantries.[5] He said, "Sir, it
shows a lack of understanding not to be able to curb one's passions
at all. Restraining them is a matter of temperament. But surely
one can manage them with discretion." He desired to see me at
Court at one. I came accordingly, and was presented. The Duke
and Duchess were plain old people. The Duke talked of "ma sœur"

[4] Perhaps for Prince Ludwig Ernst, brother of the Duke, who died on 13
August 1763.
[5] Karl (II) Eugen, Duke of Württemberg, was at this time thirty-six years
old, having succeeded in 1737 at the age of nine. His court at Stuttgart was
one of the most brilliant in Europe, and he himself was handsome and gifted;
but he was also headstrong and vicious, and the splendour of his court was
purchased by expenditures which bore heavy on his people. His young
Duchess, the niece of Frederick the Great, had separated herself from him in
1756 after eight years of marriage, whereupon (to quote the *Allgemeine
Deutsche Biographie*) "his life really took on the aspect of a gallop: despotism, extravagance, sensual excesses of the wildest sort prevailed to an alarm-
ing degree.... Not content with his large provision of courtesans (mainly
Italian), he sacrificed daughters of good German houses to his lust, and so
brought heavy misfortune on many families, against whom he threatened
vengeance if they dared to oppose him." It was this duke of Württemberg
who forbade Schiller to write plays and ordered him to practice medicine;
Schiller ran away from him in 1782.

(the Princess of Wales) just like a good Scots nobleman. The Hereditary Prince was mild and quiet; the other, Prince Auguste, very brisk. He was just arrived from getting himself installed Knight of the Teutonic Order. The Princess was ugly, but easy and comical.[6]

It was a fine old castle. We had a very good dinner. The grand passage was lined with honest-looking guards, quite comfortable. After dinner I retired to my inn. At seven we returned to Court, and chatted and played cards. They made a whist-party for me. I found the style of this court easy and cordial. I am already well with Chambellan Helmolt (a fine fellow like Lord Cassillis), the Grand Écuyer, the Grand Échanson[7] Forstern, the Baron von Schlegel, and my good friend the Maréchal. The ladies are also very agreeable. At supper I sat by Mademoiselle de Bilow, who was educated at Strelitz with the Queen.[8] She was very like Mrs. Hamilton of Bangour. She had fine eyes. She had much sentiment. She begged of me to tell the Queen that I had heard her praised by one who had the best opportunity of knowing Her Majesty.

THURSDAY 18 OCTOBER. At twelve I went and saw the Duke's cabinet of medals. It is nobly arranged in cases with drawers in which are divisions for each medal. The heads of the emperors in plaster bronzed make a very suitable ornament to the cabinet. It contains about fifteen thousand pieces. It is very rich in Greek and Latin medals, and contains some very curious ones. There is here an Alexander the Great with his own head, and five pieces of Tiberius. The gentleman who has the care of the cabinet was very

[6] The Duke (an uncle of George III) was sixty-five; the Hereditary Prince, Ernst Ludwig, was nineteen, and his brother August, seventeen. Ernst Ludwig became Duke in 1772, and achieved a considerable reputation as a mathematician and astronomer. August became a soldier and patron of letters; Wieland dedicated *Oberon* to him. The Princess (aged twenty-three) was named Friederike Luise.

[7] *Chambellan* is perhaps "Gentleman of the Bedchamber"; *Grand Écuyer*, "Master of Horse"; *Grand Échanson*, "Chief Butler."

[8] Charlotte Sophia, who married George III in 1761, was the niece of the Duke of Mecklenburg-Strelitz.

intelligent. He told me that he could discover counterfeit antiques because the veritable antiques were round in the edges, as anciently they coined in a different manner from what they do now. I found here also several English coins, and a few old Scots ones. This day the Hereditary Prince of Hesse-Philippsthal dined at Court.

After dinner Monsieur de Schlegel carried me to wait on the Grande Maîtresse,⁹ who was a woman of *beaucoup d'esprit;* but she talked with affected, refined grief on the death of her only daughter, and had the disagreeable manner to *s'écouter,*¹ as a French author says. It is a sad fault. I have it in some measure. All affected people have it, and as I was ill educated, I am obliged to affect more genteel manners and so have learnt the habit of playing a part. Schlegel and I then went and saw the garden, which is very well. All the German princes are very magnificent, and at every court you find things worth seeing. I indulged agreeable reflections how I should talk of Saxe-Gotha to the Princess of Wales, how I should remind her of the pretty Zee Bergen near the Palace, the romantic Thuringer Valken at a distance, as also the Insuls Berg,² on the top of which is a cottage, but as it is very cold, one can go there only in the heat of the summer, and the house must be warmed some days before.

At night we had a ball at Court. We were in dominoes, and I pleased myself with the idea of being in Spain. Monsieur le Grand Écuyer was kind enough to lend me a very genteel domino, white with red ribbons. We were very happy. I must observe that my journal serves me not so much as a history as it serves me merely as a reservoir of ideas. According to the humour which I am in when I read it, I judge of my past adventures, and not from what is really recorded. If I am in gay spirits, I read an account of so much ex-

⁹ Juliana Franziska von Buchwald, a famous blue-stocking who numbered among her friends Frederick the Great, Voltaire, Wieland, Herder, Goethe, and others. Her daughter, the Countess of Werthern, had died in the previous January.
¹ Talk as though she liked to hear herself.
² The Seeberg, Thüringer Wald (Thuringian Forest), and the Inselsberg.

istence, and I think, "Sure I have been very happy." If I am gloomy, I think, "Sure I have passed much uneasy time, or at best, much insipid time." Thus I think without regard to the real fact as written.

THURSDAY 18 OCTOBER[3]

> I wish, my Muse, thou could'st be more sedate,
> And at more leisure poetry create;
> For this same rapid rhyming much I fear
> May make a very sloven of my dear;
> May make thee learn to hobble up the hill
> Like lumpish Johnny of my father's mill,
> Who trudges slow along the plashy way,
> Each foot well loaded with a pound of clay.
> No, may'st thou ever march with bounding strides,
> And, like thy Poet, equal him that rides.

FRIDAY 19 OCTOBER. I went and saw the Duke's Library, which is very large, in excellent order, and contains some curious pieces. There is a French book entitled *La Truandise* (i.e., in old French, *pauvreté*) *de l'âme*, where there is an allegorical picture of a poor soul which comes to receive from the Holy Church the alms of grace. The Soul is painted as a woman, stark naked, who presents herself before five or six sturdy priests and holds a bag to put their alms in. The book is in manuscript. There is also a German Bible which formerly belonged to the Elector of Bavaria. It is a manuscript written an age before the Reformation. It is in two volumes. The first contains the historical books of the Old Testament. It is probable that there has been another volume in which the rest of the Old Testament has been written. This first volume is decorated with paintings in an odd taste, but finely illuminated and richly gilded in the manner of that ancient art, which is now

[3] These indifferent verses are included because of their sharply realized picture of "lumpish Johnny," the Auchinleck work-horse. To a student of Boswell's life such flashes of memory are precious because they are rare. Boswell seldom records his recollections of childhood in any but a general way.

totally lost. Some of the designs are truly ludicrous. When Adam and Eve perceive that they are naked, God comes in the figure of an old man with a pair of breeches for Adam and a petticoat for Eve. One would almost imagine that the painter intended to laugh at the Scriptures. But in those days it was not the mode to mock at the religion of their country. The genius which is now employed to support infidelity was then employed to support piety. The imagination which now furnishes licentious sallies was then fertile in sacred emblems. Sometimes superstition rendered them extravagant, and sometimes weakness made them ridiculous, as I have now given an example. The second volume contains the New Testament complete. It is illuminated by the same hand as the first volume, as far as the history of Our Saviour's passion in the fourteenth chapter of St. Mark. It has been reckoned that the gold employed in illuminating the two volumes may amount to the value of a thousand ducats. It is probable that the ancient painter has died when he had got as far as the fourteenth of Mark. The Duke of Bavaria has however taken care that the work should not be left imperfect. At the end of this volume the arms of Bavaria are painted, and there is an inscription bearing that Otto Henry, Duke of Bavaria, caused the remaining part of the Sacred Oracles to be adorned by a more modern painter, *anno* 1530–1532 — for it took two years to finish it. The work of the last painter has not the advantage to be illuminated with gold in the ancient manner, as was the work of the former painter. But the modern has been a much superior genius. His designs are remarkably well conceived, and executed with accuracy and taste. His colours are fresh and lively. He has however now and then fallen into little absurdities. The Evangelist tells us that when Mary Magdalene found Our Saviour after his resurrection, she supposed him to be the gardener, for which reason the painter has drawn Christ holding a spade. Now Mary supposed him to be the gardener because he was in a garden. Had he had a spade in his hand, it was impossible to doubt of it. But how suppose that Jesus had a spade? Upon the whole, this Bible is one of the noblest books that I have ever seen.

There is here another remarkable book, *Magnum opus continens numismata imperatorum Romanorum, a Jacobo de Strada Mantuano elaboratum, anno 150–.*[4] This work was executed by order of the Count de Fugger, whose family was in Germany what the family of the Medici was in Italy. The work consists of thirty-one volumes, in each of which is from 300 to 500 leaves. For each leaf the Count de Fugger paid a ducat, so that at the least it must have cost 9,300 ducats. It would seem that there have been more copies of this work, for some of the first volumes are to be found in the Libraries of Vienna and Dresden. The library-keeper at Gotha is a very learned man, simple, quiet, and obliging.

I was this day dressed in a suit of flowered velvet of five colours. I had designed to put on this suit first at Saxe-Gotha. I did so. It is curious, but I had here the very train of ideas which I expected to have. At night the Princess made me come to the table where she sat at cards, and said, "Mr. Boswell! Why, how fine you are!"[5] She is a good, lively girl. I am already treated here with much ease. My time passes pleasantly on. Between dinner and evening court I read the *Nouvelle Héloïse;*[6] I write; I think.

SATURDAY 20 OCTOBER. Rousseau gives me an enthusiasm of feeling which I thought was all over with poor melancholy Boswell. Thus agitated, my heart expands itself and feels the want of an object to love. Zélide is next my heart. She presents herself to my imagination with all her advantages. I see the daughter of one of the first nobles of Holland. I see a foreign lady of genius, science, and fortune. I see the amiable companion of my winter at Utrecht, who might make an amiable companion for life. But then again I recollect that she studies metaphysics and mathematics; that she despises the common affairs of life, which form the sum total of

[4] "An extended study of the medals of the Roman Emperors, made by Jacopo de Strada of Mantua, in the year 150–."

[5] The memoranda, however, show that the Princess advised Boswell to put on a black ribbon and to wear a different sword-knot.

[6] He has begun to prepare himself for his meeting with Rousseau. The memoranda for 20 October conclude, "You're to consult Rousseau on diseased mind."

terrestrial happiness; that her imagination is so strong that there is no depending upon her conduct; and that her constitution is naturally bad, and has been rendered worse by an irregular education. My heart then starts back from such an alliance, and rests contracted within itself. It is uneasy to be so. Fancy comes kindly to its relief, and amuses it with pleasing pictures of tender felicity with a Spanish or an English lady. Thus flows my existence at present. As to the future part of it, I can as yet say nothing. I may be thrown into situations which may give me quite a new turn of thinking, make me quite a new man. I have already experienced this in some degree. Since I parted from Mr. Samuel Johnson at Harwich, what a variety of minds have I had!

This day I was in excellent frame. I had a cordial regard for the worthy Court of Saxe-Gotha. I must remark a curious form here. Before and after dinner, the Marshal posts himself opposite the Duke and Duchess, and at his side has one of the pages. The Marshal makes a signal, and the page says grace. I think this form very decent. But I could wish that their Highnesses would not talk, but remain in decent silence. We dined always in a large old room. There were in it two alcoves opposite each other. In the one was the furnace, and in the other a buffet, which by candle-light had an excellent effect. The table here at dinner was excellent. At supper it was moderate. After dinner I took leave of the Duchess, who said, "I am sorry that you are leaving us. Perhaps you will come back some day." I also took leave of the ladies of the Court. Mademoiselle Schlotheim said, "I think you have ease of manners." Her grandmother, Madame de Rüxleben, educated the Princess of Wales.

I am somewhat of a virtuoso. Wherever I am, I make a collection of the silver specie struck the year in which I have been in the country. I went and waited on the Master of the Mint, who had been in England and spoke English tolerably. He supplied me with new coins, and treated me with good Rhenish wine. He was one of your old, staunch Germans.[7] How curious is it to think that every

[7] In the memoranda Boswell describes him as an "ugly dog but civil."

man is of infinite importance to himself, and yet groups of indi-
viduals serve only to furnish amusing speculation for me. I then
returned and took leave of the Duke and of the gentlemen. They
were all extremely kind. The Grand Écuyer said, "You ought to
stay longer. You know that you are welcome here." I went to my
inn, undressed, and wrote till four in the morning. Slept only
two hours.

[Boswell to John Johnston]

Saxe-Gotha, 20 October 1764

MY DEAR JOHNSTON, . . . What think you, Johnston, of writing my epitaph? In these enlightened days when the arts are advanced to a degree almost incredible, when calculation reigns and
a man builds a house for thirty years as exactly as a cook makes a
dinner for thirty people, what think you of writing an epitaph for a
man who is to be dead only two days? It must neither have the
sadness of one upon a man who is dead for good and all, nor must it
be so liberal in eulogiums, as our dead man is to get up again very
soon, and may probably give them the lie. It must be a short, decent
composition, as thus:

EPITAPH ON MR. BOSWELL, DEAD FROM SATURDAY TO MONDAY

> Ye who the gen'rous lively Boswell knew,
> With kind regret this gloomy object view;
> But let not hopeless grief your bosoms pain,
> For in two days he'll be alive again.

I ever remain, my dear friend, yours with all affection,

JAMES BOSWELL.

SATURDAY 20 OCTOBER

> Thy bread, Westphalia, thy brown bread I sing,
> Bread which might make the dinner of a king;
> Though one of those whom Englishmen call dogs,
> One whose nice palate had been us'd to frogs,
> Could not, forsooth, digest a stuff so coarse,

But call'd it good provision for his horse.
An etymologist, who pokes his nose
Into dark holes which Time has wish'd to close,
May learn that "Niccol" was the horse's name,
Hence the bread's title, "Bon pour Niccol," came.[8]

SUNDAY 21 OCTOBER. I got up at six. I heard the noise of an organ. I entered the great church. I found there a numerous congregation, a great many well-dressed people, lustres lighted. This morning worship had a fine effect. I then mounted my old friend the post-wagon. I was in the sweetest spirits. 'Tis strange that want of sleep should produce such an effect. But so I find it. I drove two miles to Langensalza, where the wagon was to stop all day. I dismounted, went to my inn, and sent a card to the Grand Maître of the Princesse Frédérique of Saxe-Gotha, Douairière de Saxe-Weissenfels, a house now sunk into that of the Elector.[9] I only notified that a Scots gentleman wished to be presented to the Princess. The Grand Maître sent immediately to know my rank, and was told I was a baron, upon which I was asked to come to his house at twelve and afterwards go to Court. I went accordingly to him; he spoke only German. He carried me in a coach to Court. I found the Princess very civil. I was quite the man of fashion. I was placed by her Highness. The table was plentiful and the servants numerous. She

[8] The etymology of the word "pumpernickel" is uncertain, but that presented by Boswell may safely be dismissed. He did not invent it, but probably found it in Nugent's guide-book, frequently quoted in these notes: "Westphalia in general is a good country, abounding in all necessaries of life, and yet there is no part of Germany where the peasants live in a more miserable manner. Their bread is of the very coarsest kind, ill baked, and as black as a coal, for they never sift their flour. The people of the country call it *Pumpernickel,* which is only a corruption of a French name given it by a gentleman of that nation who passed through this country. It is reported that when this coarse bread was brought to table, he looked at it and said *qu'il était bon pour Nickel,* that it was good for Nickel, which was the name of his horse" (Thomas Nugent, *The Grand Tour,* 2d ed., 1756, ii. 80).

[9] Of Saxony. *Douairière* means "dowager": she was the widow of the last Duke of Saxe-Weissenfels.

is pretty old. She has public table only three days a week. She has her Dame d'honneur. We had officers and other honest Germans. I was here quite at my ease in the house of the sister of the Princess of Wales, and the aunt of my king. After dinner I took leave politely, saying I should be happy to tell the Princess of Wales that I had the honour of paying my respects here. I had one of her Highness's coaches to conduct me to my inn. Was not this a rare adventure? I called this "shooting a princess flying." I was indeed the person in motion and her Highness the person at rest. I was in a moment again in my travelling-dress. Her Highness's chaplain, who had dined with us, waited upon me, and carried me to take a walk and see the town. It is the dirtiest that I ever saw. Its streets are overflowed with liquid mud, and with difficulty you step along a narrow path on each side. The chaplain was a laughing fellow, tolerably knowing.

At six we parted. I was somewhat splenetic, and dreary apprehensions as to my conduct distressed me. I swore solemnly neither to talk as an infidel nor to enjoy a woman before seeing Rousseau. So I am bound a month at least. I was very heavy-headed from having had no sleep last night; and as I did not know when the wagon might set out, I threw myself on the bed, leaving orders to Jacob to call me. I slept till eleven, and got up unhinged. But a glass of cold water and a walk up and down the room set me to rights. By long study I shall be quite master of spleen. Between eleven and twelve at night I set out.

MONDAY 22 OCTOBER. Sad travelling. About twelve at night as the wagon was rumbling down a hill, one of its wheels fell into a deep hole, and there we stuck fast and had almost been overturned. We could not get the horses to pull out the wagon. Luckily we were within a little of our station, the village of Helsa. The postilion went to bring help. He returned with a man and a horse. Still it would not do. He went once more. He was an old creature and mighty slow. It was a dreadful rain. We remained upon the hill more than two hours. It was quite serving a campaign. The postilion, I do believe, would have allowed us to remain a-soaking till daybreak. But at last we walked to the village, and sent a man to watch our baggage. I kept my temper. I went to bed and slept pretty sound.[1]

MONDAY 22 OCTOBER

> Behold, ye Hessians, from the Shire of Ayr
> A laird whom your moustaches have made stare!
> While a mere child, nor yet advanced to taw,
> You in Edina's ancient town he saw,
> When the Rebellion[2] you came o'er to quell
> And send, forsooth, the monster back to hell;
> While Arthur's Seat resounded with your drums,
> I saw you buying breeches for your bums;
> But, with your breeches, you were not so stout
> As the bold Highlanders who went without.

TUESDAY 23 OCTOBER. My last night's adventure had fermented my blood. I dreaded a fever. We drove through a pretty wild country to Kassel. As I approached it, I thought of the last war.[3] Its three divisions situated on eminent ground have a good effect. I put up at the Stockholm, a very good inn. I sent immediately to the Grand Maréchal du Rosey. My reception was cold, for a girl went with my card, and he asked if I had no servant. One perceives in trifles the style of a court, as the character of a man. He sent me notice that the Landgrave was out of town, but that he would let me know when his Highness returned. I passed the evening at home, and wrote a good deal. I was curious to see the Land-

[1] He paid four groschen to a man who guided him to the village, four more to the man who watched the baggage, and six groschen for lodging and brandy (Expense Account).

[2] One would have expected the Rebellion of 1745, which occurred when Boswell was five years old, to have made a profound impression on him, but as a matter of fact his papers contain only four or five personal recollections of that time, these verses being one of the instances. "Nor yet advanced to taw" (line 3) means "not old enough yet to play at marbles."

[3] Because the surrender of Kassel to the Anglo-Prussian army on 1 November 1762 had marked the end of the war so far as Great Britain was concerned.

grave. After the King of France, he is the prince in Europe who tires the most. My chairman told Jacob that his Highness used to say, "Oh! Ih hab lang syde. Der Syde valt meer lang."[4] He said too that since the Prince changed his religion, he had no peace, and that he would willingly give up Popery, but his *Régence* will not allow him. In short, that they will oblige him to be damned. What absurd ideas enter into the heads of the vulgar!

WEDNESDAY 24 OCTOBER.[5] I waited on Monsieur du Rosey, and found him an elderly Swiss gentleman, mighty polite and genteel. I found that a recommendation was necessary, for he was cold till I told him that I had a letter for Madame de Wintzingerode. He told me, "Some time ago we had a trick played on us here. A gentleman came who called himself the son of Duke Hamilton. However, he had neither carriage nor servant, not even proper clothes. He was in a riding-coat. We gave him equipment. He was presented at Court. He had good enough manners; but after his departure we discovered that he was neither English nor Scotch, but a foreign adventurer who had learned a little of the language." I said, "Sir, if one receives such a man as that, one deserves to be taken in."

I then called on Monsieur de La Porte, French minister[6] here, brother to Monsieur de La Porte whom I knew at Utrecht. I found him at dinner. He promised to come to me after dinner. He did so,

[4] "Ach, ich habe lange Zeit! Die Zeit fällt mir lang!" ("Oh, I am bored! Time seems endless to me.") Friedrich II (1720–1785), Landgrave of Hesse-Kassel, had been in Scotland in 1746 with Hessian troops to help in suppressing the Jacobite rebellion; it was he who hired out Hessian soldiers to England during the War of American Independence. The discovery in 1754 of his secret conversion to Roman Catholicism caused a rupture in his family, he himself being exiled from Hesse until his succession in 1760, and the County of Hanau-Münzenberg being sequestered in the name of his estranged wife, Mary of England (daughter of George II), and her sons, under the guardianship of England, Prussia, Sweden, Denmark, the Corpus Evangelicorum, and the States General (the chairman's "Régence").

[5] " . . . Get *Héloïse* from La Porte" (Memorandum, 24 October). See p. 146 *n*. 6.

[6] Not "envoy" but "minister of the Gospel" — a Protestant clergyman.

and proved to be a knowing, sagacious man, very plain, very obliging, and very deliberate. He resembled somewhat Mr. Clow at
Glasgow.[7] He carried me to see the Maison des Modèles, which is
a singular thing. You have here models of all the buildings and
gardens of the Prince, in particular, however, of the grand waterfall, which is not yet completely executed. But there are here many
pieces yet unexecuted. The waterfall must be a work of prodigious
expense. The water issues from a hill and flows down a flight of
steps till it reaches a basin; from thence it again is conveyed to a
flight of steps. In short, this alternation will be carried on a vast
way. On each side of the fall are evergreens, verdant banks, and a
serpentine stair. On the top of the hill, or rock, is a large statue of
Hercules, in the inside of which is a stair. The statue is so large that
a man may stand in the head of it. It was the grand-uncle of this
Landgrave who caused make the waterfall. His son, the King of
Sweden,[8] came to see him, and was immediately carried to view
the fall. His father asked him, "Is it not beautiful? Can you imagine
anything that is lacking here?" The King replied, "Nothing, except a gibbet for the man who planned this for your Highness."
This pleasantry however was taken seriously ill by the old Prince,
and His Majesty of Sweden was obliged to decamp without taking
leave. We then saw the *orangerie*. Before it stand some ancient
statues in bronze, four I think, on the terrace. There are here also
some very pretty figures of white marble, which came from Italy
a good time ago but have not been brought hither till very lately,
by reason of the war. There were a parcel of sweet little children,
and three grand pieces, a Narcissus, a Venus de Medicis, and a
group of boys with grapes. We then saw the menagerie, which is
very well. I remarked in a room ten or a dozen apes, and in another
the various kinds of parrots. We then viewed some pretty walks on

[7] Professor of Logic at the University.

[8] There is some mistake here, for Friedrich I of Sweden was the son of "this"
Landgrave's grandfather, Karl, not the son of his grand-uncle, Wilhelm VII,
who died six years before the King of Sweden was born. Friedrich obtained
his regal title through his marriage to the daughter of Charles XII of Sweden.

the side of the hill. They are done with taste. I saw here a grotto. Here it was that the Landgrave used to have his private devotions before it was discovered that he was Catholic. It was concealed seven years. His valet de chambre was much vexed, and told him, "Sir, the moment that it becomes known, I shall quit you."[9]

I was very desirous to know from good authority the real character of the Landgrave. De La Porte said, "Sir, take my word for it that he is a good prince. He has had many misfortunes. He has been treated very severely. There was an English lady of the Court who was largely responsible for bringing about the separation between his Highness and a princess whom he adored.[1] He needs only sensible and clever people to guide him. He is unable to give his attention to everything; and sometimes affairs go badly enough." I then asked him to explain the reason of his Highness's change of religion. He said, "He was very ill educated. Donop, who was his tutor, admitted, 'I need a tutor myself.' He was a pretty man, but without solid principles. Thus the Prince was not grounded in a manner which one could depend on." I found De La Porte prudently avoided to seem convinced of the real reason of this change, which was indeed his Highness's attachment to a certain Countess of the Catholic religion, who insisted that his Highness should surrender his soul to her before she would give him up her body. By this means, I suppose, she made matters easy with her conscience, or with her vanity. She either imagined that gaining a prince to her communion might atone for her sin of gallantry, or

[9] Professor Warnock reports that the Director of the Landesbibliothek at Kassel, Dr. Wolf von Both, had not heard this story of the grotto, and is very sceptical of it. He cannot conceive of a grotto near enough to the Palace for the Landgrave to have gone to it seven years unperceived.

[1] The phrase which I have translated "lady of the Court" is in the original *dame d'honneur*, Boswell having recorded La Porte's speech entirely in French. The reference is possibly to Lady Rochford, with whom Friedrich was carrying on a flirtation in 1746. Before her marriage in 1740 she had been Maid of Honour to the Princess of Wales, and her husband held various high Court appointments. But the Landgrave did not separate from his wife until several years after 1746.

that the rank of her lover might bear her up against the contempt of being a mistress.[2]

De La Porte gave me several anecdotes of the Landgrave. He told me he had been with him at the *bains* in the neighbourhood, and that the Prince had talked to him a great deal. "He has studied thoroughly the controversy between the Catholics and the Protestants. He knows the history of the Church well, and one must be well equipped by special study to be able to dispute with him. His memory is filled with dates and little anecdotes, and if you do not know them, he triumphs. Moreover, he refers you to Bossuet for an explanation of difficult subjects. If you know nothing about the books of which he speaks, he advises you to study his religion, because you are unfamiliar with it. It is in this way that he gets rid of German pastors. However, one can well believe that his Highness is not entirely fixed in his principles, and that sometimes he is even sorry for what he did. There was a certain pastor who wrote him a very rude letter. He showed it to me. It was an unmannerly piece. He spoke to him about his change of religion without observing the slightest decorum. And he intruded some political matters, with which he certainly had nothing to do. I told his Highness my sentiments on the subject. He said to me, 'Sir, I don't believe everything the priests tell me. Surely, at the Day of Judgment, the worthy men of all religions will be saved. And as for my change of religion, that's not a matter to make such a great noise about.' I said to him boldly, 'Sire, if a man changes his religion for another which he believes false, God is justly offended.' He gave me no answer.

"One day he said something that struck me singularly. He said to me, 'David and Peter were both pious, yet one committed adultery and the other betrayed his Master.' 'Yes, Sire,' I answered, 'but they were sincerely penitent.' He hesitated for some time.

[2] Friedrich's father, reproaching the Elector (and Archbishop) of Cologne for receiving his son into the Roman Communion, refers to the wiles of "a certain Countess." Dr. Theodor Hartwig cautiously identifies her as a Countess Leiningen, but thinks that the Roman Catholic mistress was still another.

Then he said, 'Yes, one should imitate them in their piety, and not in their vices. Good day, Monsieur de La Porte.' And he went away. I was astonished, for he had never treated me like that. I was afraid of having offended him. But a few days later a gentleman of the Court said to me, 'His Highness is very fond of you.' So I supposed that his Highness had had some stirring of remorse, and it was that that made him go off so abruptly. He has however a strong dash of superstition, for he said to me one day, 'Sir, do you not believe that we can obtain favours from heaven by prayers to the saints? I shall give you an instance. Once I asked something from God through the intercession of the Virgin Mary. It was something of consequence, and I obtained it.' I replied without ceremony, 'Your Highness is very much indebted to God: first for having granted the thing that you desired, and in the second place for having granted it for such a prayer.' " Is not Monsieur de La Porte a very fine fellow? Indeed he is. He came with me to my inn and drank a glass of wine.

THURSDAY 25 OCTOBER. All the morning I wrote. My method is to make a memorandum every night of what I have seen during the day. By this means I have my materials always secured. Sometimes I am three, four, five days without journalizing. When I have time and spirits, I bring up this my journal as well as I can in the hasty manner in which I write it.[3] Some years hence I shall perhaps

[3] This method had evolved gradually and experimentally. The early journal, of which the great example is the London journal of 1762–1763, appears to have been written up from memory, in the main without recourse to notes of any sort. The daily memoranda, which were contemporaneous in origin with the London journal of 1762–1763, at first contained no reference to events past, but were programmes for the day ahead. Boswell, I think, wrote them the first thing in the morning before putting on his clothes. In Holland he began the practice of reviewing the events of the previous day and of awarding himself praise or blame for his behaviour, before setting down his admonitions for the day ahead. The memoranda of this period always begin with the word "Yesterday," and appear still to be written in the morning. The memoranda of the German tour are identical in character with those written in Holland, but there is no reason to doubt Boswell's statement that he was now writing them at night. Either he habitually went to bed after midnight, or he deliberately anticipated.

abridge it in a more elegant style. I take up too much time in writing letters. I am resolved to guard against this. I shall make my correspondence valued by making it scarce. Yet while I am abroad it is pleasant to have a variety of correspondents, and it will also be pleasant when I am settled at home. Well, then, why make grave, proud resolutions of writing little? I was in the wrong, and there's an end on't.

At one I went to Court. The Palace is an old building but large, and the rooms are magnificent. I was pleased to find here a family picture of the present House of Brunswick done by [Johann Heinrich Tischbein],[4] the Landgrave's painter. I was curious to see the Landgrave, who as Prince of Hesse was in Scotland in the year 1745. He appeared at last, and I was presented to him. He scarcely spoke, in order to keep up his dignity. I dined. The table was very good. I took particular notice of a ham with pears well boiled in sugar. It made an excellent dish, and I eat of it very heartily. The Grand Écuyer and some more of the courtiers were very civil to me. At five I was presented to the Princess Charlotte, cousin of the Landgrave. She was mighty lively and affable. I saw also Madame de Wintzingerode, for whom I had a letter from Mademoiselle de Stang, Lady of Honour at Brunswick. We had a very good concert. But I perceived the Landgrave a-tiring; for he was continually calling to him his courtiers, and whispering to them. Then we returned to the apartment and played cards. They made a party of whisk[5] for me. I supped at Court.

FRIDAY 26 OCTOBER.[6] At eight I saw the Maison des Sciences, in which are several rooms of curiosities, rich but inferior much to the museum at Dresden. There is a good many antiques. A collec-

---

[4] Boswell neglected to fill a blank here. The picture he is referring to is the fine one reproduced at p. 14. It is still at Kassel.

[5] The older spelling of *whist*, which is the form Boswell generally uses.

[6] " . . . Swear few letters. *Think*, and be Johnson, Temple, and Gray. Is not *Britain* noble? Restrain envoy ideas. Auchinleck and jaunts each year. Gardens, pictures, Miss Bosville" (Memorandum, 26 October). "Miss Bosville" was a young lady from Yorkshire, daughter of an English squire whom Boswell regarded as head of the Boswell clan. He had not met her, but for some time had been indulging fantasies of making her his wife.

tion of old musical instruments, an odd enough conceit. There is a fine picture by Rosa[7] of the great Landgrave's menagerie. It is very large, and immensely full, without any confusion. Rosa lived here three years to paint this picture, for which I was told he had thirteen hundred ducats. I saw an exceeding large burning-glass which burns a foot under water. I saw several curious pieces invented by the great Landgrave himself, amongst others a clock in the form of a man which, at whatever hour you please, fires a pistol and lights a lamp; so that you are awaked in the night and have a light immediately. I next saw the gallery of pictures, amongst which are some noble pieces, chiefly of the Flemish School. I never see a portrait of a comely Dutchwoman but I think with kindness of Zélide. What a fancy!

I next waited on De La Porte, and saw his sister, a good hearty old maiden; then saw the marble bath, which in its kind is truly *une chose unique*. The outside has nothing remarkable, but within there is an octagon room with four superb statues and four panels richly carved, besides intermediate pieces of marble. The floor is also marble. In the middle is the bath, an octagon too, adorned with other four statues. In short it is a most magnificent work.

I was not asked today to dine at Court. It is not the custom to send to strangers. They must pay their respects at Court, and perhaps they are invited to the table, perhaps not. It is not a true hospitable court, although it is however not amiss. At six I went to the *comédie*. On entering the house I was surprised to hear the *orchestre* play one of Lord Kellie's[8] concertos. They however played it very ill. The pretty, slow parts they made a country dance of. The piece was *Tartuffe*, and pretty well performed. I was asked by a general who speaks good English why I had not been this morning at Court. I said I had been seeing fine things. I supped at Court. Before supper I took leave of the Landgrave. He was very hypochondriac. For most part, he talks too freely. But all he said

[7] Not the celebrated Salvatore Rosa, but Johann Melchior Roos (1659–1731).
[8] Thomas Alexander Erskine, sixth Earl of Kellie, Boswell's acquaintance and brother of his close friend Andrew Erskine, was one of the most gifted musical composers of the day. He had studied in Germany.

to me when presented first, was, "Where do you come from last?" and when I took leave, "Where do you go from here?"[9] He seemed gloomy. Kassel has been but so-so.

SATURDAY 27 OCTOBER. I breakfasted at honest La Porte's; and as I told him that I never drank tea or coffee, there was wine and bread and butter and Geneva confections. What kindness! Worthy people! I was quite my father. At one I set out for Frankfurt. The wagon was covered with leather, but it was a monstrous machine. One could see nothing from its little openings, for it had no glasses. It jolted most horridly, and as it was constructed with iron bars, when I attempted to sleep, I received most severe raps and was really in danger of having my head broke. In short, it was a trying machine, worse than my good friends the open post-wagons, for upon them I could see the country, feed on the fresh air, and sleep like a mariner on the top of a mast.

I am surprised how I neglected to mention that one of my chairmen at Kassel had been in the Hessian troops who were in Scotland in 1745. He talked of *Bart*, by which he meant to say Perth. I had with me in the wagon a French servant, a blackguard, impudent dog. Yet at night I supped with him and my servant. Such is my hardy plan on my German travels. I also lay down with them on the straw. It was terrible. The heat of an iron stove rendered the straw musty and the air hot, and this, joined to the breaths of a good many people by no means of the most clean race, rendered the room most abominable. I could not sleep. One sad circumstance in the *Stube*, or common room of a German inn, is being obliged to sleep with a tallow candle or a coarse lamp a-burning. I had recourse to the Stall Knecht[1] and got a place in the hayloft, where I slept sound though cold.

SATURDAY 27 OCTOBER

Here am I, sitting in a German inn,[2]
Where I may penance do for many a sin,

[9] Almost exactly what his relative George III used to ask Boswell when they met at Court, to Boswell's great annoyance.
[1] Ostler, stableman.
[2] At Werkel, a small village near Fritzlar.

For I am pester'd with a thousand flies,
Who flap and buzz about my nose and eyes.
A lumpish landlord has the easy chair;
Hardly he speaks, but wildly does he stare.
In haste to get away, I did not dine,
And now I've had cold beef and cursed wine,
And in five minutes, or a little more,
I shall be stretch'd on musty straw to snore.

SUNDAY 28 OCTOBER. In the afternoon we got rid of the Frenchman, and I and Jacob came to Marburg,[3] a large city. I was out of order. I knew not what to make of my existence. I lay down between two feather beds and resigned myself to my fate.

MONDAY 29 OCTOBER.[4] This day we were joined by the Camer dienar[5] of the Hereditary Prince of Hesse-Kassel, quite a Bruce Campbell, as also a tall, roaring dog who had studied law, but was now going into the Darmstadt Guards. We jogged well on. At night we were laid thirteen in a room, besides a Danish woman and three children. I could not bear this, so the postmaster gave me his own bed.

TUESDAY 30 OCTOBER. We jogged well on. The roaring dog taught me a comical German song, "Want du myn Swager wilt werden," &c.[6] About two I arrived at Frankfurt-on-the-Main. I was in bad humour. Jacob asked me why I waited in the courtyard. I said, "To look after the baggage." He replied with a kind of sneer, "Yes, to look after the baggage!" I was irritated. I wished to turn him off. Yet I considered, he is a most excellent servant; and a fellow of common sense and activity in his duty cannot have the supple politeness of one who has a kind of genteel sentiment and at the

[3] Boswell wrote *Warpurg.*
[4] Boswell's twenty-fourth birthday.
[5] Gentleman of the Bedchamber.
[6] Literally, "If you will be my brother-in-law." But *Schwager* had various slang meanings: (1) boon-companion, crony; (2) coachman, postilion; (3) rival for, or co-partner in, the favours of a mistress. Since the song was "comical" and the singer "a roaring dog," the last meaning may be suspected.

same time is negligent and perhaps dishonest. It was certainly true that my staying in the courtyard could do no good, and the *naïf* fellow could not help telling me so. I made him understand that he had done wrong, and he was sorry and seemed very desirous to do his duty.

And now comes a good anecdote. I had brought with me from Berlin sixty-eight louis, with which I imagined I might complete my tour through Germany to Geneva. When I had got as far as Dresden, I perceived that my money would run short. I wrote to my Lord Marischal my situation, begged his Lordship's advice whether I should proceed from Frankfurt directly to Neuchâtel, or should visit the courts of Mannheim, Durlach, and Stuttgart, and, if he thought it proper for me to visit those courts, begged he might send me to Frankfurt a bill for thirty louis. This afternoon I sent to the post and had the pleasure to receive an obliging letter from his Lordship with the bill enclosed, and besides that, an order on Neuchâtel for thirty louis more, in case I should want more. I was filled with gratitude to the venerable Earl. I felt myself a man of worth to be regarded by him. I strolled with pleasant *étourderie* in the streets of Frankfurt.

[Received 30 October, Lord Marischal to Boswell]

Potsdam, Wednesday, about the middle of October[7]
I THIS MOMENT RECEIVE the honour of yours and write this note in advance, because I go to Berlin tomorrow, where I shall get the bill and enclose it, for thirty louis of twenty-four livres. Don't go to Stuttgart, go on to Neuchâtel, where if you should want money, I add a postscript for other thirty louis. Perhaps you would do as well to remain in Neuchâtel as go to Geneva among a number of young English, until you hear from my Lord, your father, but this as you find the company of Neuchâtel. Colonel Chaillet is a brave, honest-hearted man; and for women, Madame la Colonelle Sandoz is worth the whole town of Geneva, men, women, and children;

[7] 17 October.

tell her so from me, she understands English. *Bon soir.* The rest at Berlin.

Berlin, 20 October 1764

Here enclosed goes a bill, value thirty louis. Good night, good journey, and all good things, may they accompany you.[8]

Sir: — If Mr. Boswell, my friend and countryman, has need of money, I beg you to give him thirty louis of twenty-four francs, to the account of your very humble servant,

THE MARISCHAL OF SCOTLAND.

To Monsieur le Conseiller Rougement,
at Neuchâtel

[Boswell to Lord Marischal]

Frankfurt, 30 October 1764

My Lord, — I return you many thanks for your bill, which I received this evening and have already converted into gold. It is agreeable to think that I am travelling with your Lordship's louis. Brown,[9] who is a fatalist and deals in rhetorical figures, would call them so many golden links in the chain of my existence.

I have kept most stoically to the post-wagons. Instead of grumbling, I took to rhyming. Allow me to give your Lordship a specimen:

No more, my friend, your gaping wonder keep
To hear that I on German post can sleep.
Not with more pleasure does he close his eyes
Who on soft down luxuriously lies;
For know, the roughly rumbling wagon wild
Is just to me as cradle to a child.
As on the rugged roads I bouncing reel,

[8] The paragraph following is in French in the original.
[9] The Reverend Robert Brown, a Scotsman, pastor of the English-speaking church at Utrecht. Boswell had dined in his family regularly during the winter of 1763–1764.

My firm corporeal strength with pride I feel,
And while my back upon the boards is knock'd,
I think, 'twas thus great Hercules was rock'd.[1]

I think my comparison between the rumbling of a post-wagon
and a cradle is good; nor is it amiss to suppose that such rude rock-
ing could lull to sleep none but a Hercules. I ever remain, &c.

TUESDAY 30 OCTOBER

Ye who with fortune ever are at strife,
And make a noise about the ills of life,
What had you said if ye like me had been
With lubbers stretch'd on straw, in all thirteen?
Some roaring Germans in a drunken tone
Still rudely bawl'd, "Vie slaft der Herr Baron?"[2]
Myself of mighty consequence to make
A Baron's title I forsooth must take;
And for my vain indulgence, as you hear,
I now and then must pay a little dear.

WEDNESDAY 31 OCTOBER. The cold had got into my head. I
rose with a sad headache. I took chaise and drove to Hanau with
intention to wait on the Landgrave of Hesse-Kassel, the Princess
Mary of England.[3] Du Rosey had given me a recommendation to
the Court. I sent it between eleven and twelve to the Maréchal, saying that I was obliged to go next day. He sent his compliments, and

[1] The ten-line verses for 15 October.

[2] "How's his Lordship the Baron sleeping?" The "lubbers" believed Boswell
to be an impostor because no German baron would have travelled in so
plebeian a style. But he was quite right in maintaining that his status in
Scotland was at least as high as that of a Baron (Freiherr) in Germany. Because of the fact that all the children of a nobleman there inherited his title,
titles of nobility were very common. A British peer was almost the equivalent
of a German prince.

[3] Mary had separated from her husband after the disclosure of his conversion, and lived with her sons at Hanau. Boswell generally uses the French
feminine forms Landgrave, Margrave in preference to the English forms
Landgravine, Margravine.

was sorry that it was an hour too late. I had a hint that a stranger from the Court of Kassel could not be very welcome. I could not retract what I had said as to my departure, so I missed seeing the court here. I was sorry not to see a daughter of George the Second, and the young Landgrave with his Danish princess.[4] I composed myself to patience. My headache was dreadful. It was as severe as I can imagine. I resolved to stand it firm. I did so. Yet at night I dreaded seriously that I should take a fever and perhaps die. I was alarmed with *real terror — something new.* I cleared up at night. I thought of my own character, and I was revived with this thought: "A sapling is not an oak, but it will most certainly become one. I am the sapling of a philosopher, and want only experience. Some years hence, I shall undoubtedly be a solid, happy man. But I must take care to preserve myself, so that time may have fair occasion to exert its influence, and form me into a mellow character." With this thought I fell asleep.

THURSDAY 1 NOVEMBER. Early this morning I left Hanau and returned to Frankfurt, where I got into the boat for Mainz. My headache was better. I met in the boat with Mr. Barnard, a Dunkirk merchant, grandson to the great Sir John.[5] He was a good, lively fellow. We had a pleasant sail of about eight hours. We stopped an hour at a village, where we dined. We saw in our passage the village of Hochheim, which, though situated on the banks of the Main, gives name to the best old Rhenish. When we arrived at Mainz, I heard that the Elector was from home, and would not return for a fortnight. I was sorry at this, as I had a letter for one of his chamberlains, and wished to see an ecclesiastical court.[6] Pa-

[4] Wilhelm IX, Hereditary Prince of Hesse-Kassel, had married a daughter of the King of Denmark less than two months before. The young couple had only just arrived at Hanau.

[5] Lord Mayor of London and for many years its representative in Parliament; vigorous and respected opponent of Sir Robert Walpole. He died on 29 August of this year.

[6] The Archbishop of Mainz, primate of Germany, was also Elector of Mainz and president of the Electoral College. Emmerich Joseph von Breidbach, a prelate of liberal tendencies, had been consecrated to the see in the previous November.

tience was again my kind comforter. Barnard and I went and viewed the town. It contains some very good houses, and it has a certain air very becoming in an ecclesiastical town. It was All Saints' Day. We went into two churches, which were both grand. My soul was elevated to devotion by the solemn vespers. Barnard and I supped at my inn. We had with us a French traveller. We were hearty.

FRIDAY 2 NOVEMBER. The French traveller was Monsieur Bertollon, a merchant of fine stuffs at Lyons. He and I and my servant and a German woman got into an extra post for Mannheim. The Frenchman had a Pomeranian dog called Pomer whom he was mighty fond of. He was a singular Frenchman, a great lubberly dog with a head like a British tar. He sung most outrageously. He was jolly. The German *Frow* was oldish and very fat. When he sung, she was like to choke with laughing, and when she recovered her breath cried, "Er is ein lustiger Mensch."[7] I do not remember to have met with a more ludicrous scene, for the Frenchman and the *Frow* mutually laughed at each other. I was highly diverted, though my headache still continued. It was a heavy cold. I was in a real fever. I was just transported like a sack.

We dined at Worms. A Jew came into the parlour. He exchanged German money with me. I gave him some pieces which would pass only in the states which I had left, and he gave me pieces which would pass everywhere. By way of being generous to the poor Israelite, I gave him six batzen.[8] He went away. I found he had cheated me to the value of some batzen. O Israel! Why art thou ever so dishonest? At night we arrived at Mannheim, and put up at the Prince Frédéric. I eat a wine soup and tumbled into bed.

SATURDAY 3 NOVEMBER. I sent to the General de Fürstenberg a card of recommendation which I had to him from a Monsieur de Franckenberg at Kassel. He returned me an absurd, extravagant card, full of respect for a man whom he knew nothing of. He said he was confined to his bed, but referred me to Monsieur Harold, Gentleman of the Chamber, and Irish by nation. I waited on

7 "He's a droll man."
8 About a shilling in English money.

Harold, and found him a hearty old fellow full of anecdotes. He has been abroad a great many years. He has been thirty years in the Elector Palatine's service. He taught his Highness to read English. He told me that I could not be presented till Monday, as the Elector was gone a-hunting this day, and as tomorrow was his *jour de fête,*[9] when nobody was presented. I dined at the ordinary of my inn. My fever flew out upon my lips. I was a disagreeable figure. I was fretted. At three Mr. Harold's nephew waited upon me. He had been long in the French service and was now a captain in the Elector Palatine's. He was a genteel young fellow, knew a good deal, and talked well, though with affectation. He carried me to hear the opera rehearsed. I was well amused for some hours, and then returned to my inn, and read English newspapers which old Harold sent me. While abroad, I am often long without seeing a London paper. Now and then I come to a place where I get a budget of them. At Dresden I got one. Here I got one. It is curious how ideas are effaced and renewed. I had not thought of Chace Price since I left England, till I read tonight in the papers that his house had been robbed.[1] It made me laugh from the queer light in which I viewed it. I had written none for three days, and this night could absolutely do nothing. The nervous fluid was disordered.

SUNDAY 4 NOVEMBER. To cure my cold I kept my chamber all day. At five Captain Harold paid me a visit. My fellow-traveller of Lyons was in the next room. He used to come to me at night crying, "Sacré bleu! Je m'ennuie."[2] He amused me with little particulars.

MONDAY 5 NOVEMBER. My cold was much better. It prevented me yesterday from hearing superb mass in the Elector's Chapel. However, by keeping my room, I have shunned a fever. At eleven Harold carried me to Court. The Palace is large and elegant. There is a gallery, a passage round the whole of it, prodigiously

[9] That is, the feast of St. Charles Borromeo, the Elector's baptismal saint.

[1] "On Sunday night some villains broke into the house of Chace Price, Esq., in Curzon Street, Mayfair, and stole out of the same plate and linen to a considerable value, with which they got off undiscovered" (*London Chronicle,* 9 October 1764). Price, a wit and politician, was a friend of Samuel Foote, John Wilkes, and Charles Churchill.

[2] "Damn, but I'm bored!"

long. There were a great many people at Court. Harold talked of
not presenting me till tomorrow. After having already waited two
days, this piqued me not a little, and had I not been presented this
day, I should have bluntly set out next morning. However the
Grand Chambellan presented me to the Elector. His Highness
asked me from whence I came. He was very swarthy, and very
high and mighty. I was presented to the Électrice, who was much
painted, and also exceeding lofty.[3] I saw here the Prince of Nassau-
Weilburg. He recalled to my mind The Hague and all its ideas. At
night I was at the opera. It was indeed superb. I had the ideas of the
Palatine Court which Sir Adam Fergusson gave me.[4] When I came
home, I could neither read nor write. I was truly splenetic and went
to bed. How frail is this existence of mine! how easily changed!

TUESDAY 6 NOVEMBER. Why do I not talk of the beauty of
Mannheim? of its streets *tirés à cordon*[5] and lighted better than

[3] Carlyle calls Karl Theodor, Elector Palatine (1724–1799), "a poor idle
creature, of purely egoistic, ornamental, dilettante nature: sunk in theat-
ricals, bastard children, and the like." His Electress, whom he had married
in 1742, was the Princess Elizabeth Augusta, eldest daughter of the Count
Palatine of Sulzbach. The Elector Palatine was *ex officio* chancellor and
dean of the Electoral College, and became automatically Reichs-Vikar (in-
terim representative of the Imperial dignity) when the Imperial throne
fell vacant. A Reichs-Vikar enjoyed the power of creating titles as high as
Count of the Holy Roman Empire. Karl Theodor was three times Reichs-
Vikar, and during those periods sold titles freely. The "Karl-Theodor counts"
constituted a special class in the Empire: they were not considered quite
genuine, though their honours were legally unassailable. In 1777, by the
death of the Elector of Bavaria without heirs, Karl Theodor became also the
sovereign of Bavaria, which he tried to trade with the Emperor in return
for provision for his illegitimate children. This brought on a war, the last
in which Frederick the Great engaged. Karl Theodor's reign in the
Palatinate was no less disastrous. He surrendered Mannheim and other
towns treacherously to the French Revolutionary armies, met from the
French Government the same bad faith he had shown towards his own
subjects, and had to flee to Saxony.
[4] Sir Adam had visited Mannheim briefly in 1757, while on the Grand
Tour.
[5] Properly *au cordeau:* laid out perfectly straight and intersecting at right
angles.

any streets that I have seen? I am in bad humour. The Court here is insupportable after the polite reception which I have met with at others. No invitation to dine with the Elector. I told Harold his court was not hospitable, and extolled that of Brunswick. At night I was at the *comédie.* There was a comic actor there the very image of Lord Kames. He had his size, his countenance, his voice, his manner. I never saw so strong a likeness.

TUESDAY 6 NOVEMBER

> Five winter days at Mannheim shall I be,
> And in my lines that city shan't you see?
> Shall not the Elector Palatine be prais'd
> And to the skies his noble court be rais'd?
> No, faith, my friend, to be exceeding plain,
> Such scurvy courts deserve no tuneful strain.
> Raise it? Why, faith, I'd raise it to the skies,
> As the bold eagle made the tortoise rise —
> That he might let it drop upon the stones,
> And to a jelly bruise its flesh and bones.

WEDNESDAY 7 NOVEMBER. I went and saw the Jesuits' Church, which is a very elegant piece. The outside is of white stone, with some fine carving and one or two good statues. The inside is very fine both in painting and gilding, though a little gaudy. Some of the panels were green. The painting is either crucifixion pieces or pictures in honour of the order. You find here a representation of the holy consolation afforded by the Jesuits and of their conversions in different parts of the globe. They seem to triumph far and near. There are here some elegant altar-pieces of marble.

I then went to see the Jesuits' College. I had heard that there was here a French Jesuit, Père Monier. I asked for him. He came to me immediately. He was a black, handsome man, between thirty and forty. He showed me their *réfectoire*, but told me that although their college had a good outside, it was but poor within. He showed me their garden, where he and I walked an hour. He had been in

Canada. He was shrewd and lively. He talked cleverly on the political affairs of Europe. He talked of the error of the French in having banished his order.[6] He said, "I am not angry at them. I pity
them. But soon they will open their eyes. They will see the terrible
consequences. They will see the decline of literature. Not precisely
that the Jesuits sustained it all alone, but they aroused emulation.
Now the other colleges will fall into neglect." He asked me if I was
Catholic. I told him, "No. But I hope I shall not be damned for
that" (striking him gently on the shoulder). "Do you really believe that I shall be damned?" He replied, "Sir, it is hard; but it is
absolutely necessary for me to believe it. You have not the excuse
of a poor peasant. You are enlightened." I smiled modestly. He immediately entered on the favourite subject of Jesuits, the Catholic
controversy. He run on with arguments which I do not conceive
any Protestant, truly attached to his religion as the only means of
salvation, could answer. I told Père Monier that I was of no sect.
That I took my faith from Jesus, that I endeavoured to adore God
with fervency; that I found my devotion excited by grand worship,
and that I was happy to worship in a Romish church. I said my notions of God made me not fear him as cruel. The Père said, "I am
really sorry that you are not a Catholic." He was so agreeable I almost regretted that I could not make him happy by thinking as he
did. But I took him by the hand, and said, "Sir, I shall have the
pleasure of meeting you in heaven."

I asked Captain Harold today why the Court here did not ask
strangers to dine. He said, "Sir, our Court preserves its grandeur by

[6] Because the constitution of the Society of Jesus places obedience to its own
General above that to civil or episcopal authority, the Jesuits have frequently been in conflict with Church and State in Roman Catholic countries.
France, after an investigation by a royal commission of archbishops and
bishops, had just suppressed the order entirely, but had allowed its members
to remain in the country as secular priests. In 1767 the Jesuits were expelled
from France, Spain, Naples, and Parma, though they still enjoyed the protection of the Pope, Clement XIII. Clement XIV, elected in 1769, suppressed
the order in all parts of the world, and it was not again restored to formal
legal existence till 1814.

not having many strangers at its table." "Sir," said I, "if the Elector believes that, he is very much deceived; for I shall always find more grandeur at a court where there is a superb table than at a court where there is none at all." In the evening we had what is called the Académie de Musique. It was very full, and the music was excellent. I quitted this court quite discontented.

[Boswell to John Johnston]

Mannheim, 7 November 1764

My dear Johnston, — To find Boswell in bad humour is no new thing for you. You have seen him sulky as a Welshman who has been rejected in the Heralds' Court, as an Englishman who has had his dinner spoiled, as an Irishman who has been detected in uttering five bulls and in forming a project to carry off a rich widow, and as a Scotsman who has lost an election or who has got a younger officer put over his head. I could give you many comparisons as excellent as these, should I come upon the Continent. But at present I would not choose to go out of His Majesty's dominions. If you ask me in a respectful manner why I am in bad humour, I shall tell you. I say, "in a respectful manner," because when a man is sulky he is also proud, and requires particular attention to be paid him, even by his best friends. Well do you know this, Johnston. Well may you remember how I begged of you one evening at Thom's[7] not to lean upon the table, because it gave me pain.

I am in bad humour in Mannheim because I have found here a very bad court. The Elector wants, forsooth, to be a prodigious great man. He gives an opera and a French comedy and a concert, or an Academy of Music as he calls it, all which entertainments are really magnificent. But then he treats strangers with a distance which makes some of them laugh at him and others curse him, according to their temperaments. For my own part, I have had an inclination to do both. As to his table I can say nothing. Strangers

[7] A tavern in Edinburgh.

are very seldom invited to dine there. I have not been asked once. What an inhospitable dog! I have been obliged to dine at an ordinary, amongst fellows of all sorts and sizes. It was one of the best tables in town, but the company disgusted me sadly. O British, take warning from me and shun the dominions of the Elector Palatine.

I remain, my dear Johnston, ever yours,

JAMES BOSWELL.

WEDNESDAY 7 NOVEMBER[8]

> Yes, be it bruis'd! It is a stranger's pray'r;
> And let th' Elector its destruction share!
> Burnt be his palace to the very ground,
> And let no vestige where it stood be found!
> For hospitality ne'er enter'd there,
> But studied grandeur, to make blockheads stare.
> At noon his Highness with dark face appear'd,
> And much he wanted to be greatly fear'd;
> His cringing courtiers play'd the shameful farce,
> But I still seem'd to bid him kiss my a———.

THURSDAY 8 NOVEMBER.[9] My ill humour continued. I was angry at myself. I saw my weakness. In such cases one must open. I said to Jacob, "I should not like to go to Switzerland in this humour." "Ah, Sir," said he, "when you see the peasants with their great breeches and long beards, the humour will pass off quickly enough." It was a dreary day. I stopped at an inn opposite to which was a convent of Capuchins. I heard them at mass. It made me solemn. After passing some very bad road, I arrived at Karlsruhe, the residence of the Court of Baden-Durlach. I put up at the Darmstädter Hof, a very good inn. I supped well, and recovered my good humour.

[8] Continuing the verses for 6 November.

[9] "Chairman, rhubarb, and thread, 17 groschen; powder, heavy paper, pens, 13 groschen; nails for mending the trunk, 2 groschen; diachylon [adhesive plaster] and eau de senteur [toilet water], 10 groschen; *Drink Gelt* at the Prince Frédéric, one crown twenty groschen" (Expense Account).

[Boswell, probably to Baron von Wachtendonck.
Original in French]¹

[Between Mannheim and Karlsruhe, 8 November 1764]

Sɪʀ: — Although my French is still far from good, I cannot refrain from expressing the infinite gratitude I owe his Highness the Elector Palatine for the courtesies with which I have been honoured at his court.

I hope, Sir, that you will have the goodness to excuse my French. My expression will perhaps be very imperfect. But my feelings are very clear. Be assured, Sir, that they come from the heart.

It is a standing jest against the English that they are somewhat uncivilized because strangers who come among them do not find the most agreeable of receptions. I fear that this jest is only too true, but I like to think that with time our rude islanders will become more civilized. Let them come to Mannheim. Let them be presented to the Court there. They will see there perfect politeness of manners; they will experience the charm of that politeness, and when they return home, they will try to imitate so fine an example. It is at Mannheim that one sees a gracious prince. It is there that one is convinced that a great prince, by being affable, loses no portion of the respect due to him. It is true that at Brunswick his Grace the Duke speaks to strangers, and that he has an absurd idea

¹ The manuscript of this piece of elaborate irony (a draft) is undated and records neither the place of writing nor the name of the intended recipient. It seems likely, however, that Boswell is addressing himself to the Grand Chambellan of the Court of Mannheim, for the person in question must have been in some way responsible for the entertainment of strangers at that court, and Boswell would probably have used English in writing to old Mr. Harold. In the absence of any certain evidence, I have assumed that he wrote it at that inn between Mannheim and Karlsruhe, where he stopped, presumably to wait for horses. I doubt that he actually sent it. The memorandum of 10 November ends, "Be prudent; swear *not* letter till Stuttgart," which may mean, "Don't send your letter to Mannheim till you have put more road between yourself and the Elector."

that when a man keeps his mouth shut, strangers may suspect that it is more prudent for him to do so than to open it—and perhaps also his Highness thinks he does well to show a little good sense and wit, as if those qualities were not entirely useless in a prince. Besides, the family of Brunswick is only a minor family, almost unknown in Europe. It is true that it has produced heroes of the greatest distinction and that it has made the most illustrious of alliances. But that is nothing to the Elector Palatine. Show me another prince in Europe who has a face as black as his. No, Sir, you will not find one. It is that that constitutes his Highness's unique glory; and a stranger is sufficiently rewarded in coming to Mannheim if he obtains permission to look half an hour a day at the celebrated black face of the Elector Palatine. I shall never forgive a remark of one of my countrymen, a man who had been at other courts and imagined that he would find similar manners at the great Court of Mannheim. When some one asked him, "Are you not satisfied? Did you not see his Highness's black face?" he replied brusquely, "Black face? Black face? The devil take it! Can't I buy a negro who has a face two degrees darker than his?"

It is also true that at Brunswick strangers eat at the Duke's table. His Highness does not think that strangers come there to be fed, for if a man were looking for ways to save money, he would hardly think of spending twenty louis on the road so as to be able to save five at Brunswick; but his Highness thinks that young noblemen on their travels would rather acquire polish in high company than pass their time at an inn. His Highness takes pleasure in helping young noblemen from abroad, and he finds that he has not diminished his grandeur in the least by having at his table people of good family who will everywhere express their delight at his goodness. But, as I have already had the honour to tell you, Brunswick is only a very, very small court. I hold in sovereign contempt the high officials, the ladies-in-waiting, and the gentlemen of that court who make it their business to speak immediately to strangers and to make their stay agreeable. But I admire the style of your antechamber, which resembles a café — I should say a very grand café. That's where one sees worthy people. You do not utter a word to a stranger, and no doubt he thinks you all oracles.

I commission you, Sir, to throw yourself at the feet of the Elector Palatine and to assure him of my gratitude in the terms which I have just stated to you. Do so, Sir, and you will infinitely oblige your most humble servant.

FRIDAY 9 NOVEMBER. The Baron de Thüngen, Maréchal of the Court of Gotha, had given me a letter for his sister, Madame de Schmidburg. She was not in town; so I was here without any recommendation. I sent a card to Monsieur de Stetten, Overschenk (Grand Échanson). He returned me for answer that he would mention me to the Margrave, and that he did not doubt but what I would be received at Court. A little after, he sent to me that the Margrave would be glad to see me, and that a coach would come at twelve to carry me to Court. A little after, Monsieur de Stetten paid me a visit. He was a colonel in the Margrave's service. He was a frank, polite, honest man. At twelve I had a coach and servant from the Court. I was a little hipped, but took resolution. I was presented to the Prince Brother,[2] who has a regiment in the Dutch service, a silent genteel man, and to the Prince Eugene, uncle to the Margrave *à la mode de Bretagne*, that is to say, cousin to his father. This Prince is in the Sardinian service.

Just before dinner the Margrave entered.[3] I was presented to him. He had a reserved, modest, amiable address. Monsieur de Stetten acted as Maréchal, and carried his cane, with which he

[2] Wilhelm Ludwig.

[3] Karl Friedrich (1728–1811), one of the most intelligent princes of his day. He supported the new German literature, was visited frequently by Voltaire, and attempted unsuccessfully to put the teaching of the Physiocrats into practice. He greatly increased his territories during his reign. In 1771, through the death of the Margrave of Baden-Baden without issue, he united Baden-Baden to Baden-Durlach. In 1805 he went over to the side of Napoleon, quadrupled the area of Baden, and assumed the style of Elector and later of Grand Duke. His grandson and successor married Napoleon's adopted daughter, Stéphanie de Beauharnais.

gave two distinct knocks on the floor; then the company said a silent grace; then we sat down to table, which was very well served. After table the Maréchal again gives his strokes, grace is said, the Prince retires a moment, coffee is ready, he returns and talks as long as he chooses. He told me he had been in England twice. He spoke English remarkably well. He talked of Lord Wemyss, Sir James Steuart, Lord Dunmore (all Scots, bravo!), and my Lord March, too.[4] His Highness knew well the present literature of Scotland. I talked to him of the Select Society, of my having been a member of it, of the same society with Hume and Robertson, &c. He was very attentive to every little anecdote. I found that I was truly agreeable to him. Monsieur de Stetten said to me, "Sir, the Margrave does not sup in company. But if you care to come to the *table du Maréchal* we shall be highly honoured." At eight I went to the Maréchal's table,[5] where I found Stetten, the Grand Écuyer, and a good jovial company. I was placed at the head of the table. Much respect was paid me. There was here a major, a Swede, as like Sir Joseph Yorke as a natural face can be to an artificial. Nature had given them both a good countenance. The Major's was better than the Ambassador's, and was not rendered ridiculous by affected airs. I was mightily amused with two young courtiers who wanted to be smart before me. One of them said, "You have read La Fontaine's *Fables?*" The other replied mincingly, "No, I am too much given to realities."

SATURDAY 10 NOVEMBER. At ten this morning Monsieur de Schmidt, a Swiss, Conseiller de la Cour, waited upon me and car-

[4] Lord Wemyss (the title had been forfeited) and Sir James Steuart were active Jacobites who fled to the Continent after the failure of the '45. Wemyss was one of Belle de Zuylen's suitors; Steuart is still known for his *Inquiry into the Principles of Political Economy*. Lord Dunmore had been a page of Charles Edward, but in view of his extreme youth at the time, had been pardoned; he later became Governor of Virginia. Lord March, later Duke of Queensberry, is notorious as "Old Q" or "the Star of Piccadilly."

[5] Boswell's French and English equivalents for German *Marschallstafel* are so literal as to be misleading. The word does not really mean "the Marshal's table," but rather the table of the grand officials of the court.

ried me to the Margrave's Library. I saw a very pretty collection. But one half of his Highness's books are at Bâle, where he has a palace. Monsieur Molter, the library-keeper, was very civil. He has travelled in Italy. He has a good deal of learning and some genius. He is just finishing the third volume of a German miscellany. He has in it odes of his own, and pieces which he has translated from the English. Schmidt proves to be a mighty knowing little man, especially in antiquities. He has gained several prizes before the Academy. He has the charge of the Margrave's cabinet. He told me his Highness said, "This gentleman pleases me greatly. He is a true philosopher." He had given orders to Schmidt to show me all he could and to Molter to give me out what books I pleased, and to send me a parcel of London newspapers. I saw a collection of curiosities, some of which were valuable enough. But the cabinet of medals is noble. We began this day to look at the ancient medals. Schmidt knows them perfectly. Were I a couple of months with him, I should be a tolerable antiquary. It is a pleasing study.

This day I was presented to the Prince Christoph, an Austrian general, brother to Prince Eugene. He was a plain, hearty cock. I talked with the Margrave on the gloomy religion of Holland, on the old method of preaching such as that of Bishop Latimer, and the strange method of talking to the Almighty of trifles, like the *auld* Scots *Gospel*-ministers. It has been still sad weather here. This afternoon it cleared up. I went and saw the stables, which are excellent. I walked in the wood and pheasant preserve, beautiful and wild. The Baron de Munzesheim, a genteel, lively young Gentleman of the Bedchamber,[6] lent me the *Nouvelle Héloïse* and *Émile*. I read two or three hours in the evening. I am perfectly happy here. I improve and am rationally amused. I came hither with intention to stay three days, and then go to Stuttgart. I will not go to Stuttgart. I will remain five or six days more here. I did not go this night to the Maréchal's table.

SUNDAY 11 NOVEMBER.[7] Last night I had resolved to go this

6 Descendant of a natural son of Friedrich VI (Margrave 1659–1677).
7 " ... Yesterday ... home and read *Héloïse*. ... Prepare for Rousseau. Keep

morning and see the Prince's decoy. It rained immensely. However, I went afoot attended by trusty Jacob, my *domestique de la Cour*, and old Seyfert, my *leyn lacquay* (my *valet de louage*), a good, steady, quiet fellow. A *valet de louage* is of no use here, but it is the mode to have one. So I must peaceably pay a florin a day on that account.[8] I saw the decoy, and some ducks taken. It is mighty simple. They take a vast number here. It shocked me to see the keeper twist about the necks of the ducks and toss them upon the grass to tumble in agonies till dead. When I got back again, I was wet to the skin. I dressed, went and had another college on medals. Then to table. This was a grand court day; the servants were richly dressed. There were many more covers. We had two ambassadors from the Court of Rastatt to enquire after the young princes, who have the smallpox. The Margrave was taken up today with public people. I had no conversation with him. I entered the chapel of the Court. It is handsome. I paid some visits, passed the evening at an assembly *chez* Monsieur de Gemmingen, Président de la Chambre de Finances. Supped Maréchal's table. It is taken kind in me to go there.

MONDAY 12 NOVEMBER. I have quite the disposition for travelling. When I find a court agreeable, I wish to remain there for life. I would be *attaché*. Were I but so fixed, O how tired would I be! I must however learn to keep my place at Auchinleck. It is my duty, as I am born a laird. Were all the German princes to go and live in the delicious Spain, their families would fall, and I would find no courts. This day I talked with the Prince on fate and

---

your valet if necessary; get habit of living as *grand seigneur*, and do so in London" (Memorandum, 11 November).

[8] Besides his permanent servant, Jacob Hänni, the Swiss who travelled with him, Boswell often engaged by the day in places where he made an extended stay a temporary or local servant whose main function was to act as guide. Among the Boswell papers at Yale is a leaf on which he has recorded the names of as many of these *valets de louage* as he could remember at the end of his tour, and has added characterizing comments in French. Le Jeune, at The Hague, was "clever"; Seyfert at Karlsruhe, "heavy, careful, intelligent, honest."

free will. I was clear and lively and strong. His Highness talked
with me today a long time. My morning was passed among the
medals and books. My evening in reading Rousseau,[9] and supping
at the Marshal's table.

TUESDAY 13 NOVEMBER. It is needless for me to mention
every day the medals and the Maréchal's table. I had much conversation today with the Prince. I told him how I obtained the acquaintance of Mr. Samuel Johnson. I told him how I had formerly
been an excellent mimic, but that I had given it up absolutely, as
it debased my character and procured me enemies. During dinner
we had talked much of Newmarket. I amused them mightily with
anecdotes of that place.[10] After table, Mr. Tanner, Honorary Professor of English at Strasbourg, paid his respects. He had been four
and twenty years in England, had learned the language extremely
substantially, but spoke with a most croaking accent. He talked of
having seen Mr. Garrick at Strasbourg. This evening I drank too
much Rhenish at supper. I was heated. I was alarmed lest my inclination for drinking should return. Why fear thus?

WEDNESDAY 14 NOVEMBER. Munzesheim had carried me
yesterday to visit a Conseiller de la Cour, where were two ladies
who sung. This morning Professor Tanner waited upon me. I was
quite a genteel *literatus.* I paid a visit to the young Prince's preceptor, a knowing, sharp little man, but somewhat of a German wit.
His name is *Ring* and he has written a treatise concerning *Rings;*
and as a ring is the image of eternity, so his name must be immortal. His wife was a poor, pale, little, insipid, good being. I was
amused to see Munzesheim place himself by her and coquet it with

[9] This reading, as we have seen, was not casual: the memorandum for 13
November again contains the injunction, "Prepare for Rousseau."
[10] At the time of Boswell's first visit to London in 1760 (see the editorial
narrative, p. 1), Lord Eglinton had taken him to the spring meeting at
Newmarket, a place famous for horse-races. There he had been admitted to
the Jockey Club, had met many of the sporting peers and gentlemen, and had
composed a rather silly burlesque poem, *The Cub at Newmarket,* which he
later published with a dedication to the Duke of York, brother of George III,
a young man of about his own age.

all the attention and all the airs of vanity which I have displayed to the finest women. It was pleasing and ridiculous. How finely varied are tastes! She however sung a very tender German song, the words by the brave Kleist, who was killed in the King of Prussia's wars: "Sie fliehet fort," &c.[1]

I then went with Schmidt, and saw a new building which does honour to this court. Below is a cabinet for natural curiosities, nobly contrived. This belongs to Madame the Margrave. Above is the Margrave's Library. I must have a draught of both these rooms. After dinner his Highness and I talked of religion. I gave him freely my notions. I maintained the religion of Jesus as displayed in the four Gospels. I maintained that it was intrinsically good. I talked with vehemence against David Hume and other infidels who destroyed our principles and put nothing firm in their place. His Highness said it was the most difficult thing to know if the Bible was really the word of God. He seemed to be a moderate sceptic. We talked very long this day. I had sent my respects to Madame the Margrave by Monsieur Schmidt, begging to be allowed the honour of waiting on her Highness. She was gracious enough to fix this afternoon for that honour. I mounted accordingly and found her comely, clever, easy, lively. I wished to have such a wife. She

[1] The opening words of the idyll "Amynt" by Ewald Christian von Kleist, officer in the Prussian Army, mortally wounded at the Battle of Kunersdorf, 1759. The first stanza runs as follows:

> Sie fliehet fort! Es ist um mich geschehen!
> Ein weiter Raum trennt Lalagen von mir.
> Dort floh sie hin! Komm, Luft, mich anzuwehen!
> Du kommst vielleicht von ihr.

(She flees away! I am in misery! A wide expanse separates Lalage from me. Thither she fled! Come, air, blow towards me! You come perhaps from her.) The Boswell papers at Yale contain a literal French version of the entire poem in Boswell's hand, and a manuscript, now defective, which once contained a notation of the air and the entire German text, written in German script. The composer of the air has not yet been identified. Max Friedländer, *Das deutsche Lied im achtzehnten Jahrhundert*, 1902, records settings before 1764 by C. P. E. Bach, J. P. Kirnberger, and F. W. Marpurg, but this is still another.

showed me a very fine cabinet of small pieces of the Flemish School. She showed me a Venus in crayon of her own painting. It was extremely fine, as also a little portrait of his Highness which she had taken from the life.[2] They were both excellent. I talked of her cabinet of curiosities. She said, "You can help to fill it. The Margrave tells me that you have promised to return here." "Madame, I shall indeed have that honour." "Now, you have made me a promise. A promise to two is more binding than to one." The Margrave entered and seemed pleased to see her Highness so much admired. One would scarcely believe that a princess could paint so. A young courtier passed the evening at my lodging.[3] He owned himself an infidel and a materialist, without any notion of futurity. I talked to him with firm vivacity; I showed him how inferior he was to me. And that if he reasoned right from his principles, he should steal my louis d'ors if he could conceal the theft.

THURSDAY 15 NOVEMBER. A sad cold has again taken possession of my head. Munzesheim gave me one of his horses, and he and I went to Durlach.[4] It is not a bad old town. It has some trade. It is lighted with lamps hung on ropes across the street. The Palace has been immensely large. We mounted a hill on which stands an old castle. From hence we had a most extensive view.

During dinner today, I talked with the Prince on planting. I had seen his new garden for all sorts of fruit-trees. It will be very noble. I was a little hipped today, and began to imagine the Margrave not so kind. Despicable weakness! I however talked with him on the human soul. He observed that we were absolutely ignorant how it was produced. "When the act of generation is performed," said he, "is there some Power ready to put in a soul at the critical minute, and to take it out again if the experiment fails?"[5] We

[2] The portrait reproduced opposite this page.

[3] The memoranda show that this was the Baron von Munzesheim. Boswell's suppression of the name probably means that at the moment he was more than usually conscious of a scheme to use the journal for writing a book of travels. For other indications of the same sort, see p. 137 ("I hope there's no offence") and p. 212 ("I hope no good Catholic will be offended").

[4] It had been the residence of the margraves until 1715.

[5] As has been explained above, p. xix, most of the conversation of Boswell's

Karl Friedrich, Margrave of Baden-Durlach, later Elector and Grand
Duke of Baden, from a red chalk drawing by his wife, the Margravine Karoline Luise, in the possession of H.R.H. Berthold, Margrave of Baden, Schloss Salem, Salem, Baden. (See opposite page.)

laughed very heartily at this speculative pleasantry, and I regained my good humour. I then waited once more on Madame the Margrave, and saw her pictures to great advantage. I then went to President Gemmingen's and heard some music. Then went home, but could do nothing. Made my excuse this evening to the Marshal's table.

FRIDAY 16 NOVEMBER. Munzesheim again carried me out to ride. It was charming weather. I was lively. I was amused to hear, "His Highness loves the girls. He likes something big and fresh that he can get without giving himself trouble, for he is modest."

And now let me record my talents as a courtier. From my earliest years I have respected the great. In the groves of Auchinleck I have indulged pleasing hopes of ambition. Since I have been in Germany it has been my ardent wish to find a prince of merit who might take a real regard for me, and with whose ennobling friendship I might be honoured all my life. I pleased myself with thinking that among the variety of princes whom I intended to visit such a one might be found. After having been at a number of courts, I had almost given up my idea. At the last court but one, my utmost wish has been fulfilled. I have found a grave, a knowing, and a worthy prince. He has seen my merit. He has shown me every mark of distinction. He has talked a great deal with me. Some days ago, I said to him, "Is it possible, Sir, that after I am gone from this I may give you any mark of my gratitude?" He answered, "I shall write to you sometimes; I shall be very glad to receive your letters." The Prince of Baden-Durlach has an order to give. He creates Knights of the Order of Fidelity. They wear a star and a ribbon hanging from their necks. My Lord Wemyss has this order. I fixed my inclination upon it. I was determined if possible to obtain it. When the Prince honoured me so far as to grant me his correspondence, I thought he would surely grant me his order. I asked him once *en passant* if only counts could have it. He said, "It is enough

---

German and Swiss tour was recorded by him in French and has been translated in this volume without special notice. The English of the conversations with Karl Friedrich, however, is Boswell's own, those conversations having been conducted in English.

to be a good gentleman." Munzesheim had told me that the Prince
was a little nice in giving it. This being my last day here, I was presented to take leave. The Prince said, "I cannot ask you to stay
longer, as I am afraid you would tire." I said, by no means, but I
was a little hurried at present, and would return again and pass a
longer time. I then took courage and said, "Sir, I have a favour to
ask of you, a very great favour. I don't know whether I should mention it." I was quite the courtier, for I appeared modest and embarrassed, when in reality I was perfectly unconcerned. He said,
"What, Sir?" I replied, "Your Highness told me that a good gentleman might have your Highness's order. Sir, might I presume to ask
you that, if I bring you proof of my being a very good gentleman,
I may obtain the order?" He paused. I looked at him steadily. He
answered, "I shall think of it." I said, "Sir, you have already been
so good to me that I flatter myself that I have the merit for obtaining such a favour. As to my rank, I can assure you that I am a very
old gentleman" (some days ago I had given his Highness a history
of my family) "and it may sound strange, but, Sir, I can count kin-
dred with my sovereign from my being related to the family of
Lennox and the royal family of Stuart.⁶ Sir, I am one of your old
proud Scots. If you grant me this favour, you will make me happy
for life, in adding honour to my family; and I shall be proud to
wear in my own country the Order of Fidelity of such a prince." He
seemed pleased. I said, "I hope, Sir, you do not take amiss my having mentioned this. I was anxious to obtain it, and I thought it was
pity to want what I valued so highly, for want of boldness to ask
it." He said, "Let me have your genealogy attested, and when you
return, we shall see." Oh, I shall have it.⁷ I took leave of his Highness with much respect.

⁶ True; he was descended on his mother's side from the Earls of Mar, and
they from the Earl of Lennox, grandfather of Lord Darnley, the father of
James I (VI). Sophia, Electress of Hanover, progenitress of the Hanoverian
kings of England, was grand-daughter to James I (VI). On his father's side
Boswell was descended from the Earl of Arran, whose mother was Mary
Stuart, eldest daughter of James II of Scotland.
⁷ This was something more than mere vanity; if he had returned to Karlsruhe,

I then went to President Gemmingen's, where I heard music and danced and was gay. I have a weakness of mind which is scarcely credible. Here amidst music and dancing I am as cheerful as if nothing had ever vexed me. My mind is like an air-pump. which receives and ejects ideas with wonderful facility. Munzesheim went home with me a little. I told him in confidence my proceedings with his sovereign as to the Order. He told me I would obtain it when I returned. I bid him speak plain. He assured me that I might depend upon having it. I supped at the Marshal's table, where I am much liked. It has been observed that the Grand Écuyer has spoken more to me than to any stranger. He is silent and backward. I have put him at his ease, led him on to talk of horses, of which I am, by the by, completely ignorant. But I had address enough to make that conversation go well on.

After supper I took leave of them all very kindly and said, "Gentlemen, I should be very unhappy at leaving this room if I thought I should not come back," and upon my word I thought so. Jacob is a most excellent fellow. I had mentioned to him my wish to have the Order. He wished it as much as I did, and to obtain it said he would walk a certain length, give a certain sum of money, or do some other extravagant thing which I do not remember. When I told him tonight that I was to have it, the fellow was quite overjoyed. I piqued his vanity by saying, "You shall have a master with a star."

SATURDAY 17 NOVEMBER. I had sitten up all night to journalize. As usual I felt myself immediately bettered by it. I discharged my bill. Last night I chose to make a figure, and gave to my coachman and *domestique de la cour* each a louis for the common purse of the servants, and each a ducat to himself. I had given them, besides, a bottle of wine a day. So that I have paid pretty well for my state. I set out composed and mild like my Lord Marischal. The

---

he might well have obtained his desire. In 1767 there were sixty-six knights of the Order of Fidelity, many of whom had no more impressive claims than Boswell. But he was debarred from returning by a complication of circumstances that will be explained later (p. 316).

Prince's Italian *coureur*, who resembled Lord Galloway, ran before my chaise a good way. I gave him what silver I had. The rogue knew how to flatter "Monsieur le Baron." I drove to Rastatt, the residence of the Margrave de Baden-Baden, the elder branch of the Baden family.[8] As he has no heirs, upon his death my worthy Margrave of Baden-Durlach will be the first of the family and will obtain an accession of country equal to what he has at present. My landlord gave me no very favourable account of his sovereign. He said he was very extravagant, and was always borrowing money, and was owing to butchers and bakers and the servants of the Court.

I caused myself be announced. The *fourrier*[9] came and told me in Latin that I should be welcome, and had a coach for me before six. I went, and found a very elegant palace in the outside, and pretty well within. The Prince was a neat, little, lively old fellow, quite easy and free. It was impossible to be bashful before him. The courtiers were very gracious. At six we went to a little theatre in the Palace, and saw a German play. One scene was ludicrous enough. A sort of Drawcansir[1] made a row of lubberly fellows stand behind each other and each take the left foot of his neighbour under his arm. Thus ranged, he bastinadoed them, and made them hop off the stage in a group. As I understood very little of the play and had been a night out of bed, drowsiness overpowered me and I fell sound asleep by the side of a very pretty young lady. We had a splendid supper.

SUNDAY 18 NOVEMBER. I went to the Prince's Chapel. The roof is very finely painted. He is a Catholic prince, so we had mass. There were seven masses at a time. The music was excellent. I was

[8] August Georg (1706–1771) succeeded his brother Ludwig Georg in 1761. He had originally been destined for the Church and had proceeded to the subdiaconate, but was permitted by a Papal bull to resign his orders and marry. He was of benevolent disposition, but rather weak, and completely under the control of his clergy.

[9] Officer charged with making arrangements for important visiting personages — an obsolete usage.

[1] Swashbuckler; so named from a character in the Duke of Buckingham's famous burlesque play, *The Rehearsal*.

very devout, and fully relished the contrast between *Affleck Kirk* and the Romish worship. Then went to Court, where I met with the two ambassadors whom I had seen at Karlsruhe: Monsieur de Freyberg, Chambellan, a kind, honest fellow; and Monsieur de Tetbourn,[2] officer of hussars, a tall, well made, worthy young fellow. We had a most excellent dinner, after which coffee; then the ladies retired, and the Prince and all we gentlemen went to the billiard-room, where we had billiards and faro, and now and then a glass of wine was served to the princes. The two Prince Uncles of Baden-Durlach were here. They come often. They love this court much better than their own. They have much more merriment and much more ease. The Margrave calls them "Mes chers princes." Today he called to one of them, "Christophe," quite familiar. I lost a louis at faro. Cards make me always melancholy. It is an instantaneous effect like a Presbyterian sermon.

Lest I may have forgotten it in its place, I now record that when at Berlin I made a most extraordinary experiment.[3] I composed a discourse against fornication quite like an old Scots minister. I said to myself, what damned stuff is this! and was clearly convinced that I said what was certainly true. I then read it aloud with the Presbyterian tone, and upon my word frightened myself. Ought not this to prevent me from being any more rendered dismal by a *domine?* No; for, as my Lord Marischal said, "A sermon is to me like a doleful tune, which I cannot resist."

In the evening we had a concert and cards. There is at this court the Margrave's niece, the Princess Elizabeth, a good civil princess.[4] The Prince has a particular regard for a Madame de Weyfelt;[5] and

---

[2] This probably should be Tettenborn.

[3] Probably after the adventure of 11 September, which was much more of a moral crisis than the flippancy of the entry indicates.

[4] The daughter of his brother and predecessor, the Margrave Ludwig Georg. The German principalities generally followed the rule of male succession.

[5] This should probably be spelled Weveld. A Baden Calendar for 1766 lists a Lotharius Baron von Weveld, Chamberlain to His Imperial Majesty, Privy Councillor to the Elector of Trier and the Court of Baden-Baden, Grand Master of the Chase for the hither and the farther County of Sponheim. Boswell's "Madame de Weyfelt" may have been the wife of this much-titled personage.

censorious people go the length to say that there is love between them. She is not handsome; but the idea of her being a mistress to the Prince made me think of her with a kind of desire, and even imagine her very well. There is here a Mademoiselle de Geismar, a charming creature, tall, handsome, good humoured, the only beauty I ever met with who had no caprice. I sat by her at supper, and gay we were.

MONDAY 19 NOVEMBER.[6] This, being St. Elizabeth's Day, is kept splendidly on the Princess's account. In the morning the troops paraded, and a fine figure they made. At ten we had a grand mass, with music still more noble than what we had yesterday. After all former woe, I was fully content. The troops discharged. We had a grand dinner, being all in gala, and having first paid our respects to the Princess. After dinner a fire broke out in the guard-room, and to extinguish this amused us some time. We then went to the billiard-room. Grünberg (Grand Maître to Madame la Margrave, who is always indisposed) is a very agreeable fellow. He made very nicely the distinction between temperament and humour. "Temperament is a certain constitution of the body. It has a great influence upon humour. But it does not wholly produce it. For one can have a bad temperament and good humour, if one has had a sound education. Look at the French. Without doubt some of them are restless by nature. However, you observe all of them to be good humoured." He was for a little more ease in the German courts, which he approves of as the great resource for the *noblesse*, which is truly the case. He told me that in a court where there is good order one never wearies. This court is the easiest that I have yet seen. They don't embarrass themselves by taking a ceremonious care of you. They leave you to your own choice. You have all sort of good things, and when you chat with them, they are polite and obliging. I see that if I had nothing else in view but to pass time, I might stay half a year here without any fear of strange looks or signs. It would give them pleasure.

[6] On this day Boswell records the purchase of six pairs of shoes at 1 crown 10 groschen a pair (Expense Account).

Yesterday I saw the Prince's treasure. He has a number of antiques of a size for seals and rings. I observed two pillars of about a foot and a half each, all surrounded with these antiques. He has a variety of very valuable things, but his glory is to possess the third diamond in Europe; after that of the King of France and that of the Emperor comes that of the Margrave of Baden-Baden. It is very large. It is fixed in a hat. This day was entirely filled up at Court. One might say not very profitably, but I answer I am forming my manners. I should have mentioned that I left some of my verses with the Margrave of Baden-Durlach.[7] This night I took leave here. I remember Mr. Brown told me that I should see a prodigious difference between the Protestant and Popish towns of Baden. I could not perceive it.

TUESDAY 20 NOVEMBER.[8] Set out early and drove to Strasbourg; was amused to find myself in the dominions of the French King, and to see on bills posted up, "De par le Roi."[9] My inn was L'Esprit. I wrote all the evening.

WEDNESDAY 21 NOVEMBER. I waited on young Monsieur Gayot, son of the Préteur Royal.[1] Monsieur Tanner had desired me to present his compliments. Monsieur Gayot was a genteel, black little man, much of the gentleman and the man of the world, quite *fait* as the French say. His father had been employed to take care of the provisions of the French Army, and he had resided much at Kassel, where he formed a friendship with Dr. Armstrong, Physician to the Army. He corresponds with him. He described the Doctor with great justness. "He is a man of hypochondriac cast whose physical constitution greatly influences his spirits. Before dinner he is quite dejected. But when he has had a bottle of good wine, he begins to come alive; he stretches his wings, he mounts like an

[7] A two-page sequence from the ten-line verses, entitled "London Verses." Professor Warnock found them in the summer of 1952 still reposing among the Margravine's papers at Karlsruhe.

[8] "... Enter not Suisse till Germany journalized" (Memorandum, 20 November).

[9] "In the King's name."

[1] The Governor of the city.

eagle. When he was like that, I would take him in my carriage outside Kassel. We would throw ourselves on the grass at our ease, and
he would harangue in the liveliest manner, with a celestial fire."
The Doctor has given a fine character of Monsieur Gayot in his
Epistle called *Day*.[2] Mr. Garrick had passed lately some time at
Strasbourg and had been much with Monsieur Gayot, who he said
had stolen his villa at Hampton, for Monsieur Gayot's is much the
same. Monsieur Gayot spoke good English, though his accent was
foreign. He has studied that language much. He observed that the
English put the pronoun possessive in the gender of the possessor
and not in that of the thing possessed: as, *his* mare, *her* horse,
which is very clear; whereas in all other languages the pronoun
possessive takes the gender of the thing possessed. Garrick had
owned that this was a perfection in our tongue which he had not
before attended to. I explained it to Monsieur Gayot and showed
him that we had but one pronoun possessive (*my*) which changes
not its termination. As for *his*, it is only the genitive of *he*; and *her*
is also the genitive; the *s* is not added on account of the harsh pronunciation.[3]

I found myself mighty well with Gayot. He asked me to dine
with him. He presented me to his lady, a young, pretty, sweet creature without any airs. She charmed me by calling her husband
always "Mon bon ami." We had with us also Monsieur le Docteur,
a physician, a great admirer of Dr. Pringle's, on account of his

[2] Yet Kassel else no sad retreat I find,
While good and amiable Gayot is my friend,
Generous and plain, the friend of humankind;
Who scorns the little-minded's partial view,
One you would love, one that would relish you.
With him sometimes I sup, and often dine,
And find his presence cordial more than wine.
John Armstrong, *Day: an Epistle to John
Wilkes*, the concluding section

[3] Not a very impressive testimonial to the linguistic knowledge of a man who
proposed to compile an etymological dictionary. The genitive of feminine
nouns and pronouns in Old English was regularly formed without *s*, as in
modern German. Hence such survivals as "Lady-chapel," where the "Lady"
is historically genitive ("Our Lady's chapel").

knowledge, judgment, and vivacity of style. He had studied man
as a machine,[4] and said, "Man depends on the position in which he
finds himself." We had an agreeable friendly dinner, after which
Monsieur le Docteur gave me some arguments for materialism
which I could not answer. Monsieur Gayot sent for Professor
Schoepflin, Royal Historiographer. He is of the country of Baden-
Durlach and has lately written an elegant Latin history of the
principality of Baden. It consists of five or six volumes and is elegantly printed at Karlsruhe. This gentleman was a tall figure, full
of knowledge, healthy and lively. We went to his house, and saw
his library, which is immensely rich in history and antiquities.[5]
He said, "Your sceptics say, 'Why study so much the facts of history? Perhaps they are not true.' To that I reply, 'Let us suppose,
gentlemen, that they are fables; still, they are fables which everybody talks about, and of which you ought not to be ignorant.' I shut
their mouths by speaking thus, and spare myself the considerable
trouble of explaining to them the force of faith in history." This
was putting the matter in a new light with great justice. Monsieur
Gayot was kind enough to offer me his coach while I remained at
Strasbourg. But I did not put him to that trouble.

THURSDAY 22 NOVEMBER. I went and saw the Cathedral,
which is one of the noblest pieces of Gothic architecture that I ever
beheld. Mr. Garrick had written verses expressing his indignation
at seeing little shops built round it. Monsieur Gayot showed me the
verses, and I answered them. I entered a little and heard solemn
service. I then waited on Schoepflin. He is really an able man, and
his attachment to the Margrave of Baden-Durlach makes me regard him particularly.[6] A student and his governor entered. I be-

[4] See p. 115 *n.* 10.

[5] Jean Daniel Schoepflin (then in his seventieth year) was one of the most
famous university professors of the time. Boswell does his library no more
than justice: it contained twelve thousand volumes and was considered one
of the best historical collections owned by an individual in his day. He later
presented it to the city of Strasbourg. It was burned in the Prussian bombardment of the city, 24 August 1870.

[6] If he hoped to induce Schoepflin to mention him favourably, he succeeded.
On 29 November 1764 Schoepflin wrote to Karl Friedrich as follows (original

came a little splenetic. There needs no more to turn the course of my ideas.

Gayot paid me a visit, and then carried me home to his house, where I dined. We had Monsieur l'Abbé, uncle to Madame Gayot, and our good friend Monsieur le Docteur. We were gay and cheerful. I should have mentioned yesterday that Madame Gayot made me a present of a collection of prints representing the rejoicings of Strasbourg on the arrival of the King.[7] I could not carry them with me. She promised to give me them as I returned to Karlsruhe or to send them for me to England. This day after dinner Monsieur Gayot showed me a genteel room, saying, "Now then, when you return, here is your room. It is better than L'Esprit. You will either stay here, or at my house in the country." Was there ever more civility? And he had not a crumb of the usual flattery. He is a noble fellow. He told me I had a French air, and that I would undoubtedly speak good French. He bid me speak slow to avoid the hissing pronunciation of the British. He told me he had been early accustomed to suffer, and so had acquired calm fortitude of mind. He told us several good stories. I passed the evening at the *comédie*, which is not very brilliant here. I was pleased with one song, "Maudit Amour," &c.[8] I was sorry not to find there the Marshal Contades who was the French general at the Battle of Minden. He is at present commander here.

---

in French): "Mr. Boswell the Scotsman, who has passed through Strasbourg, has the most active sense of the favours which you have heaped on him. He is a young man who will go far. He has knowledge and good judgment. I have laid out his route for him. On his return from Italy, he will go by Vienna, Munich, Ratisbon, Stuttgart, to Karlsruhe, and from there by way of Strasbourg to Paris" (*Brieflicher Verkehr*, ed. Richard Fester, 1906, p. 172).

[7] Louis XV, after his recovery from smallpox at Metz had gained him the title of "le Bien Aimé," made a triumphal entry into Strasbourg, 5 October 1744, ostensibly as the deliverer of Alsace from the Imperial Army, which had actually evacuated it some weeks before. The "collection of prints" was a magnificent album engraved by Weis: *Représentation des fêtes données pour la convalescence du Roi, &c.*

[8] "Accursed Love," a song from *Le Peintre amoureux de son modèle*, words by Anséaume, music by Duni, 1757.

UPON SEEING STRASBOURG CATHEDRAL
EXTEMPORE BY A STRANGER
(DAVID GARRICK, ESQ.)[9]

That hallow'd spire which rises to the skies
Fills ev'ry heart with rapture and surprise;
Approach the temple — round its rev'rend base
Vile traffic shops God's edifice disgrace.
Are there still Goths in this enlighten'd age
Who dare oppose and scorn the sacred page?
Who by one impious act at once express
Their want of virtue, taste, and righteousness?

[ANSWER BY BOSWELL]

Stranger, why storm so fierce because around
This grand cathedral our poor shops are found?
Why call us Goths? Why rank us among those
Who would the sacred oracles oppose?
　In times of old, the greedy sons of gain
Their booths set up in Judah's lofty fane;
The place of pray'r most impiously made
A crowded scene of bustling, babbling trade;
Till the Messiah came with awful rod,
And drove the thieves from out the house of God.
But we the temple would not dare defile:
We hold in honour this majestic pile;
With humble rev'rence by its walls we stay,
In honest business to employ the day;
And, while thus cover'd by its holy shade,
Say, "To do wrong, who would not be afraid?"

[9] An early version of Garrick's lines. He later added a couplet and made some other changes. Boswell's answer is now printed for the first time.

BOSWELL WITH

ROUSSEAU AND VOLTAIRE

1764

Boswell with
Rousseau and Voltaire, 1764

ROUSSEAU AND VOLTAIRE. Jean Jacques Rousseau, who has sometimes been said to have influenced history more profoundly than
any other human being born in the Christian Era, was a Swiss of
French stock, born in Geneva in 1712, and was consequently fifty-
two years old when Boswell penetrated his retreat at Môtiers. After
having spent the first thirty-eight years of his life in obscurity as
footman, teacher, secretary, musical composer, copier of music,
hack writer, and vagabond, he emerged into fame with a *Discourse
on the Arts and Sciences*, in which he maintained with infectious
eloquence the paradox that the savage state is superior to the state
of advanced civilization. In three large works, *The New Héloïse*,
Émile, and *The Social Contract*, all published within a period of
eighteen months in 1761–1762, he presented revolutionary views
on the most important of all subjects: government, education, religion, sexual morals, and family life. He became at once the most
powerful force in European letters, and because of the revolutionary character of his ideas, collided violently with Church and
State. For some years before the publication of *Émile* (a section of
which, entitled "The Creed of a Savoyard Vicar," contains the full-
est statement of his views on religion), he had been living in Paris;
and he published the book there, with the assurance of protection
from powerful friends, at the end of May, 1762. It was promptly
condemned, and an order issued for his arrest. With the connivance
of the authorities, he fled from Paris to Yverdon, a dependency of
the state of Berne. Geneva (the most powerful of the states of the

Swiss confederation) in turn condemned him, and brought pressure on Berne to order his expulsion. On 10 July 1762 he took refuge nearby in Môtiers, a small mountain village in the territory of Neuchâtel, which at that time was not a part of the Swiss confederacy but an independent principality, its sovereign being the King of Prussia. The Governor was none other than our old friend Lord Marischal, who extended to the harassed author his own tactful friendship and the guarantee of protection from Frederick.

If we are to see Rousseau as Boswell saw him early in December, 1764, we must erase from our minds nearly everything we know about his private life. This knowledge comes mainly from *The Confessions*, which were not yet written, and were not published until after Rousseau's death. Some twenty years before, he had taken as concubine an illiterate French girl named Thérèse Le Vasseur, a servant at an inn. According to Rousseau's own account, which has been doubted but apparently without good reason, Thérèse bore him five children between 1746 and 1755. All, immediately after their birth, were placed in the Foundling Hospital in Paris, only the first being given any mark of identification. Rousseau's justification at the time was that he was so wretchedly poor, and Thérèse's relations were such a bad lot, that he thought the children would have a better chance in the hospital than under his own care. He *was* very poor, and he appears to have been justified in his judgment of Thérèse's relations; he was also ashamed of his connection with Thérèse and unwilling to publish it; he did not wish to be bothered with the care of children; finally, he was afflicted all his life by a perverse disinclination to do the right thing at the right time. Later on, when he was writing his great books, he passed through an intense moral struggle and emerged as the "savage philosopher," genuinely ascetic in theory and practice. (In 1758, he had indicated his change of heart by a tract condemning the theatre.) In 1761 he revealed his secret to Madame de Luxembourg. He had, he told her, ceased his intercourse with Thérèse some time since. The thought of the abandoned children filled him with remorse, and he begged her to try to find them. She made such search as was possible, but in vain. Unfortunately, three or four other people knew the secret, and one of them used it as a weapon to strike him down at a time when he little expected such a blow.

At Môtiers Rousseau was situated in what for him were nearly ideal conditions. He was a neurasthenic who found it necessary sooner or later to quarrel with every one who put him under obligation, and at Môtiers he was better able than in Paris to fend for himself and avoid either courting favours or accepting them. He could spend more uninterrupted time at his desk there, an important point for a professional man of letters whose sole income came from his pen. As a recluse he could manage somewhat better his chronic physical complaint — a congestion or constriction of the urethra, which caused frequent painful urination and made him at all times uneasy. (For one thing, he could at Môtiers wear with less embarrassing notice the Armenian caftan — a cassock-like gown — which he had adopted as a measure of relief and convenience.) But beyond all this, he loved country scenery passionately for its own sake, both as affording an outlet for the nature-mysticism of which he was one of the earliest exponents, and as providing opportunity for his hobby of botanizing.

In brief, Rousseau at long last had won his way to decency and self-respect, and was living a quiet, frugal, productive, and tolerably happy life. Boswell saw him at the very height of his unclouded fame: saw him as a fearless and virtuous philosopher, persecuted by civil tyranny and ecclesiastical bigotry, a figure deserving the homage of the young, the generous, and the ardent.

Rousseau could probably have continued to enjoy his retreat at Môtiers indefinitely if he had been willing to keep quiet, but to keep quiet was not in his nature. In a published reply to the Archbishop of Paris, he continued to air his religious views, which were equally offensive to orthodox Catholics, orthodox Protestants, and atheist *philosophes*; he defiantly and publicly renounced his Genevan citizenship, and encouraged a numerous party of supporters at Geneva in what amounted to a democratic revolt against the

Government. Jean Robert Tronchin, a member of the Genevan Council, defended the condemnation of *Émile* in *Letters Written from the Country*, to which Rousseau replied in *Letters Written from the Mountain*, an eloquent and inflammatory attack on the ruling oligarchy of the city. As we shall see, Boswell's travelling-companion from Strasbourg to Bâle, a Monsieur Boily, was bringing Rousseau some advance copies of this work. It reached Geneva on 18 December 1764, in the interval between Boswell's last conversation with Rousseau and his own arrival there. To continue the narrative one must now turn to the other great object of Boswell's Swiss quest.

François Marie Arouet, a Parisian, universally known by his assumed name of Voltaire, by many degrees the most famous man of letters then living in the western world, had recently celebrated his seventieth birthday. In English-speaking countries at the present day the first section of his extremely voluminous works that one thinks of is the ironic prose tales, of which *Candide* is the supreme example, but in 1764 one thought of him first of all as epic and dramatic poet (he wrote over fifty plays in verse, among them some of the most admired tragedies in the French classical tradition); then also as historian, philosopher, critic, and controversialist. His entire life was spent in sniping from not-too-precarious hide-outs at the political and religious orthodoxy of his country. In 1726, to escape imprisonment for having spoken back to a powerful nobleman, he exiled himself in England, and remained there for three years, moving in distinguished society, learning the language, and observing with appreciative eye the English tradition of free speech. From 1751 to 1753 he was domiciled with Frederick the Great in Potsdam, leaving after a quarrel that appears not to have been very creditable to either of them.

The epithet most commonly applied to Voltaire in the eighteenth century was that most commonly applied to him now: sceptic. He was a deist, but a deist of the hard-minded variety, and never passed up an opportunity to mock at all particular scriptures and all particular religions. Mockery, indeed, was his forte. He is never more hilarious than when he engages in one of his completely unscrupulous dead-pan expositions of the content of literary works that he dislikes: Shakespeare's *Hamlet*, the book of the prophet Ezekiel, Rousseau's *Nouvelle Héloïse*.

In 1758 Voltaire settled at Ferney, about four miles from Geneva, but on French soil. At Ferney he could enjoy both the social liberty of France and the political liberty of Geneva; and he prepared for these states' turning on him simultaneously by purchasing houses also in the Canton of Vaud and the Kingdom of Sardinia, both close at hand. His writings and his shrewd business dealings had brought him great wealth, and he lived in a château like a seigneur, amidst a constant crowd of guests — thin as a skeleton, toothless, with a long nose and with youthful eyes flashing out from under his wig. Altogether a very different sort of man from the prickly hermit of Môtiers.

Rousseau had begun as a warm-hearted admirer of his brilliant elder, but had come gradually to abhor his mocking scepticism. Though his own affirmative beliefs did not go beyond deism, he never publicly ridiculed any religion, and in fact believed that without some kind of established church, morality and civic virtue were impossible. His animosity was sharpened when in 1755 Voltaire settled at Les Délices, just outside the gates of Geneva, became the city's idol, built a private theatre, and stirred up his friend D'Alembert to attack the Genevan prohibition of dramatic performances. Rousseau, instigated partly by jealousy but in the main by sincere belief, replied to D'Alembert in a famous *Letter* in which he accused Voltaire of corrupting the Spartan virtue of his native city. In 1760 he sent one of his characteristically brilliant and savage letters to Voltaire himself: "In short, I hate you, since you will have it so." That, for Rousseau, would have ended the matter. It was his habit to quarrel very freely, but he was incapable of subterfuges or of taking any practical action to harm an enemy. In attacking Voltaire he had foolishly pitted himself against one of the most tenacious, devious, and ruthless minds in Europe. Voltaire began, under a pseudonym, by subjecting the *Héloïse* to coarse ridicule, and was probably instrumental in bringing about the Genevan condemnation of *Émile*. Voltaire's personal physician, Dr. Theodore Tronchin, cousin of the author of *Letters Written from the Country*, was one of the four or five living persons who knew the sad secret of Rousseau's infants. He seems, directly or indirectly, to have informed Voltaire; and on 27 December 1764 Voltaire published a pamphlet, *How the Citizens Feel*, ostensibly composed by a devout Genevan pastor, attributing Rousseau's complaint to venereal disease, accusing him of having exposed his children, of killing Thérèse's mother by his heartless treatment, and of abusing Thérèse herself. Rousseau read this pamphlet on 31 December (a little more than two weeks after Boswell's departure), and from that time was a broken man, frequently insane, always on the verge of insanity. The remaining fourteen years of his life were mainly occupied by frantic flights from persecutors, who seem, after 1765, to have been wholly imaginary. Boswell's visit could not have been more dramatically timed. Had he come only a little later, he would almost certainly have missed the charming and gentle domestic idyll (the dinner in Rousseau's kitchen) which is the high point of his interviews.

Boswell's manœuvres to secure extended conversations with Voltaire are fully explained and commented on in his own records. There are no hidden currents moving under the surface of those interviews. But the reader will perhaps be helped at the outset if the random and sometimes cryptic references to Rousseau in the journal and memoranda prior to December, 1764 are pulled together into an explicit statement.

Boswell came to Rousseau as a disciple to a master, as a patient to a physician, in a sense as a penitent to a confessor. Though he had made up his mind to visit Rousseau as far back as the summer of 1763, there is no clear evidence that before the autumn of 1764 he knew any of Rousseau's writings except "The Creed of a Savoyard Vicar," and he may not have actually read that. When he left Berlin and started on a tour which was to bring him to Môtiers by definite stages in ten weeks or less, he began, after his usual fashion, to prepare himself for the interview. As he moved along through the German courts and into Switzerland, he read straight through the *Nouvelle Héloïse* and *Émile*. He had intended only to equip himself with the knowledge necessary to ask good questions; he experienced a violent conversion. As early as 27 September he was counselling himself to "see Rousseau and get full advice." *Full* advice, which of course implied that Rousseau should first have given a patient and careful hearing to the whole story of Boswell's most extraordinary life. There is consequently an unexpressed comedy being played throughout the first three interviews: Boswell is trying to manœuvre Rousseau into the confessional; Rousseau, uneasy from his malady and on pins and needles to get back to his desk, is showing alarmingly resourceful resistance, and is eluding Boswell whenever he brings the conversation towards a propitious opening. How Boswell managed a reversal of situation and finally got a hearing for his confession had best be left for the reader to discover in its place.

―――――――――

FRIDAY 23 NOVEMBER.[1] I said last night to Jacob, "Do let us get off once without being hurried." We did so today. My rogue of a coachman had engaged a Frenchman to go in my machine, and to pay him twelve livres to Bâle. I was very angry, and wanted to keep him out. But hearing that he had not paid the coachman, I took him in on condition that he should pay me ten livres and give the coachman nothing. He was a very genteel, clever young fellow, an engraver, who had passed three years in Holland. He was knowing and lively, modest for a Frenchman.[2] We had a good day's journey to ———.[3]

[1] "... This day, all packed — no haste. Set out. Read. *Retenu,* but cheerful. Never own changes. Plan Rousseau" (Memorandum, 23 November).
[2] This gentleman, Charles Ange Boily, had a commission for Rousseau, though Boswell apparently did not discover it. He was to deliver to Rousseau eight advance copies of the *Lettres écrites de la montagne,* from the Amsterdam publisher Rey, and to take Rousseau's portrait for an engraving. He seems, however, not to have gone to Môtiers, but to have sent the packet by other hands.
[3] Probably Colmar.

SATURDAY 24 NOVEMBER. We were very gay. Monsieur Boily, my Frenchman, made a very just distinction between his nation and the British. "The English think themselves superior to other people, and hold them in sovereign contempt. The French have no scorn for others. But it is certain that they think themselves superior to all other nations." He taught me a song. He was a materialist too, forsooth. He made scarcely any distinction between master and servant. He had no judgment to know when to speak and when to hold his tongue.

We now entered Switzerland. They are a phlegmatic nation. Jacob showed no signs of lively joy at the sight of his country.[4] We arrived at Bâle and put up at the Three Kings, finely situated on the bank of the Rhine. Imhof, our landlord, was a most original fellow. He was prodigiously fluent in the praises of his town, which he said deserved to be seen at great length, so that I should stay with him several days. He went out and took a turn with us, expatiating on all that he saw. We supped at his table d'hôte, where he harangued on the number of people and on the distinguished savants who had been in his house. He said, "Voltaire came here. He went to bed. I asked his servant, 'Does your master wish any supper?' 'I don't know. It all depends. Perhaps yes, perhaps no.' Well, I had some good soup made, and a chicken dressed. Monsieur Voltaire wakes up; he asks for supper. I serve him the soup. He takes it. He refuses it. Then he takes it again. 'It is excellent soup!' A gentleman had come in, and I gave him half the chicken. I serve the other half to Monsieur Voltaire. He takes it. He refuses it. Then he takes it again. 'It is an excellent chicken!' He is annoyed because he has not a whole chicken, and keeps saying, 'Half a chicken is no chicken! Half a chicken is no chicken!' In short, he was very

[4] "Jacob was a Bernese, and for a Bernese, Switzerland means the Canton of Berne. Bâle or any other part of Switzerland would leave him quite unmoved. Right enough, when they get to Berne, Boswell has occasion to observe that Jacob rejoiced to find himself in his own capital. Another proof of Boswell's accurate reporting" (Dr. Fritz Güttinger of Zürich, translator of Boswell into German, in a letter to the editor).

well pleased with my house." There goes a specimen *Eloquentiae Imhoffianae.* He amused me much, and I concluded him to be either a very honest fellow, or a very great rogue.[5] I had a most excellent bedchamber.

SUNDAY 25 NOVEMBER. I read with attention Rousseau's "Creed of the Savoyard." I was struck with its clearness, its simplicity, and its piety. I went and saw the famous Dance of Death, which has been called the work of Holbein, as that painter was of this city, but it was in reality painted by Jean Klauber. It is very old, but has been so often mended that, like William the Lion's chair at Aberdeen, it has very little remaining of the first work. I bought a book of the designs and inscriptions. It is in a covered gallery, with rails in front, that the Death's Dance is placed. Malicious boys now and then get at it with stones, and spoil it.[6] I dined with our *hôte* who raged, "A man must live. We make nothing here." I then went and saw the Arsenal, which contains a great many arms kept in the best order. They shone like a looking-glass. There are here many arms taken from the Duke of Burgundy.[7] I then waited on Monsieur Wolleb, President of the Chamber of Justice. I had been recommended to him by Professor Gottsched at Leipzig. I found him a German-Swiss *literatus,* full of animal spirits. I put him at his ease, and he talked away with much volubility.

[5] Casanova thought him a rogue. He kept a register in which he characterized as scoundrels all his guests who did not give him as large tips as he thought they should have done.

[6] This painting was destroyed by a mob in 1806.

[7] At the battles of Grandson and Morat, in the year 1476. These famous victories over the greatest warrior prince of the time demonstrated decisively the superiority of the armies of the republican burghers and peasants of the Swiss confederation to those of their monarchical and feudal neighbours. Charles the Bold, Duke of Burgundy, who was brother-in-law to Edward IV of England and for years treated with Louis XI of France as with an equal, was so badly defeated by the Swiss that the power of Burgundy was broken, and Louis XI was able to seize the Duchy. See Byron's *Childe Harold,* III. lxiii–lxiv and (for a popular treatment of Charles's last war) Scott's *Anne of Geierstein.*

He told me a most curious anecdote. The clock of the city of Bâle is about an hour before all the clocks in the country, and indeed before the sun himself, by which they are regulated; so that when a stranger sets out from Bâle at noon, after travelling a league, he finds it noon still. Various are the causes assigned for this particularity of the Bâle clock. Some say that there was a conspiracy of the citizens to rise in arms at a certain hour, and that the magistrates, having had notice of it, advanced the clock an hour; so that some of the conspirators came to the rendezvous too late, and others too soon, and in short were all in confusion. Some again maintain that the enemy was at their gates, and were to be let in at a certain time by some wicked malcontents, but that a miracle was wrought in the favour of Bâle, and the clock advanced an hour. This tradition is highly natural. It flatters their vanity and pleases their superstition to suppose such an interposition of Providence. No less a man than the late famous mathematician Bernoulli set himself to account for this strange mensuration of time. He supposed that they had taken a dial which was not just to regulate the clock of the Cathedral by. By this means the Cathedral clock has been put wrong, and the others have followed. But this account will not suffice; for if the dial for the Cathedral clock had been bad, it would have been corrected by the others. Wolleb said that most probably the clock had been advanced during the Council of Bâle, that the ecclesiastics might meet an hour sooner, perhaps with design to be an hour sooner with their mistresses. As the Council lasted ten years, the irregularity of the clock became a custom.[8] I asked if they did not think to correct this absurd custom. A grave gentleman of authority in the city gravely replied that not a year ago the affair had been debated in Council, and some of the members had maintained that the clock should not be changed, as it might perhaps bring ruin upon their republic. Is it possible that such darkness can remain in an age so enlightened?

[8] The Council, the third of the reforming councils of the fifteenth century, actually sat at Bâle for seventeen years, 1431–1448. But it is now believed that the eccentricity of the Bâle clock was a survival of the mediaeval method of counting the hours.

Wolleb said that the servants and workmen would lie longer abed by the change; as to rise at five would appear terrible, although they really rise at present at that hour by the name of six.

I must give a specimen of Wolleb's wit. When in England he said, "You English don't love the foreigners; and yet had it not been for a foreigner, you would be damned. You own there is no salvation but through Jesus Christ." — "Yes, sure." — "Well, Jesus Christ was a foreigner. Ha! ha!" This is wit like Kennicott's.[9]

[Boswell to the Margrave of Baden-Durlach][1]

Bâle, 25 November 1764

Sir: — I am persuaded that no man ever obtained what he valued very highly without feeling a strong degree of agitation when he prepared to enjoy it. Therefore, Sir, I am not surprised to feel myself a good deal embarrassed when I sit down to write to the Margrave of Baden-Durlach. Permit me to assure your Highness of my gratitude for all your goodness towards me. The gracious reception which I met with at the Court of Karlsruhe was more than I could expect. But to be honoured with your Highness's correspondence is a favour so great, a distinction so flattering, that I must be excused for not expressing my sense of it to the Prince himself; for, let me write with as much delicacy as I could, there would still be an appearance of adulation. I am the more proud of the honour done me that I obtain it without my asking it, without giving any hints that I wished for it. A man rarely wishes for what is very far beyond his reach; and I assure you, Sir, that this honour appeared so to me. Allow me however to say that it would have given me pain to have quitted your Highness for ever. The conversations after dinner had insensibly attached me to a worthy philosopher whom Providence had made a prince. Your Highness will pardon my manner of talking. It is impossible for me to avoid

[9] Apparently Benjamin Kennicott (1718–1783), the biblical scholar. His controversial style was extremely blunt.

[1] From a photostat of the original, among the Margrave's papers in the Grand-Ducal Family Archives at Karlsruhe. Boswell's draft, which is among the papers at Yale, shows only trifling differences from the letter as sent.

it without subjecting myself to a cold restraint, and, instead of expressing my natural sentiments, composing a formal epistle which might serve for any other man as well as for myself.

I passed two days at Strasbourg, where I procured a copy of Mr. Garrick's verses on the Cathedral. I beg leave to present them to your Highness, with my answer to them. Garrick is very angry that there are shops kept around the Cathedral. I immediately undertook the cause of the shopkeepers and wrote their answer. But I went next morning to view the Cathedral, and I found that I was in the wrong. Like an honest advocate who has undertaken an unjust cause, I am very happy not to be successful in my pleadings. It gives me much satisfaction to hear that the shops are soon to be removed. . . .

May I presume to beg of your Highness to offer my most humble respects to Madame the Margrave, whose elegant genius and amiable affability charm my remembrance by turns and make me doubt which of them to admire most. I ask pardon for writing so much and saying so little.

I have the honour to be, with the most perfect respect, your Highness's most faithful, humble servant,

JAMES BOSWELL.

In care of Messieurs Cazenove, Clavière et fils, à Genève.

MONDAY 26 NOVEMBER. Bâle makes me think of my worthy father, as Erasmus and Frobenius lived here.[2] Wolleb waited upon me. We talked of Rousseau's idea of teaching nothing to a child before twelve or fourteen, because before that age a child has no inclination to learn, and he should never be forced. "But," said Wolleb, "a child may have an inclination to learn earlier. For example, I have a daughter. I always used to say, 'Are you in the humour?' If she said yes, I taught her something; if not, I left her alone." I asked him if he took no method to force her inclination.

[2] Lord Auchinleck collected and read fine old books, and the great Dutch humanist Erasmus (?1466–1536) was one of his favourite authors. Johann Froben (?1460–1527) of Bâle, a famous printer, was a friend of Erasmus and printed many of his works.

"I own that I said to her, 'You must not often be out of the humour.' " "Ah, Sir," said I, "you spoil everything."

I went and saw a private collection of pictures, some of which were good. I then saw at the Maison de Ville a picture by Holbein, the Sufferings of Christ, in eight pieces. I wrote a description of it.[3] I then saw the Cathedral Church, one of the venerable Gothic buildings. The pulpit is of stone curiously carved. In those times when this church was built, superstition run high, but morals were at a very low ebb. There is carved in this church a monk in most gross copulation with a nun. Wolleb also showed me an old Popish chapel on the Pont du Rhin. Above the door was a niche in which was formerly placed a statue of the Virgin, and under this niche, by way of ornament, was carved a woman's thighs wide open and all her nakedness fully displayed. It has appeared so indecent that they have effaced it a little, yet still the *ipsa res* appears. At two we went and saw the College Library, which is very numerous, and has a good many manuscripts. I asked for a manuscript Anacreon.[4] But, O strange penury! There was here neither manuscript nor

[3] There seems to be no compelling reason for including this description in the present edition, but it exists among the Boswell papers at Yale in two forms: Boswell's own note, made with lead pencil, and a copy in ink made some years later by his clerk, James Brown. The fact is that the content of the note is less interesting than the medium in which it was recorded, Boswell manuscripts in pencil being relatively rare. In all the great mass of documents at Yale, perhaps not more than a dozen are in pencil, though many of those in ink were obviously jotted down in places where a desk and the ordinary furniture for writing with ink would not have been available. Boswell clearly carried some kind of portable ink-horn and pen with him most of the time, and used this pocket-pen regularly in preference to a pencil. — Hans Holbein's altar-piece, often considered his masterpiece, is now in the Holbein Room of the Museum at Bâle.

[4] Boswell's friend and mentor, Sir David Dalrymple, had thoughts of preparing an edition of the Greek lyrics, and had asked Boswell to consult the manuscripts of the Library of the University of Leyden, including a manuscript of Anacreon, and to send him a note on their contents. Lord Auchinleck, who was a good classical scholar, also took a special interest in Anacreon. See *Boswell in Holland*, Index, under Anacreon.

printed Anacreon. But this library has a vast treasure in possessing a great many capital pieces of Holbein, amongst others, a suite of Christ's Sufferings better done than in the Town Hall, particularly where Our Saviour is bound and scourged. In the Town Hall he is a poor shrinking figure, like a real malefactor. Here he preserves his dignity amidst all the ignominious treatment of his foes.[5] There is here a large book of drawings by Holbein; they ought to be engraved. As also a *Moriae encomium* of Erasmus, which belonged to a school-master who used to have Holbein often at his house, and he, to amuse himself, made most excellent designs on the margin. There are plates done after them to embellish several printed editions. Poh! what language is this, a printed edition! One might as well say a written manuscript. But I journalize in haste, so let errors be pardoned. At five I set out for Soleure.

TUESDAY 27 NOVEMBER. Boily, my Strasbourg French companion, lies down at night and rises in the morning with a full persuasion of the materiality of his soul. What a poor being is he to think thus! He still accompanies me. We lay last night at a little village. This day we travelled along excellent road. We had on all hands grand mountains and rocks and now and then a castle.

I must not omit the dress of a Swiss country girl. She has a petticoat and short gown, fixed on the fore part with buttons or clasps; a little straw hat stuck on her head, and her hair plaited threefold and hanging at full length. If her hair is not long enough, she adds a piece of black ribbon, for it seems indispensably necessary that a Swiss girl have a queue down to her heels.

At Soleure I put up at the Couronne. I sent a letter of recommendation from Monsieur de Schmidt at Karlsruhe to Monsieur de Barthès de Marmorières, Secretary to the French Embassy. He politely waited upon me, and we chatted easily. He was a little man, well bred and clever, a proof of which is that he is the only secretary of his nation not chosen by the Ambassador, but sent out

[5] The pictures and drawings which Boswell saw are now in the Museum at Bâle. Of the five scenes from the Passion, Baedeker attributes only two to Holbein himself.

by the King. He invited me to dine tomorrow with the Ambassador. Boily re-entered. We were of the same age. "But," said he, "You are much more mature than I am." It is true. It gives me pride and pleasure. I shall be every day more so.[6]

WEDNESDAY 28 NOVEMBER. Soleure pleases me because it is the first place I have come to mentioned by Mr. Addison in his Travels. I just take a contrary route from his. He begun at Marseilles and ended at Soleure and the other Swiss towns, with a little of Germany. I begin at Soleure and shall end at Marseilles. I saw Soleure with a kind of classical pleasure when I thought the Spectator has been here. I had Addison's Travels with me. I shall compare his *Remarks*[7] with every place which I visit.

I walked out this morning early. I saw the Jesuits' Church which was a-building when Mr. Addison was here. As he was here more than sixty years ago, the church does not seem new. The front of it was built by the munificence of Louis XIV and Louis XV, as an inscription bears. Where the old Cathedral stood, they are now building a magnificent church. When Mr. Addison was here, there was a church a-building. When Mr. Boswell is here, he finds the same thing. There is a stroke of real vanity. Mr. Addison mentions two Tuscan pillars which stood at the ascent to the Cathedral. One of them is still standing. I mounted a tower and saw the town. It is not large. I took a walk on the ramparts. Mr. Addison says, "The whole fortification of Soleure is faced with marble." It is indeed faced with a hard stone which may be called marble, but which is so coarse that the term marble should hardly be given to it.

At twelve I waited on Monsieur de Barthès. He complained much of his situation. He said that Soleure was divided in politics. The French party hates the Spanish; and they live ill together.[8]

[6] Another quarrel with Jacob occurred on this day, as the memoranda show: " ... Jacob again, settling accounts, called francs florins. Chid him. He said, 'Monsieur might make a mistake like that himself.' Very angry at him. Take care. Be on quite decent footing with the frank fellow. Don't joke with him but very rarely ... " (Memorandum, 28 November).

[7] *Remarks on Several Parts of Italy,* 1705.

[8] Boswell's reference to opposed French and Spanish parties at Soleure is

He complained much of the Swiss, who he said had lost their morals and had no longer their attachment to the French nation. He called them a dull, mean people. He said, "We prefer the noble hatred of the English to that of the Swiss, who hate us like snakes." He said, "Un de ces paysans sur sa rude montagne vous dirait que le Roi de France peut lui lécher le cul." I must say this in English. The Swiss are now very little in the interest of France. The vulgar are taught to despise that renowned monarchy; so that it is common enough for "a peasant on his rude mountain to bid the King of France kiss his backside."

I was presented to the Ambassador, Monsieur Buisson de Beauteville, a tall, lean man, quite French, quite *formé*. He had the most finished smoothness of manners. I am a physiognomist. I am sure he is a good sort of man. I found here the Chevalier Arregger, to whom I had compliments from my Lord Marischal. He has been long in the service of Spain. He was once taken by the Algerines, and lived as a slave for five years, till they lowered his price, and his friends ransomed him. He now lives at Soleure. We had here a large company of the chiefs of the Canton and others. There was here a genteel young man, a Genevois, Monsieur Buisson. He and I chatted a good time together. He gave me a letter to a Monsieur Huber at Geneva. I said, "Sir, you at Geneva are much changed. If John Calvin should come back, he would not recognize you." "No," said he; "upon my word, he would have a bad time of it!"

Arregger carried me to a party at the home of a Madame de Rhole.[9] I stayed there some time, and then went home and wrote two hours. At eight I returned to the Ambassador's. He had asked me, "Are you staying here some time?" "No, Sir, I leave tomor-

---

obscure to me, for it is generally assumed that the Bourbon monarchies were at this time pretty much in accord in matters of foreign policy. "French and Austrian" would seem to make better sense than "French and Spanish." But the Bourbon Family Compact was recent, and the party animosities roused earlier in the century by the War of the Spanish Succession no doubt lingered on.

[9] Probably Maria Anna Ludovica von Roll (b. 1737), who has been identified as the heroine of one of Casanova's adventures.

row." "You will come back for supper, though?" We had an elegant dinner. Our supper was very genteel. The Ambassador was quite agreeable. Monsieur le Chevalier, his nephew,[1] and I were well together. I imagined myself in Paris. I have talents to appear well in that brilliant capital.

[Boswell to John Johnston]

Soleure, 28 November 1764

MY DEAR JOHNSTON, — Man is a curious animal; and I am not at all amazed that many philosophers have tried to define him and Pope written a poem upon him, as the philosophers, as well as the poet, were men themselves. But whatever may be the essential nature of man, sure I am that his happiness or misery, his abilities or his weakness, depend almost entirely on his position. This evening, Johnston, you are shivering with cold at Edinburgh, while I bid defiance to winter at Soleure. You are probably thoughtful and gloomy. I am thoughtful and gay. And whence comes this mighty difference between two men who in many hours of their existence have differed less than most men? Why, from no other cause but position. You are in a Scots town. I am in a Swiss town. You are in a dirty town. I am in a clean town. You have passed the day in uniformity. I have passed the day in variety.

I have walked the ramparts. I have viewed from a tower the environs. I have been in the Jesuits' and Franciscan Churches. I have been at a card assembly. I have kissed (but no more) a comely healthy maid at my inn. I have dined and supped at the French Ambassador's. There is my day. . . .

My dear Johnston! "Live well," as the good German says, and believe me ever, your most sincere affectionate friend,

JAMES BOSWELL.

THURSDAY 29 NOVEMBER. At five I set out and had a pleasant drive to Berne.[2] Jacob rejoiced not a little to find himself in his own

[1] Presumably the Genevese Monsieur Buisson mentioned earlier in the entry.
[2] We learn from the memoranda that Boswell had "sitten up" till three, presumably to bring up his journal.

capital, within two miles of which he was born. I put up at the Faucon. Berne is a pretty town. The houses are excellent; good stone without and wood within. They are very warm. This town has a singular convenience in having on each side of the principal streets spacious piazzas, so that one can traverse the whole town in the worst weather without suffering any inconvenience. This afternoon I had a return of my gloom. I walked out and was very uneasy. I returned to my inn, journalized, and recovered.

FRIDAY 30 NOVEMBER.[3] Whom should I meet today but Lombach, my Utrecht acquaintance. For a moment he recalled to me some dreary ideas. He carried me to see the Arsenal, where there are arms for one hundred thousand men, notwithstanding that every peasant is obliged to have his arms in good order. Such a group of mortal engines made me feel some horror. But let me not now philosophize. The arms here are not so bright as at Bâle. There are here a vast many suits of armour; as also many a figure of the bear, the crest of this canton, from which it takes its name. *Bern* in German is a bear.[4] The Bernois have a prodigious affection for this animal. They have figures of him in all quarters, and in different attitudes. They have two live bears in a *fossé* by the fortifications of their town. I hope no good Catholic will be offended with me for saying that the bear appeared to me like the tutelar saint of this people.

I was amused with the history of a gigantic figure in wood, which stood in one of their churches, as the representation of some holy person or other. At the Reformation, instead of destroying this

[3] " . . . Prepare for Rousseau. Be composed. Recall Utrecht contemplations. Then ask him *how O how* to behave with the daughter of your respected friend — the wife of the amiable ――――. Put the case of her threatening to tell him. In short, pass some rich days at Môtiers" (Memorandum, 30 November). This is the love-affair alluded to twice previously (pp. 42, 123). He did give Rousseau an account of the whole business, as will appear in the proper place.

[4] This is only folk-etymology. Berne was probably named from the ancient Italian city of Verona, which, as "Bern," figures prominently in German heroic legend.

figure amongst other remains of idolatry, they mounted him upon one of their gates and made him represent Goliath of Gath, and upon a well just opposite to the gate they have placed a figure of David ready to sling at him.

Lombach dined with me at my inn, after which we went and saw the great church, an old Gothic building by the same architect who built the Cathedral at Strasbourg. But the tower here is not built; for the architect fell from one of the corners, and was killed on the spot.[5] We then waited on Monsieur Sinner, library-keeper, to whom I had a letter from Schmidt. He carried us to the Library, which is noble, but has no manuscript Anacreon, though rich in manuscripts. Sinner has given one volume of a catalogue of them in an excellent form. He gives, of each manuscript, the title, the size, and when he can, the year in which it was written, as also the persons to whom it has belonged. This is curious and useful. In the catalogues of other libraries the simple title of a manuscript is given, and a man knows not whether it can be of use to him or not without going to see it. In the catalogue of the King of France's Library, I find "Anacreontis Odae," but I can have no notion whether it is a manuscript of the fifteenth century or of fifty years ago.

I must here remark that in this and all the principal libraries that I have seen abroad, they have shown me a present of books sent them by a certain unknown whimsical Englishman. He is no doubt a most prodigious Whig, for he has sent Milton's prose works (which I suppose he prefers to his poetry), Toland's *Life of Milton*, Algernon Sidney's works, and several other such dainty pieces of British republican writing. The books are bound in red morocco, and adorned with gilded stamps of the cap of liberty, pitchforks, swords, and I know not what other terrible instruments of fury. I am surprised that he has not thought of introducing the scaffold, the block, and the axe. He might have adorned a whole board with

[5] Lombach (or Boswell's guidebook) was badly informed. The Cathedral of Strasbourg is much older than the Minster of Berne. The tower was finished at the end of the nineteenth century.

a representation of the murder of King Charles. He has, however, a stamp of Great Britain, as she is usually seen portrayed upon our halfpence; to render her, however, complete, he has subjoined this sensible and sublime inscription, "O Fair Britannia! Hail!" Lest Sidney, Milton, and Toland should not be strong enough in the good cause, our enthusiast has now and then added notes of his own, and quotations from others like himself. He has taken care to copy an apt passage in the poetry of Mr. Richard Glover. In short, he has made me laugh very heartily.[6]

As Jacob's friends are only two leagues from this, he had written to them to come and meet him. This day his mother, his sister, and three brothers arrived. He entertained them well. He insisted that I should show myself to them. I did so, and was highly pleased to see this picture of family affection. Gruner, an old Dutch Swiss colonel, to whom I had a letter from Schmidt, carried me to two societies at Berne, like those at The Hague. I passed there some hours dully enough. Then Lombach carried me to sup with him at an inn where were some handsome female merchants, for it was now the Fair of Berne.

SATURDAY 1 DECEMBER.[7] Betimes I set out in a good coach and in agreeable indolence drove to Neuchâtel. I sent to Colonel Chaillet a letter which my Lord Marischal had given me to him.[8] He asked me to sup with him. But I had already eaten heartily of excellent trout.

SUNDAY 2 DECEMBER. I waited on Colonel Chaillet, whom I found to be a sensible, hearty, brave old fellow. I dined at my inn, the Treize Cantons, with my landlord, Meuron. I was a little

[6] The "unknown whimsical Englishman" was Thomas Hollis, a wealthy gentleman of republican principles, who according to Dr. Johnson, "might have exuberated into an atheist" if he had had a little more time. He sent his presents of books to Harvard College as well as to the libraries on the Continent, and one of the pre-Revolutionary buildings at Harvard is named for him.

[7] " . . . This day calm. At inn, journal. Neuchâtel, prepare Rousseau, serious, delicate" (Memorandum, 1 December).

[8] See pp. 88, 161.

hipped. At four Madame Chaillet carried me to a company where we played cards.

MONDAY 3 DECEMBER. I let Jacob go for a week to see his relations, which made him very happy. One great object which I have ever had in view since I left Britain has been to obtain the acquaintance, and if possible the regard, of Rousseau. I was informed that he lived in a wild valley, five leagues from Neuchâtel. I set out early this morning, mounted on a little horse, with a *Reysesac*[9] which held some shirts. I was joined by Abraham François, a merchant here. My horse was lazy; he lent me a spur and a whip, and on we jogged very cordially. He taught me a French song, "Sous le nom de l'amitié, Phillis, je vous adore," to a minuet tune.[1] I amused myself with him, and this amusement formed an excellent contrast to the great object which occupied my mind.

We had a fine, hard road amidst mountains covered with snow. We stopped at Brot, the half-way inn. Monsieur Sandoz, the landlord, had a handsome daughter, very lively and very talkative, or rather chatty, to give the young lady a lighter word. She told us, "Monsieur Rousseau often comes and stays here several days with his housekeeper, Mademoiselle Le Vasseur.[2] He is a very amiable man. He has a fine face. But he doesn't like to have people come and stare at him as if he were a man with two heads. Heavens! the curiosity of people is incredible. Many, many people come to see him; and often he will not receive them. He is ill, and doesn't wish to be disturbed. Over there is a pass where I have gone with him and Mademoiselle Le Vasseur. We have dined there. He will walk in such wild places for an entire day. Gentlemen who have come here have asked me a thousand questions: 'And his housekeeper, is she young? Is she pretty?' " All this chat of Mademoiselle helped to frighten me.

There was here a stone-cutter who had wrought for Voltaire.

[9] Portmanteau.
[1] From *La Clé du caveau*, words by Jean Joseph Vadé, music by Adolph Blaise.
[2] Here and elsewhere in this volume Boswell actually wrote "Mademoiselle Vasseur."

The most stupid of human beings will remember some anecdote or other of a great man whom he has had occasion to see. This stone-cutter told me, "Sir, there used to be a horse that pulled a cart at Ferney, and Monsieur Voltaire always said, 'Poor horse! you are thin, you are like me.' " Any trifle of such a genius has a value.

Abraham François and I drank a glass of good wine and pursued our journey. We passed one place exactly like Killiecrankie and another where a group of broken rocks seemed every moment ready to tumble down upon us. It will most certainly tumble ere long. Monsieur Rousseau lives in the village of Môtiers. A league on this side of it, Abraham parted from me, after I had returned him his whip and his spur. I advanced with a kind of pleasing trepidation. I wished that I might not see Rousseau till the moment that I had permission to wait upon him. I perceived a white house with green window-boards. He mentions such a one in *Émile*.[3] I imagined it might perhaps be his, and turned away my eyes from it. I rode calmly down the street, and put up at the Maison de Village. This inn is kept by Madame Grandpierre, a widow, and her two daughters, fat, motherly maidens. The eldest received me. I told her, "I have let my servant go and see his friends and relations, so I am alone. You must take good care of me." Said she, "We shall do our best."

I asked for Monsieur Rousseau. I found he kept himself very quiet here, as my landlady had little or nothing to chatter concerning him. I had heard all that could be said as to his being difficult of access. My Lord Marischal had given me a card with compliments to him, which I was sure would procure me admission.[4] Colonel Chaillet had given me a letter to the Châtelain,[5] Monsieur Martinet, the Principal Justice of the place, who could introduce me without difficulty. But my romantic genius, which will never

[3] Near the end of the Fourth Book: Rousseau's description of the kind of house he would prefer to all others.

[4] The brief note printed on p. 104.

[5] Lord of the Manor of Val de Travers; the Squire. Colonel Chaillet's letter has not been recovered.

be extinguished, made me eager to put my own merit to the severest trial. I had therefore prepared a letter to Monsieur Rousseau, in which I informed him that an ancient Scots gentleman of twenty-four was come hither with the hopes of seeing him. I assured him that I deserved his regard, that I was ready to stand the test of his penetration. Towards the end of my letter I showed him that I had a heart and a soul. I have here given no idea of my letter. It can neither be abridged nor transposed, for it is really a masterpiece. I shall ever preserve it as a proof that my soul can be sublime. I dressed and dined and sent my letter *chez* Monsieur Rousseau, ordering the maid to leave it and say she'd return for the answer, so that I might give him time to consider a little, lest perhaps he might be ill and suddenly refuse to see me. I was filled with anxiety. Is not this romantic madness? Was I not sure of admittance by my recommendations? Could I not see him as any other gentleman would do? No: I am above the vulgar crowd. I would have my merit fairly tried by this great judge of human nature. I must have things in my own way. If my bold attempt succeeds, the recollection of it will be grand as long as I live. But perhaps I may appear to him so vain, or so extraordinary, that he may be shocked by such a character and may not admit me. I shall then be in a pretty situation, for I shall be ashamed to present my recommendations. But why all this doubt and uneasiness? It is the effect of my melancholy timidity. What! can the author of *Eloisa* be offended at the enthusiasm of an ingenuous mind? But if he does admit me, I shall have a very difficult character to support; for I have written to him with unusual elevation, and given him an idea of me which I shall hardly come up to.[6]

[6] This passage illustrates one of the most remarkable features of Boswell's journal. It was written some time — perhaps several days — after the episode he is describing. But in posting his journal Boswell seldom writes from the point of view of the actual date of composition. He goes back and describes each moment as it was lived, carefully excluding knowledge of what happened later. This must be very rare among diarists, who generally give to the experiences they record the emotional tone of the moment of writing.

[Boswell to Rousseau. Original in French][7]

[Môtiers] Val de Travers, 3 December 1764

SIR: — I am a Scots gentleman of ancient family. Now you know my rank. I am twenty-four years old. Now you know my age. Sixteen months ago I left Great Britain a completely insular being, knowing hardly a word of French. I have been in Holland and in Germany, but not yet in France. You will therefore excuse my handling of the language. I am travelling with a genuine desire to improve myself. I have come here in the hope of seeing you.

I have heard, Sir, that you are very difficult, that you have refused the visits of several people of the first distinction. For that, Sir, I respect you the more. If you admitted all those who from vanity wished to be able to say, "I have seen him," your house would no longer be the retreat of exquisite genius or elevated piety, and I should not be striving so eagerly to be received into it.

I present myself, Sir, as a man of singular merit, as a man with a feeling heart, a lively but melancholy spirit. Ah, if all that I have suffered does not give me singular merit in the eyes of Monsieur Rousseau, why was I made as I am? Why did he write as he has written?

[7] My translation of this famous letter follows the text of the original in the Public Library at Neuchâtel, as printed by Professor C. B. Tinker, *Letters of James Boswell*, 2 vols., Clarendon Press, 1924, i. 58–61. With the kind permission of Professor Tinker and the publishers, I have appropriated at will phrases from Professor Tinker's translation in *Young Boswell*, The Atlantic Monthly Press, 1922, i. 50–52. The newly recovered Boswell papers contain several drafts which are printed in an appendix (p. 323), so that any reader who wishes may see how hard Boswell worked to achieve the precise effect of enthusiastic naïveté which he thought most likely to ensnare the author of the *Nouvelle Héloïse*. The whole series of documents is also one of the best demonstrations extant of the speed of Boswell's writing even when he was taking pains and writing in a foreign language. The memoranda show that he did not arrive at Môtiers till one o'clock. Between that time and his appearance at Rousseau's door, which could hardly have been later than five, he changed his shirt, dined, rewrote his letter twice, redrafted and expanded the last page, copied it out, and strolled for half an hour by the Areuse, waiting an answer.

Do you ask if I have recommendations? Surely you do not need them? In the commerce of the world a recommendation is necessary in order to protect people who lack penetration from impostors. But you, Sir, who have made such deep study of human nature, can you be deceived in a character? I think of you thus: excepting for the incomprehensible essence of the soul, you have a perfect knowledge of all the principles of body and mind, of their movements, their sentiments; in short, of everything they can do, of everything they can acquire which truly affects man as man. And yet, Sir, I dare present myself before you. I dare to put myself to the test. In cities and in courts, where there are numerous companies, one can disguise one's self, one can sometimes dazzle the eyes of the greatest philosophers. But for my part, I put myself to the severest test. It is in the silence and the solitude of your sacred retreat that you shall judge of me, and think you in such circumstances I shall be able to dissimulate?

Your writings, Sir, have melted my heart, have elevated my soul, have fired my imagination. Believe me, you will be glad to have seen me. You know what Scots pride is. Sir, I am coming to see you in order to make myself more worthy of a nation that has produced a Fletcher of Saltoun and a Lord Marischal.[8] Forgive me, Sir, I feel myself moved. I cannot restrain myself. O dear Saint-Preux![9] Enlightened Mentor! Eloquent and amiable Rousseau! I have a presentiment that a truly noble friendship will be born today.

I learn with deep regret, Sir, that you are often indisposed. Perhaps you are so at present. But I beg you not to let that prevent you from receiving me. You will find in me a simplicity that will put you to no trouble, a cordiality that may help you forget your pains.

I have much to tell you. Though I am only a young man, I have

[8] Andrew Fletcher of Saltoun (1655–1715) was a Scots patriot who had strongly opposed the Union with England. He was one of the heroes of Lord Marischal, who had suggested to Rousseau that Rousseau write his life.
[9] The hero of the *Nouvelle Héloïse*. He is the teacher, as well as the lover, of Julie, the heroine.

experienced a variety of existence that will amaze you. I find myself in serious and delicate circumstances concerning which I eagerly hope to have the counsel of the author of the *Nouvelle Héloïse*. If you are the charitable man I believe you to be, you cannot hesitate to grant it to me. Open your door, then, Sir, to a man who dares to tell you that he deserves to enter it. Place your confidence in a stranger who is different. You will not regret it. But I beg you, be alone. In spite of all my enthusiasm, after having written to you in this fashion, I know not if I would not prefer never to see you than to see you for the first time in company. I await your reply with impatience.

BOSWELL.

MONDAY 3 DECEMBER [continued]. To prepare myself for the great interview, I walked out alone. I strolled pensive by the side of the river Reuse[1] in a beautiful wild valley surrounded by immense mountains, some covered with frowning rocks, others with clustering pines, and others with glittering snow. The fresh, healthful air and the romantic prospect around me gave me a vigorous and solemn tone. I recalled all my former ideas of J. J. Rousseau, the admiration with which he is regarded over all Europe, his *Héloïse*, his *Émile:* in short, a crowd of great thoughts. This half hour was one of the most remarkable that I ever passed.

I returned to my inn, and the maid delivered to me a card with the following answer from Monsieur Rousseau: "I am ill, in pain, really in no state to receive visits. Yet I cannot deprive myself of Mr. Boswell's, provided that out of consideration for the state of my health, he is willing to make it short."

My sensibility dreaded the word "short." But I took courage, and went immediately. I found at the street door Mademoiselle Le Vasseur waiting for me. She was a little, lively, neat French girl and did not increase my fear.[2] She conducted me up a darkish

[1] Or Areuse.

[2] One would hardly infer Thérèse's true age (forty-three) from this description. She must have been much more attractive in appearance than has generally been assumed.

stair, then opened a door. I expected, "Now I shall see him" — but it was not so. I entered a room which serves for vestibule and for kitchen. My fancy formed many, many a portrait of the wild philosopher. At length his door opened and I beheld him, a genteel black man in the dress of an Armenian. I entered saying, "Many, many thanks." After the first looks and bows were over, he said, "Will you be seated? Or would you rather take a turn with me in the room?" I chose the last, and happy I was to escape being formally placed upon a chair. I asked him how he was. "Very ill. But I have given up doctors." "Yes, yes; you have no love for them." As it is impossible for me to relate exactly our conversation, I shall not endeavour at order, but give sentences as I recollect them.[3]

BOSWELL. "The thought of your books, Sir, is a great source of pleasure to you?" ROUSSEAU. "I am fond of them; but when I think of my books, so many misfortunes which they have brought upon me are revived in my memory that really I cannot answer you. And yet my books have saved my life." He spoke of the Parlement of Paris: "If any company could be covered with disgrace, that would be. I could plunge them into deep disgrace simply by printing their edict against me on one side, and the law of nations and equity on the side opposite. But I have reasons against doing so at present." BOSWELL. "We shall have it one day, perhaps?" ROUSSEAU. "Perhaps."

I was dressed in a coat and waistcoat, scarlet with gold lace,

[3] Boswell jotted down hints for these conversations with Rousseau in his memoranda, in French, and then, still using French for the dialogue, entered them in his journal. But even in the journal he did not bring them up to the style of the conversations in the London journal of 1762–1763 or even of those in the earlier portion of the present manuscript. He does not always make clear who is speaking, and the condensation of his record gives an abruptness to certain portions that is not characteristic of his most careful work. The translated text here given, which expands the French slightly and inserts the names of the speakers, is in the main that of the late Geoffrey Scott; it first appeared in 1928 in the 4th volume of Colonel Isham's privately printed *Private Papers of James Boswell.* The footnotes continue to be by Frederick A. Pottle.

buckskin breeches, and boots. Above all I wore a greatcoat of green camlet lined with fox-skin fur, with the collar and cuffs of the same fur.[4] I held under my arm a hat with a solid gold lace, at least with the air of being solid. I had it last winter at The Hague. I had a free air and spoke well, and when Monsieur Rousseau said what touched me more than ordinary, I seized his hand, I thumped him on the shoulder. I was without restraint. When I found that I really pleased him, I said, "Are you aware, Sir, that I am recommended to you by a man you hold in high regard?"

ROUSSEAU. "Ah! My Lord Marischal?" BOSWELL. "Yes, Sir; my Lord furnished me with a note to introduce me to you." ROUSSEAU. "And you were unwilling to take advantage of it?" BOSWELL. "Nay, Sir; I wished to have proof of my own merits." ROUSSEAU. "Sir, there would have been no kind of merit in gaining access to me by a note of Lord Marischal's. Whatever he sends will always find a welcome from me. He is my protector, my father; I would venture to say, my friend."[5] One circumstance embarrassed me a little: I had forgotten to bring with me from Neuchâtel my Lord's billet. But a generous consciousness of innocence and honesty gives a freedom which cannot be counterfeited. I told Monsieur Rousseau, "To speak truly, I have forgotten to bring his letter with me; but you accept my word for it?"

ROUSSEAU. "Why, certainly. Numbers of people have shown themselves ready to serve me in their own fashion; my Lord Marischal has served me in mine. He is the only man on earth to whom I owe an obligation." He went on, "When I speak of kings, I do not include the King of Prussia. He is a king quite alone and apart.

[4] Boswell wore the same coat and greatcoat when he sat for the portrait painted by George Willison at Rome the following May.

[5] Rousseau wrote of Lord Marischal in his *Confessions*, "How many affectionate tears have I shed on my path as I thought of the goodness, the lovable virtues, the gentle philosophy of that venerable old man! I called him my father, he called me his child. These two names give some idea of the attachment which bound us together, but they fail to express the need which we had of each other, and of our unremitting desire to be in each other's company."

Jean Jacques Rousseau, from a mezzotint by David Martin in the Metropolitan Museum of Art, after a painting (1766) by Allan Ramsay.

That force of his! Sir, there's the great matter, to have force — revenge, even. You can always find stuff to make something out of. But when force is lacking, when everything is small and split up, there's no hope. The French, for example, are a contemptible nation." BOSWELL. "But the Spaniards, Sir?" ROUSSEAU. "Yes, you will find great souls in Spain." BOSWELL. "And in the mountains of Scotland. But since our cursed Union, ah — " ROUSSEAU. "You undid yourselves." BOSWELL. "Truly, yes. But I must tell you a great satisfaction given me by my Lord. He calls you Jean Jacques out of affection. One day he said to me, 'Jean Jacques is the most grateful man in the world. He wanted to write my brother's life; but I begged him rather to write the life of Mr. Fletcher of Saltoun, and he promised me he would do so.' "[6] ROUSSEAU. "Yes, Sir; I will write it with the greatest care and pleasure. I shall offend the English, I know. But that is no matter. Will you furnish me with some anecdotes on the characters of those who made your Treaty of Union, and details that cannot be found in the historians?" BOSWELL. "Yes, Sir; but with the warmth of an ancient Scot." ROUSSEAU. "By all means."

He spoke of ecclesiastics. "When one of these gentlemen provides a new explanation of something incomprehensible, leaving it as incomprehensible as before, every one cries, 'Here's a great man.' But, Sir, they[7] will tell you that no single point of theology may be neglected, that every stone in God's building, the mystic Jerusalem, must be considered as sacred. 'But they have added stones to it. — Here, take off this; take off that! Now you see, the building is admirably complete, and you have no need to stand there to hold it up.' 'But *we* want to be necessary!' Ah! —

"Sir, you don't see before you the bear you have heard tell of. Sir, I have no liking for the world. I live here in a world of fantasies,

[6] Lord Marischal, whose admiration for Rousseau's genius did not blind him to the dangers of having him as a biographer, was naturally slow to entrust to him the reputation of his beloved brother, the Field Marshal.
[7] The Catholic ecclesiastics, apparently. The next two sentences would then be the rejoinder of the Reformers.

and I cannot tolerate the world as it is." BOSWELL. "But when you come across fantastical men, are they not to your liking?" ROUS-SEAU. "Why, Sir, they have not the same fantasies as myself. — Sir, your country is formed for liberty. I like your habits. You and I feel free to stroll here together without talking. That is more than two Frenchmen can do. Mankind disgusts me. And my house-keeper tells me that I am in far better humour on the days when I have been alone than on those when I have been in company." BOSWELL. "There has been a great deal written against you, Sir." ROUSSEAU. "They have not understood me. As for Monsieur Vernet at Geneva, he is an Arch-Jesuit, that is all I can say of him."[8]

BOSWELL. "Tell me, Sir, do you not find that I answer to the description I gave you of myself?" ROUSSEAU. "Sir, it is too early for me to judge. But all appearances are in your favour." BOS-WELL. "I fear I have stayed too long. I shall take the honour of returning tomorrow." ROUSSEAU. "Oh, as to that, I can't tell." BOSWELL. "Sir, I shall stay quietly here in the village. If you are able to see me, I shall be enchanted; if not, I shall make no com-plaint." ROUSSEAU. "My Lord Marischal has a perfect understand-ing of man's feelings, in solitude no less than in society. I am over-whelmed with visits from idle people." BOSWELL. "And how do they spend their time?" ROUSSEAU. "In paying compliments. Also I get a prodigious quantity of letters. And the writer of each of them believes that he is the only one." BOSWELL. "You must be greatly surprised, Sir, that a man who has not the honour of your

[8] Jacob Vernet, pastor and professor at Geneva, had criticized Rousseau pri-vately for receiving the Communion at the hands of Pastor Montmollin two years before. Though not especially intolerant himself, he held that Rous-seau's religious views were as incompatible with orthodox Calvinism as with Roman Catholicism, and that to present himself for the Communion implied a lack of sincerity. There is some reason, however, for thinking that Boswell misunderstood Rousseau, and that the "Arch-Jesuit" was another pastor of very similar name, Jacob Vernes, who had drawn up what amounted to the official censure of the Genevese pastors on Rousseau: *Lettres sur le christia-nisme de J.-J. Rousseau.* It is significant that Rousseau attributed the *Senti-ment des citoyens* (see p. 200) to Vernes.

acquaintance should take the liberty of writing to you?" ROUSSEAU. "No. I am not at all surprised. For I got a letter like it yesterday, and one the day before yesterday, and others many times before that." BOSWELL. "Sir, your very humble servant. — What, you are coming further?" ROUSSEAU. "I am not coming with you. I am going for a walk in the passage. Good-bye."

I had great satisfaction after finding that I could support the character which I had given of myself, after finding that I should most certainly be regarded by the illustrious Rousseau. I had a strange kind of feeling after having at last seen the author of whom I had thought so much. I sat down immediately and wrote to Dempster. I sat up too late.

[Boswell to George Dempster]

[Môtiers] Val de Travers, 3 December 1764

MY DEAR DEMPSTER, — Where am I now, think you? In the village which contains Rousseau. I arrived here this day at noon from Neuchâtel, in order to wait upon the Wild Philosopher. I had heard all that could be said of his being difficult of access, but was not a bit discouraged. I wrote him a letter which I was sure would recommend me, for I told him my character and claimed his regard as what I had a title to. I wrote with manly confidence, and told him I was not afraid to stand the test of his penetration. . . .

Dempster, I have been with him. I have been most politely received. Would you see easy elegance, see the author of *Héloïse*. . . . I must not pretend to give you in a hasty letter an idea of our conversation. Let me only assure you of one fact. The Corsicans have actually applied to Monsieur Rousseau to give them a set of laws. He has answered, "It exceeds my powers but not my zeal." He is like to break his heart at this French invasion. . . . ⁹ Oh, Dempster,

⁹ This discussion of Corsican affairs is not recorded in the memoranda or the journal, but it is certainly authentic, and proved in the long run to be for Boswell the most important result of his meeting with Rousseau. The island of Corsica had long been in a state of armed revolt against the Republic of Genoa, and under the leadership of a remarkable general and dictator,

how much pain did it give me to see Rousseau distressed; and yet an
hour and a half run on ere I could think of quitting him. We have
made an agreement. I shall stay quietly in this village for some
days, and he will see me as much as his health permits. I am here in
a beautiful wild valley surrounded by immense mountains. I am
supremely happy. I write this partly from a pardonable vanity,
partly from a desire to give you pleasure. Adieu, Dempster. A good
Parliament.

BOSWELL.

TUESDAY 4 DECEMBER. After taking a walk in the *vallon,* I
went to the door of Monsieur Rousseau. Mademoiselle Le Vasseur
was abroad, and I could not get in. I met her on the street, and she
said, "Monsieur Rousseau will let you know this afternoon at what
hour he can see you." I dined at the table d'hôte with a Monsieur
Durey, a Parisian, son to a rich financier, but obliged to fly on account of *lettres de cachet* which were taken out against him by his
sister's influence, who is married to a man in power and wants to
have all the fortune of her father. This same Durey is, however, a
sad dog. He has spent a vast deal of money upon women, and upon
absurd plans for the Young Pretender. He is a kind of author,

---

Pasquale de Paoli, had virtually established its independence. Rousseau, in
his *Social Contract,* had remarked that there was only one country left in
Europe that was capable of sound legislation, and that was Corsica. Matteo
Buttafoco, a Corsican officer in the French Army, wrote to him inviting him
to come to Corsica and draw up a constitution for the island. Paoli probably
did not know of this invitation until after it had been made, and in any case
had no intention of giving any one *carte blanche* to provide Corsica with a
system of government, but he seconded the invitation to Rousseau to come to
the island because he hoped to secure his services as historian and propa-
gandist. Rousseau had only recently received Buttafoco's letter when Boswell
called upon him. — The French had not "invaded" Corsica in 1764, though
it may well have seemed so to persons not familiar with the complicated
politics of the situation. Genoa had finally lost control of all of the island except certain fortified coastal towns, which the insurgents could not take because of a lack of ships and artillery. France, ostensibly to discharge a debt
to Genoa, took over the defence of these towns. The French troops in Corsica
had as yet made no attempt to occupy territory not held by the Genoese.

writes you a criticism in the *Journal encyclopédique*, and even composes you a system of education on a plan entirely new. This last has not yet seen the light. Small will be the light which it will impart — "Not light, but rather darkness visible."[1] Monsieur Durey lives snug at Môtiers and eats in the inn, when some good friend does not invite him.

My other companion was Monsieur de Turo, who has an estate in the neighbourhood, has travelled a good deal, has a good deal of knowledge, and is a tall, stout young fellow. But with the whim of an English oddity, he lives constantly in this inn. The inhabitants of the village have named him their Governor, an office of small authority but of consequence enough to make Monsieur de Turo hold his head extremely high. I have seen him grant a pass to a beggar with great dignity. He generally keeps a parcel of dogs, and goes a-hunting on the hills. Scandal says that he is intimately connected with my youngest landlady. Perhaps I have done him an injury in the spelling of his name. Perhaps he writes it Thurot, and possibly may be a near relation of the gallant Captain Thurot who during the last war awed and dismayed the coasts of Caledonia.[2] After dinner I waited on Monsieur Martinet, the Châtelain, a knowing, hearty fellow. He engaged me to sup with him.

At five I went to Monsieur Rousseau, whom I found more gay than he had been yesterday. We joked on Mademoiselle Le Vasseur for keeping him under lock and key. She, to defend herself, said he had another door to get out at. Said he, "Ah, Mademoiselle, you can keep nothing to yourself."

He gave me the character of the Abbé de Saint-Pierre, "a man who did good, simply because he chose to do good: a man without

---

[1] *Paradise Lost*, i. 64.

[2] "Monsieur de Turo" was probably Charles Auguste du Terreaux, mayor of the nearby village of Les Verrières. Rousseau did not love him, and stigmatized him in the last book of *The Confessions.* — François Thurot, French naval officer commanding a small fleet sent out to harass English commerce, eluded greatly superior English strength for two years. He finally suffered a fatal wound while fighting against great odds off the coast of Ireland, 28 February 1760.

enthusiasm. One might say that he was passionately reasonable.
He would come to a discussion armed with notes,[3] and he used to
say, 'I shall be sneered at for this,' 'I shall get a hissing for that.' It
was all one to him. He carried his principles into the merest trifles.
For example, he used to wear his watch suspended from a button
on his coat, because that was more convenient. As he was precluded
from marriage, he kept mistresses, and made no secret of it. He had
a number of sons. He would allow them to adopt none but the most
strictly useful professions; for example, he would not allow any son
of his to be a wig-maker. 'For,' said he, 'so long as Nature continues
to supply us with hair, the profession of wig-making must always
be full of uncertainty.' He was completely indifferent to the opinion of men, saying that they were merely overgrown children.
After paying a long visit to a certain lady, he said to her, 'Madam,
I perceive I am wearisome to you, but that is a matter of no moment
to me. You amuse me.' One of Louis XIV's creatures had him
turned out of the Academy for a speech he had made there. Yet he
perpetually visited this man. 'For,' said he, 'he acted in his own interests, and I bear him no grudge for that. He amuses me. He has
no grounds for being offended with me. I have grounds for offence
against him, but I am not offended.' In short, he continued to call
on this Academician, until the latter put a stop to it because he
found it disagreeable to see a man whom he had injured. He had
plenty of good sense, but a faulty style: long-winded and diffuse,
yet always proving his point. He was a favourite with women; he
would go his own way independently, and he won respect. If you
become a Member of Parliament, you must resemble the Abbé de
Saint-Pierre.[4] You must stick to your principles." BOSWELL. "But,

[3] Doubtful: Boswell's French is, "on le voyoit à porter des mémoires." Mr.
Scott translates, "He was seen writing his memoirs."
[4] Much of this closely parallels what Rousseau had said of Saint-Pierre in
Émile. He had known Saint-Pierre only briefly and at the end of Saint-
Pierre's long life, but had examined his voluminous manuscripts with the
intention of publishing an edition of his works. In the end he prepared merely
abstracts and criticisms of two of the more important of Saint-Pierre's works,
but his own thinking was deeply affected by this study.

then, one must be very well instructed." ROUSSEAU. "Ah, sure enough. You must have a well-furnished head." BOSWELL. "But, Sir, a Member of Parliament who behaves as a strictly honest man is regarded as a crazy fool." ROUSSEAU. "Well then, you must be a crazy fool of a Member; and believe me, such a man will be respected — that is, if he holds consistently by his principles. A man who changes round on every occasion is another affair."

He talked of his *Plan for Perpetual Peace, taken from the Abbé de Saint-Pierre.* I frankly owned that I had not read it. "No?" said he — then took one down from his bookcase and gave it me. I asked him smilingly if he would not put his name upon it. He laughed heartily at me. I talked to him of the German album and how I had been forced to take one; but that except what was written by the person who gave it me, there was nothing in it. Said he, "Then your album is *album.*"[5] There was a sally for you. A precious pearl; a pun made by Rousseau. He said, "I have seen the Scottish Highlanders in France. I love the Scots; not because my Lord Marischal is one of them but because he praises them. *You* are irksome to me. It's my nature. I cannot help it." BOSWELL. "Do not stand on ceremony with me." ROUSSEAU. "Go away."

Mademoiselle always accompanies me to the door. She said, "I have been twenty-two years with Monsieur Rousseau; I would not give up my place to be Queen of France. I try to profit by the good advice he gives me. If he should die, I shall have to go into a convent." She is a very good girl, and deserves to be esteemed for her constancy to a man so valuable. His simplicity is beautiful. He consulted Mademoiselle and her mother on the merits of his *Héloïse* and his *Émile.*[6]

I supped with the Châtelain. He said, "We two are alone, so as

[5] *Album* is Latin for "white," or, to use the word derived from the French equivalent, "blank."

[6] Boswell, who had a very winning way with women of Thérèse's class, had already got her on his side. The memoranda add, as part of her speech, "You may come both morning and evening," and Boswell's comment, "She your friend."

to be free to talk of my Lord Marischal and nothing else." We were hearty.

WEDNESDAY 5 DECEMBER. When I waited upon Monsieur Rousseau this morning, he said, "My dear Sir, I am sorry not to be able to talk with you as I would wish." I took care to waive such excuses, and immediately set conversation a-going. I told him how I had turned Roman Catholic and had intended to hide myself in a convent in France. He said, "What folly! I too was Catholic in my youth.[7] I changed, and then I changed back again. I returned to Geneva and was readmitted to the Protestant faith. I went again among Catholics, and used to say to them, 'I am no longer one of you'; and I got on with them excellently." I stopped him in the middle of the room and I said to him, "But tell me sincerely, are you a Christian?" I looked at him with a searching eye. His countenance was no less animated. Each stood steady and watched the other's looks. He struck his breast, and replied, "Yes. I pique myself upon being one." BOSWELL. "Sir, the soul can be sustained by nothing save the Gospel." ROUSSEAU. "I feel that. I am unaffected by all the objections. I am weak; there may be things beyond my

[7] See p. 1. We know none of the details of Boswell's conversion; even in the sketch of his life, soon to be mentioned, which he wrote for Rousseau, he was no more explicit than here. Rousseau's vagaries are much better documented. He was brought up a Calvinist. In 1728, running away from Geneva at the age of sixteen, he came to Annecy in Savoy, and there fell in with Madame de Warens, a recent convert to Catholicism, who was engaged in securing further conversions. At her instigation he entered the Hospital of the Holy Ghost at Turin, where, eleven days after his arrival, he was baptized and received into the Roman Church. His account of this episode furnishes one of the most brilliant and most repulsive passages in the *Confessions*. From then until 1742, still under the influence of Madame de Warens, his *maman*, protector, and mistress, he remained an apparently contented Catholic. During the next twelve or thirteen years in Paris, under the influence of the Encyclopaedists, his ideas changed in the direction of emotional deism. In 1754, on the occasion of a brief visit to Geneva, probably more as a profession of civic than of religious faith, he received Communion again in his national church. His developed views on religion were stated in "The Creed of a Savoyard Vicar," the fourth book of *Émile*, which, as has already been said, proved as shocking to Calvinists as to Catholics.

reach; or perhaps the man who recorded them made a mistake. I say, God the Father, God the Son, God the Holy Ghost."[8]

BOSWELL. "But tell me, do you suffer from melancholy?" ROUSSEAU. "I was born placid. I have no natural disposition to melancholy. My misfortunes have infected me with it." BOSWELL. "I, for my part, suffer from it severely. And how can I be happy, I, who have done so much evil?" ROUSSEAU. "Begin your life anew. God is good, for he is just. Do good. You will cancel all the debt of evil. Say to yourself in the morning, 'Come now, I am going to *pay off* so much evil.' Six well-spent years will pay off all the evil you have committed." BOSWELL. "But what do you think of cloisters, penances, and remedies of that sort?" ROUSSEAU. "Mummeries, all of them, invented by men. Do not be guided by men's judgments, or you will find yourself tossed to and fro perpetually. Do not base your life on the judgments of others; first, because they are as likely to be mistaken as you are, and further, because you cannot know that they are telling you their true thoughts; they may be impelled by motives of interest or convention to talk to you in a way not corresponding to what they really think." BOSWELL. "Will you, Sir, assume direction of me?" ROUSSEAU. "I cannot. I can be responsible only for myself." BOSWELL. "But I shall come back." ROUSSEAU. "I don't promise to see you. I am in pain. I need a chamber-pot every minute." BOSWELL. "Yes, you will see me." ROUSSEAU. "Be off; and a good journey to you."

About six I set out.

[EDITORIAL NOTE: The reader may well wonder what Boswell was doing in the interval between the end of his visit to Rousseau,

[8] This sounds a great deal more orthodox than the Savoyard Vicar, but Boswell has probably omitted some qualifying phrases. Universal natural religion, Rousseau taught, is based on three articles of faith: the existence of a benevolent God, free will, and the immortality of the soul. In addition to these, a man will do well to accept trustfully as much of the religion of his country as is compatible with universal tolerance. He probably means here, "I am willing to repeat without equivocation the Christian formula of the Trinity, though I regard all such dogmas as uncertain, and abhor any attempt to make them exclusive."

which could not have lasted much past noon, and six o'clock. The answer can be supplied: he was at the Maison de Village, writing. As we have seen, he had come to Môtiers with a determination to spread his whole life before the Sage and to secure the Sage's counsel. But after three interviews he had come to realize that Rousseau was simply not going to *listen* to his confession. It occurred to him that if he wrote it out, left it with Thérèse to give to Rousseau, and then went away for a few days, Rousseau would certainly *read* it; and if Rousseau had read it, he might discuss it. Consequently Boswell spent the afternoon composing a long and elaborate "Sketch of My Life" and a covering letter. The covering letter follows, with the portion of the "Sketch" that deals with that episode in his life on which he principally desired Rousseau's comment: the intrigue with a married woman in Scotland. After that comes a vaunting letter to John Johnston. This letter is a striking illustration of the lengths to which Boswell was prepared to go in order to invest his records with the authority of literal circumstance. Johnston would not see it for months, and would probably have been just as grateful if Boswell had written it in retrospect from Neuchâtel. The month was December, the night was getting steadily darker, it was raining, Boswell had a considerable stretch of mountain road to negotiate without a guide, but after finishing the "Sketch" he delayed his departure still further in order to provide his faithful friend with a report as "authentic" as circumstances could make it.]

[Boswell to Rousseau][9]

[Môtiers, Val de Travers, 5 December 1764]

Sir: — I am as grateful as man can be for your really gracious reception.

If you can, I beseech you to help me. I am leaving you a sketch of my life. It is hastily written. In it you have facts merely; had I

[9] Translated from the original letter, now in the Public Library of Neuchâtel, as printed in Professor C. B. Tinker's *Letters of James Boswell*, 2 vols., 1924, i. 62–63. If Boswell kept a copy, it has not been recovered.

entered on feelings, it would have been too diffuse. You do not love to be bothered by any one's company, but my papers may perhaps be admitted. After all that I have done, I still have my health; I still have for the most part a very healthy mind; I have a soul that incites me to be a man. Oh, vouchsafe to preserve a true Scot! My Lord Marischal is old. That illustrious Scottish oak-tree must soon fall. You love that ancient country. Preserve a sapling from it. I shall return with my Lord's portrait.[1] You will see me, and I shall go out from your retreat into the world with two or three simple and noble principles, and I shall be a man all the rest of my days. You will be so generous as to keep my secret. Imperfect as I am, I consider myself an excellent man in the world as it exists. But I have an idea that it is possible to rise above the world as it is; and until I do, I shall not be content.

You will have the goodness to return my sketch.

During my spell of melancholy at Utrecht, I made the acquaintance of a young lady, very rich and of the first rank. I behaved in such a fashion as to be honoured with the reputation of a philosopher. Oh, how deceitful are appearances! If you wish to amuse yourself by reading some pieces by that young lady, you will find them in a little packet by themselves.[2] I should very much like to have your opinion of her character. You are the only one to whom I have shown her papers. I could trust you with anything.

I am, with a respect and an affection which you will not doubt, your eternal admirer.

[1] Probably a character-sketch. But it is possible that in his luggage at Neuchâtel he had an engraved portrait of Lord Marischal which he was willing to sacrifice for another interview.

[2] The "pieces" probably were the two letters he had so far received from Belle de Zuylen, plus the other compositions of hers that are still among the Boswell papers: namely, some verses, the "Portrait of Zélide," and a "portrait" of Madame Geelvinck. All of these except the verses are printed in *Boswell in Holland.*

[5 December, Extract from "Sketch of My Life."
Original in French][3]

. . . I loved the daughter of a man of the first distinction in Scotland.[4] She married a gentleman of great wealth. She allowed me to see that she loved me more than she did her husband. She made no difficulty of granting me all. She was a subtle philosopher. She said, "I love my husband as a husband, and you as a lover, each in his own sphere. I perform for him all the duties of a good wife. With you I give myself up to delicious pleasures. We keep our secret. Nature has so made me that I shall never bear children. No one suffers from our loves. My conscience does not reproach me, and I am sure that God cannot be offended by them." Philosophy of that sort in the mouth of a charming woman seemed very attractive to me. But her father had heaped kindnesses on me. Her husband was one of the most amiable of men. . . .[5] I was seized with the bitterest regrets. I was sad. I was almost in despair, and often wished to confess everything to Monsieur de ———, in order to compel him to deprive me of my wretched life. But that would have been the most fatal of follies. I opened my heart to Madame de ———. Although she was affectionate and generous, she was set in her ideas. She reproached me for my weakness. What could I do? I continued my criminal amour, and the pleasures I tasted formed a counterpoise to my

[3] This "Sketch" fills fourteen quarto pages of the same size as the contemporary journal. Boswell also preserved two outlines, an incomplete first draft, and various rejected leaves.

[4] After getting back the "Sketch" from Rousseau, Boswell carefully inked over with repeated pen-strokes all those details which pointed to the lady's identity, but with the exception of one sentence, noted below, everything that he wrote can be recovered with certainty. There seems to be little doubt that the lady was Jean Home, only daughter of Lord Kames, who married Patrick Heron of Kirroughtrie in 1760. In 1772 Heron divorced her for adultery with a young Army officer.

[5] A sentence here has not been completely deciphered. It probably says something like, "He insisted that I should make extended visits at his house in the country."

remorse. Sometimes even in my transports I imagined that heaven could not but smile on so great a happiness between two mortals. At twenty-two, my father permitted me to go to London. I was glad to escape from Madame de ——'s vicinity. I made a resolve never to write to her, and for two years we have had no news of each other, except that we are in good health. . . . Sir, I have given you in haste a record of all the evil I have done. I have told you of all there is good in me. Tell me, is it possible for me yet to make myself a man? Tell me if I can be a worthy Scots laird. If I can — heavens, how much I fear the contrary! — if I can be virtuous as regards Madame de ——. Perhaps she has changed too. O charitable philosopher, I beseech you to help me. My mind is weak but my soul is strong. Kindle that soul, and the sacred fire shall never be extinguished.

[Boswell to John Johnston]

[Môtiers] Val de Travers, 5 December 1764

MY DEAR JOHNSTON, — Art thou alive, O my friend? Or has thy spirit quitted its earthly habitation? To hear of thy death would not now distress me. I would glory to think of thy exaltation.

Johnston, I am in the village which contains Rousseau. These three days I have visited that sublime sage. He has enlightened my mind. He has kindled my soul. Yes, we are immortal. Yes, Jesus has given us a revelation. I feel an enthusiasm beyond expression. Good heaven! Am I so elevated? Where is gloom? Where is discontent? Where are all the little vexations of the world? O Johnston! Wert thou but here! I am in a beautiful wild valley surrounded by immense mountains. I am just setting out for Neuchâtel. But I return to Rousseau.

I am to be alone on horseback in a dark winter night, while the earth is covered with snow. My present sentiments give me a force and a vigour like the lion in the desert.

Farewell, my dear friend.

JAMES BOSWELL.

WEDNESDAY 5 DECEMBER [continued]. The night was such as Lady Randolph describes —

> It was dark December; wind and rain
> Had beat all night.[6]

I was firm and bold and among the wild rocks had grand thought. About nine I arrived at Brot, where Master Sandoz and his family took all care of me. I eat biscuits and drank wine. I became gay with the good folks around me, and Mademoiselle and I sung the story of *Héloïse* in verse to an old French tune,

> Quand le fier Baron d'Étange
> Sortait du Pays de Vaud, &c.

I was quite in the Highlands of Scotland. She was a Lochaber lass. Though the song is written in a ludicrous style, the recollection of the events made me cry.[7] The Sandoz are a numerous family, about five hundred. Just a clan. In a village on one of the Swiss mountains this tribe has a fund lodged for the support of their poor brethren. I was quite the gay and great man.

THURSDAY 6 DECEMBER.[8] The morning was gloomy to me as usual. But a good ride to Neuchâtel set me to rights. I had engaged to dine *chez* Colonel Chaillet either this day or Friday, I knew not which. Rousseau said jestingly, "Go and dine with him both days." I sent and learnt that it was Friday I had fixed. At three he came to me. He told me my Lord Marischal was no longer attached to the House of Stuart. "One night at Neuchâtel he was playing at piquet. They brought a *Gazette de Hollande* in which he read that the Duke of York had become a Cardinal.[9] He threw down his cards. He said,

---

[6] John Home's *Douglas*, I. i. 229–230.

[7] We have as yet found nothing further concerning this ballad. The Baron d'Étange was the father of Julie, heroine of the *Nouvelle Héloïse*.

[8] "Expenses at the Maison de Village at Môtiers, three days' lodging, three dinners, and keep of a horse, two crowns; the horse, four days, one crown" (Expense Account).

[9] Henry Benedict Maria Clement, second son of the Old Pretender, took orders in the Roman Church, and was created a cardinal in 1747, shortly after

'Now all our hopes are lost. Oh, to think that I have sacrificed my-self for that beastly family! The father is not worth six sous, which is two thousand times as much as the elder son is worth; and now the one in whom we had a little confidence turns priest!' My Lord has only contempt for Prince Charles. In the year '45 the French Court was requested to supply ten thousand men, clothing for ten thousand cavalry, clothing for twenty thousand Highlanders, arms, and a million livres. Without all that, sensible men would not have been willing to invade Scotland. The Prince had prom-ised to be firm in his demands, but he let himself be swept away, and rushed off, as we all know. My Lord wrote to his friends, 'Risk nothing. He is a madman.' The Prince however used my Lord's name, until they sent a messenger, who brought them back his true sentiments. After the Rebellion, the Prince came to Bâle, from whence he wrote asking my Lord to find him a safe place in the country of Neuchâtel. My Lord replied that he was writing di-rectly to the King of Prussia, and that he would not remain there himself. The Prince demanded his friendship. My Lord replied, 'I do not wish to dishonour myself. Can I be the friend of a man who has done such-and-such' — and he gave him a list of the shameful things which he had done. The Prince wrote him a reply in which he did not deny the facts, but promised to conduct himself better in the future. My Lord wished never to see him. When the Prince thought that his supporters in England sent him too little money, he threatened to give informations against them, unless they gave him more." What a sad picture of the descendant of *centum sex proavi!*[1]

At five we went *chez* le Capitaine Sonbrun, where we played at

---

his twenty-second birthday. At his death in 1807 the male line of the Stuarts came to an end.

[1] "One hundred and six ancestors" — the real and legendary kings of Scot-land. This highly improbable list, which begins some four hundred years before the Christian Era, may be seen at the end of *The Scots Magazine* for 1740. No. 106 is James V, the last king before the fatal succession of Mary, the first Queen Regnant of the Kingdom.

cards and supped. I had *un ennui à la mort*, but bore it. I found here Mr. Bowyer, an English sea-captain, an amiable, spirited young fellow.[2] I received this night from Geneva a packet of fourteen letters from Messieurs Cazenove, Clavière et fils, to whose care all my correspondents have written for some time. I had not heard from my father for three months, and was very uncertain if he would allow me to go to Italy. His letter this night was most kind. He agreed to my going to Italy for four months, and wrote to me as to a man. I was penetrated with his goodness. I had a letter from Sir David Dalrymple in which he scourged me with humorous severity till I was almost angry; and a letter from my brother John proposing to turn English clergyman. This vexed me greatly. I wrote to him that he might remain a curate in a little village, and that I would by no means agree to it till he assured me that he could play well enough upon the fiddle to gain him a comfortable livelihood.[3]

[Received 6 December, the Reverend Charles de Guiffardière to Boswell. Original in French][4]

The Hague, 22 November 1764

YOUR LETTER FROM GOTHA, MY DEAR SIR, came as a very pleasant surprise to me. You are really a most amiable Englishman. I

---

[2] George Bowyer, later admiral and a baronet. He commanded the *Burford* and the *Albion* during the war with the American colonies.

[3] The letters from Lord Auchinleck and Lieutenant John Boswell have not been recovered, but most of the others are among the Boswell papers. Two of the more lively will do to represent the packet and show the range of the advice that Boswell was receiving from his friends.

[4] The Reverend Charles de Guiffardière, a young French Protestant clergyman whom Boswell had met at Utrecht the previous autumn, later became French Reader to Queen Charlotte, and appears in Fanny Burney's *Diary* as "Mr. Turbulent." Boswell, whose own behaviour was uncommonly strict in Utrecht and who always held very strict notions of clerical decorum, was shocked by Guiffardière's levity, a situation which Guiffardière deliberately exploited. But the present letter shows that his antinomianism was more than mere talk. The letter which Boswell wrote to him from Gotha has not been recovered.

thought, to speak frankly with you, that the German Highnesses would have made you forget your good Dutch friends. But since I came to The Hague, I have been undeceived by so many people who esteem and love you that I burn with eagerness to make amends. It is my impression that Monsieur de Sommelsdyck, your cousin, who will forward this to you, is not among those least eager to declare themselves your friends; he speaks of you with warmth and lively interest, and I think he would give up something that he loves very much rather than not be your relation. Not to speak of the belles who weep your absence, the philosophers who debate your principles, the poets who sing your return, there are twenty houses here that extol your complaisance, your attentions, your courtesy. You have been, in a word, the man of the hour, a delicious, an adorable man whom people must have or must have had. That is the refrain of all the discussions that have been held concerning you. I shall not repeat what the amiable Mademoiselle de Zuylen told me of her friend Boswell last summer when I had the honour to see her at Utrecht. You are not at all a coxcomb, my friend, but there is a certain philosopher who would have lost his head completely on seeing himself so firmly planted in that sweet girl's heart.

Now for your letter; but before I come down to the point, allow me to exhort you to write in such a strain that I can read you without disgust. I am not referring to your style, which begins to be French; a sojourn of six months at Geneva will put the finishing touches to that. That you are often uncertain about a word, an expression, or the turning of a phrase should not surprise you. You will speak French a long time yet before you speak it well. There is in our language a delicacy, a precision, that one perceives only after much use of it and much good reading. Also a man like you who knows how to think and is not unaware of the fact that the serious study of a language is a very philosophic matter, will understand that among the crowd of people who gather to murder French, very few understand it. Besides, in France the language of the people is one thing, that of the *bourgeoisie* another, that of the Court still another; whereas in England the language of the people is the language of the nation. The reason is that with you the people is everything, but in France it hardly counts at all. That is why the English people, according to report, express themselves with much more nobility and accuracy than in any other country whatever, while in France the language of the courtier dominates that of so-called honest folk, and even sets the tone for men of letters, who, if they did not adopt it, would be considered mere pedants.

Forgive this wearisome dissertation, my dear Sir, but blame yourself for it, for you furnished the occasion. I could have wished that you had sent me a little *haircloth and bees* to make me laugh.[5]

I have been for a week here at The Hague, where we are passing the winter. I would not have believed that I should regret my hamlet so much. Tilburg is a charming retreat. I have attached myself there to a charming woman whom I adore and with whom I have passed many delicious moments. Picture to yourself the most seductive face in the world, a sparkling eye, a fresh complexion, an uptilted nose, rosy lips, and a breast of alabaster, the walk and bearing of a goddess, softness full of grace and voluptuousness in all her movements, even the least — picture to yourself all that, I say, and you will have formed in your mind a portrait far below the original. She is married to a Swiss captain, a man of very little charm, lives retired in a village three leagues from Bois-le-Duc, and is the darling of all who know her. We are intimately connected in spite of her boor of a husband, and I hope will long continue so.

[5] The italicized words are in English in the original. In *Boswell in Holland,* following 24 May 1764, where Guiffardière refers to "two volumes of *haircloth and bees,*" I have conjectured that he was making a mocking comparison of Boswell to Virgil, who wrote amatory poems (*Eclogues*) and didactic poems on farming (*Georgics*), the latter including a disquisition on bee-culture. But Boswell (I thought Guiffardière might be implying) would substitute ascetic for amatory verses. It seems to me now perhaps more likely that the phrase *haircloth and bees* is an actual quotation from some unrecovered bit of verse by Boswell which Guiffardière had seen, or from some other English poem he had read. According to Boswell, he read and spoke English with remarkable facility.

My dear Boswell, do not come wearying me to death with your morality, so sublime and so little suited to men. Believe me, our hearts' morality is the only morality we have to lead us, and that disgusting mass of precepts that people no longer read, that derive from I know not what absurd principles, is made only for those gross and clumsy souls incapable of ever attaining to the delicacy of taste which enables a well-born soul to feel all that is lovable in virtue and hateful in vice, independently of the ridiculous reasons advanced by our sages. You seem to be one of those merciless perse-cutors of the passions. You are young, my dear Sir. (Do not take offence at my bluntness.) Study mankind, and you will see that it is not in the tomes of a scholar who dissects the human heart at leisure in the gloomy depths of his study, at the risk of committing a thousand absurdities and without bothering himself whether his nonsense will bore the world or offend it —[6] Above all, devote yourself to women. You realize of course that I am not speaking of that class of women to whom young men go to purchase disgust at real pleasures, but of those women who are distinguished for their feelings, their delicacy, for that taste for the voluptuous which so well characterizes sensitive souls; for a healthy judgment, an ex-quisite finesse. That is the world in which you belong. Let books and study have their turn, but let them never serve save as pas-times.

I do not feel in speaking to you in this fashion that I have had the ill grace to read you a lecture. Always consult yourself first. You know your own interests, I suppose, better than any other being whatsoever.

If you choose to write to me at The Hague, in care of Monsieur le Comte de Hogendorp, Receiver General of the United Provinces, it will give me pleasure.

I have the honour to be, Sir, your most obedient servant,

DE GUIFFARDIÈRE.

If you see Lord Abingdon at Geneva, tender him my regards.

[6] Guiffardière lost track of his sentence, which to complete it needs some such words as "that true morality is to be found."

[Received 6 December, Sir David Dalrymple to Boswell][7]

Edinburgh, 10 October 1764

Dear Sir, — I am to thank you for your letter of the 1st September, which I ought to have acknowledged sooner, but I am sure you will excuse my silence. In your letter, after having informed me of the present situation of your mind, you desire me to inform your father of the conditions under which you propose to live and breathe in Scotland. I think they are four.

First, you must not be a *true young laird*. You say you would rather die, and this you solemnly swear. — This depends not upon your father but upon yourself, for if you are a man of business, fill up your time and think of contributing any usefulness to society, you will not be a *young laird* in your sense of the word. I remember that I formerly gave you my sentiments as to this at great length; and if I had not the good fortune to convince you at that time, it is vain for me to speak any more to you upon that subject or upon any other. There are *young lairds* of your acquaintance, and those of considerable rank, who continue so although their fathers have been long at rest. They are the idle and dissipated, who depend for their pleasure upon every trifling amusement and upon every companion as idle and dissipated as themselves and as trifling as their amusements.

Your next condition is that you shall while in Edinburgh worship God according to the rites of the Church of England, which make you think of heaven, whereas the Presbyterian worship makes you think of hell, as you once told David Hume.[8] — For my

[7] Sir David Dalrymple, Bt., a practising Scots advocate who two years later was elevated to the bench as Lord Hailes, stood midway in age between Boswell and his father, and was held in high respect by both of them: by Lord Auchinleck for his legal knowledge, industry, and ambition; by Boswell for his attainments in historical scholarship and polite letters. (He had attended Eton and had contributed essays to *The World*.) Boswell had early made him one of his mentors, and was likely to turn to him when he wanted some one to mediate between himself and his father. The letter which Sir David is answering has unfortunately not been recovered.

[8] Boswell, after a period of scepticism, had received the Communion in the

own part, I do not consider it as a matter of much moment in which
of the two ways God is worshipped, provided that he is worshipped,
the difference of the rites being in my poor opinion very inconsid-
erable. Perhaps I do not totally approve of either, but what then?
Ought I to expect that every one should dress according to my
fancy? If I should be ridiculous in expecting this, ought I to expect
that a whole nation should worship God according to my fancy?
Or ought I on this account to associate myself with people in rites
which are more pleasing to me as making me not think of hell,
while I know that the bulk of those people are men who worship
God in one particular mode either from education or in opposition
to the religious ceremonies established by law in a limited government? Shall I tell Dr. Robertson that he is a Calvinist who cannot
be pleasing in the sight of God, and that his prayers and sermons
put you in mind of hell? If you ever happen to be in any *Catholic*
country, I doubt not but that the great wax candles unlighted upon
the *altar*[9] will give you a clearer idea of heaven than any of the
rites of the Church of England ever did. My dear Sir, you are capti-
vated with show. The world is a perpetual puppet-show in your
eyes, and what is remarkable, still retaining the graces of novelty.
However, if you like the puppet-show, I suppose your father will
have no objection to your being of the Church of England, for "Ned
C———, the priest" is not in this country. You will pardon me for
thinking that your Soaping Club is at the bottom of this unphilo-

chapel of the English Ambassador at The Hague on Christmas-day, 1763.
The Presbyterian Church was established in Scotland, and the Scottish Episcopal Church still suffered under severe disabilities because its ministers refused to recognize the Hanoverian succession. But there were in Edinburgh
two or three "qualified" Episcopal chapels; that is, chapels using the rite of
the Church of England and served by priests who had been ordained in that
church. Boswell had demanded the right to attend one of these chapels
regularly on his return to Scotland. It may be added here that he never got up
his courage to do so.
[9] "*Un*lighted" seems odd, but the manuscript is clear. Had Sir David never
seen the mass celebrated? What makes his remark still more puzzling is that
in large and well-appointed Anglican churches of the time it *was* a frequent
practice to put candles on the altar and to leave them unlighted.

sophical esteem for the English ceremony.[1] The person who told you that you would one day be a Methodist philosopher[2] spoke just as intelligibly as if he had said you would be a buck man of sense, or a jockey judge. You are far from being a Methodist, because you attempt to reason; and far from being a philosopher, because you are caught with show, with the tinsel of ceremony and the hollow civility of courts.

Your third condition is *ménage à part*. My answer is, marry some woman of family and tolerable sense in your own country, and then the rest will follow of course. Believe me, without this your plan of separate family will sound ridiculous to others and in a few weeks be irksome to yourself. It will be very fine to see you soaping your own beard tête-à-tête with yourself. Positively, I will have your picture drawn in this attitude, as Sir John says; you may write the ballad under it.[3] Pray, do you remember Jerry

[1] See p. 70. Dalrymple is quoting from *Boswell, a Song*, a self-congratulatory effusion which Boswell himself had published in a miscellany in 1762. The stanza in question runs as follows:

> And he owns that Ned Colquitt the priest
> May to something of humour pretend;
> And he swears that he is not in jest
> When he calls this same Colquitt his friend.

The Reverend Edward Colquitt was one of the ministers of a "qualified" Anglican chapel in Edinburgh, "a man," as Boswell later wrote, "who had lived much in the world, and, with other qualities, was eminent for gay sociality." Lord Auchinleck clearly considered Colquitt responsible for some of his son's more troublesome vagaries. — On his return to Edinburgh from London in 1760, Boswell with several "rattling" companions, had founded in Edinburgh a society for giggling and making giggle called the Soaping Club. "Let every man soap his own beard" appears to have been current slang for "let every man do as he pleases." Colquitt had been a Soaper.

[2] This was the Reverend Archibald Maclaine, co-pastor of the English (Presbyterian) church at The Hague. See *Boswell in Holland*, 25 April 1764. By "Methodist" both Maclaine and Dalrymple meant something like "emotionalistic." In 1764 Methodism was not a sect but a revivalist movement within the Church of England.

[3] Shakespeare, *II Henry IV*, IV. iii. 52–53.

in *The Plain Dealer*, who stipulated for free egress and regress into the maids' chamber?[4] Perhaps this is the plain English of *ménage à part*. If so, I, in place of Dr. Gaubius, say, ℞ *conjugem*.[5]

The last condition is the worst of all: a journey to London once a year. But this is not your own, you got it in *Tristram Shandy*. If you were my son, I would never consent to such a journey. You mean to wind up the watch backwards, and thus undo what had been done and break the spring. If your duty as a lawyer called you to London, good. Your father then would not have the power of preventing your journey. If you was in Parliament, *vir bonus ac discretus*,[6] as the writs bear, it would be a breach of privilege to keep you away. But to stipulate that you should go annually to London whether you have anything to do there or not — if you were my son, I would as soon agree to your making an annual jaunt to Sodom and Gomorrah, where though iron swims, feathers sink. Being of this opinion, I must be excused from talking to your father on the subject.

Let me ask you as a friend what you propose to bring on your side in consequence of the demands that you make on your father. In mutual contracts something is given when something is received. To tell you the truth, I cannot interfere where I would not wish for success.

Pereat qui barbam et saponandi ritus *primus invenit!* Possibly it was some *independent* evil spirit. Think a little and you will not hold my conjecture wild. I wish the beard and the basin and the wash-balls had gone along with him into the vast profound.[7] I am afraid that this will be the ruin of our poor friend the Baron, who

[4] William Wycherley, *The Plain Dealer*, V. iv.
[5] Dr. Gaubius, a celebrated Dutch physician of Leyden, had advised Boswell "to live temperately, to take a great deal of exercise, and never to want occupation" (*Boswell in Holland*, following 22 May 1764). Sir David's prescription is simply *a wife*.
[6] "A worthy and discreet gentleman."
[7] The Latin means, "May he perish who first devised the beard and the rites of soaping!" In the letter which Dalrymple is answering, Boswell had no doubt said that he wished to be *independent* of his father.

is idle and believes himself *melancholy gentleman-like*, as Old Ben says.[8] Did you ever read Swift's cure for the vapours in the land of horses?[9] You think that I write at ease; but though I can laugh, I have of late suffered great misfortunes. What think you of two fine children cut off,[1] and a languishing dispirited dear wife? Yet I can talk to you as I have often talked, and can endeavour to rouse you to active life and usefulness.

I beg that you would circumscribe your idea of travelling. There is no occasion for you to go into Spain to see idle and ignorant gentlemen. The remains of barbarous magnificence will amuse but for a moment. You have seen more in Brandenburg than all that the caliphs and sherifs ever did. If you mean to be esteemed, you must endeavour to form and execute some plan of usefulness.

After you have reflected, let me know your plan; and whenever I can be of any service to you with your father, you may command me. I am positive that it would have hurt you had I communicated to him the substance of your last letter as you desired. Believe me your sincere friend,

Dav: Dalrymple.

friday 7 december. Captain Bowyer came and saw me. We spoke French. I said, "Sir, I am much pleased and at the same time sorry to find here such an agreeable compatriot. I prided myself upon being the wisest of all our travellers. But you are at least as wise as I." I dined at Colonel Chaillet's, where we had a great com-

---

[8] Ben Jonson, *Every Man in His Humour*, I. iii near end (Folio text).

[9] The seventh chapter of "A Voyage to the Houyhnhnms" concludes: "A fancy would sometimes take a Yahoo to retire into a corner, to lie down, and howl and groan, and spurn away all that came near him, although he were young and fat, wanted neither food nor water; nor did the servants imagine what could possibly ail him. And the only remedy they found was, to set him to hard work, after which he would infallibly come to himself . . . " (*Gulliver's Travels*, Part IV). Sir David had previously called Boswell's attention to this passage: see *Boswell in Holland*, following 5 October 1763.

[1] Apparently twins who died at birth or shortly thereafter. Sir David had been married less than a year before the date of this letter.

pany and an immense dinner. We were three hours at table. My
Lord Marischal had given me a bill upon Colonel Chaillet. Thus:[2]

SIR: — Please pay to Mr. Boswell one good fish, cooked *à la
suisse*, with one bottle of your best wine, and charge to the account
of your servant

M——.

There is *gaieté d'esprit* for you. In the evening I went to a private
ball, where I was tolerably pleased.

SATURDAY 8 DECEMBER. I waited on Madame la Colonelle
Sandoz whose husband I had seen at The Hague. She was a smart,
clever woman. I delivered her my Lord Marischal's compliments.
She was very frank with me and gave me her confession of faith
without reserve. It was much that of Rousseau. After dinner she
carried me to wait of[3] Mademoiselle Prevost, whom I was very desirous to see, as she had in some measure educated Zélide, having
been with her from eight to thirteen, and carried her to Geneva.
She was a polite old maiden and praised much her fair friend. I
was in the wrong in talking too freely of Zélide's faults both to
Madame Sandoz and Mademoiselle Prevost. I saw here a portrait
of Zélide which brought her full to my mind, and with unusual
grace. I loved her. I called on Captain Bowyer, and sat some time
there, and passed the evening at Colonel Chaillet's, where I found
Mademoiselle Prevost, who showed me a letter from Zélide in
which she talked of her having written "shocking fables," and
called the libertine D'Hermenches "her generous friend." I saw
her to be a vapourish, unprincipled girl. I was happy not to be connected with her.[4] I supped here very jolly. Chaillet recounted his
acts of severity in military discipline. He made us all shudder.

[2] Lord Marischal's "bill" was written in French.
[3] A Scotticism.
[4] " . . . Saw her a hare-brained girl, glad not to have her. What is her genius?
'Tis like playing on fiddle" (Memorandum, 9 December). — Constant
d'Hermenches, a married man of forty or so, a Swiss nobleman in the military service of the States General, enjoyed a considerable reputation as a

SUNDAY 9 DECEMBER. I had taken leave of this people last night, with intention to go today, but Jacob did not arrive as he had promised, so I passed the day at home close, writing. Chaillet however came and sat an hour with me, and told me many tales of his political prowess while in the Sardinian service. He has been a bold, active, pushing fellow. At night Jacob arrived.

MONDAY 10 DECEMBER. At twelve I walked out two leagues to Colombier, leaving orders for a chaise to take me up next morning. I went to the Maison de Village, kept by the father of Madame Froment's Lisette. Her sister Caton served me up a good Swiss dinner. I asked her, "Would you like to go to Scotland?" She said, "Yes, Sir. I don't want to stay here." She pleased me. Ibrahim, the Turk, whom my Lord Marischal educated with Ameté,[5] came to see me. He was to be a painter, but became hypochondriac and has a pension from my Lord. He was a little dark dog, laughed immoderately, and said, "I am vapourish," but talked not amiss. Old Stefan the Kalmuck whom my Lord had also from his brother, Marshal Keith, was here. He was long my Lord's valet de chambre, but drank so that he was no longer to be trusted, and now has also a pension. Innumerable are the instances of my Lord's goodness. Ibrahim looked at Stefan and said, "We have travelled a great deal. We have rolled about the globe, and here at last we have fallen into a hole."

I then waited on Mademoiselle Morel, to whom my Lord Marischal had given me a letter. She was not very young, but was soft, mild, cheerful, and uniform, and attached to my Lord like a Scots lass. Her brother, who had been a colonel in the Sardinian service, was jolly and civil. I was just in a country family in our own good island. To sit all the evening here seemed severe. I

---

lady-killer. Belle de Zuylen was carrying on a clandestine and extremely candid correspondence with him. Boswell probably knew of it; at any rate, he shows jealous dislike of D'Hermenches.

[5] The French form of Madame de Froment's Turkish name, Emet-ulla. Ibrahim is called variously a Turk and a Tibetan, a relation of the Grand Lama. His name is Turkish.

dreaded the idea of the visits which I must yet make in Scotland. They insisted that I should stay in their house.

TUESDAY 11 DECEMBER. I went to the inn and found Caton. "Were you serious when you said you would go with me to Scotland?" "Yes, Sir. When I was still a young girl, in the house of Monsieur ——, an attempt was made to force me. I escaped. I married through vexation. I never loved my husband. He spent all his money. He ran off. I can have a divorce. I should like to be far away from here. I would go with a gentleman to whom I was attached. I believe you to be a perfectly honourable man." "But you understand on what footing you will be with me? I do not wish to deceive you." "Yes, Sir; you will dispose of me as you see fit." She had two pretty children and was a fine fresh Swiss lass. I said, "Well, I make no promises; but if I find it suitable, I shall write to you." Mademoiselle Morel carried me to see the Château of Colombier, where my Lord Marischal lived. It is a large old building, and inspired me with Scottish ideas.[6]

At eleven I set out, and had a good drive to Yverdon. I sent a card to Sir James Kinloch, who was still at his country-seat. My inn at the Maison de Village was very bad. Two hours before supper the maid brought me bread and cheese and a bottle of wine. I was somewhat surprised and asked the meaning of this. She said, "So that you may *goûter*. Do you not wish to *goûter?*" I found to *goûter* was a custom in Switzerland, where they eat from morning to night. I complied with the rule and did as others do.

WEDNESDAY 12 DECEMBER. I waited on the Baron de Brackel, son-in-law to Sir James Kinloch. I found him a man about fifty, a good manly figure, grave, reserved, polite, quite a man of the world. He insisted that I should come and live in his house. He had been much with Lord Marischal, and he told me that my Lord could not stay long in a place without taking a dislike to it, and that he was of a most changeable disposition. This consoled me.

[6] In the manor-house of Colombier, across the road from the Château, Belle de Zuylen was to spend nearly the whole of her secluded and unhappy life after her marriage in 1773 to Monsieur de Charrière.

He gave me a letter from Mademoiselle Kinloch at Utrecht. It was simple and gay, and amused me.[7] I was presented to Madame de Brackel, a tall, handsome, charming woman. They had a child of some months old, a fine boy. We dined genteelly. After dinner came Madame de Coppet, another sister, and her husband, good quiet people. Company came, and cards employed the evening. I found myself in an excellent family, supped, and was pleased.

THURSDAY 13 DECEMBER. I lay down last night in calm easy spirits, and I got up this morning in the same happy frame. Madame de Brackel chose Swiss linen and employed a proper sempstress to make shirts for me. Already was I upon an easy footing here. I was proud to receive civilities from so fine a woman. I saw here a beautiful picture of family felicity. I was in an honest rage against corruption of manners, and I resolved to do my best to support conjugal virtue. At twelve Sir James Kinloch waited upon me. He has been thirty years in this country, but remains the old Scotsman, just an East Lothian Swiss laird.[8] He is a most excellent farmer. I contrived to make conversation go well on upon country affairs. He said that here lime cost them about half a crown a boll. I complained to him that we had at Auchinleck a fine grass field destroyed by rushes which made it necessary to plough it up every two or three years. He told me of an infallible remedy which he had found in an old French book of husbandry: to lay upon the field a sufficient quantity of soot. He said he had tried it and found it succeed. He said that perhaps the soot of coals would not have

[7] Marguerite Susanne Kinloch, younger sister of the wife of the Reverend Robert Brown at Utrecht, was a sprightly Swiss girl of twenty or so. During the whole of Boswell's stay in Utrecht she had been a member of Brown's family. Boswell played shuttlecock with her almost daily, and the pair engaged in raillery of a rather juvenile sort.

[8] Sir James, who at this time was fifty-nine years old, had left Scotland to escape an unfortunate marriage which he may never really have intended to enter into. He had married a Swiss woman and had raised a large family in Switzerland, but this marriage, whatever its status in that country, was not recognized as legal in Scotland. On his death the baronetcy passed to his brother, not to his son.

the same effect as that of wood, but I might try. He dined with us; after which Monsieur de Brackel presented me at the Château to the Bailiff,[9] a most sensible, knowing, respected man. We passed the evening at cards *chez* ——, and supped at home.

[13 or 14 December, Memorandum of Topics to discuss with Rousseau. Original partly in French][1]

Suicide. Hypochondria. A real malady: family madness. Self-destruction: your arguments, not answered. — Was poet, praised in journals. — Suppose not slave to appetites, more than in marriage, but will have Swiss girl, amiable, &c. Quite adventure. [I would name my natural sons] Marischal Boswell, Rousseau Boswell. Anxious to see if children sound ere marry. Hurt nobody. If clear against this, can abstain, can live as Templar in Malta. Would have no deceit, all clear. — Scots familiarity and sarcasm: used to repress it by reserve and silence, but this rendered hypochondriac. May I not be gay, and fight the first man who is rude with me? Coward from youth; how could it be otherwise? Now firm. His sentiment of duels. — Court of London? No. Envoy? No. Parliament or home, and lawyer. Old estate, good principle. Propagate family great thing of all. Shall I suffer gloom as [expiation of] evil? And you, O great philosopher, will you befriend me? Am I not worthy? Tell me. You have no interest, no *ménagement*. If I am, take care of me. I tell you that the idea of being bound even by the finest thread to the most enlightened of philosophers, the noblest of souls, will always uphold me, all my life. Come, then, let

[9] Victor de Gingins, Seigneur de Moiry, chief magistrate of Yverdon, which at that time was ruled by Berne. He wrote political memoirs and was author of a political novel.

[1] These memoranda and the other set printed at p. 256 fill three sides of two undated quarto leaves of the same size as the contemporary journal. The fourth side is occupied by a copy in Boswell's hand of a poem by Belle de Zuylen, probably made by him at Brackel's from a manuscript sent by Mademoiselle Kinloch.

us make a compact: "I will meet you in heaven." Say that, and it will suffice for my entire life.

FRIDAY 14 DECEMBER. At eight I got on horseback and had for my guide a smith called Dupuis. I said, "Since when (*depuis quand*) have you had that name?" I passed the Mountain Lapidosa,[2] which is monstrously steep and in a great measure covered with snow. I was going to Rousseau, which consideration levelled the roughest mountains. I arrived at Môtiers before noon. I alighted at Rousseau's door. Up and I went and found Mademoiselle Le Vasseur, who told me, "He is very ill." "But can I see him for a moment?" "I will find out. Step in, Sir." I found him sitting in great pain.

ROUSSEAU. "I am overcome with ailments, disappointments, and sorrow. I am using a probe.[3] — Every one thinks it my duty to attend to him." BOSWELL. "That is most natural; and are you not pleased to find you can be of so much help to others?" ROUSSEAU. "Why — "

I had left with him when I was last here what I called a "Sketch of My Life," in which I gave him the important incidents of my history and my melancholy apprehensions, and begged his advice and friendship. It was an interesting piece. He said, "I have read your Memoir. You have been gulled. You ought never to see a priest." BOSWELL. "But can I yet hope to make something of myself?" ROUSSEAU. "Yes. Your great difficulty is that you think it so

[2] This name seems to be unknown to cartographers. One would guess that since it was winter and the heights were covered with snow, Boswell would have gone up the valleys by Ste. Croix and Buttes. In that case, Mountain Lapidosa ("Rocky Mountain") would probably be Mont Chasseron (5285 ft.), one of the more spectacular peaks of the region.

[3] French, "J'ai un Sond." Boswell had arrived at one of the crises of Rousseau's complaint. He had given up doctors, but sometimes tried to relieve the condition himself by the use of a probe or urethral dilator. The journal implies that when Boswell called, the instrument was actually *in situ*. The memoranda read "Sond toujours," which is perhaps more plausible, though it may be noted that Rousseau seems not on this occasion to have walked about the room, nor even to have risen.

difficult a matter. Come back in the afternoon. But put your watch on the table." BOSWELL. "For how long?" ROUSSEAU. "A quarter of an hour, and no longer." BOSWELL. "Twenty minutes." ROUSSEAU. "Be off with you! — Ha! Ha!" Notwithstanding the pain he was in, he was touched with my singular sally and laughed most really. He had a gay look immediately.

I dined in my old room with the two boarders. After dinner I walked out. There had fallen much rain, and the *vallon* was all overflowed. Nature looked somewhat different from the time that I was first here. I was sorry that such a scene was subject to any change.

At four I went to Monsieur Rousseau. "I have but a moment allowed me; I must use it well. — Is it possible to live amongst other men, and to retain singularity?" ROUSSEAU. "Yes, I have done it." BOSWELL. "But to remain on good terms with them?" ROUSSEAU. "Oh, if you want to be a wolf, you must howl. — I attach very little importance to books." BOSWELL. "Even to your own books?" ROUSSEAU. "Oh, they are just rigmarole." BOSWELL. "Now you are howling." ROUSSEAU. "When I put my trust in books, I was tossed about as you are — though it is rather by talking that you have been tossed. I had nothing stable here" (striking his head) "before I began to meditate." BOSWELL. "But you would not have meditated to such good purpose if you had not read." ROUSSEAU. "No. I should have meditated to better purpose if I had begun sooner." BOSWELL. "But I, for example, would never have had the agreeable ideas I possess of the Christian religion, had I not read 'The Savoyard's Creed.' Yet, to tell the truth, I can find no certain system. Morals appear to me an uncertain thing. For instance, I should like to have thirty women. Could I not satisfy that desire?" ROUSSEAU. "No!" BOSWELL. "Why?" ROUSSEAU. "Ha! Ha! If Mademoiselle were not here, I would give you a most ample reason why." BOSWELL. "But consider: if I am rich, I can take a number of girls; I get them with child; propagation is thus increased. I give them dowries, and I marry them off to good peasants who are very happy to have them. Thus they become wives at the same age as would have been the case if they had remained virgins, and I, on my side, have had the benefit of enjoying a great variety of women." ROUSSEAU. "Oh, you will be landed in jealousies, betrayals, and treachery." BOSWELL. "But cannot I follow the Oriental usage?" ROUSSEAU. "In the Orient the women are kept shut up, and that means keeping slaves. And, mark you, their women do nothing but harm, whereas ours do much good, for they do a great deal of work." BOSWELL. "Still, I should like to follow the example of the old Patriarchs, worthy men whose memory I hold in respect." ROUSSEAU. "But are you not a citizen? You must not pick and choose one law here and another law there; you must take the laws of your own society. Do your duty as a citizen, and if you hold fast, you will win respect. I should not talk about it, but I would do it. — And as for your lady,[4] when you go back to Scotland you will say, 'Madam, such conduct is against my conscience, and there shall be no more of it.' She will applaud you; if not, she is to be despised." BOSWELL. "Suppose her passion is still lively, and she threatens to tell her husband what has happened unless I agree to continue our intrigue?" ROUSSEAU. "In the first place, she will not tell him. In the second, you have no right to do evil for the sake of good." BOSWELL. "True. None the less, I can imagine some very embarrassing situations. And pray tell me how I can expiate the evil I have done?" ROUSSEAU. "Oh, Sir, there is no expiation for evil except good."

A beautiful thought this. Nevertheless, I maintained my doctrine of satisfaction by punishment. Yes, I must ever think that immutable justice requires atonement to be made for transgressions, and this atonement is to be made by suffering. This is the universal idea of all nations, and seems to be a leading principle of Christianity. I gave myself full scope; for since I left England I have not had anybody to whom I could lay open entirely my mind till I found Monsieur Rousseau.

I asked him, "When I get to France and Italy, may I not indulge in the gallantries usual to those countries, where the hus-

[4] The lady of his "Sketch." See pp. 212 *n.* 3, 234.

bands do not resent your making love to their wives? Nay, should
I not be happier as the citizen of such a nation?" ROUSSEAU. "They
are corpses. Do you want to be a corpse?" He was right. BOSWELL.
"But tell me, has a virtuous man any true advantages, is he really
better off than a man given up to sensuality?" ROUSSEAU. "We cannot doubt that we are spiritual beings; and when the soul escapes
from this prison, from this flesh, the virtuous man will find things
to his liking. He will enjoy the contemplation of happy souls,
nobly employed. He will say, 'I have already lived a life like that.'
Whereas those who experience nothing but the vile passions which
have their origin in the body will be dissatisfied by the spectacle of
pleasures which they have no means of enjoying."

BOSWELL. "Upon my word, I am at a loss how to act in this
world; I cannot determine whether or not I should adopt some
profession." ROUSSEAU. "One must have a great plan." BOSWELL.
"What about those studies on which so much stress is laid? Such as
history, for instance?" ROUSSEAU. "They are just amusements."
BOSWELL. "My father desires me to be called to the Scottish bar; I
am certainly doing right in satisfying my father; I have no such
certainty if I follow my light inclinations. I must therefore give
my mind to the study of the laws of Scotland." ROUSSEAU. "To be
sure; they are your tools. If you mean to be a carpenter, you must
have a plane." BOSWELL. "I do not get on well with my father. I am
not at my ease with him." ROUSSEAU. "To be at ease you need to
share some amusement." BOSWELL. "We look after the planting
together." ROUSSEAU. "That's too serious a business. You should
have some amusement that puts you more on an equal footing:
shooting, for example. A shot is missed and a joke is made of it,
without any infringement of respect. You enjoy a freedom which
you take for granted. — Once you are involved in a profession,
you must keep on with it even though another, and apparently
better, should present itself. If you keep changing, you can
achieve nothing."

(I should have observed that when I pushed the conversation
on women, Mademoiselle went out, and Monsieur Rousseau said,

"See now, you are driving Mademoiselle out of the room." She was now returned.) He stopped, and looked at me in a singular manner. "Are you greedy?" BOSWELL. "Yes." ROUSSEAU. "I am sorry to hear it." BOSWELL. "Ha! Ha! I was joking, for in your books you write in favour of greed.[5] I know what you are about to say, and it is just what I was hoping to hear. I wanted to get you to invite me to dinner. I had a great desire to share a meal with you." ROUSSEAU. "Well, if you are not greedy, will you dine here tomorrow? But I give you fair warning, you will find yourself badly off." BOSWELL. "No, I shall not be badly off; I am above all such considerations." ROUSSEAU. "Come then at noon; it will give us time to talk." BOSWELL. "All my thanks." ROUSSEAU. "Good evening."

Mademoiselle carried me to the house of a poor woman with a great many children whom Monsieur Rousseau aids with his charity. I contributed my part.[6] I was not pleased to hear Mademoiselle repeat to the poor woman just the common consolatory sayings. She should have said something singular.

[14 or 15 December, Memorandum of Topics to discuss with Rousseau. Original partly in French]

From time to time a letter to rekindle me. — I am a fine fellow; really, I am so. — Not own *ridicules?*[7] — Yet tell, and assure me as to women. Be honest, and I'll be firm. — As to prayer, what shall I do? — How do with my neighbours? — *Émile*, is it now practicable? Could he live in the world? — Young man with Savoyard, you or not? — Voltaire rogue. — Journal seven hundred pages. — Must I force study? I appear *instruit*. — Zélide's character; pronounce at once, what is she? — Worthy father, may I travel even though [he disapproves?] — Mahomet, what? Is

[5] Rousseau did not admire greed, but in children he found it preferable to vanity, as more natural for a child's age.

[6] "Crown, poor woman" (Memorandum, 14 or 15 December, separating the memorandum printed at p. 251 from that which follows the present entry).

[7] See p. 262: "Suppose you were to walk in upon a drinking-party ... "

there expiation or not by Christ? May I not just hold my peace in Scotland, not to offend tenants? — Is it worth the trouble, an individual, all for me? I am but one.

SATURDAY 15 DECEMBER. At seven in the morning I got on horseback and rode about a league to St. Sulpice, where I saw the source of the Reuse, the river which runs through the Val de Travers. It is a prodigious romantic place. I could not determine whether the water gushes in an immediate spring from the rock, or only issues out here, having pierced the mountain, upon which is a lake. The water comes forth with great violence. All around here I saw mountains and rocks as at Hartfell in Annandale. Some of the rocks were in great courses like huge stone walls, along which grew the towering pines which we call pitch firs, and which are much handsomer than the firs of Scotland.[8]

I was full of fine spirits. Gods! Am I now then really the friend of Rousseau? What a rich assemblage of ideas! I relish my felicity truly in such a scene as this. Shall I not truly relish it at Auchinleck? I was quite gay, my fancy was youthful, and vented its gladness in sportive sallies. I supposed myself in the rude world. I supposed a parcel of young fellows saying, "Come, Boswell, you'll dine with us today?" "No, gentlemen, excuse me; I'm engaged. I dine today with Rousseau." My tone, my air, my native pride when I pronounced this! Temple! You would have given half a guinea to see me at that moment.

I returned to my inn, where I found the Court of Justice of the *vallon* assembled. I entered and was amused to hear a Justice of Peace and honest farmers and a country minister[9] all talking French.

I then went to Monsieur Rousseau. "I hope your health is bet-

[8] " . . . Source of the Reuse, immensely wild. . . . Retreat of Rousseau. He walks till he is all in a sweat, to have the pleasure of being cool there . . . " (Memorandum, 16 December).
[9] Probably the local pastor, Monsieur Montmollin. He later preached against Rousseau, with the result that Rousseau's house was stoned, and he fled from Môtiers.

ter today." ROUSSEAU. "Oh, don't speak of it." He seemed unusually gay. Before dinner we are all so, if not made to wait too long. A keen appetite gives a vivacity to the whole frame.

I said, "You say nothing in regard to a child's duties towards his parents. You tell us nothing of your Émile's father." ROUSSEAU. "Oh, he hadn't any. He didn't exist." It is, however, a real pity that Monsieur Rousseau has not treated of the duties between parents and children. It is an important and a delicate subject and deserves to be illustrated by a sage of so clear a judgment and so elegant a soul.

He praised *The Spectator.* He said, "One comes across allegories in it. I have no taste for allegories, though your nation shows a great liking for them."

I gave him very fully the character of Mr. Johnson. He said with force, "I should like that man. I should respect him. I would not disturb his principles if I could. I should like to see him, but from a distance, for fear he might maul me." I told him how averse Mr. Johnson was to write, and how he had his levee. "Ah," said he, "I understand. He is a man who enjoys holding forth." I told him Mr. Johnson's *bon mot* upon the innovators: that truth is a cow which will yield them no more milk, and so they are gone to milk the bull. He said, "He would detest me. He would say, 'Here is a corrupter: a man who comes here to milk the bull.' "[1]

I had diverted myself by pretending to help Mademoiselle Le Vasseur to make the soup. We dined in the kitchen, which was neat and cheerful. There was something singularly agreeable in this scene. Here was Rousseau in all his simplicity, with his Armenian dress, which I have surely mentioned before now. His long coat and nightcap made him look easy and well.

Our dinner was as follows: 1. A dish of excellent soup. 2. A *bouilli* of beef and veal. 3. Cabbage, turnip, and carrot. 4. Cold pork. 5. Pickled trout, which he jestingly called tongue. 6. Some little dish which I forget. The dessert consisted of stoned pears and

[1] Boswell shows considerable rashness and Rousseau great acuteness, for Johnson *had* directed the remark at Rousseau and Hume.

of chestnuts. We had red and white wines. It was a simple, good repast. We were quite at our ease. I sometimes forgot myself and became ceremonious. "May I help you to some of this dish?" ROUSSEAU. "No, Sir. I can help myself to it." Or, "May I help myself to some more of that?" ROUSSEAU. "Is your arm long enough? A man does the honours of his house from a motive of vanity. He does not want it forgotten who is the master. I should like every one to be his own master, and no one to play the part of host. Let each one ask for what he wants; if it is there to give, let him be given it; otherwise, he must be satisfied without. Here you see true hospitality." BOSWELL. "In England, it is quite another matter. They do not want to be at ease; they are stiff and silent, in order to win respect." ROUSSEAU. "In France, you find no such gloom among people of distinction. There is even an affectation of the utmost liberty, as though they would have you understand, 'We stand in no fear of losing our dignity.' That is a more refined form of self-esteem."

BOSWELL. "Well, and do you not share that yourself?" ROUSSEAU. "Yes, I confess that I like to be respected; but only in matters of importance." BOSWELL. "You are so simple. I expected to find you quite different from this: the Great Rousseau. But you do not see yourself in the same light as others do. I expected to find you enthroned and talking with a grave authority." ROUSSEAU. "Uttering oracles? Ha! Ha! Ha!" BOSWELL. "Yes, and that I should be much in awe of you. And really your simplicity might lay you open to criticism; it might be said, 'Monsieur Rousseau does not make himself sufficiently respected.' In Scotland, I assure you, a very different tone must be taken to escape from the shocking familiarity which is prevalent in that country. Upon my word, I cannot put up with it. Should I not be justified in forestalling it by fighting a duel with the first man who should treat me so, and thus live at peace for the rest of my life?" ROUSSEAU. "No. That is not allowable. It is not right to stake one's life on such follies. Life is given us for objects of importance. Pay no heed to what such men say. They will get tired of talking to a man who does not answer them." BOSWELL. "If you were in Scotland, they would begin at the very start by calling you Rousseau; they would say, 'Jean Jacques, how goes it?' with the utmost familiarity." ROUSSEAU. "That is perhaps a good thing." BOSWELL. "But they would say, 'Poh! Jean Jacques, why do you allow yourself all these fantasies? You're a pretty man to put forward such claims. Come, come, settle down in society like other people.' And they would say it to you with a sourness which I am quite unable to imitate for you." ROUSSEAU. "Ah, that's bad."

There he felt the thistle, when it was applied to himself on the tender part. It was just as if I had said, "Hoot, Johnnie Rousseau man, what for hae ye sae mony figmagairies?[2] Ye're a bonny man indeed to mauk siccan a wark; set ye up. Canna ye just live like ither fowk?" It was the best idea could be given in the polite French language of the rude Scots sarcastical vivacity.

BOSWELL. "I have leanings towards despotism, let me tell you. On our estate, I am like an ancient laird, and I insist on respect from the tenants." ROUSSEAU. "But when you see an old man with white hair, do you, as a young man, have no feelings at all? Have you no respect for age?" BOSWELL. "Yes. I have even on many occasions been very affable. I have talked quite freely with the tenants." ROUSSEAU. "Yes, you forgot yourself, and became a man." BOSWELL. "But I was sorry for it afterwards. I used to think, 'I have lowered myself.' " ROUSSEAU. "Ha! Ha! Ha!"

BOSWELL. "I have leanings towards despotism, let me tell you. give me credentials as your ambassador to the Corsicans. Will you make me his Excellency? Are you in need of an ambassador? I offer you my services: Mr. Boswell, Ambassador Extraordinary of Monsieur Rousseau to the Isle of Corsica." ROUSSEAU. "Perhaps you would rather be King of Corsica?" BOSWELL. "On my word! Ha! Ha! Not I. It exceeds my powers" (with a low bow). "All the same, I can now say, 'I have refused a crown.' "[3]

[2] Usually *figmaliries* or *whigmaleeries:* whims, crotchets.
[3] Rousseau, entering into the spirit of Boswell's game of bestowing titles, makes the satirical suggestion that Boswell's despotic temper fits him better

ROUSSEAU. "Do you like cats?" BOSWELL. "No."⁴ ROUSSEAU. "I was sure of that. It is my test of character. There you have the despotic instinct of men. They do not like cats because the cat is free and will never consent to become a slave. He will do nothing to your order, as the other animals do." BOSWELL. "Nor a hen, either." ROUSSEAU. "A hen would obey your orders if you could make her understand them. But a cat will understand you perfectly and not obey them." BOSWELL. "But a cat is ungrateful and treacherous." ROUSSEAU. "No. That's all untrue. A cat is an animal that can be very much attached to you; he will do anything you please out of friendship. I have a cat here. He has been brought up with my dog; they play together. The cat will give the dog a blow with his tail, and the dog will offer him his paw." (He described the playing of his dog and cat with exquisite eloquence, as a fine painter draws a small piece.) He put some victuals on a trencher, and made his dog dance round it. He sung to him a lively air with a sweet voice and great taste. "You see the ballet. It is not a gala performance, but a pretty one all the same." I think the dog's name was Sultan. He stroked him and fed him, and with an arch air said, "He is not much *respected*, but he gets well looked after."⁵

---

to be a king than an ambassador. Boswell counters by quoting Rousseau's own words when invited to be the lawgiver of Corsica. See p. 225.

⁴ He had, in fact, an antipathy to cats, sufficient to make him "uneasy when in the room with one." Readers of *The Life of Johnson* will remember how this adds spice to the delicious account of Dr. Johnson and his cat Hodge.

⁵ When Rousseau came to England in 1766, Sultan accompanied him, and played a major part in a characteristic episode of that visit, related by David Hume in a letter to the Marquise de Barbentane, 16 February 1766: "Soon after our arrival, I prevailed on [Rousseau] to go to the playhouse and see Garrick. Mrs. Garrick gave him her box, which is much concealed from the audience, but opposite to that of the King and Queen; and their Majesties were privately informed that they might there expect to see Monsieur Rousseau. When the hour came, he told me that he had changed his resolution, and would not go: for — 'What shall I do with Sultan?' That is the name of his dog. 'You must leave him behind,' said I. 'But the first person,' replied he, 'who opens the door, Sultan will run into the streets in search of me, and will be lost.' 'You must then,' said I, 'lock him up in your room, and

BOSWELL. "Suppose you were to walk in upon a drinking-party of young folk, who should treat you with ridicule, would you be above minding it?" ROUSSEAU. "It would put me out of countenance. I am shy by nature. I have often, for example, been overcome by the raillery of women. A party such as you describe would be disagreeable to me. I should leave it." I was comforted to find that my sensibility is not despicable weakness.

BOSWELL. "The Anglican Church is my choice." ROUSSEAU. "Yes. It is no doubt an excellent religion, but it is not the Gospel, which is all simplicity. It is another kind of religion." BOSWELL. "The Gospel, at the outset, was simple but rigorous too, as when Paul says it is better not to marry than to marry." ROUSSEAU. "Paul? But that is not the Gospel." BOSWELL. "Then you have no liking for Paul?" ROUSSEAU. "I respect him, but I think he is partly responsible for muddling your head. He would have been an Anglican clergyman."

BOSWELL. "Mr. Johnson is a Jacobite, but he has a pension of £300 sterling from the King." ROUSSEAU. "He ought not to have accepted a pension." BOSWELL. "He says that he does not drink the health of King James with the wine given him by King George." ROUSSEAU. "But you should not employ the substance given you by this wine in attacking King George."

Mademoiselle said, "Shall you, Sir, see Monsieur de Voltaire?" BOSWELL. "Most certainly." (To Rousseau.) "Monsieur de Voltaire has no liking for you. That is natural enough." ROUSSEAU. "Yes. One does not like those whom one has greatly injured. His talk is most enjoyable; it is even better than his books." BOSWELL. "Have you looked at the *Philosophical Dictionary?*" ROUSSEAU. "Yes."

---

put the key in your pocket.' This was accordingly done; but as we went downstairs, the dog howled and made a noise; his master turned back and said he had not resolution to leave him in that condition; but I caught him in my arms and told him that Mrs. Garrick had dismissed another company in order to make room for him; that the King and Queen were expecting to see him; and without a better reason than Sultan's impatience, it would be ridiculous to disappoint them. Partly by these reasons and partly by force, I engaged him to proceed. The King and Queen looked more at him than at the players" (*Letters of David Hume*, ed. J. Y. T. Greig, 2 vols., 1932, ii. 14–15).

BOSWELL. "And what of it?" ROUSSEAU. "I don't like it. I am not intolerant, but he deserves — " (I forget his expression here.)⁶ "It is very well to argue against men's opinions; but to show contempt, and to say, 'You are idiots to believe this,' is to be personally offensive. — Now go away." BOSWELL. "Not yet. I will leave at three o'clock. I have still five and twenty minutes." ROUSSEAU. "But I can't give you five and twenty minutes." BOSWELL. "I will give you even more than that." ROUSSEAU. "What! of my own time? All the kings on earth cannot give me my own time." BOSWELL. "But if I had stayed till tomorrow I should have had five and twenty minutes, and next day another five and twenty. I am not taking those minutes. I am making you a present of them." ROUSSEAU. "Oh! You are not stealing my money, you are giving it to me." He then repeated part of a French satire ending with "And whatever they leave you, they count as a gift."⁷ BOSWELL. "Pray speak for me, Mademoiselle." (To Rousseau.) "I have an excellent friend here." ROUSSEAU. "Nay, but this is a league." BOSWELL. "No league at all." Mademoiselle said, "Gentlemen, I will tell you the moment the clock strikes." ROUSSEAU. "Come; I need to take the air after eating."

We walked out to a gallery pendant upon his wall. BOSWELL. "In the old days I was a great mimic. I could imitate every one I saw. But I have left it off." ROUSSEAU. "It is a dangerous talent, for it compels one to seize upon all that is small in a character." BOSWELL. "True. But I assure you there was a nobleness about my art, I carried mimicry to such a point of perfection. I was a kind of virtuoso. When I espied any singular character I would say, 'It must be added to my collection.' " He laughed with all his nerves:⁸ "You are an odd character." BOSWELL. "I am a physiognomist, be-

⁶ The memoranda read "(something like punishment)." In a letter to Du Peyrou, 4 November 1764, Rousseau says that the book seems to him "an outrage against society, and punishable even before human courts" — perhaps the very words he employed in speaking to Boswell. Voltaire's *Philosophical Dictionary* had only just appeared.

⁷ "Ce qu'ils ne vous prennent pas, ils disent qu'ils vous le donnent." I have not identified the author.

⁸ This unusual expression is Boswell's own, being in English in the original. The memorandum reads, "Laughed from heart."

lieve me. I have studied that art very attentively, I assure you, and I can rely on my conclusions." He seemed to agree to this. ROUS-SEAU. "Yet I think the features of the face vary between one nation and another, as do accent and tone of voice; and these signify different feelings among different peoples." This observation struck me as new and most ingenious. BOSWELL. "But in time one learns to understand them."

ROUSSEAU. "The roads are bad. You will be late." BOSWELL. "I take the bad parts on foot; the last league of the way is good. — Do you think that I shall make a good barrister before a court of justice?" ROUSSEAU. "Yes. But I regret that you have the talents necessary for defending a bad case."

BOSWELL. "Have you any commands for Italy?" ROUSSEAU. "I will send a letter to Geneva for you to carry to Parma." BOSWELL. "Can I send you anything back?" ROUSSEAU. "A few pretty tunes from the opera." BOSWELL. "By all means. Oh, I have had so much to say, that I have neglected to beg you to play me a tune." ROUSSEAU. "It's too late."[9]

MADEMOISELLE. "Sir, your man is calling for you to start." Monsieur Rousseau embraced me. He was quite the tender Saint-Preux. He kissed me several times, and held me in his arms with elegant cordiality. Oh, I shall never forget that I have been thus. ROUSSEAU. "Good-bye. You are a fine fellow." BOSWELL. "You have shown me great goodness. But I deserved it." ROUSSEAU. "Yes. You are malicious; but 'tis a pleasant malice, a malice I don't dislike. Write and tell me how you are." BOSWELL. "And you will write to

[9] Music occupied Rousseau all his life. Though poorly grounded technically, he was fluent as a composer of simple melodies and perspicacious as a critic and musical theorist. Before the appearance of the three great literary works in 1761–1762, copying musical scores had been his chief means of livelihood, and achievement in opera his ambition. Of his several attempts, one (in 1752) was an enormous success: the one-act pastoral, the *Devin du village* or *Village Soothsayer*. Meanwhile he had been commissioned to write the musical articles for the *Encyclopaedia*. This he did very inadequately, but out of the effort grew his large and influential *Dictionnaire de musique*, which he was finishing at the time of Boswell's visits.

me?" ROUSSEAU. "I know not how to reach you." BOSWELL. "Yes, you shall write to me in Scotland." ROUSSEAU. "Certainly; and even at Paris." BOSWELL. "Bravo! If I live twenty years, you will write to me for twenty years?" ROUSSEAU. "Yes." BOSWELL. "Good-bye. If you live for seven years, I shall return to Switzerland from Scotland to see you." ROUSSEAU. "Do so. We shall be old acquaintances." BOSWELL. "One word more. Can I feel sure that I am held to you by a thread, even if of the finest? By a hair?" (Seizing a hair of my head.) ROUSSEAU. "Yes. Remember always that there are points at which our souls are bound." BOSWELL. "It is enough. I, with my melancholy, I, who often look on myself as a despicable being, as a good-for-nothing creature who should make his exit from life, — I shall be upheld for ever by the thought that I am bound to Monsieur Rousseau. Good-bye. Bravo! I shall live to the end of my days." ROUSSEAU. "That is undoubtedly a thing one must do.[1] Good-bye."

Mademoiselle accompanied me to the outer door. Before dinner she told me, "Monsieur Rousseau has a high regard for you. The first time you came, I said to him, 'That gentleman has an honest face. I am sure you will like him.'" I said, "Mademoiselle is a good judge." "Yes," said she, "I have seen strangers enough in the twenty-two years that I have been with Monsieur Rousseau, and I assure you that I have sent many of them packing because I did not fancy their way of talking." I said, "You have promised to let me have news of you from time to time." "Yes, Sir." "And tell me

[1] Boswell is quoting *Émile*, the twenty-fourth paragraph of the Second Book; Rousseau pretends not to recognize the allusion and makes it the occasion of a bit of irony. The passage Boswell has in mind runs as follows: "If you live according to Nature, are patient, and dismiss your doctors, you will not escape death, but you will feel it only once; whereas they bring it daily before your troubled imagination, and their lying art, instead of prolonging your life, only takes away your power of enjoying it. I shall always ask what real good the art of medicine has done to men. Some of those whom it cures would die, to be sure; but millions whom it kills would live. Sensible reader, do not invest in that lottery where the chances are so heavily against you. Suffer, die, or get well; but in any case *live* to your last hour."

what I can send you from Geneva. Make no ceremony." "Well, if you will, a garnet necklace."[2]

We shook hands cordially, and away I went to my inn. My eldest landlady looked at me and said, "Sir, I think you are crying." This I retain as a true elogium of my humanity. I replied, "[No.] Yet I am unhappy to leave Monsieur Rousseau. I will see you again in seven years." I got a-horseback and rode by the house of Monsieur Rousseau. Mademoiselle waited for me at the door, and cried, "*Bon voyage;* write to us." Good creature. I rode gravely to Yverdon contemplating how this day will appear to my mind some years hence. I was received cordially by my gallant Baron and my amiable Madame de Brackel; yet did my spirits sink pretty low. No wonder after such a high flow.

SUNDAY 16 DECEMBER. I went in the Baron's chaise with Madame de Coppet to Giez, the *campagne* of Sir James Kinloch. We found there the Baron, who had gone before us on horseback; Madame Paccotton, a daughter of Sir James, who is separated from a bad husband; and Mademoiselle Susette, the youngest daughter next to my friend at Utrecht. We dined well and sung merrily. I gave Sir James some old Scots tunes, which he also hummed as well as he could and seemed highly recreated. I could scarcely think myself out of Scotland; yet the manner of keeping Sunday marked well the difference. The Baron opposed Monsieur Rousseau's system as to the cat, "for," said he, "nothing is more certain than that it is an ungrateful animal; and as for its being free, I have seen a cat that had been trained and was as servile as any creature could become. Monsieur Rousseau is a singular man. I have heard him say that he had read nothing for twenty years. But he has cited authors who have written since that time."[3] In short, the Baron is not much his friend. He seems a disciple of Voltaire.

[2] Which he did send: see p. 310. Also, the expense account for 15 December contains a mysterious entry of four crowns "for a *certain affair*" which I suspect of being a tip to Thérèse.

[3] Such as Voltaire's *Philosophical Dictionary!*

At four we returned, dressed, and went to the Château, as is the custom here every Sunday. I found a very handsome company at cards. Fourteen in all made the company for supper. The Bailiff talked a great deal to me of Rousseau. "When he heard the decree of the Parlement of Paris, he was furious. When he came here, he wished to insert an outrageous paragraph in the *Gazette de Berne*, in which he compared Paris to Toulouse.⁴ I said to him, 'Do you realize the consequences? The French Ambassador at Soleure will lodge a complaint against you, and you will be arrested. No; you will not insert it.' He replied, 'No, I shall not do it. It may be that some day I shall feel that I am obliged to you; but now I do not feel it.' The decree of Geneva pierced his heart. He was terribly downcast. An order came from Berne for him to leave our canton. I wrote that he was ill; I wanted to gain time. A second order came. Then I communicated it to him, but tactfully. 'Are you contented here?' 'Yes, but I see too many people.' 'I think you would be better off at Môtiers.' He fixed me with his piercing gaze. 'I believe I understand you.' 'Yes, you understand me.' I had already engaged the house where he now is. He left that same day. He came to take leave of us. There were tears in his eyes. He said, 'They are tears of joy for having known you.' "

The Bailiff gave me more anecdotes of him. "I asked him, 'But how is it possible that the same man could have written the *Essay on Inequality* and *The Village Soothsayer?*' 'I am ill. I find myself in a black humour, and then my thoughts are black. I wrote the *Inequality* in a forest where for three months I had seen nobody. I was in a very gay company for three weeks; then I wrote *The Village Soothsayer*.' 'Are you Saint-Preux?' 'The story is fundamentally true. I can tell you no more now. Some day I shall tell

⁴ Where a French Protestant, Jean Calas, so recently as 9 March 1762, had been tortured and broken on the wheel on an incredible charge of having murdered his son to prevent his becoming a Roman Catholic. Voltaire had stepped forward as the champion of the dead man, and had made the case notorious throughout Europe. As a result of his indefatigable labours, the judicial action against Calas was annulled, Calas was declared innocent, and his family granted an indemnity.

you.' He owned that he was himself the young man who lived with the Savoyard curate, whose profession of faith is real. Monsieur Rousseau told me that he had put it into his own words, but that he had not added a single idea.[5] Women are his ruling passion. You see what fire he has in his eyes when he speaks of them. He considers it no crime to have a mistress. He advocates laws for the citizens of a state, but he regards himself as a being apart.[6] He says that people ought to put as much of his *Émile* into practice as they find expedient." I asked the Bailiff, "Do you think that he has done good in the world?" He answered, "He could have but he has not. For the most part he has written for fame."

We supped very well; then returned to the hall, and played at *vaut rien*, the same with tres-ace[7] in Scotland. This is a most cheerful country. The Bailiff did not scruple to skip with the best of us, and retained his dignity as much as if he had carefully preserved it in stiff and formal gravity.

MONDAY 17 DECEMBER. I wrote all morning and grew vapourish and was dull. After dinner the Baron said that if I had stayed in Holland I would have gone out of my mind. At night we had a great company at cards. So many supped: among others, the friend of Mademoiselle Kinloch at Utrecht, Mademoiselle Martin, a sweet creature.

TUESDAY 18 DECEMBER.[8] I should have gone this morning but was prevailed with to stay for a *partie* at supper *chez* Monsieur du

[5] The Vicar is believed to combine characteristics from two priests who had befriended Rousseau in the memorable period following his conversion at Turin: Monsieur Gaime and Monsieur Gatier.

[6] The memoranda add a little here: "No fatherland for him, no laws, &c. He is not obedient to his mother Geneva." According to Rousseau's own statement, Thérèse had been no more to him than housekeeper and nurse for some years previous to the publication of *Émile*. He might have avoided scandal by marrying her sooner (he put off doing so until 1768 and then did it in a left-handed fashion), but he hated irrevocable engagements, and it was not his way to do anything prudent.

[7] A game of tag, generally played by six people.

[8] " ... Shun affectation at all times. Swear run no risk by women" (Memorandum, 18 December).

Foin, a Parisian, a hearty fellow who is employed to furnish the Swiss cantons with salt. His wife is plump and lively, though vapourish even to the seeing of visions in the night.

I took a walk to Chamblon, the *campagne* of the Baron. I thought: "I am just educating for a periodical writer; I am storing my mind with anecdotes *quas mox depromere possim.*"[9] Joseph, the coachman, showed me the house. I found the rooms small; one however was locked, which the judicious Joseph, willing to support the honour of his master, would make me believe was superb. I made our family very merry with this.

After dinner the Baron went with me to the Château, where I took leave in form of the Bailiff. We returned home, where I found a Mrs. Irwine who had attended the Princess of Wales. I was in a whimsical frame, and talking of Holland said that the women in that country were perfectly round, and, as the Dutch are very frugal, it is very common to see a man rolling his wife before him through the streets like a barrel; as they are also very cleanly, he wraps *Mevrouw* in a waxcloth coverlet. What a ludicrous conceit!

We supped well at Monsieur du Foin's. The Bailiff was there. We had also a Madame de Luze of Neuchâtel, a genteel, pretty sort of woman, who writes verses. She is a great admirer of Rousseau. She had a pretty little daughter whom they called in jest "Madame Jean Jacques." I took leave of this people with regret. They are virtuous, hospitable, and gay. When we got home we were regaled with a glass of choice liqueur. The Baron was formerly in the French service in the regiment of the great Maréchal de Saxe, with whom he was very intimate.[1] I found he had been a wild rogue. He gave me some anecdotes of his life at Paris, and talked of intriguing with a kept girl when the *payeur* was absent. It is curious to see a

[9] "Which I may be able to publish by and by" (Horace, *Epistles*, I. i. 12).
[1] Maréchal de Saxe was a famous French general, the victor of Fontenoy. One of the illegitimate children of Augustus the Strong, King of Poland (see p. 107 *n.* 5), he resembled his father closely, both in his vigour and his excesses. He was chosen Duke of Courland in 1726, but was able to maintain his authority over the Duchy for no more than a year.

man, after a life of libertine conduct, turned a grave father of a family.

WEDNESDAY 19 DECEMBER. No machine was to be had, so I was obliged to stay another day. I kept snug from morning to night, except taking a walk with the Baron, whose system I combated. He is an old chieftain in Courland; but he lives in Switzerland and is even inclined to sell the estate of his fathers. At night I was too jocular. There is a great difference between intemperance of mirth and a cheerful glass of gladness.

THURSDAY 20 DECEMBER. I had last night taken leave of my amiable landlady. This morning the *brave Baron* was ready to give me the parting embrace, and very cordial it was. I had sad roads to Lausanne, where I arrived in the evening.

FRIDAY 21 DECEMBER.[2] I was curious to know what British were here. Amongst others they named me "Monsieur Graäm, Scotsman." I went and called upon young Murray, nephew to Lord Elibank, who gave me full particulars as to Lausanne; and who should this "Graäm" be but young Graham of Gartmore. I flew to see him, and happy we were to meet. He was quite gay. It pleased me to see that an advocate *may* be made a fine fellow.[3] He raged against the Scots Parliament House, and a man's passing his whole life in writing "d—mned *papers.*" I said an advocate, like a Prussian soldier, must be bred to his business and know no better.

The amusements of lawyers are not the elegant exercise of genius and the fine arts, which would unfit them for their dry business. Their entertainment consists in solid eating and drinking, and in rude and boisterous merriment, after which they return to their work like a horse after his corn. While Graham and I walked Lausanne, I was as far from being an advocate as from being a

---

[2] "Yesterday ... sickish. Joked too much with Jacob. At night, supped too free; was harassed with unclean thoughts. Again enjoyed air. Swear so no more, and live more spare ... " (Memorandum, 21 December).

[3] Graham's father, Nicholas Graham of Gartmore, resembled Boswell's father in being both advocate and landed gentleman, and young Graham (whose name was William) was following his father's footsteps. Hence Boswell's special interest in him.

captain of a man-of-war. Graham had passed the winter in France, and was full of that charming country. He seemed not a little pleased at the licking which the *Gazette littéraire* has given to Lord Kames, whom he called the most unequal-tempered man alive.

Graham was engaged at dinner. So I dined at the table d'hôte of my inn, after which I took a walk to the *campagne* of the Prince Louis Eugène de Württemberg-Stuttgart, a man of a character singularly amiable.[4] He married a comtesse, which was an unpardonable degradation. He lives here in a sweet retirement. I sent in my compliments, and begged to have the honour of paying him my respects. He received me, and I was charmed with him. He has been in the French service some time, and has got that exquisite ease peculiar to the lively nation. He is a man of parts and of letters. He admires Rousseau, and in a great measure follows his plan of education. The Princess agrees to it, and their two daughters will be examples of the new system. I had heard of this, and said, "I should like very much to see a child brought up according to Rousseau's plan." Said the Prince, "I can show you some." He then caused bring the two young ladies, the eldest of whom he has called Sophie, and a stout lass she was. The other was more delicate; but they both seemed healthy and gay. It was truly a romantic scene.[5] The chaplain had been in China and was a dry, matter-of-fact fellow. I passed an hour here with uncommon satisfaction. The Princess was a mild, agreeable little woman. This was quite an adventure. I shall perhaps write to this prince.

I then went with Graham to what is called Le Cercle, where I found about fifteen English playing at whist and making a great deal of noise.[6] They rendered me hippish. I should have mentioned

[4] Ludwig Eugen (1731–1795) succeeded his brother, the tyrannical Karl Eugen mentioned on p. 141 as Reigning Duke of Württemberg in 1793, but enjoyed his honours less than two years.

[5] Sophie was the name of Émile's beloved. One would hardly infer from Boswell's description of the "two young ladies" that they were respectively eighteen months and five months old.

[6] Gibbon, who was a member of Le Cercle, wrote of it as follows: "It is an agreeable enough society for passing one's idle hours in. It is composed of

that I went and paid a visit to Madame d'Hermenches, lady of Colonel Constant at The Hague. She received me very politely.[7] I supped with Graham at his landlord's, where lived also the two Mr. Grenvilles, quite Englishmen. A Mademoiselle d'Illens supped with us. She was acquainted with Monsieur Rousseau. She was languishing and amiable. I sat by her and enlivened myself by talking with her. Lausanne is a fine, airy, agreeable place where the society is easy and gay. So Graham assured me.

SATURDAY 22 DECEMBER. I had a good day's drive to Geneva.[8] Curious were my thoughts on entering this seat of Calvinism. I put up Aux Trois Rois. I sent immediately to Cazenove, Clavière et fils for my letters. Young Cazenove brought me a good packet, which made me a very happy man. I had letters from the Margrave of Baden-Durlach, from Rousseau, from Temple, and from Erskine.[9] What a group of ideas! I supped at the table d'hôte, where was a Monsieur de La Sale, a Parisian, with whom I chatted agreeably.

---

about eighty persons: foreigners and people of rank in the city, and three black balls are enough to exclude one. They have a handsome set of rooms where one is sure to find cards, conversation, the gazettes, the newspapers, &c. In a word, it is a select café" (*Le Journal de Gibbon à Lausanne,* 17 *août* 1763–19 *avril* 1764, *publié par* Georges Bonnard, Lausanne, 1945, p. 25, translated).

[7] Madame de Constant d'Hermenches and her husband seem by this time to have been living little together. She was seven years his senior and her health was bad.

[8] The memoranda are rather fuller here: "Yesterday had slept only two hours. Set out a little after four, really sick. Walked and grew better. Dined at Nyon with French officers. Came to Geneva at five ... " (Memorandum, 23 December).

[9] The letter from Erskine has not been recovered; the others are printed below in the order of Boswell's mention.

A Motiers-Travers 20. 9bre 1764

Voici, Monsieur, la lettre dont je vous
ai parlé. Je crois que vous serez bien aise
de voir celui à qui elle en addressée; c'est
un homme qui a de la philosophie dans
la tête et de la vertu dans le coeur.
Vous pourrez vous informer de sa
demeure à la Cour de Parme où
il est, je crois, lecteur ou Bibliothecaire
du jeune Prince. Je vous souhaite
un bon voyage et vous embrasse, —
Monsieur, de tout mon coeur.

Rousseau

J'ai reçu depuis vôtre départ deux
lettres de Mylord Mareschal: il se porte
bien et va venir passer le carnaval
à Berlin.

Letter from Rousseau to Boswell, 20 December 1764, from the original
in the Yale University Library.

[Received 22 December, the Margrave of Baden-Durlach
to Boswell][1]

Sir   It was with a great deal of pleasure j recived your obliging lettre, and j beg you would be persuadet that j value the sati-
faction of entering in corespondence with very much. You do me
to much honour Sir, by giving me the tile of a Phylosopher, a have
not learning enought to be a theoretical one, and practical Phylosopher are very rare beings, all j can do is to be a friend of Philosophical work, and Conversations, and of good and virtous men;
So you will oblige me Sir, by writing to me alwais openly and
freely, and without Ceremonie.

I am very much obliged to you Sir, for the verses you was
pleased to send me, and j was very glad to see, that after you had
so elegantly contradicdet Mr: Garik, you at last became of the
same sentiment with him

The Marg: desires me to make you her compliments, and is
very sensible of you kind remembrance, and j shall allwais be Sir:
Your most obediant humble Servant.

THE MARGGRAVE OF BAADEN DURLACH

Carlsruhe
Dec: the 9. 1764.

[Received 22 December, Rousseau to Boswell. Original
in French][2]

Môtiers-Travers, 20 December 1764

HERE, SIR, is the letter I spoke to you about. I think you will be
glad of having seen the person to whom it is addressed; he is a man
with philosophy in his head and virtue in his heart. You will be
able to find out where he lives from the Court at Parma, where he

[1] The Margrave's spelling, capitalization, and punctuation have been preserved.
[2] See the facsimile.

is, I believe, Reader or Librarian to the young Prince. I wish you a good trip and embrace you, Sir, with all my heart.

                                  Rousseau.

Since you left, I have received two letters from my Lord Marischal. He is well, and is going to pass the carnival season at Berlin.[3]

[Rousseau to Alexandre Deleyre. Original in French][4]

                           Môtiers, 20 December 1764

     I AM TAKING ADVANTAGE, MY DEAR FRIEND, of the departure of Mr. Boswell, a Scots gentleman who is going to make the tour of Italy, to send you a brief greeting and tell you how much your last letter touched and rejoiced my heart. Although I have never courted any man, I have responded so readily to the overtures of a thousand people who have courted me that I have, so to speak, thrown myself at their heads. They have all fallen off at the first rub, and, behold, almost the only one of the lot I was difficult with, stays with me, consoles me in my misfortunes and pardons me the wrongs I did him. Dear Deleyre, I have certainly been slow in writing, but if my sincere friendship still pleases you, do not look upon my dilatoriness as a loss. I will surely pay you interest.

    I am glad that Mr. Boswell and you are to make each other's acquaintance. I think you will both be grateful to me for bringing you together. In the first letter he wrote me, he told me that he was a man "of singular merit." I was curious to see a man

[3] Rousseau wrote, "et va venir passer le carnaval." I have assumed that *venir* was an inadvertency.

[4] Rousseau's editors have long known that he wrote this letter, but the original has never turned up. It is now printed for the first time from a copy made by Boswell, in translation at this point, the French text at p. 328. — Alexandre Deleyre, 1726–1797, French *philosophe*, was the author of two comedies and of books on Bacon and Montesquieu. He had known Rousseau in Paris, and had remained his loyal friend and disciple after the breach with Diderot and the other Encyclopaedists. He was bringing up his infant son according to the principles of *Émile*, and was writing Rousseau long and fervent letters, almost as enthusiastic in tone as Boswell's.

who spoke of himself in such a fashion, and I found that he had told me the truth. In his youth he got his head confused with a smattering of harsh Calvinist theology, and he still retains, because of it, a troubled soul and gloomy notions. I have advised him to devote his tour of Italy to the study of the fine arts. If you philosophize with him, I beg you to restrain your own inclinations, and to present him with moral objects only under such aspects as are consoling and tender. He is a convalescent whom the least relapse will infallibly destroy. I should have been interested in him even if he had not been recommended to me by Lord Marischal. To you I need not say more.

I am on the point of concluding a transaction which may give me peace and bread for the rest of my days. I need both; for in my present dejection of body and mind, I can no longer think or act. The business I am referring to is a general edition of my writings, which a society wishes to undertake here under my supervision, and by which I should make my final bow to the public.

One thing embarrasses me, and that is the Preface, which it is out of my power to write. Would you have the time, would you be in the humour, to assume the responsibility for this piece of work? I cannot express to you what a favour you would be doing me. It is understood, of course, that it would be you who spoke, and that you would allow it to bear your name. I should like to think that it would share the fate that awaits mine, a fate, I believe, which cannot but be honourable, for posterity is always just. Think it over and let me know as soon as you can, for your reply may determine me as to the decision I am to make.

I am not altogether of your mind concerning the impossibility of giving the Corsicans a good set of laws, and I do not at all believe that it will be necessary to resort to bigotry. Far from thinking that one should abstain from mingling in the affairs of men so as to have no reproaches to make against one's self, I think the contrary: that one prepares a very serious reproach against one's self when one neglects to do good; or at least when one fails to try, and with some hope of succeeding. But this is not the time to talk of all that, and the Corsicans today have other things to do than to establish Utopia in their midst. It must be owned that your countrymen, the French, are a very servile nation, a people thoroughly devoted to tyranny, exceedingly cruel and relentless in their pursuit of the unfortunate. If they knew of a free man at the other end of the world, I think they would go thither for the mere pleasure of exterminating him. Good-bye.

In the twenty-fourth volume of Muratori's collection, *Scriptorum rerum Italicarum*, there is a little work by P. Cyrnaeus entitled *De rebus Corsicis*. Isn't that work separately published, and would there be no way to make it better known?

[Received 22 December, Temple to Boswell]

Berwick, 13 November 1764

MY DEAR BOSWELL, . . . Your letter is the longest and the best I ever had from you. It is a true picture of yourself: full of good sense and liberal sentiment; easy, yet animated. There's compliment for compliment for you. . . .

Indeed, Boswell, you have a loyal heart. A king with you is everything, and I make no doubt but that if you had lived in the time of the first Charles, you would have been a most zealous Royalist. When you saw Frederick the Great (for I must own he deserves that name), instead of being struck with the majesty of his presence and the splendour of his actions, you should have recollected with abhorrence his ruinous ambition, his perfidy and want of principles; you should have seen not a hero who conquers but to bless, but the tyrant of his people and the enemy of mankind. Ferdinand, instead of a great general, should have appeared to you in the light of an abominable usurer, who would have sold armies or a brother for a ducat more. I wish I could allow those praises which you seem to think due to the Hereditary Prince; I admire him for his love of arms and for the name he has acquired in them, but cannot reflect upon his levity, dissipation, and lust, without contempt and pity. . . .

I begin to think your opinion of us both is very just. I own I once had formed great schemes and thought them practicable; but now I begin to despair, for I have many difficulties to struggle with, and doubt much, though I had none, that Nature ever intended me to make a figure in life. I shall now endeavour to make myself easy, to enjoy my friends and my books, and to steal through life as quietly as I can. However, had I your advantages, I would neither be so humble nor so content. We never were reckoned inferior to our fellow collegians, perhaps superior. Why then should we poorly think that it is in their power to excel us in anything if we take equal pains? . . .

And now for your matrimonial scheme. O the adorable Zélide! How can you hesitate a moment? Such a heart, such sense, such beauty, such a fortune! I am charmed with her conduct and letter; you must not have her, Boswell, no, there will be no bearing it; you shall marry Miss Bosville. However, to be serious, why may you not marry her with your father's consent? The objections you make are none. Is not her character like your own? And as to her being a metaphysician and a mathematician, she will be so only till she is married. But there are two objections which I must own appear to me to have great weight: one is your fears of being a cuckold, the other her being a handsome Dutchwoman. These, Boswell, it must be confessed, are not to be got over. This is so like you that it made me almost die of laughing.

And now for myself. My dear friend, when you know my situation, you will pity me much; you will do more, you will relieve me if you can. In my last I think I told you that after paying my father's creditors I should have left about £150 a year. So, I expect, it will turn out; but though this would do very well for myself, yet it cannot support my father and brother[5] too. They have got me here, and how can I leave them destitute? I have no friends, I do not believe they have any (though they think they have), and unless you can provide for one of them, I must be confined here the

[5] Temple's younger brother Robert was an Army officer on half pay. He and Boswell had shared Temple's chambers in the Temple in the summer of 1763.

best part of my life perhaps, or do what I cannot bear to think of. You are intimate with Lord Eglinton. He must have some interest, certainly enough to get Bob put upon full pay, or my father a moderate appointment in the Customs or in one of the public offices. He understands business very well. Boswell, I know you love me. I am miserable in my present situation. I cannot apply to my studies, I am not well, I am weary of my being. Relieve me if you can. You know I ever am your most affectionate

W. J. TEMPLE.[6]

SUNDAY 23 DECEMBER.[7] I slept till near nine. I got up in fine spirits, and sung and was gay even at the seat of Presbyterianism on a Sunday. At two, another young Cazenove came and conducted me to the Église de St. Germain, as I wished to see a true Geneva kirk. I found a large, dusky building, a precentor with a black wig like Monsieur Dupont,[8] a probationer (a *proposant*) a-reading the Bible to the congregation; in short a perfect Puritanical picture. Cazenove would have put me into a good seat, but a fat old woman would not give up her place. She made me smile with her obstinate rudeness. She was just a *Scots gracy*[9] *auld wife.*

[6] A brief postscript is omitted. — On 26 December Boswell wrote to Andrew Mitchell and the Countess of Northumberland begging them to use their influence in behalf of Temple's father and brother. See p. 296. The letter to Lady Northumberland has not been recovered; that to Mitchell (a long and moving one) appears in *Letters of James Boswell,* ed. C. B. Tinker, 2 vols., 1924, i. 64–65.

[7] "Yesterday . . . supped table d'hôte and defended Rousseau. Distressed with horrid wishes; did as in Ezekiel's punishment to show where that goes. This day, renew resolutions. At nine, church and communicate . . . " (Memorandum, 23 December). "Ezekiel's punishment" (more properly, certain painful and disgusting acts enjoined upon the prophet as signs to the captive Jews) is described in Ezekiel 3, 4, and 5. As to what Boswell meant by the reference, the reader's guess is as good as mine.

[8] Pierre Loumeau Dupont (d. 1786), a Swiss, had been since 1725 pastor of the French Protestant congregation in Edinburgh. The reason for Boswell's intimacy with him is not known, but he remained very attentive to Dupont to the end of Dupont's life, and always spoke of him with great affection.

[9] Devout, religious.

A Monsieur Le Cointe preached a good, sensible discourse. After church we walked on the Bastion Bourgeois, an excellent airy place, where the Genevois and Genevoises assemble. We then waited on Monsieur Gaussen, a banker of this city, whose wife is a hearty Aberdeenshire woman, and then we went to a society of young folks where were Cazenove's sisters. It was rather foolish. But I was amused to see card-playing on a Sunday at Geneva, and a minister rampaging amongst them. O John Calvin, where art thou now?

MONDAY 24 DECEMBER. After calling on my bankers, Cazenove, Clavière et fils, from whom I received payment of a bill granted me by Splitgerber and Daum, and on Chappuis et fils, to whom I was addressed by Messrs. Herries and Cochrane, I took a coach for Ferney, the seat of the illustrious Monsieur de Voltaire. I was in true spirits; the earth was covered with snow; I surveyed wild nature with a noble eye. I called up all the grand ideas which I have ever entertained of Voltaire. The first object that struck me was his church with this inscription: "Deo erexit Voltaire MDCCLXI."[1] His château was handsome. I was received by two or three footmen, who showed me into a very elegant room. I sent by one of them a letter to Monsieur de Voltaire which I had from Colonel Constant at The Hague.[2] He returned and told me, "Monsieur de Voltaire is very much annoyed at being disturbed. He is abed." I was afraid that I should not see him. Some ladies and gentlemen entered, and I was entertained for some time. At last Monsieur de Voltaire opened the door of his apartment, and stepped forth. I surveyed him with eager attention, and found him just as his print had made me conceive him. He received me with dignity, and that air of the world which a Frenchman acquires in such perfection. He had a slate-blue, fine frieze greatcoat nightgown,[3] and a three-knotted wig. He sat erect upon his chair, and

[1] In the MS, MDCC —.

[2] Constant d'Hermenches: see p. 247 *n.* 4. He was a correspondent of Voltaire, and had acted in plays in Voltaire's theatre at Lausanne.

[3] Boswell means that his night-gown (we would say dressing-gown) was cut like a greatcoat. See the illustration opposite p. 280.

simpered when he spoke. He was not in spirits, nor I neither. All I presented was the "foolish face of wondering praise."[4]

We talked of Scotland. He said the Glasgow editions were "très belles." I said, "An Academy of Painting was also established there, but it did not succeed.[5] Our Scotland is no country for that." He replied with a keen archness, "No; to paint well it is necessary to have warm feet. It's hard to paint when your feet are cold." Another would have given a long dissertation on the coldness of our climate. Monsieur de Voltaire gave the very essence of raillery in half a dozen words.

I mentioned the severe criticism which the *Gazette littéraire* has given upon Lord Kames's *Elements*. I imagined it to be done by Voltaire, but would not ask him. He repeated me several of the *bons mots* in it, with an air that confirmed me in my idea of his having written this criticism. He called my Lord always "ce Monsieur Kames."

I told him that Mr. Johnson and I intended to make a tour through the Hebrides, the Northern Isles of Scotland. He smiled, and cried, "Very well; but I shall remain here. You will allow me to stay here?" "Certainly." "Well then, go. I have no objections at all."

I asked him if he still spoke English. He replied, "No. To speak English one must place the tongue between the teeth, and I have lost my teeth."

He was curious to hear anecdotes from Berlin. He asked who was our Minister there. I said we had only a *chargé d'affaires*. "Ah!" said he, "un chargé d'affaires est guère chargé."[6] He said Hume was "a true philosopher."

[4] "And wonder with a foolish face of praise" (Pope, *Epistle to Dr. Arbuthnot*, l. 212).

[5] The "Glasgow editions" were editions of the classics published at Glasgow by Robert and Andrew Foulis. The Academy of Painting was another of Robert Foulis's projects. It was dissolved in 1770.

[6] A pun, essentially untranslatable, on two meanings of the word *chargé*: "put in charge" and "overloaded." Literally, "An ambassador's substitute is hardly overworked." Boswell of course should have written, "n'est guère."

Voltaire, from a statuette in marble (1764 or 1765) by
Joseph Rosset-Dupont, in the Voltaire Institute, Geneva.

As we talked, there entered Père Adam, a French Jesuit, who is protected in the house of Voltaire. What a curious idea. He was a lively old man with white hair. Voltaire cried in English, "There, Sir, is a young man, a scholar who is learning your language, a broken soldier of the Company of Jesus."[7] "Ah," said Père Adam, "a young man of sixty."

Monsieur de Voltaire did not dine with us. Madame Denis, his niece, does the honours of his house very well. She understands English. She was remarkably good to me. I sat by her and we talked much. I became lively and most agreeable. We had a company of about twelve. The family consists of seven. The niece of the great Corneille lives here. She is married to a Monsieur Dupuits.[8] The gates of Geneva shut at five, so I was obliged to hasten away after dinner without seeing any more of Monsieur de Voltaire.

At Geneva I called for Monsieur Constant Pictet, for whom I had a letter from his sister-in-law, Madame d'Hermenches.[9] I found his lady, who asked me to stay the evening. There was a company here at cards. I saw a specimen of Genevoises, and compared them with Rousseau's drawings of them. Constant, the husband, was lively without wit and polite without being agreeable. There were a good many men here who railed against Rousseau on account of his *Lettres écrites de la montagne*. Their fury was a high farce to my philosophic mind. One of them was arrant idiot enough to say of the illustrious author, "He's a brute with brains, a horse with brains, an ox with brains." "Rather, a snake," said a foolish female with a lisping tone. Powers of absurdity! did your influence ever extend farther? I said, "On my word, it is time for me to leave this company. Can *women* speak against the author of the *Nouvelle Héloïse?*" Pictet, a professor of law, father to

[7] See p. 169.
[8] Marie Dupuits de la Chaux was the grand-daughter of a cousin of Pierre Corneille.
[9] Marc Samuel François de Constant was, like Constant d'Hermenches, an uncle of the famous Benjamin Constant, who was not born until 1767. Marc Samuel wrote novels and was a friend of Voltaire.

Madame Constant, was an acquaintance of Lord Erskine's. He said he had seen Voltaire morning and evening during a severe sickness, and Madame Pictet, his wife, had watched him, and he was *toujours tranquille*. I supped here.

[Received 24 December, Lord Marischal to Boswell]

Potsdam, 18 November 1764

SIR: — I am glad you have made so good a journey and that my letter arrived in time. I shall always be glad of every occasion to serve you and show you my regard.

I was diverted with your idea of Hercules's having been rocked, by way of cradle, in a post-wagon; by this time I suppose you are grown to your strength, and I advise monsters and maids to keep out of your way; your pattern Hercules made havoc of both. You saw one dreadful[10] if you continued your proposed journey.

The Turk and Sardian[1] are well. Monsieur Macpherson saw in the newspaper that troops are raising in England, and had a mind to try his fortune. There was still a stronger reason for his return: he did not get leave to be absent (it was not refused, but not given); he might have run a risk of losing his half-pay. He is gone to London to make a push. Adieu, I am ever your most obedient humble servant,

MARISCHAL.

I received your note. My respects to Lord and Lady Stanhope, and to Lord Mahon at Geneva.

TUESDAY 25 DECEMBER. Although this was Christmas-day, I fairly fasted, nor stirred out of doors except a moment to the Église de St. Pierre, which was formerly a Catholic church and is a handsome building. Worship was over, but I heard a voluntary upon the organ. I was in supreme spirits, and a noble idea arose in my mind. I wrote a very lively letter to Madame Denis, begging to be

[10] He probably means the Duke of Württemberg at Stuttgart. See p. 141.
[1] That is, Sardinian: Monsieur de Froment, who was an officer in the Sardinian service.

allowed to sleep a night under the roof of Monsieur de Voltaire. I sent it by an express, and Voltaire wrote the answer in the person of his niece, making me very welcome. My felicity this night was abundant. My letter with the answer to it are most carefully preserved.

[Boswell to Madame Denis]

Geneva, 25 December 1764

I ADDRESS MYSELF TO YOU, MADAM, as to the friend of the stranger. I have the honour of knowing you to be such from most agreeable experience; for yesterday at dinner you not only entertained me with easy and cheerful conversation, but took care that I should have a double portion of the sweet tart which I am so extremely fond of. You may remember, Madam, that I expressed my affection for that dish in the strongest manner: "Je suis attaché à la tourte." I spoke in character, for I spoke with that honest frankness with which I declare my sentiments on great and on small occasions. At no time shall I ever deny my faith, my friend, my mistress, or my tart.[2]

I present myself in my natural character, which I find suits me the best of any. I own that I have in some periods of my life assumed the characters of others whom I admired. But, as David found the armour of Saul, I found them by much too heavy for me, and like David was embarrassed and unable to move with freedom. I hope, Madam, I may be allowed to quote the Old Testament once to the niece of a gentleman who has quoted it so often.

I do not, however, think lightly of my own character. No, Madam, I am proud enough. The French say, "Proud as a Scotsman." It shall not be my fault if that proverb goes out of use.

I must beg your interest, Madam, in obtaining for me a very great favour from Monsieur de Voltaire. I intend to have the hon-

[2] An indelicate pun would be quite in the spirit of this letter, but the historical evidence makes it highly unlikely that one was intended. "Tart" meaning "sweetie" or "prostitute" is not listed in any slang dictionary until a full century after the date of this letter.

our of returning to Ferney Wednesday or Thursday. The gates of this sober city shut at a most early, I had very near said a most absurd, hour, so that one is obliged to post away after dinner before the illustrious landlord has had time to shine upon his guests. Besides, I believe Monsieur de Voltaire is in opposition to our sun, for he rises in the evening. Yesterday he shot forth some rays. Some bright sparks fell from him. I am happy to have seen so much. But I greatly wish to behold him in full blaze.

Is it then possible, Madam, that I may be allowed to lodge one night under the roof of Monsieur de Voltaire? I am a hardy and a vigorous Scot. You may mount me to the highest and coldest garret. I shall not even refuse to sleep upon two chairs in the bedchamber of your maid. I saw her pass through the room where we sat before dinner.

I beg you may let me know if the favour which I ask is granted, that I may bring a nightcap with me. I would not presume to think of having my head honoured with a nightcap of Monsieur de Voltaire. I should imagine that, like the invisible cap of Fortunatus, or that of some other celebrated magician, it would immediately convey to me the qualities of its master; and I own to you, Madam, my head is not strong enough to bear them. His poetical cap I might perhaps support; but his philosophical one would make me so giddy that I should not know which way to turn myself. All I can offer in return for the favour which I ask is many, many thanks; or if Monsieur de Voltaire's delicate French ear would not be offended, I might perhaps offer him a few good rough English verses. Pray, Madam, give me your interest. I would also beg the assistance of my Reverend Father the young man of sixty, the student of our language, the disbanded soldier of the Company of Jesus. Sure, a lady and a priest must prevail.

I have the honour to be, Madam, your very humble servant,

BOSWELL.

Note from Voltaire to Boswell, 25 December 1764, written in the character of his niece, Madame Denis, from the original in the Yale University Library.

[Received 25 December, Voltaire to Boswell][3]

[Ferney, 25 December 1764]

Sr   You will do us much honour and pleasure. We have few beds, but you will not sleep on two chairs. My uncle, tho very sick, hath guess'd at yr merit. j know it more, because j have seen you longer.

WEDNESDAY 26 DECEMBER.[4] The worthy Monsieur de Zuylen has written me a kind but mysterious letter. I have answered him with warmth, and pressed him to be explicit. I have also sent, enclosed, a letter to my fair Zélide. What are now her ideas, I know not. She has not written me a line since the letter which I received from her at Brunswick, although I wrote to her a long letter from Berlin, in a severe tone, and one from Dessau in a tone more mild. This will undoubtedly clear up matters.[5] Temple is charmed with her character, and advises me to marry her; but he does not know her well enough. Time must try all.

I went with young Cazenove to see a Monsieur Huber, a man of great variety of talents, in particular, an amazing art of cutting paper.[6] He was too rough. He raged against Rousseau, and when I talked of his adoring his God, he cried, "Where is his God?" We then waited on Madame Bontems, sister to Mademoiselle Prevost. She was a jolly, talking woman. She had known Zélide, and said, "She has always followed the thoughts of her own little head. Now

[3] Endorsed by Boswell, "Answer by Monsieur de Voltaire, in the character of his niece." The document (which is indeed in the hand of the Sage of Ferney) is printed without editorial interference. See the facsimile.
[4] "Yesterday . . . at night, low lasciviousness. Have a care. Swear with drawn sword never *pleasure* but with a woman's aid. In Turin and all Italy you find enough. But venture not except with perfect sure people" . . . (Memorandum, 26 December).
[5] These letters are all printed in *Boswell in Holland*. Belle's excuse was that Boswell never gave her an address. Since her correspondence with him was supposed to be clandestine, she could not ask her father where to send a letter.
[6] Especially silhouettes. He could cut a profile of Voltaire without looking at him, and with his hands behind his back.

she has become so wise and so philosophical that really I am unable to keep up with her." I dined at our table d'hôte, after which Madame Gaussen introduced me *chez* Madame Pallard, a German lady, very amiable but very vapourish. She gave me a curious anecdote. "There is a young Russian here of a good family, whose father has absolutely forbidden him to see the English. His governor does not dare take him into any society where these gentlemen are." This is most excellent; so rude are the young English that the very Russians shun them. I supped at the table d'hôte. Monsieur de La Sale said he had been much with the Chevalier Ramsay, who was governor to the Prince de Turenne, who, when young, "was very witty. Once I was dining at his house. He served me with chicken. I wanted his Highness to be served first. He said, 'No, Sir, that is the right leg, and I never eat anything but the left leg.' There was finesse for you."

THURSDAY 27 DECEMBER. I waited on Professor Maurice, the friend of honest Monsieur Dupont, who lived in the house of his grandfather. I had no recommendation to him, but entered freely, and told him my connection with Monsieur Dupont, and immediately was well with him. He was a man of knowledge, of rough sense, and of that sort of fancy which sound men have in abundance. He received me well. My ideas were somewhat Presbyterian, but of the best kind. I was too lively, and was not master of my vivacity.

I then went to Ferney, where I was received with complacency and complimented on my letter. I found here the Chevalier de Boufflers, a fine, lively young fellow and mighty ingenious.[7] He

---

[7] Not the Count de Boufflers whom Boswell met at The Hague (*Boswell in Holland*, 9 May and 6 June), but the much more interesting Stanislas Jean, son of the Marquise de Boufflers, mistress of the deposed King of Poland, Stanislas I. Though only twenty-six years old, Boufflers was already the darling of Europe because of his feats as writer of light verse, as painter, as soldier, and as lover. This autumn he had taken it into his head to visit Voltaire, an old friend of Stanislas and his mother, and before arriving at Ferney had made a tour of Switzerland, travelling *incognito* as an itinerant artist, painting portraits of ladies and making love to them. In a published

was painting in crayon a Madame Rilliet, a most frolicsome little Dutch Genevoise. There was here a Monsieur Rieu, a Genevois, a heavy, knowing fellow. Monsieur de Voltaire came out to us a little while, but did not dine with us. After dinner we returned to the drawing-room, where (if I may revive an old phrase) *every man soaped his own beard.*[8] Some sat snug by the fire, some chatted, some sung, some played the guitar, some played at shuttlecock. All was full. The canvas was covered. My hypochondria began to muse. I was dull to find how much this resembled any other house in the country, and I had heavy ennui. At six I went to Père Adam's room, which was just neat and orderly as I could fancy. I know not how it is, but I really have often observed that what I have experienced has only corresponded to imaginations already in my mind. Can pre-existence be true? Père Adam has learnt English in a year's time. He read and translated a paper of *The Spectator* with surprising ease. He and Rieu entertained me with the praises of Monsieur de Voltaire's good actions in private life: how he entertains his friends and strangers of distinction, how he has about fifty people in his château, as his servants marry and have children, and how the village upon his manor is well taken care of.

Between seven and eight we had a message that Voltaire was in the drawing-room. He always appears about this time anight, pulls his bell and cries, "Fetch Père Adam." The good Father is ready immediately, and they play at chess together. I stood by Monsieur de Voltaire and put him in tune. He spoke sometimes English and sometimes French. He gave me a sharp reproof for speaking fast. "How fast you foreigners speak!" "We think that the French do

letter to his mother written about this time he refers to a guest who can hardly be other than Boswell: "an Englishman who never wearies of hearing [Voltaire] talk English and recite all the poems of Dryden." Voltaire was tremendously taken with Boufflers, and the young and the old scapegrace were exchanging gay and improper verses which can be read in their collected poems.

[8] The motto of the Soaping Club: see pp. 243, 245.

the same." "Well, at any rate, *I* don't. I speak slowly, that's what I do"; and this he said with a most keen tone. He got into great spirits. I would not go to supper, and so I had this great man for about an hour and a half at a most interesting tête-à-tête. I have written some particulars of it to Temple, and as our conversation was very long, I shall draw it up fully in a separate paper.[9] When the company returned, Monsieur de Voltaire retired. They looked at me with complacency and without envy. Madame Denis insisted that I should sup; I agreed to this, and a genteel table was served for me in the drawing-room, where I eat and drank cheerfully with the gay company around me. I was very lively and said, "I am magnificence itself. I eat alone, like the King of England."[1] In short this was a rich evening.

FRIDAY 28 DECEMBER. Last night Monsieur de Voltaire treated me with polite respect: "I am sorry, Sir, that you will find yourself so badly lodged." I ought to have a good opinion of myself, but from my unlucky education I cannot get rid of mean timidity as to my own worth. I was very genteelly lodged. My room was handsome. The bed, purple cloth lined with white quilted satin; the chimney-piece, marble, and ornamented above with the picture of a French toilet. Monsieur de Voltaire's country-house is the first I have slept in since I slept in that of some good Scots family — Kellie, indeed. I surveyed every object here with a minute attention and most curiously did I prove the association of ideas. Everything put me fully in mind of a decent Scots house, and I thought surely the master of the family must go to church and do as public institutions require; and then I made my transition to the real master, the celebrated Voltaire, the infidel, the author of so many deistical pieces and of the *Pucelle d'Orléans.*

[9] The letter to Temple and a portion of the "separate paper," with other notes on the conversation of Voltaire, will be found in this edition following the journal entry for 28 December.
[1] The memoranda record also a jest with Père Adam: "BOSWELL. 'Père Adam, will you please give me some wine?' PÈRE ADAM. 'With pleasure.' BOSWELL. 'What! you give the cup to the laity?' "

I awaked this morning bad, even here. Yet I recovered, and as I was here for once in a lifetime, and wished to have as much of Voltaire as possible, I sent off Jacob to Geneva, to stop my coach today and to bring it out tomorrow. I then threw on my clothes and ran like the Cantab in the imitation of Gray's *Elegy*, "with hose ungartered,"[2] to Voltaire's church, where I heard part of a mass and was really devout. I then walked in his garden, which is very pretty and commands a fine prospect. I then went to my room, got paper from Voltaire's secretary, and wrote to my father, to Temple, and to Sir David Dalrymple.[3] I sent to Monsieur de Voltaire a specimen of my poem called *Parliament*. I also wrote a fair copy of my *Ode on Ambition*[4] for him, and inscribed it thus: "Most humbly presented to Monsieur de Voltaire, the glory of France, the admiration of Europe, by Mr. Boswell, who has had the honour of regarding and loving him in private life at his Château de Ferney."

He was bad today and did not appear before dinner. We dined well as usual. It was pleasant for me to think I was in France. In the afternoon I was dullish. At six I applied to the secretary for a volume of Voltaire's plays, and went to my room, and read his *Mahomet* in his own house. It was curious, this. A good, decent, trusty servant had fire and wax candles and all in order for me. There is at Ferney the true hospitality. All are master of their rooms and do as they please. I should have mentioned yesterday that when I arrived, Monsieur Rieu carried me to a room where

[2] Haply some friend may shake his hoary head
    And say, "Each morn, unchill'd by frosts, he ran
With hose ungarter'd o'er yon turfy bed
    To reach the chapel ere the psalms began."
                    John Duncombe, *A Parody on Gray's
                    Elegy*, 1753, stanza 23

[3] The letters to Lord Auchinleck and Sir David Dalrymple have not been recovered.
[4] This is listed as a poem of forty-eight lines in the "Plan" prefixed to the Bodleian manuscript of Boswell's poems, but the poem itself is not preserved in the manuscript, and has not been found elsewhere.

the maids were and made me point out which of them I meant in
my letter to Madame Denis. Monsieur de Voltaire was sick and
out of spirits this evening, yet I made him talk some time. His conversation shall be all collected into one piece. I may perhaps insert
it in this my journal. I supped at the table tonight. It hurt me to
find that by low spirits it is possible for me to lose the relish of the
most illustrious genius. Hard indeed!

[Boswell to Temple]

Château de Ferney, 28 December 1764

MY DEAR TEMPLE, — Think not that I insult you when you
read the full tale of my supreme felicity. After thanking you for
your two letters of the month of October,[5] I must pour forth the
exultation of a heart swelling with joy. Call me bombast. Call me
what you please. Thus will I talk. No other style can give the most
distant expression of the feelings of Boswell. If I appear ridiculous,
it is because our language is deficient.

I completed my tour through the German courts. At all of them
I found state and politeness. At Baden-Durlach I found worth,
learning, and philosophy united in the Reigning Margrave. He is
a prince whose character deserves to be known over Europe. He is
the best sovereign, the best father, the most amiable man. He has
travelled a great deal. He has been in England and he speaks the
language in amazing perfection. During the time that I stayed at
his court, I had many, many conversations with him. He showed
me the greatest distinction. The inspector of his cabinet, his
library-keeper, and the officers of his court had orders to do everything in their power to render my stay agreeable. Madame la Margrave, who paints in perfection and has a general taste for the fine
arts, treated me in the most gracious manner. The Margrave told
me how happy he was to have me with him. I asked him if I could
do anything that might show my gratitude. He replied, "I shall
write to you sometimes. I shall be very happy to receive your let-

[5] He means November: see p. 276, where one of them is printed.

ters." He was in earnest. I have already been honoured with a letter from His Most Serene Highness. I have promised to return and pass some weeks at his court. He is not far from France.

I have been with Rousseau. He lives in the village of Môtiers-Travers in a beautiful valley surrounded with immense mountains. I went thither from Neuchâtel. I determined to put my real merit to the severest test by presenting myself without any recommendation before the wild illustrious philosopher. I wrote him a letter in which I told him all my worth, and claimed his regard as what I had a title to. "Open your door, then, Sir, to a man who dares to tell you that he deserves to enter it." Such was my bold and manly style. He received me, although he was very ill. "I am ill, in pain, really in no state to receive visits. Yet I cannot deprive myself of Mr. Boswell's, provided that out of consideration for the state of my health, he is willing to make it short." I found him very easy and unaffected. At first he complained and lamented the state of humanity. But I had address enough to bring him upon subjects which pleased him, and he grew very animated, quite the amiable Saint-Preux at fifty. He is a genteel man, has a fine countenance and a charming voice. You may believe I had a difficult task enough to come up to the idea which I had given him of myself. I had said all that my honest pride believed. My letter was a piece of true oratory. You shall see it when we meet. No other man in Europe could have written such a letter and appeared equal to all its praise. I stayed at this time three days in the village, and was with Monsieur Rousseau every day. A week after, I returned and stayed two days. He is extremely busy. The Corsicans have actually applied to him to give them a set of laws. What glory for him! He said, "It exceeds my powers but not my zeal." He is preparing to give a complete and splendid edition of all his works. When I was sure of his good opinion on my own merit, I showed him a recommendation which my Lord Marischal had given me. I talked to him with undisguised confidence. I gave him a written sketch of my life. He studied it, and he loved me with all my failings. He gave me some advices which will influence the rest of my existence. He is to correspond with me while he lives. When I took leave of him, he embraced me with an elegant cordiality and said, "Don't ever forget me. There are points where our souls are bound." On my arrival at Geneva I received a letter from him, with a letter of recommendation to an intimate friend of his at the Court of Parma, a man of uncommon value. He has left the letter open for me to read, although it contains his most important concerns and the kindest effusions of his heart. Is not this treating me with a regard which my soul must be proud of? I must give you a sentence of this letter: "I am glad that Mr. Boswell and you are to make each other's acquaintance. I think you will both be grateful to me for bringing you together. In the first letter he wrote me, he told me that he was a man 'of singular merit.' I was curious to see a man who spoke of himself in such a fashion, and I found that he had told me the truth."

And whence do I now write to you, my friend? From the château of Monsieur de Voltaire. I had a letter for him from a Swiss colonel at The Hague. I came hither Monday and was presented to him. He received me with dignity and that air of a man who has been much in the world which a Frenchman acquires in perfection. I saw him for about half an hour before dinner. He was not in spirits. Yet he gave me some brilliant sallies. He did not dine with us, and I was obliged to post away immediately after dinner, because the gates of Geneva shut before five and Ferney is a good hour from town. I was by no means satisfied to have been so little time with the monarch of French literature. A happy scheme sprung up in my adventurous mind. Madame Denis, the niece of Monsieur de Voltaire, had been extremely good to me. She is fond of our language. I wrote her a letter in English begging her interest to obtain for me the privilege of lodging a night under the roof of Monsieur de Voltaire, who, in opposition to our sun, rises in the evening. I was in the finest humour and my letter was full of wit. I told her, "I am a hardy and a vigorous Scot. You may mount me to the highest and coldest garret. I shall not even refuse to sleep upon two chairs in the bedchamber of your maid. I saw her pass through the room where we sat before dinner." I sent my letter on Tuesday by an express. It was shown to Monsieur de Voltaire, who with his own hand wrote this answer in the character of Madam Denis: "You will do us much honour and pleasure. We have few beds. But you will (*shall*) not sleep on two chairs. My uncle, though very sick, hath guessed at your merit. I know it better; for I have seen you longer." Temple, I am your most obedient. How do you find yourself? Have you got such a thing as an old friend in this world? Is he to be valued or is he not?

I returned yesterday to this enchanted castle. The magician appeared a very little before dinner. But in the evening he came into the drawing-room in great spirits. I placed myself by him. I touched the keys in unison with his imagination. I wish you had heard the music. He was all brilliance. He gave me continued flashes of wit. I got him to speak English, which he does in a degree that made me now and then start up and cry, "Upon my soul this is astonishing!" When he talked our language he was animated with the soul of a Briton. He had bold flights. He had humour. He had an extravagance; he had a forcible oddity of style that the most comical of our *dramatis personae* could not have exceeded. He swore bloodily, as was the fashion when he was in England. He hummed a ballad; he repeated nonsense. Then he talked of our Constitution with a noble enthusiasm. I was proud to hear this from the mouth of an illustrious Frenchman. At last we came upon religion. Then did he rage. The company went to supper. Monsieur de Voltaire and I remained in the drawing-room with a great Bible before us; and if ever two mortal men disputed with vehemence, we did. Yes, upon that occasion he was one individual and I another. For a certain portion of time there was a fair opposition between Voltaire and Boswell. The daring bursts of his ridicule confounded my understanding. He stood like an orator of ancient Rome. Tully was never more agitated than he was. He went too far. His aged frame trembled beneath him. He cried, "Oh, I am very sick; my head turns round," and he let himself gently fall upon an easy chair. He recovered. I resumed our conversation, but changed the tone. I talked to him serious and earnest. I demanded of him an honest confession of his real sentiments. He gave it me with candour and with a mild eloquence which touched my heart. I did not believe him capable of thinking in the manner that he declared to me was "from the bottom of his heart." He expressed his veneration — his love — of the Supreme Being, and his entire resignation to the will of Him who is All-wise. He expressed his desire to resemble the Author of Goodness by being good himself. His sentiments go no farther. He does not inflame his mind with grand hopes of the immortality of the soul. He says it may be, but he knows nothing of it. And his mind is in perfect tranquillity. I was moved; I was sorry. I doubted his sincerity. I called to him with emotion, "Are you sincere? are you really sincere?" He answered, "Before God, I am." Then with the fire of him whose tragedies have so often shone on the theatre of Paris, he said, "I suffer much. But I suffer with patience and resignation; not as a Christian — but as a man."

Temple, was not this an interesting scene? Would a journey from Scotland to Ferney have been too much to obtain such a remarkable interview? I have given you the great lines. The whole conversation of the evening is fully recorded, and I look upon it as an invaluable treasure. One day the public shall have it. It is a present highly worthy of their attention. I told Monsieur de Voltaire that I had written eight quarto pages of what he had said. He smiled and seemed pleased. Our important scene must not appear till after his death. But I have a great mind to send over to London a little sketch of my reception at Ferney, of the splendid manner in which Monsieur de Voltaire lives, and of the brilliant conversation of this celebrated author at the age of seventy-two.[6] The sketch would be a letter, addressed to you, full of gaiety and full of friendship. I would send it to one of the best public papers or magazines. But this is probably a flight of my over-heated mind. I shall not send the sketch unless you approve of my doing so.

Before I left Britain, I was idle, dissipated, ridiculous, and re-

[6] Actually seventy.

gardless of reputation. Often was I unworthy to be the friend of Mr. Temple. Now I am a very different man. I have got a character which I am proud of. Speak, thou who hast known me from my earliest years! Couldst thou have imagined eight years ago that thy companion in the studies of Antiquity, who was debased by an unhappy education in the smoke of Edinburgh, couldst thou have imagined him to turn out the man that he now is? We are now, my friend, united in the strictest manner. Let us do nothing of any consequence without the consent of each other.

And must I then marry a Dutchwoman? Is it already marked in the rolls of heaven? Must the proud Boswell yield to a tender inclination? Must he in the strength and vigour of his youth resign his liberty for life to one woman? Rather (say you) shall not my friend embrace the happiness which fortune presents to him? Will not his pride be gratified by the attachment of a lady who has refused many advantageous offers? Must he not marry to continue his ancient family? and where shall he find a more amiable wife? Is he not a man of a most singular character? and would not an ordinary woman be insupportable to him? Should he not thank the Powers Above for having shown him Zélide, a young lady free from all the faults of her sex, with genius, with good humour, with elegant accomplishments? But, my dear Temple, she is not by half so rich as I thought. She has only £400 a year. Besides, I am not pleased with her conduct. We had agreed to correspond, and she directed me to send my letters to the care of her bookseller. I wrote to her from Berlin a long letter. She did not answer it. I was apprehensive that I had talked too severely of her faults, and wrote her from Anhalt-Dessau begging pardon for my too great freedom. Still I remain unanswered. Her father is a very worthy man. He and I correspond, and we write to each other of his daughter in a strange, mysterious manner. I have trusted him upon honour with a letter to her. So I shall be sure that she receives it, and shall see how she behaves. After all, when I consider my unhappy constitution, I think I should not marry, at least for some time; and when I do, should choose a healthy, cheerful woman of rank and fortune.

I am now well, because I am agitated by a variety of new scenes. But when I shall return to the uniformity of Scotland, I dread much a relapse into the gloomy distemper. I must endeavour by some scheme of ambition, by elegant study, and by rural occupations to preserve my mind. Yet I own that both of us are sadly undetermined. However, I hope the best.

My worthy father has consented that I shall go to Italy. O my friend, what a rich prospect spreads before me! My letter is already so long that I shall restrain my enthusiastic sallies. Imagine my joy. On Tuesday morning I set out for Turin. I shall pass the rigorous Alps with the resolution of Hannibal. I shall be four months in Italy and then return through France. I expect to pass some time at Paris.

Forgive me, Temple, for having delayed to mention your concerns till almost at the end of my letter. You are sure how much I suffer from your uneasiness. I wish I could be as sure of relieving you. I know well the great, and can have no confidence in them. Lord Eglinton would forget to do anything. I have written to Lady Northumberland begging she may get Bob put upon whole pay. Lord Warkworth[7] was in General Craufurd's regiment, and both my Lord and my Lady had a great esteem of the General. I have told her Ladyship that the General had promised to take care of the young lieutenant, and that if her Ladyship puts him again in commission, "in so doing you will fulfil the intentions of him who is no more, whose memory you must ever regard. May I add that your Ladyship will give me a pleasure — a comfort — which I can hardly express? Were I at present as rich as I shall probably be, the brother of my friend should not depend for a commission on the uncertain favour of any great person alive." (She may be angry at this last period. It ought to please, it ought to rouse her.)

[7] Lady Northumberland's eldest son, later Earl Percy and Duke of Northumberland. Lady Northumberland had been personally gracious to Boswell in the winter of 1762–1763, when he was in London trying to get a commission, and he had considered her his patroness, but she had been unable or unwilling to secure the commission for him.

"O Madam! be truly great. Be generous to the unfortunate. If your Ladyship will befriend the young man sincerely, I beg to be honoured with a line," &c. I own to you I have but little hopes from her Ladyship. We shall see. I have not been mean enough to flatter her. That I am determined never to practise. I have also written to Mr. Mitchell, late Envoy at the Court of Berlin, who is just recalled. He is an old friend of my father's, and a man of the strictest probity and the warmest generosity. I have told him your story as I did to Lady Northumberland. O my Temple! how do I glory in displaying the conduct of my friend! If Mr. Mitchell can aid us, he will. I would hope he may serve either your father or brother. I have solicited him for both. Why am I not in power? I may be so perhaps, yet, before I die.

Temple, I am again as loyal as ever. I abhor a despotic tyrant. But I revere a limited monarch. Shall I be a British courtier? Am I worthy of the confidence of my king? May George the Third choose that the most honest and most amiable of his subjects should stand continually in his royal presence? I will if he says, "You shall be independent." . . . Temple, this is a noble letter. Fare you well, my ever dear friend.

JAMES BOSWELL.

[EDITORIAL NOTE: The reader whose knowledge of Boswell's method comes mainly from the London journal of 1762–1763 will probably be puzzled by Boswell's elated assurance to Temple that Voltaire's long and brilliant conversations had been "fully recorded," since in the journal as we have it those conversations are for the greater part described rather than reported. The fact is that the London journal of 1762–1763 does not represent Boswell's commoner practice, which was to content himself with rough notes of long and involved conversations and not to attempt to write them out in full dramatic form in his journal. This applied even to Johnson's conversations. Whenever one comes upon a particularly long and brilliant conversation in *The Life of Johnson,* one will be right more than half the time if one assumes that Boswell worked it up at the time of the writing of the *Life* from a rough note contemporary with the conversation. When Boswell said that his conversations with Voltaire were "fully recorded," he meant that he had made a full enough record so that he would be able at any later period to retrieve them from the depths of his re- markable memory, with the length and degree of complexity that they deserved. Judging from his practice in *The Life of Johnson*, his Voltairian notes would have been good for twenty or twenty- five printed octavo pages of conversation, dramatically cast. Un- fortunately, he never got around to writing them up, and unfor- tunately we do not now have all his records. Of the "eight quarto pages" — a record distinct from the journal, the memoranda, and the letter to Temple — which he mentions so proudly, only two pages, on paper of the size of the contemporary journal, have come down to us. They consist of notes in English in a style much more elliptical than that of the journal, but it has seemed to me that be- cause of the interest attaching to any authentic utterance of a man so famous as Voltaire, the reader will prefer to have them treated as text and not relegated to the inferior position of a footnote or an appendix. I have appended to them a portion of the memoran- dum of 28 December which fills out to some extent Boswell's state- ment in the letter to Temple, "He talked of our Constitution with a noble enthusiasm." Both notes and memorandum record the conversation of 27 December, but they are here printed after the letter to Temple of 28 December because that letter illuminates so many of their obscurities.]

[27 December, Notes of Voltaire's English Conversation]

VOLTAIRE. "Shakespeare often two good lines, never six. A mad- man, by G–d, a buffoon at Bartholomew Fair.[8] No play of his own,

[8] Voltaire's sincere belief from first to last was that Shakespeare was a bar- barian of genius, but in the years following his return from England he had more to say about Shakespeare's merits than about his defects. He urged his countrymen to follow Shakespeare in the use of historical subjects and in

all old stories." Chess. "I shall lose, by G–d, by all the saints in Paradise. Ah, here I am riding on a black ram, like a whore as I am.[9] — Falstaff from the Spaniards." BOSWELL. "I'll tell you why we admire Shakespeare." VOLTAIRE. "Because you have no taste." BOSWELL. "But, Sir — " VOLTAIRE. "Et penitus toto divisos orbe Britannos[1] — all Europe is against you. So you are wrong." BOSWELL. "But this is because we have the most grand imagination." VOLTAIRE. "The most wild. — Pope drives a chaise with a couple of neat trim nags but Dryden a coach and six, with postilions and

---

putting more action on the stage, and showed in his own plays that he had read Shakespeare to advantage. But he never doubted the vast superiority of French classical drama; and as the years passed he became alarmed at the growing popularity of Shakespeare in France, especially at heretical suggestions, raised by the fact of Shakespeare's fame, that the classic unities and classic decorum might not be absolute requirements. By 1761 (*Appeal to All the Nations of Europe*) he was engaged in a violent polemic against the idol of the English stage, and he kept it up till his death. He was full of the subject when Boswell called, for he had recently been revising the *Appeal*.

[9] Voltaire is repeating from memory a ribald English jingle (a "jocular tenure") which he had probably picked up from *The Spectator* for 1 November 1714 (No. 614). The pertinent passage runs as follows: "At East and West Enborne, in the County of Berks, if a customary tenant die, the widow shall have what the law calls her freebench in all his copyhold lands ... while she lives single and chaste; but if she commit incontinency, she forfeits her estate. Yet if she will come into the court riding backward upon a black ram, with his tail in her hand, and say the words following, the steward is bound by the custom to readmit her to her freebench:

> Here I am
> Riding upon a black ram
> Like a whore, as I am;
> And for my *crincum crancum*
> Have lost my *bincum bancum*;
> And for my tail's game
> Have done this worldly shame;
> Therefore I pray you, Mr. Steward, let me
>   have my land again."

[1] "And the Britons, completely cut off from all the rest of the world" (Virgil, *Eclogues*, i. 66).

all." Repeated well some passages of Dryden. BOSWELL. "What is memory? Where lodge all our ideas?" VOLTAIRE. "As Thomson says, where sleep the winds when it is calm?[2] Thomson was a great painter. Milton, many beauties and many faults, as there is nothing perfect in this damned world. His imitators are unintelligible. But when he writes well, he is quite clear." BOSWELL. "What think you of our comedy?" VOLTAIRE. "A great deal of wit, a great deal of plot, and a great deal of bawdy-houses." BOSWELL. "What think you of *Fingal?*" VOLTAIRE. "Why, it is like a psalm of David. But there are noble passages in it. There are in both. The Homer of Scotland."

BOSWELL. "You speak good English." VOLTAIRE. "Oho! I have scraps of Latin for the vicar. — Addison is a great genius. His character shines in his writings. — Dr. Clarke was a metaphysical clock. A proud priest. He thought he had all by demonstration; and he who thinks so is a madman." BOSWELL. "Johnson is a most orthodox man, but very learned; has much genius and much worth."[3] VOLTAIRE. "He is then a dog. A superstitious dog. No worthy man was ever superstitious." BOSWELL. "He said the King of Prussia wrote like your footboy, &c." VOLTAIRE. "He is a sensible

[2] "But still we are left quite in the dark as to the essential nature of the faculty of Memory, and the manner in which its operations are performed. When we talk of a storehouse of our ideas, we are only forming an imagination of something similar to an enclosed portion of space in which material objects are reposited. But who ever actually saw this storehouse, or can have any clear perception of it when he endeavours by thinking closely to get a distinct view of it? It is the fabric of a vision, and every candid man who has fairly tried to get at it will confess that he can have no confidence that it exists. I had the honour to have a conversation with Voltaire on this subject. I asked him if he could give me any notion of the situation of our ideas which we have totally forgotten at the time, yet shall afterwards recollect. He paused, meditated a little, and acknowledged his ignorance in the spirit of a philosophical poet, by repeating as a very happy allusion a passage in Thomson's *Seasons.* 'Ay,' said he, 'where sleep the winds when it is calm?' " (Boswell, *The Hypochondriac,* No. 67, April, 1783).

[3] "But very learned . . . worth" is an interlinear addition. Voltaire's rejoinder applies only to Boswell's statement that Johnson was orthodox.

man.[4] — Will you go and see the Pretender at Rome?" BOSWELL. "No. It is high treason." VOLTAIRE. "I promise you I shall not tell your king of you. I shall not betray you. You would see a bigot: a poor being." BOSWELL.[5] "His son is worse. He is drunk every day. He kicks women, and he ought to be kicked." VOLTAIRE. "Homer was the only man who took it into his head to write twelve thousand verses upon two or three battles. — It is diverting[6] to hear them say *Old England.*" BOSWELL. "Sir, 'Old England,' 'Old Scotland,' and 'Old France' have experienced a quite different effect from that . . ."[7]

[THURSDAY 27 DECEMBER. NOTES OF CONVERSATION WITH VOLTAIRE. Original partly in French] . . . VOLTAIRE. "You have the better government. If it gets bad, heave it into the ocean; that's why you have the ocean all about you. You are the slaves of laws. The French are slaves of men. In France every man is either an anvil or a hammer; he is a beater[8] or must be beaten." BOSWELL. "Yet it is a light, a genteel hammer." VOLTAIRE. "Yes, a pocket hammer. We are too mean[9] for our governors to cut off our heads. We are on the earth; they trample us."

SATURDAY 29 DECEMBER. I this morning visited Monsieur Rieu and Monsieur de Belle Pré, a gentleman-painter. They lived in the same room. I then visited my excellent Père Adam, who gives lessons to some of the young servants and is in all respects

[4] In *The Life of Johnson,* under date of 19 July 1763, Boswell, who was writing many years later and probably without reference to his note, gives this in the form, "An honest fellow!"
[5] This speech may also belong to Voltaire, but it is preceded by a clear mark of quotation.
[6] The manuscript reads *divering,* but I do not see what can be intended except *diverting.*
[7] The sentence perhaps continued "of 'old woman' " — that is, though "old" in English is often an epithet of respect, it is not invariably so.
[8] The manuscript reads, "he is beat." Boswell perhaps started to write, "he is beat or he beats," and then changed his construction so as to produce nonsense.
[9] The manuscript has the alternative *low.*

obliging. I talked of religion and found him to be a sincere Christian. He said, "I pray for Monsieur de Voltaire every day. Perhaps it will please God to touch his heart and make him see the true religion. It is a pity that he is not a Christian. He has many Christian virtues. He has the most beautiful soul. He is benevolent; he is charitable; but he is very strongly prejudiced against the Christian religion. When he is serious I try to say a word to him; but when he is in the humour of casting shafts of ridicule, I hold my peace." Worthy father! How strange is the system of human things! I reasoned with him against the eternity of hell's torments. He could not escape from the opinion of the Church, but his humanity made him say, "I shall be delighted if it proves to be otherwise." I then went with Rieu and saw the theatre of Monsieur de Voltaire. It is not large, but very handsome. It suggested to me a variety of very pleasing ideas. One circumstance rendered Monsieur de Voltaire's particularly agreeable to me. My association of ideas was such that I constantly thought of Temple. I can account for this. Some years ago he wrote to my father proposing that he and I should go together to study at Geneva, and should see "Voltaire! Rousseau! immortal names!" Besides, we used to talk much of Voltaire with Nicholls and Claxton.[10] Such little circumstances which recall my dear friend are valuable.

I next went with the secretary and saw Monsieur de Voltaire's library, which was tolerably numerous and in very good order. I saw there the *Elements of Criticism* and, by the secretary's denying it, I was persuaded that Voltaire had written the severe letter upon this book in the *Gazette littéraire*. The Jansenists used to publish against the Jesuits what they called *Mémoires ecclésiastiques*. Voltaire has got a thick volume of them bound up with the title of *Sottises ecclésiastiques*.[1] I saw upon a shelf an octavo with this title, *Tragédies barbares*. I was sure they must be English. I took down the book, and found it contained *Cleone, Elfrida, Caracta-*

[10] Cambridge friends of Temple whom Boswell had met in London in the summer of 1763.
[1] *Ecclesiastical Nonsense.*

cus.[2] I was mightily amused with these little sallies, which were quite in the taste of Sir David Dalrymple. I heartily wish Voltaire had titled more of his books.

I was dressed the first time at Ferney in my sea-green and silver, and now in my flowered velvet. Gloom got hold of me at dinner, in so much that I thought I would not be obliged to stay here for a great deal of money. And yet in reality I would be proud and pleased to live a long time *chez* Monsieur de Voltaire. I was asked to return when I should be at Lyons. I took an easy leave of the company. Monsieur de Voltaire was very ill today, and had not appeared. I sent my respects to him, and begged to be allowed to take leave of him. He sent to me his compliments and said he would see me. I found him in the drawing-room, where I had near half an hour more with him; at least, more than a quarter. I told him that I had marked his conversation. He seemed pleased. This last conversation shall also be marked. It was truly singular and solemn. I was quite in enthusiasm, quite agreeably mad to a certain degree. I asked his correspondence. He granted it. Is not this great?

[SATURDAY 29 DECEMBER. NOTES ON VOLTAIRE'S ENGLISH CONVERSATION][3] . . . BOSWELL. "When I came to see you, I thought to see a very great, but a very bad, man." VOLTAIRE. "You are very sincere." BOSWELL. "Yes, but the same [sincerity] makes me own that I find the contrary. Only, your *Dictionnaire philosophique* [troubles me]. For instance, *Ame*, the Soul — " VOLTAIRE. "That is a good article." BOSWELL. "No. Excuse me. Is it — [immortality] — not a pleasing imagination? Is it not more noble?" VOLTAIRE. "Yes. You have a noble desire to be King of Europe. [You say,] 'I wish it, and I ask your protection [in continuing to wish it].' But it is not probable." BOSWELL. "No, but all cannot be the

[2] The first by Robert Dodsley (1758), the second and third by William Mason (1752, 1759). As a matter of fact, they are all "regular" tragedies, and are "barbarous" only in being written in the English language.

[3] The portion of the memorandum for 30 December which records the conversation of the 29th.

one, and may be the other. [Like Cato, we all say] 'It must be so,'⁴ till [we possess] immortality [itself]." VOLTAIRE. "But before we say that this soul will exist, let us know what it is. I know not the cause. I cannot judge. I cannot be a juryman. Cicero says, *potius optandum quam probandum*.⁵ We are ignorant beings. We are the puppets of Providence. I am a poor Punch." BOSWELL. "Would you have no public worship?" VOLTAIRE. "Yes, with all my heart. Let us meet four times a year in a grand temple with music, and thank God for all his gifts. There is one sun. There is one God. Let us have one religion. Then all mankind will be brethren." BOS-WELL. "May I write in English, and you'll answer?" VOLTAIRE. "Yes. Farewell."

SATURDAY 29 DECEMBER [JOURNAL, continued]. Well, I must here pause, and as an impartial philosopher decide concerning myself. What a singular being do I find myself! Let this my journal show what variety my mind is capable of. But am I not well received everywhere? Am I not particularly taken notice of by men of the most distinguished genius? And why? I have neither profound knowledge, strong judgment, nor constant gaiety. But I have a noble soul which still shines forth, a certain degree of knowledge, a multiplicity of ideas of all kinds, an original humour and turn of expression, and, I really believe, a remarkable knowledge of human nature. This is different from a knowledge of the world as much as is the knowledge of a florist, who understands perfectly the works of Nature, from that of him who understands flowers formed by art. The florist perceives in general that the artificial flowers are not natural, but whether they are made of gummed linen, of china, or of copper, he cannot tell. So I know in general your men of the world to be artificial, but am not able to develop their different qualities. What is really Man I think I know pretty well. With this I have a pliant ease of manners which must please. I can tune myself so to the tone of any bearable man I am with that he is as much at freedom as with an-

⁴ Addison's *Cato*, V. i. 1, the opening line of the famous soliloquy.
⁵ "Matter of faith rather than of demonstration."

other self, and, till I am gone, cannot imagine me a stranger. Perhaps my talents are such as procure me more happiness than those of a more elevated kind. Were it not for my black hypochondria, I might be a practical epicurean.

I departed from this château in a most extraordinary humour, thinking hard, and wondering if I could possibly, when again in Scotland, again feel my most childish prejudices. When I got to Geneva, I was visited by young Chappuis, to whom I said, "Monsieur de Voltaire is a poet, he is a sublime poet, and goes very high. Monsieur Rousseau is a philosopher, and goes very deep. One flies, the other plunges." This is clumsily said, but the thought is not bad. I supped at Monsieur Gaussen's, where I found Lord Stanhope and Lord Abingdon and his brother. I was so-so. I had first been at Professor Maurice's, where I saw his lady, his son, and his daughter.

SUNDAY 30 DECEMBER. I sat at home all forenoon writing. At three Professor Maurice called upon me and sat an hour. We were cheerful. It was a curious idea: "This is a Geneva minister." I talked vastly well, yet I talked of my gloom with pride. He was amazed at it. He asked my correspondence. I shall write to him. Vanneck was now at Geneva with his good governor, Monat, who invited me this afternoon to the *société* of his wife. He lived in the Maison de Ville. I found here a very genteel company with true Geneva looks. After tea and coffee was a ball. The fiddle or fiddles fairly played and the company fairly danced. Was not this enough to break my most stubborn association of gloom with a Sunday at Geneva? To complete the thing, there was a clergyman in the company. This is the second young Geneva minister that I have seen. I do not at all like them. I know not if they are Arians and Socinians, but I am sure they are fops. I played a hand at whist, and after we had played and danced enough, we went to supper. I say *we* danced, for, although I was not much in spirits,[6] I danced a minuet with Madam Rilliet, whom I had seen and grown fond of

---

[6] He explains in the memoranda that he was "hipped with hunger." He seems to have gone without dinner that Sunday, as he frequently did.

at Ferney; and thus I solaced myself with the downfall of Presbyterian strictness. However the Geneva clergy are different from the Scots. Monsieur Maurice insisted, "We are not Puritans. The Archbishop of Canterbury is in communication with our Venerable Society, and whenever the Anglican Church does something of importance, he gives us notice of it." We supped in a great town hall, and eat and drank considerably. After which they pelted each other with the crumb of their bread formed into little balls. This was rather rude in a large company and in presence of a stranger. I however threw with the rest, partly to keep them in countenance, partly to indulge my whim. I asked if this was the common custom at Geneva. They said they did so only among friends. They were monstrously familiar, the men pawing the sweaty hands of the women, and kissing them too, as the minister slabbered the greasy, unwashen hands of a married woman. Had I been the husband, I should have kicked the fellow downstairs. I was disgusted much, and only consoled myself that I beheld a nauseous example of the manners of republicans. I was glad to get home.

MONDAY 31 DECEMBER. All last night I sat up and wrote letters. I do not mark in this my journal the various fluctuations of my extensive correspondence. It would be an immense labour, and my bundles of letters will explain it sufficiently. At ten young Maurice came to me, and we went and saw the Geneva Library, which is in good order, and tolerably provided with manuscripts. The professor who showed it me talked of honest Monsieur Dupont. We then mounted the tower of the Church of St. Pierre and saw the famous great clock of which I have heard Monsieur Dupont talk so much. I wrote to the good old gentleman from his favourite town of Geneva, and gave him an account of all this. Young Maurice dined with me at my inn. He was a very fine lad, sensible and obliging.

I found at my banker's a letter from my worthy father, in which he said "he longed to see me, to have my assistance in his affairs, and to explain to me every point concerning them." Although I was uneasy to think how little my distempered mind could apply to the sober business of life, this way of writing to me so warmed my heart that I felt a sudden spring of resolution, and hoped to give satisfaction to the worthiest of men.[7] I called on young Chais, who was sick and could not receive me. I was received at Lord Stanhope's and presented to my Lady. I sat some time there. I then went to Gaussen's, where I was kept to supper. I was so-so. When I got home, I was so fatigued with writing last night and walking today that I could hardly think. I sunk to sleep most sound.

[Boswell to Rousseau. Original in French][8]

Geneva, 31 December 1764

MANY, MANY THANKS, SIR, for the note with which you have honoured me. Many, many thanks for having recommended me to your intimate friend. You have spoken of me in the style that my enthusiasm would have desired. Believe me, I shall not prove you wrong.

And you left your letter to Monsieur Deleyre open. And Boswell is already the confidant of your interesting concerns and of the effusions of your heart.[9] Sir, you fill up the measure of my noble pride. You told me that all I lacked was to know my own worth. I know it now.

I have been with Monsieur de Voltaire. His conversation is the most brilliant I have ever heard. I had a conversation alone with him lasting an hour. It was a very serious conversation. He spoke to me of his natural religion in a way that struck me. In spite of all

[7] This letter has not been recovered, nor has Boswell's to Monsieur Dupont.
[8] Translated from the original letter, now in the Public Library of Neuchâtel, as printed by Professor C. B. Tinker in *Letters of James Boswell*, 1924, i. 65–68. There is among the Boswell papers at Yale a complete draft showing only trifling differences from the letter as sent. In my translation I have made grateful use of some phrases from Professor Tinker's translation in *Young Boswell*, 1922, pp. 54–58.
[9] Rousseau later informed Deleyre that he had not intended Boswell to read the letter but had left it open through absent-mindedness. There is therefore no reason to suppose that in his characterization of Boswell he was not being perfectly frank.

that has happened, you would have loved him that evening. I said to myself, *Aut Erasmus aut Diabolus.*[1]

Here I am in the city of which you were once proud to be a citizen, and which you will never be able to deprive of the glory of having borne you. Your *Letters from the Mountain* are making a tremendous noise here. I have for the most part found myself among the partisans of the magistracy, consequently among your furious enemies. I should be ashamed to repeat to you what I have heard them say in their rage against "that scoundrel Rousseau." You are the cause of a terrible ferment in this seat of learning. I consider Geneva like Athens, but an Athens during the persecution of Socrates.

You said that you were interested in me. Will you then write to me as often as your occupations and your physical and mental discomforts permit? You can do me a great deal of good. You said that there are points at which our souls are bound together. What glory for me! I have an ambition of the strongest kind to increase the number of those points.

I set out for Italy tomorrow. I beg you to give me your advice as to how to conduct myself so as to profit most in that country of the fine arts. I love antiquities. I love painting. I shall have the best opportunities for perfecting myself in both. I have a real taste for music. I sing tolerably well. I play on the flute a little, but I think it beneath me. Two years ago I began to learn to play the violin, but I found it so difficult that I gave it up. That was a mistake. Tell me, would I not do well to apply seriously to music — up to a certain point? Tell me what instrument I should choose. It is late, I admit. But shall I not have the pleasure of making steady progress, and shall I not be able to soothe my old age with the notes of my lyre?[2]

[1] "Erasmus or the Devil," the remark of Sir Thomas More when he first met Erasmus. Boswell means that if what he saw at Ferney that evening was not the true Voltaire, it must have been the Devil, for no human being was capable of the impersonation.

[2] "The vision of James Boswell in the role of Ossian, with white beard streaming to the winds, amid the romantic glades of Auchinleck, soothing his

You know me well, Sir, for you have read the sketch of my life. But I forgot to tell you an anecdote that has troubled me. Last summer I was in a large company in Germany. It was a very disagreeable company, and I was vexed at having to waste time in it. They were all praising the French, and I declaimed against that nation in the rudest terms. An officer rose, came to my side, and said, "Sir, I am French, and no one but a scoundrel would speak so of that nation." We were still at dinner. I made him a bow. I had half an hour to reflect. After dinner was over, I took the Captain into the garden. I said to him, "Sir, I am deeply embarrassed. I was very impolite; I am sincerely sorry for it. But you have made use of an expression which a man of honour cannot put up with, and I must have satisfaction for it. If it is possible to avoid a quarrel, I should be happy, for I was wrong. Will you be good enough to apologize to me before the company? I will apologize to you first. If you cannot agree to my proposal, we must fight, though I confess that I shall do it with repugnance." I spoke to him with the sangfroid of a philosopher determined to do his duty. The officer was a worthy man. He replied, "Sir, I will do everything you wish." We went back into the company. We made our apologies to each other. We embraced. The affair was over. Yet I could not be at ease until I had consulted two or three Scotsmen. I said to them, "Gentlemen, I am a simple man; I am not acquainted with the rules you follow in society, but I think I acted like a man. You are my countrymen. I ask your opinions." They assured me that the affair had been honourably adjusted on both sides. They advised me to take the scrape as a lesson for the future. Forgive me, Sir, for having told you this story. As I hope to be truly reckoned among your friends, I wish you to know all the good and all the bad of my character, so that you may cherish the one and correct the other. I am timid by temperament, and my education did everything to make me the slave of fear. But I have a soul capable of breaking these vile chains and forcing myself to feel the noble courage that belongs to a man.

---

stricken age with a lyre, is one that no kindly imagination will reject"
(C. B. Tinker, *Young Boswell*, 1922, p. 55).

What is your serious opinion as to duels? You have not said enough on the subject in the *Héloïse*.[3] There are people who would have us believe that the Gospel teaches us to be too delicate. I am a little of that way of thinking myself.

I have had a letter from Lord Marischal, full of goodness and gaiety.

You will not object if I write occasionally to Mademoiselle Le Vasseur. I assure you that I have formed no scheme of abducting your housekeeper. I often form romantic plans but never impossible ones. Tell me, can I hope to be able to write French some day?

I am truly yours,

BOSWELL.

[Boswell to Thérèse Le Vasseur. Original in French]

Geneva, 31 December 1764

I TAKE THE LIBERTY, MY DEAR MADEMOISELLE, of sending you a garnet necklace, which you will have the goodness to keep as a slight remembrance of a worthy Scot whose face you found honest.[4]

I shall never forget your worth. I shall never forget your feats of legerdemain. You weave lace.[5] You do the cooking. You sit down at table. You make easy, cheerful conversation. Then you rise, the table is cleared, the dishes are washed, all is put in order, Made-

[3] To any one who had read in the *Nouvelle Héloïse* Julie's long and burning indictment of the whole system of duelling — not to mention the account of the behaviour of Lord Édouard Bomston after receiving a challenge—this may seem an odd statement. But the *Nouvelle Héloïse* was a work of fiction, and Boswell could not be sure that it presented Rousseau's personal views. The problem of duelling was a very real one to Boswell. He brought the subject up again and again in his conversations with Johnson, and never came to a clear conclusion as to what a man of honour who professed to be a Christian should do if he were insulted or challenged.

[4] He paid eight crowns for it, entering it in his expense account under date of 1 January.

[5] "Vous travaillez avec les fuseaux": literally, "You work with bobbins." I assume that this refers to the weaving of bobbin-lace on a pillow.

moiselle Le Vasseur is with us again. Only a juggler could perform such feats.

Take good care of your charge, you who hold the Great Rousseau under lock and key. But do not be too haughty because of your station. Deign to write to me sometimes and to give me a particular account of what is happening to you. You have promised me that you will.[6] You have doubtless always believed that a promise ought to be sacred. And the Philosopher with whom you dwell teaches you no other doctrine in that regard.

Tell me how things stand with our poor family, the good woman with so many children. I am very fond of one of her daughters because it was she who came to fetch me when it was time for me to go to Monsieur Rousseau.

Farewell, Mademoiselle. Allow me to salute you with a kiss.

BOSWELL.

[6] Thérèse was practically illiterate. She could write, with very bizarre spelling, but very seldom did.

1765

TUESDAY 1 JANUARY. Voltaire had solemnly assured me that he never was afraid of death, and had desired me to ask the famous Dr. Tronchin, his physician, if he had ever seen him so.[7] Gaussen sent a card to Tronchin, asking permission for me to wait upon him, which was granted. I was to set out this morning, so went to him in boots at eight o'clock. I found him a stately, handsome man, with a good air and great ease. I said, "Sir, I am not ill, but if a man in good health may pay you his respects — " He replied, "One must indeed be at home to such men," and smiled. He said Rousseau was "a haughty, ambitious, wicked rascal, who has written with a dagger dipped in the blood of his fellow citizens. A man ruined by venereal diseases,[8] a man who affects a severity of manners and at the same time keeps a mistress. I used to be his friend, but when I found that, rather than be under obligation to any one, he exposed his own infants, I did not wish to see him any more."

[7] Theodore Tronchin, at this time in his middle fifties, was a Genevan who had studied at Cambridge and Leyden, and was now one of the leading physicians of Europe. Lord and Lady Stanhope, just mentioned by Boswell, had settled at Geneva in order that their only remaining child might be under his care. Voltaire was his fervent admirer, and frequently said that he lived through Tronchin alone. Rousseau had long been his friend and correspondent; they had been at one in their opposition to the presentation of plays in Geneva, but Tronchin's orthodoxy was shocked by *Émile* and *La Nouvelle Héloïse*, and his patriotism was violently affronted by Rousseau's attacks on the Council of Geneva. It was almost certainly he who gave Voltaire the material for the pamphlet *Sentiment des citoyens*, which had just published to the world the secrets of Rousseau's private life. It is important to remember that Boswell now hears most of the charges against Rousseau for the first time.

[8] Since Tronchin had never examined Rousseau professionally, his diagnosis of the nature of Rousseau's malady can be set down as no better than a guess. Rousseau denied it vigorously.

313

This shocked me; but I recollected that Tronchin was connected with the Geneva magistracy, whom Rousseau has so keenly attacked. Tronchin saw that I was hurt at hearing such a character of my admired Rousseau, and said, "I have plucked a feather from your happiness." I replied, "It will grow again."

I then talked of Voltaire. He said, "He is very amiable, but is never the same for two days. Sometimes he is a very good deist. But if he is vexed, if he has received a letter which has annoyed him, he hurls his shafts at Providence. I have always regarded him as an astronomer regards a phenomenon. I have marked all the nuances of his mind. I have seen him when he believed himself to be dying, and I thought so too." BOSWELL. "Indeed? And did he feel horror?" TRONCHIN. "No. The worse he is, the better deist he becomes. His illness makes him think more of God as a merciful Being." BOSWELL. "Well, I can then tell people so, on the best authority. Monsieur de Voltaire charged me to ask you if he was afraid of death, as the ministers have said." TRONCHIN. "You may indeed say that, Sir. But he is mad. I call any man mad who has no fixed principles to serve him as a compass in the great crises of life. Such a man is the weakest creature in existence." BOSWELL. "It is curious to see great men close at hand." TRONCHIN. "Sir, there are few men who can keep their glory when they are examined under the microscope. I have sent off my son on his travels.[9] He will see all the great men in Europe, and he will learn to judge without prejudice. — I once asked Monsieur de Voltaire why he did not act with more constancy according to his principles. He replied, 'If I had as strong a body as you, I should be more constant.' "

This interview was of no small value, as it enabled me to have always a hold upon the bigots who forge stories of the great Luminary of France.

I set out at eleven in a chaise mounted so high before that I was thrown back like a bishop in his studying-chair. All the chaises for passing the Alps are hung in this way. I jogged on, mighty deliberate.

[9] He later became secretary to Andrew Mitchell at Berlin.

[EDITORIAL NOTE: The journal will be continued from this point in *Boswell on the Grand Tour: Italy, Corsica, and France.* A few letters which belong chronologically to that volume are printed below because they are needed to round out two of the main organizing themes of the present volume: Boswell's relations with Voltaire and with the Margrave of Baden-Durlach.]

[Boswell to the Margrave of Baden-Durlach][1]

Turin, 15 January 1765

SIR: — I have had the honour to receive a letter from your Most Serene Highness in answer to the first which I took the liberty to write to you. You desire me to write to you "without ceremony." I take this as a genteel reproof for having expressed myself in a manner that looked like studied compliment. I own my fault, Sir. Yet be assured that I wrote as I felt, so was not insincere. My fault was in feeling too much elation at having obtained the regard of a prince. I pretend to be a philosopher; and a philosopher ought not to have the same kind of vanity that the ordinary race of men have. Accustomed to the calm contemplation of Truth, he ought not to be much dazzled by the adventitious splendour of rank. I am however able to say something in my own defence. Horace, whose philosophy is no less admirable than his poetry, tells us that

Principibus placuisse viris non ultima laus est.[2]

Had I found no prince superior to the most part that I have seen, and had all princes treated me with haughty disdain, I should most certainly have laughed at this line as at the speech of a fawning courtier; or I should have taken upon me to give it an unusual meaning, and have translated *principibus viris,* "first-rate men," not on account of their rank but of their estimable qualities. As I have however found a prince of merit and have been happy enough

[1] Printed from Boswell's draft in the Boswell papers at Yale.
[2] "To have pleased great men is not the least praiseworthy of a man's accomplishments" (*Epistles,* I. xvii. 35).

to please him, I submit to the common interpretation of the words, and with great satisfaction take the praise which Horace gives me.

Prince, refuse not my honest panegyric. Let your subjects and servants speak. Let trumpets proclaim through your dominions an assembly of your people. I am willing to have your character fairly voted. I know well what would be the general voice; and were I not afraid of again offending your delicacy, I should draw it up in the form of a vote of the British House of Commons.

Your Highness has ordered me to write to you freely. You may say what you please, but this is proof enough of your being a philosopher. I shall endeavour to make the best use of the privilege which you judge me worthy of. The longer I write to you, I shall write the better.

I passed a month in Switzerland. I have been with Rousseau and with Voltaire. I have so much to say of both that I shall delay it till I have again the honour of being in the Palace of Karlsruhe. Your Highness shall then hear a recital which I am sure will give you great pleasure.

I must ask pardon for having delayed so long to answer your Highness's letter. Methinks I have reversed your orders. You desired me *to write* without ceremony. I have taken the liberty *to not write* without ceremony. . . .

I have written to my father to send me the genealogical tree of our family, attested by the heralds of Scotland. I hope to produce it at Karlsruhe in May next, and I indulge the agreeable idea of being ever connected with your Most Serene Highness by having the honour to wear your Order of Fidelity.

I offer my best respects to her Highness the Margrave. . . .

May I beg of your Highness to write to me soon, that I may be assured of your not taking amiss my long delay. I promise that I shall never again be so much in fault.

I have the honour, &c.

[EDITORIAL NOTE: The further relations between Boswell and Karl Friedrich contain an irreducible element of mystery. The letter which Boswell sent from Turin is not now among the Margrave's papers, and it may perhaps be assumed that it was lost in the post. But the same cannot be said of two later letters which Boswell sent, one from Rome in May and one from Siena in August, 1765, for both now repose in the Grand-Ducal Family Archives at Karlsruhe. In these later letters Boswell expressed growing uneasiness at having had no further word from Karl Friedrich, though he reasserts his intention of returning to Karlsruhe. On 6 February 1766, however, at Calais, just before embarking for England, he wrote a grieved but manly Finis both to his hopes of a star and to the continuance of a relationship that at one time had promised to fulfil his utmost wishes: "I intended paying you my respects before I returned to Scotland, and in that view obtained from my Lord Marischal the enclosed recommendation, but your silence made me suppose that you had altered your opinion of me, either from bad information or from that fickleness to which the great are so unhappily subject. And upon that supposition I thought it would be better not to embarrass your Highness by making you a second visit. . . . You know, Sir, I never asked your correspondence. Your Highness asked mine and wrote to me that you *set a high value on it.* . . . " We know this letter only from the draft, the letter itself not being now at Karlsruhe. The register of letters shows that Boswell really sent it, but one could again assume that it never reached its destination. The loss on the road of two letters out of six would not be extraordinary for the Continental posts of the period. And if it were not for one circumstance, one would simply suppose that Karl Friedrich got bored with Boswell after writing one letter, and chose to terminate the correspondence by silence.

What makes the whole business really mysterious is a document preserved in the Grand-Ducal Family Archives at Karlsruhe, the copy of a letter dated 24 May 1768. It is unsigned and is in the hand of a secretary, but the author obviously was Karl Friedrich, and it bears the direction, "To Sir Boswell of Auchinleck": "After the last letter I directed to you to Geneva, I heard no more of you till I recollected some times ago from the newspapers that you returned to England. I am glad of your being now more at leisure to renew our correspondence, interrupted by your travels. For to judge from the affectuous mind you once showed to me, I dare hope that it is no oblivion which stopped the courses of this literary commerce. . . . After having enjoyed your agreeable and instructive conversation, I am now deprived of, I should be too much at a loss if you did not make me amends for by writing. In this sweet expectation, I am, with all my heart, Sir, your affectionate. . . . " Now, there is nothing whatever in the Boswell papers to show that Boswell ever received this singularly gracious epistle; and it is very hard to believe that if he had received from a reigning prince a letter ending "your affectionate," the expressions of his delight would *all* have disappeared. Yet the document at Karlsruhe is not a draft nor a letter prepared for sending but not sent; it is clearly a transcript of a finished letter, a transcript made for filing.

It does not seem very likely that Karl Friedrich could have forgotten that he had received at least two letters from Boswell in reply to the one which he himself had sent to Geneva; and the tone of his letter just quoted seems so sincere that I hesitate to accuse him of the meanness of lying. Professor Curt von Faber du Faur, whose knowledge of German court-life is unrivalled, has suggested an explanation which I should like to accept. He thinks it quite possible that Karl Friedrich's secretaries disapproved of the continuance of this familiar correspondence in English, and did not show the Margrave Boswell's later letters, though they filed them. Similarly they may have seen to it that Karl Friedrich's second letter was never actually posted. If this is true, there is a considerable element of pathos in the whole affair.

We now return to the winter of 1765, and the correspondence with Voltaire.]

[Boswell to Voltaire]

Turin, 15 January 1765

Sɪʀ: — When I took leave of you at Ferney, I asked your correspondence and you most readily granted my request. I hope you granted it as a philosopher and not as a courtier. In short, I hope you was in earnest. I now sit down to try.

You will find me the same man in my letters that you found me in conversation, singular and agreeable. Was it not so? You either liked me much, or you are the best dissembler that ever lived. I am sure you was pleased to find a man that gave you no flattery, of which you have had so much that it cannot fail to be insipid or disgusting to you. Many a high-seasoned ragout of compliment has been served up to Monsieur de Voltaire. The learned and the great of all nations in Europe have exerted their talents in this way. Surely you could give us a most humorous account of their different tastes. Did your appetite still continue, you would be obliged to publish a reward to the inventor of a new mode of adulation. People accustomed to luxurious diet are delighted with the simplicity of a rural repast. In the same manner, Monsieur de Voltaire, tired of studied flattery, relished extremely the honest praise of a good Scots laird. What I gave you was natural. It had neither spice nor perfume. It was fresh from the dairy. It was curds and cream.

I reflect with great satisfaction on my spirited candour when we talked of religion. I told you upon this occasion, "Sir, you are one individual and I another." You may remember that I showed no mean timidity; and while I maintained the immortality of my soul, did I not glow with a fire that had some appearance of being divine? I am exceedingly happy that I have had an important conversation with you. Before that, my admiration of your genius was obscured by the horror with which I had been taught to consider your character as a man. Had I not waited upon you at Ferney, I should have had a very honest detestation of you while I lived. But, Sir, since that time I have thought of you very differently. Although I am sincerely sorry at your being prejudiced against the doctrines of consolation and hope, I shall ever esteem your humanity of feeling and generosity of sentiment. I know you must be changeable. But were not the general tenor of your mind excellent, you could not have talked to me as you did during our serious evening. When I returned to Geneva, I waited upon Dr. Tronchin, and according to your desire I asked him if you had ever shown those fears of death which the zealous orthodox have affirmed to be a certain proof of your insincerity. Dr. Tronchin assured me that you never had such fears. He said of you, "The nearer death he believes himself to be, the better deist he becomes." I am now fully satisfied as to your character; and in my presence Falsehood and Folly shall no longer blacken it. I have already had more than one occasion of vindicating you. Your faults must be allowed, but I will suffer no additions.

I told you that I had written down our important conversation. It fills eight quarto pages, and does you much honour. The famous Ben Jonson came down to Scotland to see my countryman Drummond of Hawthornden, at whose seat he passed some time in philosophical and witty intercourse. Drummond marked their conversation, and afterwards published it among his works. Ben complained of this as unfair.[3] Was he not in the wrong? Would it be unfair in me should I one day oblige the world with some of the most lively and noble effusions of an illustrious author?

If you will really correspond with me, you will do me much honour, and I shall endeavour to entertain you as well as I can. I am, &c.

[Received 15 March 1765, Voltaire to Boswell][4]

11.ͤ fevrier 1765. au Chateau de ferney par genêve.

My distempers and my bad eyes do not permit me to answer with that celerity and exactness that my duty and my heart require. you seem sollicitous about that pretty thing call'd soul. j do protest you j know nothing of it. nor wether it is, nor what it is,

[3] Boswell was mistaken about this. The famous conversations were not published until long after the death of both Jonson and Drummond.

[4] The spelling, capitals, and punctuation of the original have been preserved. It was certainly dictated — perhaps written in draft — by Voltaire, but the letter sent is in the hand of his secretary, Jean Louis Wagnière, whom Boswell met at Ferney, though he did not name him. See pp. 289, 302.

Voltaire, from an etching by Captain (?John) Adlam, in the possession of Lt.-Col. Ralph H. Isham.

nor what it shall be. young scolars, and priests know all that perfectly. for my part j am but a very ignorant fellow.

Let it be what it will, j assure you my soul has a great regard for your own when you will make a turn into our deserts, you shall find me (if alive) ready to show you my respect and obsequiousness.

V.

[Boswell to Voltaire]

Rome, 4 April 1765

YOU MAY WELL BELIEVE, SIR, that I have no small pride and pleasure to receive a letter from Monsieur de Voltaire. I heartily thank you for it. Consider the difference of our ages, and let the insolence of youth speak without restraint. Abstracting from your fame, I venerate you for your antiquity. When I first heard of you, I heard of a man whose works had been long existing; and being no chronologist, I imagined you really one of the Ancients. My early prejudices still influence my imagination, so that receiving a letter from Monsieur de Voltaire is like receiving a letter from Abraham, whose reality you doubt of, or from Julius Caesar, whom you will not allow to have swum across the river with his *Commentaries* in his teeth.[5]

I am diverted to see with how little ceremony you treat the Soul, although you own that you know nothing about it. Many infidels have maintained that Ignorance is the mother of Devotion.

[5] See Voltaire's *Dictionnaire philosophique*, article "Abraham," and *Histoire de Charles XII*, Preface of the edition of 1748. Voltaire's doubt of the existence of Abraham is expressed ironically: "Abraham, renowned in Asia Minor and Arabia, is one of those names like Thoth among the Egyptians, the elder Zoroaster in Persia, Hercules in Greece, Orpheus in Thrace, Odin among the northern nations, and many others of the same kind, which are better known because they are famous than for any well-authenticated history. I speak merely of profane history, for as concerns the Jews, our masters and our enemies, whom we take our faith from and whom we detest, since the history of that people has been visibly written by the Holy Ghost, we entertain for it such sentiments as we ought to have."

Upon that principle you ought to think of the Soul with reverence, but you make a jest of it: you call it a *pretty thing*, and talk of it as lightly as if it were your little finger. It is curious after all to reflect that the Soul is really the All, the man, the thinking principle, the source of everything noble and elegant, the author of history, of poetry, and of all the fine arts. (You must forgive my zeal for immortality. I am a melancholy man, I know not how. In this world my prospect is clouded. I cheer my hours of gloom with expectations of a brighter scene after death, and I think I have a strong probability that I shall not be deceived.) May we not hope then that it shall live for ever and still attain to greater perfection and greater felicity? Is not this a plan worthy of the Lord of the Universe? It is the Soul which has given us a general sketch of the world from Charlemagne to the present times. It is the Soul which has written so many tragedies which adorn the French theatre. It is the Soul which has surprised us with so much wit against itself, and it is the Soul which diffuses kindness and joy over the domains of Ferney. There I have you. . . .

You have been obliging enough to comply with my request that you would write to me in our language. If you would rather choose to write in your own, pray do so. If Monsieur de Voltaire does me the honour to talk to me, he may be dressed either in French silk or English broadcloth. I am, with much admiration, your obliged humble servant.

P.S. Might I ask you to present my respects to Madame Denis and to Père Adam?

APPENDIX I

Successive Drafts of Boswell's
First Letter to Rousseau

[EDITORIAL NOTE: Boswell's journal (p. 217) says nothing about his labours of revision, and if read in its natural sense would indicate that he had brought with him to Môtiers a finished letter which he had intended to use to get himself into Rousseau's presence. I conclude that this was the document which is printed below as First Draft, and suggest that it was written at Neuchâtel on the evening of 2 December. It is not literally a draft but a carefully written letter, needing only to be sealed and addressed before being sent off.]

[Boswell to Rousseau. First Draft. Original in French]

[Neuchâtel, 2 December 1764]

SIR: — I am a good Scot. I am travelling for amusement and instruction. I write French badly. I speak it still worse. I have come here in the hope of seeing you.

Sir, people have discouraged me from coming here. At any rate, they have tried to. But all they have said has merely confirmed me in my resolution to ask boldly for permission to visit you in your home. "Monsieur Rousseau is odd." Certainly. "He is a misanthrope." You are mistaken. "He has refused visits from Monsieur le Marquis de ——, from Monsieur ——, from Monsieur ——," &c., &c. So much the better. So much the better. I am not like any of those gentlemen. If Monsieur Rousseau admitted everybody, especially if he admitted people of fashion, his house would no longer be the retreat of genius and of piety. And I should not be striving so eagerly to be received into it.

I am a young man twenty-four years old. Do you ask if I have

323

recommendations? Surely you do not need them? A recommendation protects people who lack penetration against impostures. But you, Sir, who have studied human nature, who are skilled in analyzing its principles and tracing their effects, can you be deceived in a character? I should have difficulty in believing so. Yet, Sir, I dare to put myself to the test, to the most severe test a man has ever undergone. Do you wish homages? I give you facts. Your writings have melted my heart, have elevated my soul, have fired my imagination, have given me ideas of life which a melancholy but lively spirit has received for celestial illuminations. Believe me, I am a character worthy of your attention. I have not been long in the world, but I have had a great deal of experience. I have much to tell you. Do not fear to expose yourself to a vapid recital of the adventures of a young rattle-brain who has the absurd vanity to imagine himself the hero of a novel. But think rather to hear a tale of embarrassing circumstances concerning which no one in the world can give me counsel except the author of the *Nouvelle Héloïse*. Will you not receive me? If you do not, it will be something to regret, on your side as well as on mine. Forgive a sudden sally. Ah, dear Saint-Preux! Ah, feeling Mentor! I have a presentiment that a truly noble friendship will be born today.

Open, then, your door, Sir, to a young stranger. I beg you, do not refuse me. I await your answer.

Boswell.

[Editorial Note: What is printed as our Second Draft could not have been written before 3 December, for it incorporates a phrase of Mademoiselle Sandoz's at Brot: "a man with two heads." (See p. 215.) After listening to Mademoiselle Sandoz's discouraging chatter, Boswell must have decided that the neat three-page letter he had brought with him was not intense enough, and have set himself, in the Maison de Village at Môtiers, to the task of expanding and revising it. After making a few interlinear changes in the letter he had brought, he discarded it and made a completely new draft, our Second.]

[Boswell to Rousseau. Second Draft. Original in French]

[Môtiers, Val de Travers, 3 December 1764]

Sir: — I am the eldest son of a Scots gentleman of ancient family. Now you know my rank. I am twenty-four years old. Now you know my age. Sixteen months ago I left Great Britain a completely insular being, knowing hardly a word of French. I have been in Holland and Germany, but not in France. You will therefore excuse my handling of the language. I am travelling with a genuine desire to improve myself. I have come here in the hope of seeing you.

I have heard all that any one can say to discourage me in my hopes, but my hopes remain none the less strong. "Monsieur Rousseau is odd and capricious. He has refused visits from Monsieur le Marquis, Monsieur le Comte, Monsieur de ———," &c., &c. Assuredly, if Monsieur Rousseau admitted everybody, his house would no longer be the retreat of exquisite genius and of elevated piety, and I should not be striving so eagerly to be received into it.

I well know, Sir, that you do not wish to exhibit yourself as a natural curiosity, a man with two heads and four legs. I well know that your delicate sensibility could not endure either coarse flatterers or vain men of the world who call on you in order to be able to say that they have had that honour.[6] But if there comes a young man of merit, the sort of merit you prize the most, I cannot doubt that you will receive him graciously. Sir, I am such an one.

Do you ask if I have recommendations? Surely you do not need them? In the commerce of the world a recommendation is necessary in order to protect people who lack penetration from impostors. But you, Sir, who have made such deep study of human nature, can you be deceived in a character? If one were to send a picture to a Raphael, ought one to assure him of its perfection of design and of colouring? No, a Raphael would discover its perfections, and its faults too, better than they could be described by any

[6] Deletion: "and perhaps — heavens, it is possible — to make you admire them."

one else. Therefore, when you send your picture to a great judge, say nothing. Sir, you will divine my meaning.

Believe me, I imagine that having studied human nature so very deeply, you have a perfect knowledge of it, excepting only for the incomprehensible essence of the soul. You know all the principles of the body and the mind, with their movements, their sentiments, everything they can acquire. You see a man, you analyze him. You know him perfectly. And yet, Sir, I dare present myself before you. I dare to put myself to the test. In cities or in courts where there are numerous companies, one can disguise one's self, one can sometimes dazzle the eyes of the greatest philosophers. But for my part, I put myself to the severest test. It is in the silence and the solitude of your sacred grove, Sir, that you shall judge me. Think you that in such circumstances I can evade your piercing gaze?

Your writings, Sir, have melted my heart, have elevated my soul, have fired my imagination. I have a spirit that is lively but melancholy, and you know how a man can suffer from such a spirit without having had great external misfortunes. Yet I have suffered misfortunes. I find myself . . . [7]

[EDITORIAL NOTE: Boswell then discarded the Second Draft and began all over again with a Third. This satisfied him except for the last page, which he again redrafted and expanded. The letter as sent (see p. 218) follows the final draft so closely that it will suffice to print here only the last page of the Third Draft as originally written.]

[Boswell to Rousseau. Third Draft. Original in French]

. . . that has produced a Fletcher of Saltoun and a Lord Marischal. Forgive me, Sir. I grow warm. I cannot restrain myself. — O dear Saint-Preux! Enlightened Mentor! Eloquent and amiable

[7] Boswell intended to add the word "in," and then conclude as in the first draft: "embarrassing circumstances concerning which," &c.

Rousseau! I have a presentiment that a truly noble friendship will be born today.

I learn with deep regret, Sir, that you are often indisposed. Perhaps you are so at present. But I beg you not to let that prevent you from seeing me. You will find in me a simplicity that will put you to no trouble, a cordiality that will alleviate your pains.

I have much, very much, to tell you. Though I am only a young man, I have had a variety of experience that will amaze you. I find myself in delicate circumstances concerning which I conceive there is no one in the world who is capable of giving me counsel except the author of the *Nouvelle Héloïse*. I repeat again, I deserve to have it. Open your door, then, Sir, to an old Scot. Put your trust in a stranger who is different. But I beg you, be alone. With all my enthusiasm . . .

APPENDIX II

Letter of Rousseau to Alexandre Deleyre

[EDITORIAL NOTE: The present volume contains in translation two letters of Rousseau that so far as I know have never previously appeared in print. Even though this edition is not planned for scholars, there would seem to be some impropriety in publishing translations from so famous an author without also making the texts available in the language in which he wrote them. The facsimile opposite page 272 provides the French text of one of the letters, and the French of the other is printed below. As explained above (p. 274), our manuscript is not Rousseau's original, which Deleyre kept, but a copy made by Boswell. The spelling, capitalization, and punctuation of the manuscript have been preserved.]

A Motiers le 20 X^{bre} 1764

Je profite, cher Ami, du depart de M. Boswell Gentilhomme Ecossois qui va faire son tour d'Italie, pour vous donner un petit bon jour et vous dire combien votre derniére lettre a touché et rejoui mon Cœur. Quoique Je n'aye jamais recherché Personne, J'ai repondu si vivement aux avances de mille gens qui m'ont recherché que Je me suis pour ainsi dire jetté á leur tête. Tous ont disparu au premier revers, et voila que le seul presque avec lequel Je me suis rendu difficile, me reste, me console dans mes malheurs, et me pardonne mes torts. Cher DeLeyre, J'ai bien tardi sans doute, mais si ma sincére amitié vous flate encore, ne regardez pas ces retards comme une perte, Je vous en payerai bien l'interest.

Je suis bien aise que M. Boswell et vous fassiez connoissance; Je crois que vous m'en saurrez gré tous deux. Dans la premiére lettre qu'il m'ecrivit il me marqua qu'il etoit un homme *d'un merite singulier*. J'eus la curiosité de voir celui qui parloit ainsi de lui-même, et J'ai trouvé qu'il m'avoit dit vrai. Il a eu dans sa Jeunesse la tête enfarinée de la dure Theologie Calviniste, et il lui en reste une ame inquiete et des[8] idées noires. Je lui ai conseillé de consacrer son voyage d'Italie à l'etude des beaux arts. Si vous philosophez avec lui, Je vous prie de vous contraindre sur vos propres penchans, et de ne lui presenter les objèts moraux que par ce qu'ils ont de consolant et de tendre. C'est un Convalescent que la moindre rechute tueroit infailliblement. Je m'interesserois á lui quand il ne m'aurroit pas eté recommandé par My Lord Marischal. Je n'ai pas besoin de vous en dire davantage.

Je suis sur la point de conclurre une affaire qui me donneroit du repos et du pain pour le reste de mes jours. J'ai besoin de l'un et de l'autre; car dans l'abbatement de corps et d'esprit ou Je suis, Je ne puis plus penser ni agir.

Il s'agit d'une Edition generale de mes ecrits qu'une Societé veut entreprendre ici sous mes yeux, et par laquelle Je prendrois mon dernier congé du Public.

Une chose m'embarrasse, c'est la Preface, que Je suis hors

[8] Boswell wrote *des des.*

d'etat de faire. Auriez vous le tems, seriez vous d'humeur á vous charger de cette besogne? Je ne puis vous exprimer quel bien vous me feriez. Bien entendre, toutefois, que ce seroit vous qui parleriez, et que vous permettriez qu'elle portai votre nom. J'aimerois á penser qu'il partageroit avec le mien le sort qui l'attend, et que Je crois ne pouroit etre qu'honorable, parce que la Posterité est toujours juste. Voyez, et repondez moi quand vous le pourrez; car votre reponse peut me decider sur le parti que J'ai á prendre.

Je ne suis pas tout à fait de votre avis sur l'impossibilité de donner une bonne institution aux Corses, et Je ne crois point qu'il soit necessaire d'y employer la fanatisme. Loin de penser qu'il ne faille point se meler des affaires des hommes, pour n'avoir point de reproche á se faire, Je pense au contraire qu'on s'en prepare un trés grand quand on neglige de faire le bien, ou du moins d'y tacher avec quelque espoir de reussir. Mais ce n'est pas maintenant le moment de parler de tout cela, et les Corses ont aujourdhui autres choses á faire que d'etablir l'Utopie au milieu d'eux. Il faut avouer que vos françois sont un peuple bien servile, bien vendu á la Tyrannie, bien cruel et bien acharné sur les malheureux. S'ils savoient un homme libre á l'autre bout du Monde, Je crois qu'ils iroient pour le seul plaisir de l'exterminer. Bon Jour.

Il y a dans le 24 Vol. du recueil de Muratori *Scriptorum Rerum Italicarum* un petit ouvrage de P. Cirneo intitulo *de rebus Corsicis.* Cet ouvrage n'est il point imprimé separément, et n'y auroit il pas moyen de le deterrer?

INDEX

This is in the main an index of proper names, with few subject articles, but Part I of the article BOSWELL, JAMES collects and digests Boswell's references to his states of mind, traits of character, opinions, &c; and the articles ROUSSEAU and VOLTAIRE both contain the general heading *Topics of conversation*. Observations on persons and places are generally entered under the person or place in question; for example, Boswell's opinions of Frederick the Great will be found under Frederick II and not under Boswell. Churches, inns, streets, counties, mountains, &c. are given separate articles in the main alphabet. Emperors, kings, electors, and British princes of the blood are entered under their Christian names; other princes (even when sovereign), noblemen, and lords of session and their wives, under their titles. The styles chosen are usually those proper to 1764. German forenames have been anglicized in a few cases where it was thought that English-speaking readers would be more accustomed to the English forms. Maiden names of married women are given in parentheses. Titles of books are listed under the author's names, except where the author has not been identified in the text or notes, in which case a cross reference is given from the title to the author. The following abbreviations are employed: D. (Duke), E. (Earl), M. (Marquess), V. (Viscount), JB (James Boswell).

Index